CORNELL STUDIES IN SECURITY AFFAIRS

edited by Robert J. Art *and* Robert Jervis

The Tet Offensive

INTELLIGENCE FAILURE IN WAR

James J. Wirtz

Cornell University Press

ITHACA AND LONDON

First published 1991 by Cornell University Press.

International Standard Book Number 0-8014-2486-0
Library of Congress Catalog Card Number 91-55048
Printed in the United States of America
*Librarians: Library of Congress cataloging information
appears on the last page of the book.*

⊗ The paper in this book meets the minimum requirements
of the American National Standard for Information Sciences—
Permanence of Paper for Printed Library Materials, ANSI Z39.48–1984.

Contents

Acknowledgments

Many individuals and organizations have eased the task of preparing this manuscript. Robert Jervis, Richard Betts, Warner Schilling, Jack Snyder, and Robert Art not only provided comments that significantly improved the quality of this work but also served as fine examples of how one approaches the discipline of political science. Jervis and Betts often went beyond the call of duty in providing both encouragement and help in securing the resources needed to undertake the project.

I am indebted especially to Samuel P. Huntington, the John M. Olin Foundation, and the staff of the Center for International Affairs at Harvard University for providing the perfect research environment. By supplying funding for the 1985 and 1986 academic years and eight weeks of summer research, the Olin Foundation greatly facilitated the completion of this project. Sam Huntington deserves special praise for taking a keen interest in the pre-doctoral fellows at the CFIA and for creating a setting conducive to research and intellectual growth.

While I was at the CFIA, Tom Fintel, Ira Klein, Timothy Lomperis, Douglas Macdonald, and Edward Rhodes were kind enough to read first drafts of many chapters; they caught several silly mistakes before they could cause me embarrassment. Even after the end of our days at the CFIA, Lomperis, Macdonald, and Rhodes continued to read chapters and to encourage me. Michael Handel and Richard Valcourt, who both share my interest in intelligence analysis, also provided encouragement and advice. Additionally, I thank George Allen, Walt Rostow, and Robert Ruhl Simmons for offering insights into several key events during the war. I also benefited from Glenn Palmer's comments on several chapters.

I thank the Lyndon Baines Johnson Foundation for a grant that allowed me to use the documents maintained at the LBJ Library in Austin, Texas. David Humphrey was a masterful guide to the materials on the Vietnam War maintained at the library. His help allowed me to compress months of research into a matter of weeks. Similarly, I am grateful to Stephen Eldridge of the Department of the Army, who guided me through the records maintained by the Department of the Army and the National Archives. Both men showed extreme patience in the face of naive questions.

As the manuscript reached its final stages, I benefited greatly from the computer support offered by Robert Friedrich. I thank Holly Baily, Patty Peltekos, and Kathleen Moschak at Cornell University Press for their assistance. They were kind to a first-time author, and their efforts greatly improved the manuscript.

My parents, Charles John Wirtz and Elizabeth Goffa Wirtz, and my sister, Mary Elise Wirtz, deserve a special note of thanks since they continue to support me in my decision to pursue an academic career. By bearing more than their share of my financial and emotional burdens, my parents greatly eased the task of preparing this manuscript in its initial stages.

Finally, I thank my wife, Janet Ayden Wirtz. Not only did she help me in a thousand different ways, she directly contributed to the completion of the work by painstakingly proofreading the manuscript. Her confidence in my abilities never wavered, and for this I am truly grateful.

JAMES J. WIRTZ

Monterey, California

Abbreviations

ARVN   Army of the Republic of [South] Vietnam
CDEC   Combined Document Exploitation Center (allies)
CIA   Central Intelligence Agency (U.S.)
CICV   Combined Intelligence Center, Vietnam (allies)
CIDG   civilian irregular defense group (allies)
CINCPAC   Commander in Chief, Pacific (U.S.)
CMD   Capital Military District (RVN)
CMEC   Combined Material Exploitation Center (allies)
CMIC   Combined Military Interrogation Center (allies)
CMR   Capital Military Region
COMUSMACV Commander, U.S. Military Assistance Command, Vietnam
CORDS   Civilian Operations and Rural Development Support
COSVN   Central Office [Communist party] for South Vietnam
CTZ   corps tactical zone
DIA   Defense Intelligence Agency (U.S.)
DMZ   demilitarized zone
FFV   Field Force, Vietnam (U.S.)
FWMAF   Free World Military Assistance Forces (allies)
GVN   government of [South] Vietnam
J-2   military intelligence staff
JGS   Joint General Staff (RVN)
LOC   lines of communication
MACV   Military Assistance Command, Vietnam
MAF   Marine Amphibious Force (U.S.)
NVA   North Vietnamese Army
NIE   National Intelligence Estimate (U.S.)
NLF   National Liberation Front
NSA   National Security Agency (U.S.)
NVN   North Vietnam
PERINTREP   *Periodic Intelligence Report* (CICV)

PRP   People's Revolutionary party
RD   Rural Development [pacification] program (RVN)
RVN   Republic of [South] Vietnam
RVNAF   Republic of [South] Vietnam Armed Forces
SAC   Strategic Air Command (U.S.)
SIGINT   [electronic] signals intelligence
SVN   South Vietnam
USARV   U.S. Army, Vietnam
VC   Vietcong
VDRN   *Viet-Nam Documents and Research Notes*
VWP   Vietnamese Worker's [Communist] party

The Tet Offensive

Introduction

On 31 January 1968, during the Tet holiday, communist forces simultaneously attacked urban areas, military installations, and government facilities throughout South Vietnam. By the time the offensive's intensity began to wane on 13 February, 1100 Americans had been killed in action, and members of the Johnson administration and the American public had been stunned by the fury of the Tet attacks. Following the offensive, the official U.S. government investigation into the circumstances surrounding the Tet attacks concluded that, "although warning had . . . been provided, the intensity, coordination, and timing of the enemy attack were not fully anticipated."[1] U.S. and South Vietnamese officers and intelligence analysts failed to anticipate the nature of the Tet offensive. This failure not only contributed to the initial military gains enjoyed by the communists but also increased the shock produced by the attack. Ultimately, it was the surprise, not the short-term military advantages, that reduced the willingness of the American public and political elite to continue to prosecute the war in Vietnam.[2]

The Tet offensive was the decisive battle of the Vietnam War because of its profound impact on American attitudes about involvement in Southeast Asia. In the aftermath of Tet, many Americans became disillusioned with the Johnson administration's conduct of the war. To the American public and even to members of the admin-

[1]U.S. Congress, House Select Committee on Intelligence, *U.S. Intelligence Agencies and Activities: Risks and Control of Foreign Intelligence*, 94th Cong., 1st sess. 1975, pt. 5, app. 4, 1995.

[2]Headquarters, United States Military Assistance Command, Vietnam, *Command History 1968* (San Francisco, 1969), 1: 129; and George C. Herring, *America's Longest War: The United States and Vietnam, 1950–1975* (New York, 1979), p. 188.

[1]

istration, the offensive demonstrated that U.S. intervention in the ground war had produced a negligible effect on the will and capability of the Vietcong and North Vietnamese to continue in their struggle to unite Vietnam. The Tet offensive seemed to indicate to most observers that the three years of "big-unit war" that followed the deployment of U.S. ground forces in 1965 had produced only a steady stream of casualties on all sides. On the battlefield, Tet marked the turning point between U.S. escalation and withdrawal from the war.

In the realm of domestic politics, the consequences of the offensive were also profound. Tet discredited the Johnson administration, reinforcing the president's decision not to run for reelection. For many Americans, Tet enhanced the credibility gap between the electorate and government officials as battlefield developments apparently contradicted the claims of progress in the war made by the Johnson administration and the military. The offensive turned disengagement from the struggle in Vietnam into the American political priority for the next five years. Over the longer term, Tet marked the beginning of what Ronald Reagan called the "Vietnam syndrome": a period of public disillusionment with military intervention, defense spending, and an active anticommunist approach to foreign affairs. In a sense, the Tet offensive quelled the crusading spirit that characterized America's postwar rush to intervene in conflicts in the Third World.

Given the political impact of the Tet attacks, it would be logical to assume that the offensive dealt a devastating military setback to U.S. forces and their South Vietnamese allies. Dire consequences usually follow a disastrous defeat. Ironically, the allies defeated the communists decisively during Tet. From the communist perspective, the offensive was a gamble, even a desperate gamble, taken to offset the overwhelming resources, mobility, firepower, technological sophistication, and professionalism of their opponent. The North Vietnamese and Vietcong hoped that the attacks would foster a revolt of the southern population against the government, thereby adding tens of thousands of combatants to the communist side. When the offensive failed to spark this insurrection, communist commanders lacked the resources needed to attain their ambitious objectives, and the allies defeated their widely scattered forces piecemeal. Even though the Tet attacks failed to unfold as planned, the offensive eventually produced the outcome desired by the communists.

The communists intended the surprise inflicted against the allies during Tet. They adopted a sophisticated strategy of deception, misleading their opponents about their intentions in a quest to eliminate or reduce the effectiveness of responses to the offensive. In wartime,

[2]

the active or passive effort to mislead, misinform, or confuse an opponent about one's capabilities or intentions can take several forms. A nation contemplating an attack can try to make its adversary locate its forces in the wrong place. In such instances, deceptive operations embody all the signs of a real assault, to cause an opponent to believe that the pretended hostile activities are genuine. The Japanese attack on the Aleutians on 3 June 1942, an effort to lure the U.S. Navy away from the Japanese forces that would conduct the planned amphibious landings on Midway, is an example of this type of operation. Deception during war also can be used to force an opponent to violate the principle of economy of force. Such cases involve the attempt to cause the adversary to squander resources on nonexistent targets or in unimportant directions. During the Battle of Britain, for example, the British succeeded in channeling German air attacks away from actual facilities by constructing fake installations and by interfering with the Luftwaffe's electronic navigational aids. Cover, another type of deception, is intended to lull an opponent into a false sense of security so that one can seize the element of surprise. Here deception centers on the effort to disguise preparations for attack by convincing the opponent that genuinely hostile activities are harmless. Before Operation Barbarossa, the German invasion of the Soviet Union, the Nazis maintained normal diplomatic and economic relations with the Soviets in an ultimately successful effort to hide their preparations for invasion. Before Tet, the communists used a mix of active and passive deceptive strategies to mislead the allies about the location of the offensive and to hide preparations for the coming attacks. This strategy was insufficient to secure military victory for the communists, but it did help to obtain the element of surprise.[3]

If the communists failed to win the Tet offensive, what then accounts for its effect on American perceptions of the war in Vietnam? Ultimately, the shock it produced was the catalyst that led to the reevaluation of U.S. policy. The Tet attacks failed on the battlefield, but U.S. forces did not anticipate fully the scope, intensity, targets, and timing of the offensive. The allies suffered a failure of intelligence during Tet, a failure that set the stage for changes in U.S. strategy.

Why were the United States and its allies surprised by the Tet attacks? Intelligence analysts, soldiers, and political officials are gener-

---

[3]Charles Cruickshank, *Deception in World War II* (Oxford, 1979), p. xi; Michael Handel, *Military Deception in Peace and War* (Jerusalem, 1985), pp. 9–11; Gordon W. Prange, *Miracle at Midway* (New York, 1982), p. 116; Samuel Eliot Morison, *History of United States Naval Operations in World War II*, vol. 4. *Coral Sea, Midway and Submarine Actions* (Boston, 1949), p. 77; and Barton Whaley, *Codeword BARBAROSSA* (Cambridge, Mass., 1973).

[3]

ally surprised by their opponent's initiatives if they fail to accomplish four tasks, sometimes referred to as the "intelligence cycle": collection of information, analysis, response, and dissemination of warning. The first task is the collection of accurate information about the opponent's intentions and capabilities. There are, of course, a variety of ways to collect information about potential adversaries, from simply reading the foreign press to using advanced technology to monitor the opponent's communications. Yet collection can be arduous because governments bent on surprising their opponents strive to prevent accurate information from reaching their victim. Even though the notion is tautological, surprise can occur because the victim lacks information about the opponent. In any event, one should not dismiss this most parsimonious explanation for a failure of intelligence without first demonstrating that information that could have warned the victim of what was about to unfold was available.[4]

It could be argued that, on balance, U.S. intelligence organizations enjoyed several advantages simply because they were already at war. Certain methods of collecting information obviously were not available; U.S. diplomats and journalists could not wander Hanoi listening for the latest rumor about the regime's intentions. But during war, events on the battlefield can produce an intimate, albeit sometimes painful, awareness of the opponent's idiosyncrasies and standard procedures. Other sources of information generally unavailable in peacetime—reconnaissance overflights, captured documents, and prisoner interrogations—also become available during hostilities. Although it was formidable, the task of collecting information before Tet was not insurmountable from the U.S. perspective.

The second task, the analysis of evidence of enemy intentions and capabilities, is crucial, given the assumption that all information is inherently ambiguous. Current developments in widely scattered regions must be combined into a meaningful pattern. Past events must be linked to reports of future plans. Analysts also must differentiate between *signals* (accurate information about the enemy) and *noise* (inaccurate or irrelevant information) in attempting to predict the opponent's moves. In devising estimates, however, analysts are subjected to a variety of pressures. For example, the "cry wolf" syndrome, a set

---

[4]Michael Handel, "The Politics of Intelligence," *Intelligence and National Security* (October 1987), 5; Walter Laqueur, *A World of Secrets* (New York, 1985), pp. 20–37; and Ariel Levite, *Intelligence and Strategic Surprises* (New York, 1987), pp. 8–9. It should be noted that the specification of intelligence requirements, the decision to attempt to collect certain kinds of information, is usually included in discussions of the intelligence cycle. The listing of intelligence requirements did not, however, play a part in the surprise suffered by the allies during Tet; battlefield operations often generated more captured documents and prisoners than intelligence organizations could handle.

of consequences that flow from the fact that a price must be paid for the sounding of false alarms, can complicate the analytical process. For analysts, this syndrome creates an incentive to make deliberately vague estimates to avoid the professional censure and personal ridicule involved in offering clear, but inaccurate, analyses. In effect, the intellectual challenges involved in predicting the opponent's behavior can be daunting.[5]

The third task, the decision to respond to a warning issued in the analytical stage, is usually the responsibility of policy makers. To be effective, the response chosen must be attuned to the developing threat. In selecting an effective response and ordering its implementation, policy makers also have to overcome obstacles. The "cry wolf" syndrome can again exert an influence. Repeated false alarms can desensitize policy makers to warnings, causing them to fail to respond to an accurate warning. Moreover, because the United States was already at war, the false alarm rate could easily have soared. Analysts could be expected to see the greatest peril in the most mundane events, forcing policy makers to differentiate between the gravity of repeated warnings. Another obstacle is concern about miscalculated escalation; initiatives taken to lessen the impact of an attack could be perceived as threatening by a potential adversary, provoking the opponent to launch a preemptive attack in a crisis that otherwise would have been solved peacefully. Before the outbreak of the October War, for example, the Israelis delayed ordering a general mobilization because of their concerns about miscalculated escalation. Similar concerns also tempered the British response to indications that Argentina was planning to invade the Falkland Islands in 1982. During war, however, concerns about miscalculated escalation should not preoccupy policy makers; it is difficult to imagine how preparations to meet an attack could further exacerbate a conflict once hostilities have started. Ironically, the response of the Johnson administration to warnings of impending attack was shaped by concerns about miscalculated escalation.[6]

The fourth stage of the intelligence cycle is the dissemination of the order to respond to individuals, in this case field commanders. This is

[5]Roberta Wohlstetter, *Pearl Harbor: Warning and Decision* (Stanford, Calif., 1962), pp. 1–3; Ephraim Kam, *Surprise Attack: The Victim's Perspective* (Cambridge, Mass., 1989), pp. 186–187; and Levite, *Intelligence and Strategic Surprises*, pp. 17–18.

[6]Kam, *Surprise Attack*, 187–189; Richard Betts, *Surprise Attack* (Washington, D.C., 1982), p. 145; Janice Gross Stein, "Calculation, Miscalculation, and Conventional Deterrence II: The View from Jerusalem," in *Psychology and Deterrence*, ed. Robert Jervis, Richard Ned Lebow, and Janice Gross Stein (Baltimore, 1985), p. 62; Michael Handel, *Perception, Deception and Surprise: The Case of the Yom Kippur War* (Jerusalem, 1976), p. 41; and Richard Ned Lebow, "Miscalculation in the South Atlantic: The Origins of the Falklands War," in *Psychology and Deterrence*, ed. Jervis et al. pp. 100–102.

[5]

no small task: warning is likely to be ignored if the alert is not convincing or if the actions ordered do not seem relevant to the situation confronting the local commander. Moreover, because hundreds, even thousands, of small-unit commanders need accurate and appropriate information, the dissemination of warning throughout a command, even aided by modern communications, is a huge enterprise. Alerting a large army is like stopping a large truck. The driver can spot the danger ahead and even apply pressure to the brakes, but the time and distance needed to avoid the danger may not be available. Similarly, analysts and policy makers may recognize and warn of an impending threat, but the time needed to reorient the army to meet an attack may not exist. In a sense, analysts and policy makers face a point of no return; after a certain time, alerts issued in response to indications of attack produce diminishing results. Even though the point of no return is scenario-specific, the greater the number of individuals who need to be warned about an impending initiative, the earlier the point of no return arrives before an attack. Because the U.S. leadership had to advise not only their own army but several allied contingents (the South Vietnamese and Koreans) prior to Tet, the need to issue an alert before the point of no return was particularly challenging.

One final observation should be made about the completion of each stage of the intelligence cycle. Those attempting to anticipate an opponent's actions face an inherent disadvantage: a time lag exists between the moment an opponent undertakes preparations for an initiative and the point when these preparations can be first detected. Time elapses before preparations for an attack generate enough signals to stand out against the noise produced by normal levels of activity or efforts at deception. In other words, opponents obtain a head start over victims' attempts to predict their actions, and this inherent disadvantage is further exacerbated by the relatively slow process of collecting and analyzing information and selecting and disseminating a response. Intelligence organizations and policy makers are in a race to catch up with their opponents. They fail to win the race if they are unable to anticipate their opponent's initiatives before crossing the point of no return, the point when it becomes impossible to avoid the operational consequences of surprise.[7]

The intelligence cycle must be completed to avoid surprise; thus, it

---

[7]Levite, *Intelligence and Strategic Surprises*, pp. 13–15; Michael Handel, "Intelligence and the Problem of Strategic Surprise," *Journal of Strategic Studies* 7 (September 1984), 237–241; and Edwin T. Layton, Roger Pineau, and John Costello, *"And I Was There": Pearl Harbor and Midway—Breaking the Secrets* (New York, 1985), p. 22.

can be used as a tool to identify an intelligence failure. Each stage of the cycle must reflect an accurate and timely analysis of six empirical issues: (1) identity of the adversary; (2) probability of attack; (3) type of action involved; (4) location of the attack; (5) timing of the action; and (6) motivation behind the initiative. If these issues are not adequately addressed at each stage of the cycle, then the probability of a surprise increases dramatically. In a sense, then, these problems can be used to identify specific shortcomings at each stage of the intelligence cycle.[8]

Because they were already in a war, the Americans' empirical intelligence problems were relatively modest. After hostilities have commenced, the likelihood of continued attack can be assumed to be high. Because the communists lacked airborne, naval, amphibious, aircraft, and nuclear capabilities, U.S. analysts could assume that any offensive would take the form of infantry and artillery attacks. The identity of the opponent to be faced was also clear; the North Vietnamese and Vietcong had already been identified as the enemy. Paradoxically, intelligence analysts would have been better served by contravening conventional wisdom and entertaining the possibility that new adversaries (the South Vietnamese army and civilians) would join the communists during Tet by staging a revolt against the government. In any event, to avoid surprise, the allies needed to develop an accurate and timely response to only four questions: who was the opponent, and where, when, and why (in the sense of avoiding some disaster or to take advantage of some opportunity) would their opponent attack.

Because the problem of averting surprise attack in wartime is at least theoretically simpler than that of averting surprise at the outbreak of hostilities, the Tet offensive is a critical test of an explanation of intelligence failure. Stated simply, since U.S. forces were already at war with the North Vietnamese and the Vietcong, they confronted a situation in which a successful surprise attack was least likely, a situation in which the probability of some hostile action by the opponent could be taken as given. Still, they were surprised. An analysis of their intelligence activities in terms of the intelligence cycle should indicate why nations often fall victim to surprise attack. An inaccurate analysis of information or a failure to predict the location of an attack does not, however, completely explain the surprise during Tet. To address this kind of event, scholars have used theories drawn from

---

[8]Alexander George, "Warning and Response: Theory and Practice," in *International Violence: Terrorism, Surprise, and Control,* ed. Yair Evon (Jerusalem, 1979), pp. 12–24; Levite, *Intelligence and Strategic Surprises,* pp. 2–3; and Kam, *Surprise Attack,* p. 8.

several levels of analysis. These theories identify variables that often determine whether nations attempting to avoid surprise attack are successful: situational factors peculiar to the production of intelligence estimates, bureaucratic imperatives that shape the production of intelligence estimates, and the way individuals interpret information.

The situational level of analysis explores the way the pressures, concerns, and impediments inherent in the enterprise of intelligence analysis can determine whether accurate estimates are produced. The "cry wolf" syndrome, already mentioned, is just one of these factors. Analysts can also be affected by the "ultra" syndrome, a tendency to become overly reliant on sources with a reputation for providing accurate and timely information. Additionally, analysts can be affected by the "intelligence-to-please" syndrome, a tendency to produce intelligence estimates that support current policy even though information indicates that policy is failing. This syndrome usually stems from difficulties encountered in maintaining a division of labor between intelligence analysis and policy formulation. In theory, intelligence estimates should be totally divorced from policy formulation. In practice, however, analysts must be aware of current policy initiatives if their intelligence estimates are to have any relevance. Since pleasing estimates are often rewarded, intelligence analysts are motivated to produce estimates that support policy makers' preferences. Sometimes the "intelligence-to-please" syndrome is a result of outright pressure from intelligence "consumers" for estimates that support existing preferences. Allegations exist, for example, that civilian and military intelligence analysts were pressured by senior officers and administration officials to provide evidence that U.S. policies toward Vietnam were succeeding.[9]

Theories at the bureaucratic level explain how the behavior and perceptions of individuals are influenced by their organizational affiliation. Such explanations are based on the notion that individuals tend to modify their objectives, attitudes, and conduct so that they match the missions, procedures, and goals of their organization. Depending on the particular bureaucracy, the qualities valued by an organization may not be useful in helping to predict the future moves of an opponent. Additionally, bureaucracy itself—hierarchy, specialization, centralization, routine, secrecy, and especially compartmentaliz-

[9]Kam, *Surprise Attack, p.* 42; Levite, *Intelligence and Strategic Surprises,* pp. 16–17; Laqueur, *World of Secrets,* pp. 102–109; Richard K. Betts, "Intelligence for Policymaking," *Washington Quarterly* 3 (Summer 1980), 119; T. L. Cubbage II, "Westmoreland vs. CBS: Was Intelligence Corrupted by Policy Demands?" (Paper presented at the Intelligence and Military Operations Conference, U.S. Army War College, May 1987); and Samuel Adams, "Vietnam Cover-up: Playing with Numbers," *Harper's,* May 1975.

ation—can all work to impede analysis. Theories on this level also explore the severe disruption bureaucratic rivalry can bring to the production of intelligence estimates.[10]

In this book, situational and bureaucratic explanations for failures of intelligence are treated as second-order, not primary, explanations for the surprise suffered during Tet. Instead, my analysis focuses on the theory of unmotivated biases, a cognitive explanation of decision making that posits that individuals do not follow a rational process in making decisions.[11] The theory of unmotivated biases suggests that a belief system acts to insulate the decision maker from information that contradicts the system. When used in the context of the theory of unmotivated biases, the term "belief system" denotes the ideas held by individuals concerning the nature of the world and the motives of other actors. Individuals usually form these beliefs by drawing on either stereotyped interpretations of dramatic historical events, especially wars and revolutions, or powerful personal experiences. When individuals make a decision, they attempt to place ongoing events in the context of preexisting beliefs, beliefs that often take the form of historical analogies. This phenomenon tends to shape decision making in three important respects. First, belief systems filter the individual's receptivity to information. Decision makers pay attention to information that confirms their beliefs and dismiss information that disconfirms them. If a particular belief system is used to interpret a

[10]Graham T. Allison, *Essence of Decision: Explaining the Cuban Missile Crisis* (Boston, 1971); Morton Halperin, with Priscilla Clapp and Arnold Kanter, *Bureaucratic Politics and Foreign Policy* (Washington, D.C., 1974); and Kam, *Surprise Attack*, pp. 163, 176–86.

[11]Although expositions of rational-actor theory emphasize different factors, they usually share theoretical assumptions. Foremost among these is that individuals use information in an honest fashion to choose the best alternative among a set of options. Four other assumptions are also prominent. First, individuals identify all possible alternatives, or at least they search for alternatives until the process begins to waste resources. Second, individuals estimate the probability that an alternative will be successful and assess the impact of a chosen alternative on the values they seek to optimize. Third, decision makers integrate new information into their effort to make an effective decision, allowing them to make more sophisticated judgments about the implications of various alternatives. Fourth, individuals realize the need to make choices between the benefits and costs of competing alternatives to select the best policy. Even though individuals can only approximate a rational decision-making process in real life, rational-actor theory provides a highly demanding set of criteria that is still advanced as an ideal way to make decisions; see Allison, *Essence of Decision*, pp. 28–38; Richard Ned Lebow, *Between Peace and War* (Baltimore, 1981), p. 101; Irving L. Janis and Leon Mann, *Decision Making: A Psychological Analysis of Conflict, Choice and Commitment* (New York, 1976), pp. 13, 29; Janice Stein and Raymond Tanter, *Rational Decision-Making* (Columbus, 1980), p. 27; Helmut Jungermann, "The Two Camps on Rationality," in *Judgment and Decision Making*, ed. Hal R. Arkes and Kenneth R. Hammond (Cambridge, 1986), pp. 627–641; and Alexander L. George, *Presidential Decisionmaking in Foreign Policy: The Effective Use of Information and Advice* (Boulder, Colo., 1980), pp. 22–23.

given situation, it continues to filter new information in a manner that confirms the applicability of the belief system to developing events. Second, decision makers choose before sufficient information has been collected or evaluated. As a result of this premature cognitive closure, according to Richard Ned Lebow, "policy-makers will proceed a long way down a blind alley before realizing that something is wrong."[12] In other words, individuals tend to make a decision when they possess information that confirms their preexisting beliefs, even though this information may fail to describe adequately the present situation. Finally, belief systems can desensitize individuals to the need to make value trade-offs. Because of a lack of sensitivity to information that calls into question their preexisting beliefs, decision makers are likely to assert that a preferred option will simultaneously support all their goals.[13]

In this book, the theory of unmotivated biases is used to explain how analysts and policy makers addressed the empirical questions confronting them during each phase of the intelligence cycle surrounding the Tet offensive. I examine U.S. officials' beliefs about the situation in Vietnam and the information they possessed. Was the U.S. response to unfolding events appropriate to the information available, or does it reflect U.S. policy makers' belief systems? Part I addresses this question by examining the Tet offensive from the communist perspective. Chapter 1 describes the bruising strategic debate that preoccupied the communist leadership following U.S. intervention in the ground war. I advance a proposition that has largely been overlooked in the literature on Vietnam: U.S. intervention was a significant obstacle in the path of the communist effort to unite Vietnam. The communists launched Tet not only to take advantage of weaknesses in the opposing alliance but also to break a military stalemate, a stalemate that was slowly eliminating their ability to use offensive military action to influence the course of the war. Chapter 2 examines another issue largely overlooked in the literature on the war, the communists' strategy of deception. By clarifying the communist motiva-

---

[12]Lebow, *Between Peace and War*, p. 105. For a discussion of premature cognitive closure, see Robert Jervis, *Perception and Misperception in International Politics*, (Princeton, 1976), pp. 187–191.
[13]Jervis, *Perception and Misperception*, pp. 117–124; "Perceiving and Coping with Threat," in *Psychology and Deterrence*, ed. Jervis et al., pp. 18–24; and "Political Decision Making: Recent Contributions," *Political Psychology* 2 (Summer, 1980), 86–100; Ole R. Holsti, "The Belief System and National Images: A Case Study," *The Journal of Conflict Resolution* 6 (1962), 244–252; Wohlstetter, *Pearl Harbor*, pp. 397–401; Handel, "Intelligence and the Problem of Strategic Surprise," pp. 249–251; Robert Axelrod, *Structure of Decision: Cognitive Maps of Political Elites* (Princeton, 1976); and Richard E. Neustadt and Ernest R. May, *Thinking in Time* (New York, 1986).

tions and preparations for launching the surprise offensive, this section illustrates the problems confronting the allies as they attempted to predict future battlefield developments between June 1967 and January 1968.

In Part II, the analysis moves to the Americans' beliefs about the status of the allied and communist war efforts and communist behavior during truces, and to the analogies U.S. commanders used to explain and predict communist initiatives. Chapter 3 traces the origin of these beliefs and describes the expectations they created among the U.S. leadership about future communist activity on the battlefield. Chapters 4 and 5 describe the information available to U.S. officials and officers before the Tet attacks and the way preexisting beliefs guided their interpretation of indications that the communists were about to launch a major offensive. Chapter 6 shows the U.S. military and intelligence reaction to the Tet attacks, including the lingering influence of beliefs held before the offensive on the way some individuals interpreted enemy intentions. As we also see in Chapter 6, some analysts learned from the surprise suffered during Tet and successfully predicted that the communists would renew their offensive during February and May 1968.

In the Conclusion, the question that frames this analysis—why were the Americans surprised by the Tet attacks?—is answered. The communists' deceptive strategy is evaluated, thereby tracing the parameters of the problem U.S. intelligence had to overcome to avoid surprise. At what point in the intelligence cycle Americans failed is identified. Relying on the theory of unmotivated biases, the conclusion explains why the Americans did not develop an accurate response to the empirical issues that underlie the intelligence cycle.

Given its theoretical approach and structure, this book is intended not only to contribute to the history of the Vietnam War but to follow in a tradition of inquiry that has long fascinated political scientists, the study of intelligence failure. Starting with the Roberts commission, which convened on 22 December 1941, the effort to understand and prevent a repetition of the surprise attack suffered at Pearl Harbor has attracted the attention of many scholars. These efforts produced dozens of analyses, culminating in a major study of intelligence failure, Roberta Wohlstetter's *Pearl Harbor Warning and Decision*. Wohlstetter's work set the tone for future studies in identifying three factors in the failure of intelligence: the signal-to-noise ratio, or the strength of sources of accurate information relative to the strength of confusing or distracting background stimuli; the expectations of the observers; and the rewards and disadvantages of recognizing and correctly analyzing signals. Richard Betts, in his more recent *Surprise Attack*, has added to this list of factors the difficulty inherent in communicating warnings throughout a chain of command and the consequent slowing or even prevention of an effective response.[14] Complimenting Wohlstetter's work is Allen Whiting's classic *China Crosses the Yalu*, an examination of the motivations, perceptions, and policy deliberations that shaped the Chinese decision to intervene in the Korean War. Whiting's analysis addresses the topic of intelligence failure, not from the victim's perspective, but from that of the side that intends to inflict a surprise. Similarly, Barton Whaley and Michael Handel have described the impact of an opponent's deceptive strategies on the likelihood of intelligence failure.[15]

The study of the failure of intelligence suffered by the United States during the Tet offensive can contribute to an understanding of intelligence failure in international relations. In examining the Tet offensive from both the allied and communist perspective, an obvious yet often unexpected fact that sometimes contributes to failures of intelligence is revealed. To avoid surprise, it is often necessary to anticipate the opponent's mistakes. Nations sometimes surprise their opponents by reaching for overly ambitious objectives. Although they often fail to gain these objectives, they may surprise their opponents in the attempt to attain them. But the effort to anticipate the opponent's mistakes, confronts analysts with an extremely difficult problem. Not only must they recognize that the opponent is about to launch an initiative based on faulty information or inaccurate estimates; they must also convince policy makers that the opponent is about to undertake some enterprise that is likely to fail. Instead of responding to indications that the opponent is about to undertake an irrational endeavor, the victim of the looming surprise becomes preoccupied with concerns about enemy deception.

Before Tet, the possibility that the communists miscalculated became more than just hypothetical. Joseph Hovey, an analyst with the Central Intelligence Agency, developed an accurate prediction of the Tet offensive months before the attacks unfolded. His analysis was

[14]Wohlstetter, *Pearl Harbor*; and Betts, *Surprise Attack*. The damage done by international crises on the ability of statesmen to communicate and interpret intended and unintended signals has also been identified as a factor in intelligence failure in Lebow, *Between Peace and War*; "Windows of Opportunity: Do States Jump through Them?" *International Security* 9 (Summer, 1984), 147–186; and *Nuclear Crisis Management: A Dangerous Illusion* (Ithaca, 1987); Jack Snyder, "Civil-Military Relations and the Cult of the Offensive, 1914 and 1984," *International Security* 9 (Summer, 1984), 108–146; and Glenn Snyder and Paul Diesing, *Conflict among Nations* (Princeton, 1977).

[15]Allen S. Whiting, *China Crosses the Yalu: The Decision to Enter the Korean War* (Stanford, Calif., 1960); Whaley, *Codeword BARBAROSSA*; and Handel, *Military Deception in Peace and War*.

circulated among senior officers and officials in the Johnson administration, including the president. Even though his warning of an offensive of unprecedented scope was generally viewed as well reasoned and provocative, all his observations, save one, were dismissed. Hovey's explanation of the communists' motivation for launching the offensive—that they were in dire straits—was viewed as the key analytical element in his estimate. As strange as it appears, his prediction of a major offensive was interpreted as a welcome development, a sign that U.S. policies in Vietnam were succeeding. It would, then, be wrong to underestimate the gravity of the intelligence task faced by the allies as they attempted to anticipate their opponents' next move on the battlefield. Indeed, even under ideal conditions, intelligence analysts face an intellectual problem of enormous difficulty. Immersed in day-to-day events, overwhelmed by administrative details, and bombarded with erroneous and trivial information, they must retain the analytical detachment, the ability to see "the big picture," needed to recognize unexpected patterns and trends. Worse still, hindsight makes their errors of omission and commission all too painfully obvious and obscures the small analytical triumphs that can minimize failures of intelligence. It would also be wrong not to state at the outset that U.S. intelligence agents missed avoiding the operational consequences of surprise by just a few hours. They almost got it right. Given these circumstances, little effort is made to apportion blame among individuals and organizations for the surprise suffered during Tet. Those looking for villains in this book will be disappointed.

PART I

"THE BIG VICTORY,
THE GREAT TASK"

[1]

The Communist Debate
over Strategy

One of the many questions about the Vietnam War that remains to be settled is why the North Vietnamese decided to launch the Tet offensive. The question is intriguing because the communist offensive was both a dismal military failure and a brilliant political success. The U.S. military quickly recovered from the surprise it suffered and decimated the Vietcong (VC) forces that bore the main burden of the attack. In the aftermath of the offensive, however, the American public and the Johnson administration seriously questioned the costs and objectives of the war. In this respect, the Tet offensive acted as a catalyst, setting in motion a chain of events that would lead to negotiations, a halt in the bombing of North Vietnam, and a deescalation of the U.S. combat role in South Vietnam. "Tet did not end the war for the communists," according to Richard Betts, "but it created the necessary conditions for political victory."[1]

Although students of the Vietnam War do not dispute the military outcome of the Tet offensive or its political impact, they have not achieved a consensus about the attack's objectives. Two interpretations of communist goals have dominated the debate. The first main-

[1]Richard Betts, "Strategic Surprise for War Termination: Inchon, Dienbienphu, and Tet," in *Strategic Military Surprise*, ed. by Klaus Knorr and Patrick Morgan (New Brunswick, N.J., 1983), p. 159. The offensive received its name because it was launched during Tet, the beginning of the oriental lunar new year and the most important Vietnamese holiday, cherished by every religious group and social class. For a description of the importance of the Tet celebrations to the people of Vietnam, see Don Oberdorfer, *Tet!* (Garden City, N.Y., 1971), p. 70; and Herbert Y. Schandler, *The Unmaking of a President* (Princeton, 1977), p. 71. For a description of the reevaluation of U.S. policy toward Southeast Asia which began after Tet, see Schandler, *Unmaking of a President*, pp. 105–289; Townsend Hoopes, *The Limits of Intervention* (New York, 1969); and Clark Clifford, "A Vietnam Reappraisal," *Foreign Affairs* 47 (July 1969), 601–622.

tains that the shift created in American public and elite opinion was an intended rather than an unintended consequence of the offensive. Many leading commentators on the war, for example, Gen. William C. Westmoreland, the commander of the U.S. Military Assistance Command, Vietnam (MACV) at the time of the offensive, Col. Harry G. Summers, Leslie Gelb, and Richard Betts, claim that the attitudes of the American public and members of the Johnson administration were the ultimate targets of the offensive.[2]

The second interpretation maintains that an improvement in the military situation or even the immediate domination of South Vietnam was the primary objective behind what the communists called their "general offensive–general uprising." Stanley Karnow, for example, notes that, at a maximum, the communists hoped to overthrow the Saigon regime and replace it with a neutralist coalition dominated by the VC. Once in place, the new regime would work to eliminate U.S. presence and put Vietnam on the path to unification under communist control. U. S. Grant Sharp, former commander in chief, Pacific (CINCPAC), believes that the communists intended to destroy the South Vietnamese administrative structure so that it would no longer function even with U.S. aid. Sharp also notes that the North Vietnamese hoped for a large-scale defection of South Vietnamese troops, facilitating the communist domination of large portions of the country. According to Patrick McGarvey, Tet was intended to improve the position of the North Vietnamese in future negotiations by placing the two northernmost South Vietnamese provinces under communist control, setting the stage for the eventual domination of the country.[3]

Neither of these interpretations is particularly compelling. The first is misleading because it ignores the probable existence of a communist theory of victory and seems to suggest that the North Vietnamese expected to tip the political scales in their favor just by demonstrating their willingness to stand up to their opponents' firepower. It fails to account for any realistic North Vietnamese military objectives, the logical prerequisite for an effort to influence American opinion. In contrast, the second explanation, which focuses on the military objectives of the offensive, fails to acknowledge the deteriorating situation faced by the North Vietnamese and VC forces on the eve of Tet.

[2]William C. Westmoreland, *A Soldier Reports* (Garden City, N.Y., 1976), p. 322; Harry G. Summers, *On Strategy* (Novato, Calif., 1982), p. 133; and Leslie Gelb with Richard Betts, *The Irony of Vietnam: The System Worked* (Washington, D.C., 1979), pp. 333–334.

[3]Stanley Karnow, *Vietnam: A History* (New York, 1983), p. 537; U. S. Grant Sharp, *Strategy for Defeat* (San Rafael, Calif., 1978), p. 214; and Patrick McGarvey, *Visions of Victory* (Stanford, Calif., 1969), p. 50.

NORTH
VIETNAM

DMZ

Quang
Tri

THAILAND

LAOS

Hue
Thua
Thien

I CTZ

Quang
Nam

Quang Tin

Quang
Ngai

Kontum

Binh
Dinh

Pleiku

II CTZ

CAMBODIA

Phu
Bon

Phu
Yen

Darlac

SOUTH VIETNAM

Khanh
Hoa

Quang
Duc

Tuyen
Duc

Ninh
Thuan

Phuoc
Long

Binh
Long

Lam Dong

Binh
Thuan

Tay
Ninh

Binh
Duong

Long
Khanh

Hau
Nghia

Bien
Hoa

Binh
Tuy

Kien
Phong

Kien
Tuong

Long
An

Saigon

Phuoc
Tuy

South
China
Sea

Chau
Doc

An
Giang

Sa
Dec

Dinh
Tuong

Go Cong

Gia
Dinh

III CTZ

CMD

Vinh
Long

Kien Hoa

Dau Phu Quoc
(Kien Giang)

Phong
Dinh

Kien
Giang

Chuong
Thien

Vinh
Binh

Ba
Xuyen

Bac
Lieu

IV CTZ

An
Xuyen

Con Son

International boundary
Province boundary
CTZ boundary
National capital

0   50 Miles
0   50 Kilometers

SOUTH VIETNAM

[19]

Moreover, both interpretations largely ignore the insights into communist objectives offered by the concept of a "people's war," especially the Vietnamese version of this strategy.[4]

My purpose in this chapter is to examine the communist debate over strategy that led to the Tet offensive. For two years before the decision to launch the offensive, a bitter debate took place among communist military leaders over the appropriate tactical and strategic response to U.S. intervention in the ground war in the south. As communist leaders witnessed the erosion of their hard-won military gains during successive compaign seasons, they were unable to select a strategy to overcome the strengths of, and take advantage of the weaknesses of, their new opponents. Throughout the course of this debate, though, a slow but steady movement toward the strategy and tactics of the Tet offensive can be detected.

My examination of this communist debate illustrates three aspects of the decision to launch the Tet offensive, aspects largely overlooked in previous analyses. First, the decision was probably motivated by a desire to end a divisive military debate over the proper response to U.S. intervention; an offensive that utilized the entire range of military assets in the south would serve to appease all sides in the strategy debate by incorporating everyone's pet project and military organization. Second, the decision was motivated by the military leadership's perception that they were no longer making significant progress toward the unification of Vietnam under communist rule; both the North Vietnamese and VC leadership realized that, if current military trends continued, they would eventually lack the resources needed for an offensive strong enough to affect the military situation in the south. Finally, the examination of the debate over strategy demonstrates that the Tet offensive was the first major initiative adopted by the communists in response to U.S. intervention in the ground war. The communist leadership hoped that Tet would actually win the war in the south. At worst, they probably expected that the attacks would stop the momentum of allied offensive operations, buying the time needed to lay the groundwork for an extended war of attrition.

[4]According to Bernard Brodie, if Gen. Vo Nguyen Giap, in planning the Tet offensive, "really intended what he in fact achieved, then he must stand out as one of the most brilliant strategists in all history. That may be allowing him too much; on the other hand, those who hold that he was expecting a tactical victory and had no idea that his inevitable tactical defeat would nevertheless bring in its train fabulous strategic and political gains are setting him down as stupid—a conclusion that ill accords with the other accomplishments of this man, including the 1954 victory at Dien Bien Phu"; Brodie, "Tet Offensive," in *Decisive Battles of the Twentieth Century*, ed. Noble Frankland and Christopher Dowling (London, 1976), p. 305.

The Vietnamese Approach to People's War

Throughout the war, U.S. observers failed not only to recognize the martial traditions that influenced the communists' conduct of the war but also to understand their opponents' military strategy. Speaking years after the conclusion of the conflict, Gen. Phillip Davidson, chief of MACV intelligence during the Tet offensive, remarked that "the great deficiency of our entire operation . . . was [that] we really didn't have any experts on Vietnam who could tell us about these things."[5] To an extent, Americans can be forgiven for this shortcoming. Couched in convoluted terminology best understood by cadres long schooled in Marxism-Leninism, communist military writings did more than just communicate the latest twist in military strategy emanating from Hanoi; the rhetoric created by communist strategists also was meant to have a political impact by bolstering morale among their forces in the south and by winning the global propaganda battle. U.S. intelligence analysts failed to understand their adversary because they focused on only two aspects of their opponent's strategy: the Vietnamese application of people's war, which relied heavily on the ideas articulated by Lin Piao and Mao Tse-tung; and the military aspects—especially military operations involving conventional units—of the communist effort to unite Vietnam.[6]

Although the Soviets exerted a strong influence on the Vietnamese communists during the 1930s, the three-phase strategy of people's war devised by the Chinese communists eventually provided a framework for communist activities in South Vietnam. In phase one of the Chinese plan, the insurgents remain on the defensive but attempt to establish control of the population and conduct terrorist and guerrilla operations. In phase two, regular military forces are formed, the tempo of guerrilla activity increases, and isolated government forces are engaged. In the final phase, the insurgency is victorious as large military units, organized along conventional lines, go on the offen-

---

[5]Phillip Davidson, Oral History I, 30 March 1982, interviewed by Ted Gittinger, p. 42, LBJ Library; Laqueur, *World of Secrets*, p. 185. On the Vietnamese martial tradition, see Neil Sheehan, *A Bright Shining Lie: John Paul Vann and America in Vietnam* (New York, 1988), pp. 159–160.

[6]Douglas Pike, *PAVN: People's Army of Vietnam* (Novato, Calif., 1986), p. 19; and Andrew F. Krepinevich, Jr., *The Army and Vietnam* (Baltimore, 1986). D. Michael Shafer even suggests that the focus on the doctrine of people's war served U.S. analysts badly because the doctrine itself is a poor guide to the factors that fueled the insurgency in Vietnam; see Shafer, *Deadly Paradigms: The Failure of U.S. Counterinsurgency Policy* (Princeton, 1988), p. 110.

sive, destroying the government's forces and establishing full control of the population.[7]

The Vietnamese, however, developed their own version of people's war. They succeeded, according to Douglas Pike, in devising a strategy that eliminated the distinction between soldiers and civilians, uniting both in the *dau tranh* (struggle) against the enemy. Everyone was to participate in at least one of the two prongs of people's war: *dau tranh vu trang* (armed struggle, or "violence program") and *dau tranh chinh tri* (political struggle, or "politics with guns"). Political action was directed against three specific targets. *Dich van* (action among the enemy) was intended to undermine support for the war among the population in enemy-controlled areas—to win the propaganda war for the hearts and minds of the South Vietnamese and for the sympathy of the American public. *Binh van* (action among the military) was at a minimum intended to undermine morale in the opponent's army, thereby reducing its effectiveness in combat. At a maximum, the communists hoped that *binh van* would cause South Vietnamese soldiers to defect to the communist side, or even to defect in place by supplying weapons and information about allied military operations to the VC. *Dan van* (action among the people) was to bolster support for the cause in communist-controlled areas in order to harness the manpower and material resources these regions could supply.[8]

Although the proper mix of armed and political struggle in each phase of people's war was often the subject of intense debate within the communist hierarchy, the intensity of both activities was intended to increase as the battle moved toward the culmination of phase three: the general offensive–general uprising. The phrase is appropriate: the general offensive implies overwhelming military pressure; the

---

[7]William J. Duiker, *The Communist Road to Power in Vietnam* (Boulder, Colo., 1981), pp. 45–55, 128–131; and Westmoreland, *Soldier*, p. 54. General Giap described his strategy during the war against the French as follows: "Our strategy was, as we have stressed, to wage a long-lasting battle. A war of this nature in general entails several phases: in principle, starting from a stage of contention, it goes through a period of equilibrium before arriving at a general counter-offensive. . . . To maintain and increase our forces, was the principle to which we adhered, contenting ourselves with attacking when success was certain, refusing to give battle likely to incur losses to us or to engage in hazardous actions. We had to apply the slogan: to build up our strength during the actual course of fighting"; Vo Nguyen Giap, *People's War People's Army* (New York, 1962), p. 29.

[8]Pike, *PAVN*, pp. 215–220, 233–252; Douglas S. Blaufarb, *The Counterinsurgency Era: U.S. Doctrine and Performance* (New York, 1977), p. 12, 231 n. 2; Douglas Pike, *History of Vietnamese Communism 1925–1976* (Stanford, Calif., 1978), pp. 116–117. For a history of struggle movements conducted by the NLF, see Douglas Pike, *Viet Cong* (Cambridge, Mass., 1966), pp. 385–397.

opponent is subjected to the full force of the conventional units that have taken the field during the third phase; the general uprising is the culmination of years of political *dau tranh*. As envisioned by the Vietnamese, thousands of civilians would burst onto the streets of the cities and villages of South Vietnam in an outpouring of revolutionary fervor. Joined by individual defectors from the South Vietnamese army or even entire units, the general uprising would sweep the Saigon regime from power.[9]

The concept of a general uprising represents the major Vietnamese contribution to the theory of people's war. Historically, the Vietnamese had employed this tactic against Chinese rule at least ten times before C.E. 940. In more recent times, they also fostered a mass revolt against the French in the August uprising of 1945 and against the South Vietnamese regime in 1959 and 1960. In fact, during the 1960 uprising the communists timed their attacks to coincide with the Tet holidays, imitating a precedent set by Nguyen Hue when he led a surprise attack in 1799 against the Chinese occupiers of Hanoi. The decision to launch a general uprising against U.S. forces was, however, a point of contention within the communist hierarchy. Timing (*thoi co*, or "opportune moment") was crucial. If military and political conditions were not favorable, efforts to launch a general offensive–general uprising could end in disaster. Still, the communists believed that this was their ultimate weapon.[10]

Although in hindsight it might appear that the communists attained their objectives by simply progressing through each phase of people's war, in fact their strategic decisions often involved heated debate. Differences of perspective between northern and southern communists often served as a source of tension. Both the Central Office for South Vietnam (COSVN), initially established in 1951 as the communist military headquarters in South Vietnam, and the southern branch of the Vietnamese Worker's (communist) party (VWP), the

---

[9]Pike, *PAVN*, pp. 218–219; Duiker, *Road to Power*, pp. 72–73. For an idealized description of the general offensive–general uprising, see Tran Van Tra, *Vietnam: History of the Bulwark B2 Theatre*, vol. 5: *Concluding the 30-Years War* (Ho Chi Minh City, 1982), translated by Foreign Broadcast Information Service (JPRS 82783, 2 February 1983), pp. 96, 110.

[10]Pike, *PAVN*, p. 18; Oberdorfer, *Tet*, pp. 46–48; Karnow, *Vietnam*, pp. 100, 146; and William Broyles, Jr. "The Road to Hill 10," *Atlantic Monthly* 225 (April 1985), 103. For discussion of the evolution of NLF doctrine concerning the general uprising, see Pike, *Viet Cong*, pp. 76, 92, 104. For a discussion of the 1960 Tet attacks and general uprising, see Wallace J. Thies, *When Governments Collide* (Berkeley, 1980), p. 238; and Jeffrey Race, *War Comes to Long An* (Berkeley, 1972), pp. 113–115. The peasant revolts during late 1959 and early 1960 were quickly quelled by the regime in Saigon; see Duiker, *Road to Power*, pp. 190–193. For the North Vietnamese perspective on the requirements for a successful general uprising, see Giap, *People's War*, pp. 81–82, 87.

[23]

People's Revoltuionary party (PRP), established in 1962, were created to prevent southerners from straying from the political and military line set by the regime in Hanoi. A "Red vs. expert" debate also flared among officials in Hanoi. Faced with an opponent that possessed advanced weaponry and huge material resources, military and political leaders constantly debated whether ideological purity and revolutionary zeal were more important than technical expertise and sophisticated weaponry. Finally, argument over the proper mix of armed and political *dau tranh* influenced virtually every decision made by the communists in conducting the war, especially the ultimate decision to launch the general offensive–general uprising.[11]

VICTORY DENIED

Although a detailed examination of the events leading to the U.S. involvement in the ground war is beyond the scope of this analysis, a brief description of the military situation on the eve of U.S. intervention is a logical starting point for a history of the communist debate over strategy. In the few months before the intervention, communist forces nearly succeeded in uniting the country by overwhelming the Army of the Republic of Vietnam (ARVN). The loss of this nearly victorious position would haunt communist officials as they worked to develop an appropriate response to the influx of U.S. combat units.

Early Communist Successes

South Vietnam was in dire straits on the eve of U.S. intervention. In the words of Gen. Nguyen Xuan Hoang, the principal North Vietnamese army historian of the war, "by the end of 1964 our forces in the South had defeated the puppet troops. The war could have ended then, without so much bloodshed and suffering."[12] Communist forces had made steady progress in their effort to unite Vietnam by following the three-phase strategy of people's war. In fact, as the communists moved through the succeeding stages of their strategy, the military fortunes of the South Vietnamese deteriorated.

The communists began the first phase of their strategy in 1959

---

[11]Duiker, *Road to Power*, pp. 138, 213; Pike, *PAVN*, pp. 174–175, 223; William J. Duiker, *Vietnam: Nation in Revolution* (Boulder, Colo., 1983), pp. 85–86; "The People's Revolutionary Party in Rural Areas," *Viet-Nam Documents and Research Notes (VDRN)*, (Saigon, 1967), doc. 6, p. 1; Westmoreland, *Soldier*, p. 206; and Gabriel Kolko, *Anatomy of a War: Vietnam, the United States, and the Modern Historical Experience* (New York, 1985), p. 182.

[12]Nguyen Xuan Hoang quoted in Broyles, "The Road to Hill 10," p. 103.

when "regroupees," South Vietnamese communists who had moved to the north after the conclusion of the 1954 Geneva Accords, began to return south to aid the communists who had remained there. The southerners, who clamored for help from the north, were fighting for survival after Ngo Dinh Diem launched an anticommunist campaign in 1957. Even though the campaign alienated many South Vietnamese peasants, who were unjustly caught in Diem's efforts to eliminate all forms of political opposition, it did succeed in decimating communist ranks. The communists responded by increasing their program to exterminate traitors, specifically eliminating government officials. Under these circumstances, the initial phase of people's war—avoiding government units while conducting a terrorist campaign to eliminate the officials responsible for the decimation of communist ranks—matched the needs of the indigenous southern communists. As the VC gained strength, the number of officials killed per year rose from 193 in 1958 to 1,400 in 1960.[13]

In January 1961, Radio Hanoi announced the creation of the National Liberation Front (NLF) in South Vietnam. This announcement reflected the decision, made at the Third National Congress of the VWP held in Hanoi during September 1960, to become more active in the south. COSVN, which had been abolished in 1954, was also reactivated under the direction of Gen. Nguyen Chi Thanh. In the wake of these developments, the VC switched to the second phase of people's war and began to use large units in their insurgency. VC strength continued to grow throughout 1961, reaching 26,700 at year's end; by early 1962, attacks by thousand-man units were not uncommon.[14] The ARVN, trained by its U.S. advisers to repel a conventional invasion, found itself ill equipped to deal with the rising insurgency. Moreover, during the switch to tactics more suited to counterinsurgency warfare, ARVN operations lost momentum. As a result, the number of officials killed or abducted by the VC reached 1,000 per month by the end of 1962.[15]

Although the deterioration of the military and political position of

[13]Duiker, *Vietnam*, p. 54; and *Road to Power*, pp. 183–193; Ronald H. Spector, *Advice and Support: The Early Years of the U.S. Army in Vietnam 1941–1960* (New York, 1985), pp. 310–316; Kolko, *Anatomy of a War*, pp. 99–101; George McT. Kahin, *Intervention: How America Became Involved in Vietnam* (Garden City, N.Y., 1987), pp. 96–97; and U. S. Grant Sharp and William C. Westmoreland, *Report on the War in Vietnam* (Washington, D.C., 1968), p. 78.
[14]Duiker, *Road to Power*, pp. 193–199; and Sharp and Westmoreland, *Report*, pp. 78–79.
[15]Spector, *Advice and Support*, pp. 275–302; Cao Van Vien and Dong Van Khuyen, *Reflections on the Vietnam War* (Washington, D.C., 1980), p. 10; Krepinevich, *Army*, pp. 21–26; and, Sharp and Westmoreland, *Report*, p. 80.

the South Vietnamese government accelerated during 1963, the communists were not particularly responsible for these setbacks. Instead, domestic political turmoil was the major source of trouble for the government. During the summer, martial law was imposed to quell rioting that followed Buddhist protests. After the November coup that ousted President Ngo Dinh Diem and his brother, Ngo Dinh Nhu, conditions worsened as political infighting repeatedly erupted in coups.[16] This struggle for power had a bad effect on the government's war effort. ARVN units that had previously battled the VC were now used by military cliques in their competition for power in Saigon. After each successful coup, ARVN commanders and district and province chiefs were replaced, further hampering the battle against the VC. Thus, as the political turmoil continued into 1964, the government began to lose control of rural areas. Strategic hamlets, the fortified villages constructed under the Diem regime, were overrun, and local paramilitary units melted away into the population.[17]

In this context of growing unrest in South Vietnam, Ho Chi Minh and his senior aides met in December 1963 to evaluate recent developments and plan strategy. Southern cadres were becoming disillusioned because the Saigon regime failed to collapse after the fall of Diem and because the United States did not abandon its weakened ally. After much debate, the politburo called for a change of strategy. The North Vietnamese apparently decided to give added weight to armed *dau tranh* because political *dau tranh* had failed to destroy the Saigon regime. The politburo wanted to capitalize on VC progress by introducing North Vietnamese Army (NVA) units into the conflict, but it did not overlook the probable U.S. reaction to the movement of NVA units into South Vietnam. North Vietnamese leaders believed that the United States would be unlikely to end its material and advisory effort, and that it might even respond by deploying up to 100,000 combat troops to South Vietnam—but they dismissed this latter possibility as remote. They may have concluded, according to William Duiker, that by escalating the conflict they would reduce the likelihood of massive U.S. intervention. By selectively applying analogies drawn from Mao's victory in China and the compromise that had ended the war in Korea, the politburo apparently reasoned that, as

---

[16]Krepinevich, *Army*, pp. 84–94; Duiker, *Road to Power*, pp. 219–221; Kahin, *Intervention*, pp. 122–235; and Douglas Macdonald, "'Adventures in Chaos': Reformism in American Foreign Policy" (Ph.D. diss. Columbia University, 1987), especially pt. 4.

[17]Hoang Ngoc Lung, *The General Offensives of 1968–69* (Washington, D.C., 1981), p. 1; and Sharp and Westmoreland, *Report*, pp. 81, 92.

the crisis in Vietnam deepened, the United States would cut its losses in a deteriorating situation.[18]

The North Vietnamese decision to exploit the deteriorating situation in South Vietnam by committing entire NVA units to the conflict marked a shift in communist strategy. Armed *dau tranh* would now overshadow political *dau tranh* until the eruption of the Tet offensive in January 1968. This change in strategy also marked a shift to the third phase of people's war. Bolstered by an infusion of modern weaponry, personnel, supplies from the north, and by the end of the year NVA regiments, VC units inflicted a series of defeats on ARVN. In April 1964, for example, VC units overran the district capital of Kien Long in the southern tip of the Mekong delta, killing over three hundred ARVN soldiers. In July, the VC attacked several U.S. Special Forces camps, overrunning bases near the demilitarized zone (DMZ) and in Pleiku province. On 28 December, 1964, the VC 9th Division seized the village of Binh Gia in Phuoc Tuy province and virtually destroyed two ARVN battalions and inflicted heavy casualties on the armored force that attempted to relieve the beleaguered units. This engagement at Binh Gia was a turning point in the war—the first time a VC unit engaged in sustained combat against large ARVN forces.[19]

By the beginning of 1965, the pressures generated by political turmoil, a weak administrative structure, a collapse in ARVN combat capability, and a growing communist insurgency placed the South Vietnamese government in an untenable position. By defeating ARVN units in several battles in the central highlands and around Saigon, the VC and NVA exhausted ARVN's tactical reserve. Casualties among poorly led ARVN troops were mounting and their morale was declining, making it increasingly clear that the South Vietnamese could no longer handle the situation. The regime controlled only the cities and towns, leaving most of the countryside to the insurgents. The north–south lines of communication, such as roads and railroads, were cut in dozens of places, especially in heavily populated coastal areas. Normal social and economic life was disrupted, and ARVN struggled to defend the district and provincial capitals, which were swollen with refugees from the countryside. Additionally, there were indications that the enemy was preparing to seize

---

[18]Duiker, *Road to Power*, pp. 221–223, 226; and Karnow, *Vietnam*, pp. 327, 329–330. Karnow apparently relies on a 1981 interview with Vietnam's prime minister Pham Van Dong for his evaluation of North Vietnamese estimates of the likelihood of a U.S. response to the North Vietnamese invasion of South Vietnam.

[19]Sharp and Westmoreland, *Report*, p. 93.

large areas south of the DMZ and in the central highlands. According to Bruce Palmer, who toured all four South Vietnamese corps tactical zones in February 1965, "the overall picture was clear [that,] unless the situation was reversed soon, South Vietnam would not survive. To the Americans on the scene in Vietnam it seemed obvious that if the United States wanted to preserve the Republic of Vietnam, the only means available was to commit U.S. ground combat troops."[20]

The North Vietnamese Reaction to U.S. Intervention

On 8 March 1965, the United States sent the 5,000-man 9th Marine Expeditionary Brigade to South Vietnam to defend the airbase at Da Nang. After this initial deployment, the U.S. military presence rapidly expanded in the south. By the beginning of 1966, MACV already had 116,700 soldiers and 41,000 marines in Vietnam. Yet this was only a prelude to the major buildup that would occur that year. In 1966, two marine divisions, six army infantry divisions, the 1st Brigade of the 101st Airborne Division, the 173d Airborne Brigade, the 11th Armored Cavalry Regiment, and the 196th and 199th Infantry Brigades were also deployed. The buildup continued throughout 1967, and on the eve of the Tet offensive there were about half a million U.S. troops in Vietnam.[21]

The North Vietnamese leadership was surprised not only by the U.S. intervention but also by the scope and pace of the buildup of ground forces. They had made a crucial mistake in figuring that the United States would not intervene decisively to save the Saigon regime. In fact, U.S. intervention was probably the first major surprise of the war (the other instances being the Tet offensive and the 1972 Christmas bombing of Hanoi and Haiphong). Le Duan, secretary general of the Lao Dong (Communist Workers) party, coolly admitted long after 1965 that "the situation had developed more rapidly than we had anticipated."[22] Dave Palmer, a noted observer of the war, described the North Vietnamese reaction in more emotional terms: "The leaders in Hanoi were dumbstruck by Washington's reaction. Consternation and disbelief were their initial reactions. Aspirations for

[20]Bruce Palmer, *The 25-Year War* (Lexington, Ky., 1984), p. 39; McGarvey, *Visions of Victory*, p. 9; and Sharp and Westmoreland, *Report*, p. 81.

[21]Shelby L. Stanton, *The Rise and Fall of an American Army* (Novato, Calif., 1985), pp. 31–32, 65; and Sharp and Westmoreland, *Report*, p. 197.

[22]Robert Shaplen, *Time out of Hand* (New York, 1969), p. 376. Another senior communist official, writing under the pseudonym Anh Sau (probably Gen. Nguyen Chi Thanh), noted in a letter written in 1966 that "things do not always develop in strict accordance with our subjective judgement and intentions"; quoted in Duiker, *Road to Power*, p. 243.

early victory dimmed as U.S. units streamed ashore." The U.S. intervention was clearly a turning point that shocked the communists and
enormously increased the difficulties they faced in their effort to unite
the country.[23]

The new situation presented the North Vietnamese and VC leadership with an immense problem. They had to devise a response that
would negate the advantages in resources, mobility, and firepower
enjoyed by their new enemy. The search for a successful answer to
this problem would occupy communist leaders until the decision to
launch the Tet offensive, in July 1967, but the first step was the selec-
tion of strategy and tactics for the 1965 campaign. In their initial discussions, communist leaders working in the north and south held
different views about the impact of U.S. involvement and the best
way to respond to it, setting a pattern that would be mirrored in future discussions. The North Vietnamese leadership questioned the
ability of the VC and NVA to continue to take the offensive against
U.S. forces. Instead of continuing the large-unit operations called for
in the third phase of people's war, they believed that it would be
prudent to return to the guerrilla tactics of phase two until they could
take full measure of their new adversary. For example, Gen. Vo
Nguyen Giap, now North Vietnam's defense minister, apparently argued that communist forces should go on the defensive in order to
buy time for the further buildup of NVA forces. On the other side,
Gen. Nguyen Chi Thanh, overall commander of NVA and VC forces
in the south, wanted to continue the third-phase tactics, which had
been successful during the 1964 campaign season. According to Patrick McGarvey, Thanh believed that "to pause when the troops were
flushed with many recent victories would deprive them of the psychological momentum necessary to counter the influx of American
troops."[24]

Although it is impossible to determine the exact rationale behind
the decision, three factors probably influenced the communist deci-

---

[23]Dave Richard Palmer, *Summons of the Trumpet* (San Rafael, Calif., 1978), p. 84; Duiker, *Road to Power*, pp. 240–243; Kolko, *Anatomy of a War*, pp. 153–154; and Summers,
On Strategy, p. 153. According to Patrick McGarvey, "the move that caused the greatest
anxiety among Vietnamese Communist leaders—if the sheer volume of writing is an
accurate guage—was the sudden influx of American ground forces in South Vietnam in
mid-1965"; McGarvey, *Visions of Victory*, p. 5.

[24]McGarvey, *Visions of Victory*, p.8; and William O. Staudenmaier, "Vietnam, Mao
and Clausewitz," *Parameters* 7 (1977), 52–53. Disagreements over strategy existed between Thanh and Giap since the early 1960s; see Timothy J. Lomperis, *The War Everyone Lost—and Won* (Baton Rouge, 1984), p. 57. For biographies of Giap and Thanh,
including the positions and pseudonyms they adopted in the debate over strategy, see
Pike, *PAVN*, pp. 339–343, 348–351.

sion to approve Thanh's plan. First, the communists faced severe time constraints. Any new strategic and tactical approach had to be designed before the beginning of the 1965 winter-spring offensive. The fact that the communists had only limited time to devise and implement a new policy might have worked in Thanh's favor. Second, in the previous campaign season Thanh had already demonstrated that third-phase tactics could be effective. In the absence of overwhelming contradictory evidence, it might have seemed reasonable to believe that Thanh would enjoy similar success again. Finally, implicit in the strategy advanced by Giap and other northerners was the idea that the military should go on the defensive, a move that could result in the loss of hard-won objectives. The leadership was probably reluctant to move back one phase in the overall strategy of people's war unless it was absolutely necessary. In any event, the communists apparently found Thanh's arguments convincing. The 1965 campaign opened with the large-scale attacks advocated by Thanh.

THE 1965 WINTER-SPRING CAMPAIGN

Although the efficacy of U.S. military tactics and strategy in Vietnam remains a controversial issue, much of this debate overlooks the fact that the intervention had a tremendous impact on the communist military effort. U.S. forces made a good deal of progress toward the goals outlined by General Westmoreland. In his memoirs, Westmoreland notes that his strategy was divided into three phases:

Phase One: Commit those American and Allied forces necessary "to halt the losing trend" by the end of 1965.
Phase Two: "During the first half of 1966," take the offensive with American and Allied forces in "high priority areas" to destroy enemy forces and reinstitute pacification programs.
Phase Three: If the enemy persisted, he might be defeated and his forces and base areas destroyed during a period of a year to a year and a half following Phase II.[25]

The shifts between the phases of Westmoreland's strategy roughly correspond to the conduct of allied operations intended to blunt successive communist winter-spring offensives. A brief description of the outcome of the 1965 dry-season campaign illustrates the first step in

---

[25]Westmoreland, *Soldier*, p. 142.

the progression through the first two phases of Westmoreland's strategy.

Major U.S. Operations

During the 1965 dry season, Westmoreland attained his first objective by denying victory to the communists. In a series of engagements collectively known as the battle of the Ia Drang valley, which lasted from mid-October to late November, the NVA suffered a stunning defeat.[26]

The North Vietnamese intended to commit three NVA regiments in a drive from Cambodia across central Vietnam. The drive itself was supposed to terminate in Binh Dinh province, placing the central highlands under communist control and effectively cutting South Vietnam in half. The communists might have hoped that a victory of this proportion would cause the South Vietnamese government to collapse, thereby ending organized ARVN resistance. To secure these objectives, Gen. Chy Huy Man, commander of the NVA units in this offensive, developed a three-stage strategy. Initially, Man intended to use the 33d NVA Regiment to overrun outposts along the Cambodian border and then the 32d NVA Regiment to ambush allied relief columns. During the second stage, the 66th NVA Regiment was to exploit these allied setbacks by destroying isolated units and capturing key towns left unguarded as allied troops moved to relieve the besieged outposts. In this manner, Man planned to extend communist control over the Pleiku plateau. In the third stage of the campaign, a link-up between all three NVA regiments would be undertaken in the final drive toward the sea. The battle opened on 19 October when the U.S. Special Forces camp at Plei Me, 40 kilometers southwest of Pleiku, was struck by artillery fire. Almost from the outset, Man's plan went awry. NVA units failed to overwhelm Plei Me after a week-long siege. The garrison was relieved by an ARVN force, which succeeded, with the help of reinforcements from the U.S. 1st Air Cavalry Division, in fighting its way through an NVA ambush. In the wake of this initial failure, Man called off the operation. On about 26 October, NVA units began retiring westward toward the Cambodian border, and for four days they avoided detection by reconnaissance units

---

[26]Sharp and Westmoreland, *Report*, p. 281. The annual winter-spring offensive established a pattern throughout the war. Weather was critical in determining the pace of military operations; offensive operations tended to be confined to the period from November to May, when the northeast monsoon brought dry weather to the area west of the coastal plains of South Vietnam (the Tet offensive, for example, constituted the 1967 winter-spring campaign).

[31]

from the 1st Cavalry Division. On 1 November, however, a company-size action developed after U.S. troops landed to investigate a helicopter reconnaissance report of movement along the Tae River. During this engagement, the allies captured a document that identified the location of NVA units consolidating for their withdrawal toward Cambodia. The U.S. forces went on the offensive. In a series of battles between 3 and 6 November the NVA was engaged by elements of the 1st Cavalry that were now positioned to block the communist withdrawal.[27]

At this juncture, General Man mistook the rotation of units of the 1st Cavalry as evidence of a retreat. He again decided to go on the offensive. The biggest engagement of the campaign then ensued on 14 November around a small clearing in the Ia Drang valley, dubbed landing zone X-ray. In the two-day battle, which resulted in at least 600 NVA and 79 U.S. troops killed in action, a battalion of the 1st Cavalry, with the aid of reinforcements, heavy artillery, and airstrikes, defeated successive NVA assaults. The soldiers at landing zone X-ray also succeeded in buying the time needed to deploy additional allied troops. Five ARVN battalions were helicoptered into positions across the communists' line of retreat. NVA units, after breaking off the engagement around landing zone X-ray, ran headlong into this ARVN force and suffered heavy casualties. In effect, the battle of the Ia Drang valley broke the back of the 1965 winter-spring offensive.[28]

The Impact of U.S. Operations on Communist Forces in the South

Although communist forces suffered from supply, morale, and organizational difficulties before U.S. intervention—the communists had lamented the decline in the performance of cadres since the end of the war against the French—the growing number of U.S. soldiers only compounded the problem. The attempt to match U.S. firepower taxed the communists' logistical capabilities, and U.S. operations disrupted their supply system. Moreover, the VC infrastructure apparently reacted sluggishly to the new demands created by the increased

---

[27]Palmer, *Summons*, pp. 91–97; Karnow, *Vietnam*, pp. 479–480; J. D. Coleman, *Pleiku: The Dawn of Helicopter Warfare in Vietnam* (New York, 1988); and Lung, *General Offensives*, p.2.

[28]The month-long operation resulted in 1,771 known enemy and 300 U.S. troops killed; see Sharp and Westmoreland, *Report*, p. 281; and Westmoreland, *Soldier*, p. 157. Official U.S. reports of enemy killed must be taken with a grain of salt, however; for a discussion of this issue, see Martin Van Creveld, *Command in War* (Cambridge, Mass., 1985), pp. 253–254. For an evaluation of the battle of the Ia Drang valley, see Palmer, *Summons*, pp. 98–103.

tempo of combat during the 1965 dry season, with exposure to immense firepower contributing to a decline in morale among soldiers in both VC and NVA units.[29]

An insight into the impact of U.S. operations on NVA units during the 1965 campaign is provided by a diary captured in Binh Dinh province. The diary was kept by Ha Xuan Dai, a medical corpsman of the 7th Battalion of the NVA Quyet Tam Regiment. The battalion was involved in three engagements between 21 and 24 November. Subjected to repeated artillery and airstrikes over a four-day period, Dai described his impressions of the battle:

23 November: I stayed at the foot of the mountain, about two kilometers from an enemy post, to take care of our wounded. M113 APC's began to sweep near the foot of the mountain. Only 100 meters separated them from our shelter; it seemed as if we would be captured. Helicopters, observation planes and F-105s bombed near us throughout the day. We could not eat or drink.

24 November: At Nui Hon where we assembled our wounded, one comrade died due to hunger and cold. I had to go back to our base to ask for personnel to carry the wounded soldiers. We have had no food since 22 (November). There was only one bowl of fried rice for three men. I thought of having to eat tasteless wet rice. The first battle has been most difficult and complicated.[30]

Following its November 1965 encounter with allied forces, Dai's unit withdrew to the Nui Lon forest in the Mo Doc district. At about the end of January 1966, Dai's unit was caught by what he termed an "enemy sweep" (probably Operation Masher/White Wing/Thang Phong II). This operation, conducted in Binh Dinh province by the 1st Cavalry Division, ARVN forces, and units from the Republic of Korea, resulted in 2,389 known enemy casualties.[31] One of these casualties was probably Dai. His final diary entry:

30 January: I engaged in a counter assault battle with M.11B's. It was a most fierce battle. We retreated to Duc Pho, Quang Ngai province. Two comrades, Nho and Dao, are missing. Bao was wounded. Kahn was left on the battlefield to take care of wounded. I was in charge of the mission to look after the whole battalion. It was very hard. We were out of rice,

[29]Pike, *History of Vietnamese Communism*, p. 71.
[30]"Out of Rice, Ammunition and Bandages: Notes of a VC Veteran," *VDRN* doc. 13, pp. 1, 4–5.
[31]Operation Masher/White Wing/Thang Phong II was being conducted in the area where Dai's unit was located; see Sharp and Westmoreland, *Report*, p. 281.

ammunition, bandages and cotton. How long would it take us to break up the 8,000 man sweep of the enemy. I don't worry. The party will provide leadership.[32]

Although the exhaustion of supplies in Dai's unit resulted from the intense engagement with U.S. forces, the VC experienced more wide-spread problems that reduced their ability to offer material and psychological support to main force units. As a result, the PRP convened a meeting of COSVN in July 1966 to discuss the difficulties encountered during the 1965 campaign. At the conclusion of the meeting, COSVN issued a study document intended to correct several problems. The document, notes that "all Party chapters have shown signs of separation from the masses in a very alarming way." Cadres were becoming indifferent to their work and often fulfilled only the minimal requirements of party directives. Individual cadres, according to COSVN, had taken a passive attitude toward adapting party initiatives to local circumstances and preferred to wait for orders from higher echelons. The study also noted that remedial efforts had been ineffective: "Some Party chapters were designed to be improved with the help of a team of cadres sent down by higher echelons, but the work was done well only in the presence of the teams and stopped being effective immediately after the latter's withdrawal." To overcome these deficiencies, COSVN recommended that centralized party control replace the administrative structure at the local level, thereby increasing the responsiveness of cadres to the party's policies.[33]

Following the 1965 offensive, the communists apparently believed that a reluctance to engage well-trained and well-equipped U.S. troops caused a drop in individual morale and a decrease in the combat capability of units. To overcome these difficulties, they instituted an "emulation campaign." In a document captured by the 3d U.S. Marine Division in Quang Nam province on 5 May 1967, for example, the NVA 2d Division outlined its program to "counter dread of protracted war, reluctance, hesitation, neglect, dejection and inactivity," and to "put an end to situations of desertion, rallying [taking advantage of the allies' Open Arms (*Chieu Hoi*) amnesty program], surrender and suicide." This program was based on a communist version of the "body count": individuals and units would be rewarded for the number of allied soldiers they killed in battle. To win the title "Good" in the NVA 2d Division program, a battalion had to "annihilate one US company or one adequate or inadequate puppet [ARVN] battalion outside of its fortifications." A "Fair" rating could be earned by anni-hilating "two US squads or one puppet platoon."[34] A VC document dated 6 May 1966 captured by the III U.S. Marine Amphibious Force on 20 July 1966 in Thua Thien province also listed the criteria used to award honorific titles to units and individuals engaged in both com-bat and support missions. In contrast to the NVA program, the VC emulation campaign specifically targeted U.S. troops: "To obtain the title 'heroic American killing squad,' the unit must meet one of the following 3 requirements: The squad must consist of 4 heroic Ameri-can killers; kill 15 Americans or more in one battle or kill 40 Ameri-cans or more in more than one battle."[35]

Some of the communists' difficulties in the aftermath of the 1965 winter-spring campaign, such as the "fear of protracted war" and supply shortages, were probably the direct result of increased combat intensity. The logistics, morale, and organizational problems encoun-tered by the communist forces in the south, however, were the symp-toms of a general loss of offensive momentum in the wake of the communists' first encounter with U.S. combat units. Without this mo-mentum, such problems would likely worsen with additional encoun-ters with U.S. forces and the general disruption caused by a growing U.S. military presence. The communist military leaders were aware of these problems, which only added a sense of urgency to their effort to assess the 1965 strategy and develop plans for the 1966 dry season.

The Communist Leadership's Reaction to the 1965 Campaign

Although the North Vietnamese leadership supported General Thanh's choice of strategy for the 1965 winter-spring offensive, they apparently held him accountable for the failure of the campaign. In prompting a response from Thanh, the military leadership in Hanoi sparked a public debate over the choice of an appropriate strategy to deal with the U.S. intervention. Two sides emerged in the debate.

On the one hand, General Thanh defended the appropriateness of the 1965 strategy and advanced a similar plan for the next year's of-fensive. Thanh and his supporters—mostly cadre and other officers serving in the south—argued that, despite obvious advantages in fire-

[34]"Troop Training and Combat Competition Campaign—An Emulation Plan," *VDRN* doc. 15, pp. 1–6; and Westmoreland, *Soldier*, p. 101.
[35]"Translation of a Document Captured by Elements of the 3rd USMC Amphibious Force on July 20, 1966 in Thua Thien Province," Documents Presented to North Viet-nam by W. Averell Harriman, May 1968. Doc. 68, film W1484, Government Documents Collection, Widener Library, Harvard University, pp. 1, 3.

power and material resources, the United States and its allies suffered from serious weaknesses that could be exploited. Thanh also believed that main-force communist units could successfully assault large allied units and bases. He argued that he could eliminate the U.S. advantage in firepower if his troops engaged allied soldiers in hand-to-hand combat.

On the other hand, several communist leaders who remained in the north, including General Giap, wanted a return to the second phase of people's war. Deeply affected by the setback at the Ia Drang valley, Giap argued that guerrilla attacks against allied lines of communication and supply depots would disrupt U.S. search-and-destroy operations. Giap also worried about a lack of coordination between main-force units and VC guerrillas. He apparently believed that coordination between these two types of forces could serve as a force multiplier that would impede allied offensive operations. Main-force units would adopt a "coordinated fighting method" that entailed medium-sized attacks against relatively important targets. These attacks were intended to dampen morale and the overall political climate within the allied camp. Guerrilla units would adopt an "independent fighting method" whereby dozens of small-scale actions would occur daily, not only generating casualties among allied units but also disrupting allied efforts to go on the offensive. In effect, Giap was suggesting a new approach to armed *dau tranh*.[36]

The first round in this debate is marked by a letter written by General Thanh in March 1966 under the pseudonym Anh Sau. Thanh warned that it was important to remember the U.S. setbacks in China, Korea, Cuba, and Laos; the opponent should not be overestimated. Because it faced competing demands as a global power, the United States could not devote unlimited resources to the conflict in Southeast Asia. Although Thanh recommended that the communists take the initiative on the battlefield, he suggested that the revolutionary forces concentrate on the destruction of ARVN and the Saigon regime, the weak link in the allied war effort. Thanh repeated the idea, apparently still popular among senior communists, that the United States would withdraw following the collapse of its client.[37]

Thanh offered a more detailed defense of the 1965 strategy in a June 1966 issue of *Quan Doi Nhan Dan* (People's Army Daily), the official organ of the NVA.[38] Written under the pseudonym Truong

---

[36]Pike, *PAVN*, pp. 226, 342.
[37]Duiker, *Road to Power*, pp. 243–244.
[38]"Truong Son on the 1965–66 Dry Season," *Quan Doi Nhan Dan* (Hanoi), June 1966, in McGarvey, *Visions of Victory*, pp. 72–91.

Son (the Long Mountain Range), the article criticized an unnamed person—probably General Giap—who evaluated the enemy in a "mechanical bookish way." Thanh also claimed that the North Vietnamese leadership gave its tacit approval of his plans for the previous offensive by failing to provide an alternative. Lacking a viable option, Thanh had simply proceeded with the strategy used the previous year. The "Truong Son" article also advanced a detailed defense of the previous campaign strategy. Offensive operations, it stated, had interfered with U.S. efforts to establish base areas and to begin a systematic offensive. If the allies had been allowed to implement their plans without interference from NVA and VC units, argued Thanh, the communists would have faced a disastrous situation. Thanh had saved the day by applying "the policy of attacking, resolutely attacking, and continuously attacking to gain time by taking the initiative of attacking the enemy first, thus causing him to lose his initiative at the outset. This was consistent with a basic view of revolutionary military strategy as attack, attack and only attack."[39]

The article also provided a comparison of the strengths and weaknesses of the communists and allies. Thanh argued that the decision to intervene while the South Vietnamese regime was losing had placed the United States in an inferior position:

> At the outset of the [1965] dry season, the war situation developed in a way advantageous to us. . . . the Southern armed forces and people were strategically in a victorious and offensive state. The Americans were strategically in a state of defeat and passivity. . . . Thus, facing defeat, the Americans had to introduce their troops to participate directly in combat. The . . . [United States] entered the war in a state of strategic defeat and passivity appropriate to a policy filled with contradictions. Thus, the Americans had [words indistinct] many political and military problems, which were made immeasurably difficult by a very disadvantageous situation.[40]

Thanh also described the specific political problem facing the allies: a master–servant relationship between the United States and South Vietnam that would interfere with their prosecution of the war. In contrast, the major problem facing the communists was the need for greater coordination between political and military initiatives. Thanh stated, however, that the communists were solving this problem.

In terms of the future, Thanh paid little attention to guerrilla operations. Instead, he proposed the continuation of NVA and VC main-

[39]Ibid., p. 86.
[40]Ibid., p. 73.

force attacks; quick and concentrated attacks on allied lines of com-munications, supply depots, and airbases would disrupt U.S. offen-sive operations. By engaging the enemy in hand-to-hand combat, maintained Thanh, NVA and VC units could defeat their opponents by depriving them of their superior firepower.

In an article published in the party journal *Hoc Tap* (Studies) in July 1966, Thanh (this time under his own name) defended his choice of strategy by first noting that he was not solely responsible for the plan-ning of the 1965 campaign. Thanh maintained that a collective deci-sion had been made to continue the main-force operations that were successful during the "special war," the period when U.S. involve-ment was merely advisory. Thanh admitted, however, that some members of the North Vietnamese leadership had resisted the contin-uation of the 1964 campaign strategy. Thanh built on this theme by criticizing an anonymous individual—again probably General Giap—whose "conservative spirit prevented him from discovering the facts." This person, according to Thanh, "devoted himself to working in ac-cordance to old customs" and "mechanically copied his own past ex-perience." He linked this resistance to a tendency to focus on Ameri-can strengths at the cost of ignoring their weaknesses. Finally, Thanh described weaknesses that limited the ability of the United States to exploit fully its superior firepower and combat mobility. The allied war effort, according to Thanh, would inevitably suffer from the "contradictions" (racial tensions, economic strain, antiwar protests) generated by the attempt to wage an "aggressive" war. Thanh re-peated the point advanced in the "Truong Son" article that, by inter-vening when the communists held the initiative, U.S. forces were placed in an inferior position. Thus Thanh suggested that his strategy was based on an accurate assessment of U.S. strengths and weak-nesses and was designed to exploit the problems created by the U.S. decision to aid the losing side (a military inept, politically disunited and corrupt South Vietnamese government) in the war.[41]

---

[41]"General Nguyen Chi Thanh on the South's Ideological Task," *Hoc Tap* (Hanoi), no. 7, July 1966, in McGarvey, *Visions of Victory*, pp. 61–72. The idea that the United States would encounter "contradictions" in its effort to wage an "aggressive" war was a cen-tral theme of North Vietnamese analyses and was repeated continually throughout the war. In August 1967, the CIA reported: "The race riots and the emergence of the 'Black Power' movement in the United States, which the North Vietnamese government con-siders the beginning of a popular revolution in the United States, have had a most salubrious effect on the North Vietnamese morale. The North Vietnamese government believes the civil rights disturbances will force the United States to divert money and manpower from its commitment in the Vietnam war"; see CIA, Intelligence Informa-tion Cable, TDCS DB-315/03415-67 28 August 1967, in NSF Country File Vietnam, Box 252, 258, 259, Folder: Vietnam CIA Intelligence Information Cables 7/27/67–08/31/67,

On 10 July 1966, Radio Hanoi transmitted Vuong Thua Vu's analysis of Thanh's position. Vu, who specialized in technical military matters, identified the areas of agreement and disagreement between Thanh's analysis and that of the North Vietnamese leadership. Vu agreed that, despite the introduction of U.S. forces, NVA and VC units still retained the military and psychological advantages created by the successes of the 1964 campaign. NVA and VC units, according to Vu, were still in a position to pursue the main military objectives outlined by the North Vietnamese leadership; inflict casualties on U.S. forces, increase the amount of territory under communist control, and defend controlled areas against allied encroachments. Vu objected, however, to Thanh's failure to mention the role of guerrillas in the coming campaign. By congratulating the southern commanders on their effort to coordinate attacks between main-force units in the central highlands and VC guerrillas in populated areas, Vu identified a type of operation that General Giap and his supporters wanted included in the coming offensive. Moreover, Vu warned that Thanh's plan for the 1966 campaign needed to be developed more fully. In other words, the North Vietnamese leadership was not fully satisfied with Thanh's suggestions for the 1966 campaign.[42]

In a commentary transmitted on 7 September 1966 by the clandestine Liberation Radio in South Vietnam, an anonymous Cuu Long (Mekong river) attempted to reassure the North Vietnamese leadership by describing the factors that led him to believe that a few modifications in Thanh's tactics would result in a successful 1966 offensive. Cuu Long believed that VC and NVA units still retained the psychological edge gained in the 1964 campaign and that the allies were becoming demoralized. In support of this proposition, he claimed that frustration over setbacks in the central highlands motivated the U.S. decision to bomb oil installations near Hanoi and Haiphong in the summer of 1966. Cuu Long also noted specific allied problems that could be exploited in the coming offensive. He maintained, for example, that the United States and South Vietnam were

---

doc. 113, LBJ Library. Ho Chi Minh's order for the implementation of the Tet offensive, released to cadres in November 1967, provides a fine description of the "problems" created by the U.S. decision to aid the losing side in the war: "In regard to the 'puppet' government, even though a president and vice-president have been 'created', serious contradictions [political rivalry] between civilian and military leaders continue to exist in spite of US reconciliation efforts. This situation will worsen due to the continued purges which take place in the (GVN) internal organization"; see CDEC Bulletin 8319, 7 December 1967, pp. 2–3, in NSF Country File Vietnam, Box 153, Folder: Vietnam CDEC Bulletins, vol. 2, doc. 39, LBJ Library.

[42]McGarvey, *Visions of Victory*, p. 12. For a biography of Vuong Thau Vu, see Pike, *PAVN*, pp. 355–356.

ravaged by political turmoil that would impede their response to the 1966 campaign. American workers, according to Cuu Long, might even rebel when they were eventually forced to pay the costs of the war. He also believed that the timidity of the South Vietnamese government would hamper the allied war effort. In terms of future strategy, Cuu Long explained, North Vietnamese concerns had been dealt with by Thanh's plan. He noted that VC ranks had been depleted during the 1965 campaign and that only senseless carnage would be produced by frontal attacks on U.S. outposts. As an alternative, he believed that the communists should exploit the length of the U.S. logistics pipeline by attacking vulnerable points along lines of communication. By launching diversionary attacks and using hand-to-hand combat, NVA and VC units could successfully attack allied supply bases. In this manner, the communist forces could disrupt search-and-destroy operations, preventing the allies from taking the offensive.[43]

Radio Hanoi had the last word in the debate before the new campaign season. On 9 October 1966, it transmitted a commentary that raised serious concerns about Thanh's strategy. The commentary, written by the pseudonymous Le Ba, apparently reflected the views of either someone close to Giap or Giap himself. Le Ba claimed that the VC guerrillas resented Thanh's practice of using them as a manpower pool for VC and NVA main forces and that this policy wasted an important communist resource. VC guerillas, according to Le Ba, were the only forces to enjoy a degree of offensive success during the summer of 1966. Their harassing attacks kept the allies off balance throughout the rainy season. In effect, Le Ba was probably warning Thanh that VC guerrilla units should be used to shield preparations for the coming offensive. Unless they were distracted by harassment from the VC, the Americans might attack main-force units in their staging areas, preempting the 1966 winter-spring offensive.[44]

The debate over strategy that preceded the 1966 campaign season did not produce either agreement or a major innovation to counter U.S. intervention. Each side defended its past performance, claiming that the appropriateness of their prescriptions would be demonstrated if they were applied in the coming campaign. The debate did, however, describe areas of allied weakness: political instability, alliance relations, and a vulnerable logistics system. Yet, in the limited

[43]"Cuu Long on Strong Offensive," broadcast by Liberation Radio to South Vietnam, 1000 GMT, September 7, 1966, in McGarvey, *Visions of Victory*, pp. 82–100.

[44]McGarvey, *Visions of Victory*, pp. 14–15. See CIA, Intelligence Information Cable, TDCS DB-315/03415-67 28 August 1967.

time available between dry seasons, the communists were unable to develop a strategy that would strike at these weaknesses. In a sense, the debate ended in a deadlock; serious disagreements remained about the suitability of main-force assaults against American units, the use of VC guerrillas in the campaign, and the need to coordinate main-force and guerrilla operations.

After they made some concessions, Thanh and his supporters were allowed again to use the strategy adopted during the 1965 campaign. Offensive operations would be carried out by either main-force or guerrilla units, depending on the local situation. Main-force units would limit their offensive to the area near the 17th parallel, while VC guerrillas would attack scattered targets throughout South Vietnam. Giap's new approach to armed *dau tranh* was apparently interpreted as a step backward into the second phase of people's war, reducing its attractiveness to the regime in Hanoi. Moreover, when the Chinese communists suggested that North Vietnamese military operations return to the second phase of people's war, support for Giap's position probably began to wane. The North Vietnamese interpreted the advice offered by the Chinese as an effort to prevent the war in Vietnam from spreading to the People's Republic of China. When Secretary General Le Duan rejected this Chinese advice, the chances that Giap's prescriptions would be adopted before the start of the next campaign season were greatly reduced. Thus the 1966 winter-spring offensive represented a continuation of the strategy followed since 1964.[45]

THE 1966 WINTER-SPRING CAMPAIGN

After the 1965 winter-spring offensive, the tempo of U.S. operations declined until the following November. General Westmoreland had taken a calculated risk by rapidly introducing combat forces in Vietnam in 1965, before a suitable logistics base had been constructed. As a result, much of 1966 was devoted to the construction of a logistics network and the buildup of manpower. Working around the clock, U.S. Army engineers and private contractors constructed six deep-draft harbors, hundreds of helicopter pads, scores of airfields and warehouses, an intricate communications grid, and even a 600-acre island in the Mekong delta that was intended to serve as a secure

---

[45]McGarvey, *Visions of Victory*, p.8; Memo to Ambassador Henry Cabot Lodge from John Hart, 6 March 1967, in DSDUF Vietnam Box 3, doc. 53, LBJ Library; and Duiker, *Road to Power*, p. 245.

and dry base camp. The logistics buildup was a necessary prelude to the shift to offensive operations, the second phase of Westmoreland's strategy, undertaken during the 1966 dry season.[46]

Numerous search-and-destroy missions (a phrase Westmoreland later lamented) were conducted throughout the 1966 dry season. The primary purpose of these operations was to engage NVA and VC units and either destroy them or force them to surrender. During the course of these operations, allied units often found secret VC base areas and supply caches. In fact, search-and-destroy operations were more successful at destroying the enemy's logistics system than the enemy units themselves.[47]

The Impact of U.S. Operations on Communist Forces in the South

Allied forces conducted at least five major search-and-destroy operations during the 1966–67 dry season: Operation Attleboro (14 September–24 November), Operation Paul Revere IV (18 October–30 December), Operation Thayer II (25 October–12 February), Operation Cedar Falls (8–26 January), and Operation Junction City (22 February–14 May). These five operations alone accounted for over 7,000 known enemy casualties and the destruction of vast amounts of enemy stores.[48]

Junction City was the largest operation conducted by U.S. forces during the 1966 season. Even though it failed to neutralize permanently War Zone C, located Northwest of Saigon in Tay Ninh province, as a base for enemy operations, the operation shattered three regiments of the 9th VC Division. Moreover, the operation demonstrated that enemy base areas within South Vietnam were no longer secure from attack and that in the dry season armor and mechanized infantry could operate in many areas. Junction City also had an immediate impact on the NVA and VC logistics and command structure in the south. In fact, in the aftermath of Junction City the enemy moved many of its training centers, supply depots, hospitals and even COSVN itself into Cambodia.[49]

Although the search-and-destroy operations conducted throughout this season rarely resulted in the destruction of NVA and VC units,

---

[46]Karnow, *Vietnam,* p. 436.
[47]Westmoreland, *Soldier,* p.83.
[48]Bernard W. Rogers, *CEDAR FALLS–JUNCTION CITY: A Turning Point* (Washington, D.C., 1974); Sharp and Westmoreland, *Report,* pp. 283–284; S. L. A. Marshall, *Ambush* (New York, 1969), p. 6; Palmer, *25-Year War,* p. 59; Westmoreland, *Soldier,* p. 206; and Stanton, *Rise and Fall,* pp. 147–153.
[49]Palmer, *25-Year War,* p. 60.

the operations disrupted the communists' logistics system. In contrast to conventional supply systems that move soldiers and material along well-defined lines of communication, NVA and VC logistics were based on the prepositioning of supplies and the support of the rural population. The enemy had to prepare the battlefield before carrying out offensive operations. Months of effort were needed to either coerce or cajole the local population into providing the food, intelligence, and secure staging areas needed to launch successful attacks. Allied commanders became adept at destroying this logistics infrastructure. The allies "worked the system," seizing forward supply catches and interfering with the messengers, radio communications, and supply couriers that not only provided support for main-force attacks but also kept the VC underground political and administrative structure supplied and informed.[50]

The U.S. Marines also contributed to the disruption of VC logistics in their area of responsibility just below the DMZ. The marines, through their rice-protection program dubbed Golden Fleece, prevented the VC from seizing part of the local rice crop. The failure to obtain this local food supply slowed the 324B NVA Division in its attempt to cross the DMZ and invade the provinces of Quang Tri and Thua Thien. Lacking a prepared battlefield, the NVA unit was defeated by the marines in Operations Hastings and Prairie toward the end of the 1966 season.[51]

By about mid-1967, U.S. and South Vietnamese leaders believed that the situation had improved. "After only little more than a year of fighting relatively sizeable numbers of American troops," wrote Westmoreland, "communist losses were mounting drastically, with nothing tangible to show for it."[52] Indeed, the communists had suffered serious setbacks in their encounters with U.S. forces, especially the disruption of their logistics system. Once disrupted, the VC infrastructure was not easily replaced. Search-and-destroy operations also tended to drive VC main forces and NVA units into remote areas, separating them from the infrastructure and guerrilla units they needed for support. Thus the combination of disrupted logistics, increasing casualties, and a feeling among VC and NVA soldiers that the end of the war was not yet in sight resulted in a decline in the morale and combat capability of communist units.[53]

There were also signs that the political and economic situation was

[50]*Ibid.*; and Shaplen, *Time out of Hand*, p. 377.
[51]Stanton, *Rise and Fall*, pp. 125–126; and Shaplen, *Time out of Hand*, p. 378.
[52]Westmoreland, *Soldier*, p. 311.
[53]Sharp and Westmoreland, *Report*, p. 135.

improving within South Vietnam. By mid-1967, the South Vietnamese population, usually wary of foreign troops, began to accept the large numbers of American soldiers. This change of heart, especially among the urban population, was prompted by the security and economic prosperity that tended to follow in the wake of the U.S. military buildup. Moreover, pacification efforts started to show positive results by the latter half of 1967. Approximately 67 percent of the South Vietnamese population were reportedly living under government control, and of the 242 districts in the south, 222 were considered secure. Officials involved in the pacification program also considered 8,650 out of 12,600 hamlets across the south to be pacified. Overall, a feeling of cautious optimism reigned among U.S. officials in Vietnam as they assessed the outcome of the 1966 campaign. Robert W. Komer, director of the pacification program, informed President Johnson on 28 February 1967, that "wastefully, expensively, but nonetheless indisputably, we are winning the war in the South. Few of our programs—civil or military—are very efficient, but we are grinding the enemy down by sheer weight and mass."[54]

Various NVA and VC units suffered a decline in combat capability caused by a drop in morale after the 1966 campaign. For example, in a diary belonging to Mai Van Hung, captured by the U.S. 25th Infantry Division in May 1967, the author recorded the loneliness, food shortages, disease, and fear of death that often led to despair among many of the NVA soldiers in his unit. Faced with these hardships, Hung apparently began to question the sincerity and capability of his officers. His suspicions intensified after he was hospitalized with an illness and was accused of malingering by his superiors.[55] Another diary belonging to an NVA soldier, captured by the 3d Marine Division in Quang Tri province on 11 October 1967, provides additional insight into the morale problems in NVA units. In this diary, the author recorded the pep talks given by his superiors, thereby identifying the problems his officers considered serious. Of particular interest are the instructions to fight fear and weariness, which were repeated often in the lectures. The troops were also admonished not to contemplate defecting to the allied side. The last entry in the diary indicates that the unit had not yet met the expectations of its officers: on 4 October 1967, the unit was again criticized for exhibiting "weak ideology," fear

[54]"Komer Report to Johnson after February Trip to Vietnam," *The Pentagon Papers as published by The New York Times* (New York, 1971), p. 558; Lung, *General Offensives*, p. 8; and Vien and Khuyen, *Reflections on the Vietnam War*, p. 50.
[55]"Diary of an Infiltrator," *VDRN* doc. 1, pp. 1, 5.

of hardship, poor sense of organization, poor observance of regulations, and poor execution of orders.[56]

An official insight into morale problems is provided by a document captured on 10 January 1968 by the 1st Air Cavalry Division. The document is a report on the self-criticism effort mounted from September to November 1967 by the 3d NVA Division, which operated in Quang Ngai and Binh Dinh provinces. It mentioned that the sight of troops lying around gradually disappeared, organization and discipline were tightened, and malingering and begging were reduced. There were also examples of individual courage, when even some "comrade nurses, medics and cooks" acted as "heroic American-killing fighters." Balancing these improvements, however, were persistent shortcomings: "Wavering in the determination to fight, lack of conviction in our mission and about our leaders' determination . . . poor execution of orders and compliance with discipline . . . poor internal unity, fear of hardships and difficulties, [poor] relations between old-timers and the new people, between upper level and lower level." The report also mentioned numerous instances of cowardice under fire. In one incident soldiers had abandoned their positions, and in another they had fled from an ambush as soon as U.S. troops appeared. According to the report, "waverers" abandoned their positions under fire because "these people fear enemy air and artillery actions and fierceness of combat. They are enthusiastic in shouting slogans . . . but when the time comes to put these slogans into practice, they do their job carelessly.[57]

In addition to damaging morale and combat capability, allied search-and-destroy operations disrupted the enemy's logistics. In a letter dated 23 June 1967, for example, a VC agent in Phu Yen province described the impact of allied operations in the Song Cau district. The letter contained a description of a recent sweep that resulted in the deaths of fifteen VC guerrillas and three civilians. Moreover, 68 guerrillas defected during the operation, turning over eight weapons to the allies. "These defectors have denounced our activities to the enemy," according to the VC agent, "thus at present the enemy knows our operating procedures and is creating many difficulties for us."[58]

The problems mentioned by this VC agent are also reflected in a

[56]"From Poetry to Reality: A North Vietnamese Soldier's Notebook," *VDRN* doc. 10, pp. 4, 11.
[57]"Self-Criticism: Report From a North Vietnamese Division," *VDRN* doc. 19, pp. 1, 3–6.
[58]"Pacification and the Viet Cong Reaction," *VDRN* doc. 12, pp. 1, 3–5.

document captured on 17 January 1967 which contained the minutes of a meeting held by the VC supply council, Chau Thanh district, Binh Duong province, to discuss the supply difficulties encountered in the ongoing campaign. According to the minutes, civilian participation in supply operations had been badly affected. "The enemy," according to the supply council, "is directing his attacks toward our entry and exit points, especially Phu Canh and Dinh Hoa, where they have captured all three of our food procurement and supply centers." The supply council also complained that the allies poisoned much of the locally produced rice crop and physically prevented them from gathering the unspoiled portion of the remaining paddy. In addition to these supply difficulties, the minutes of the meeting described a growing problem in the VC's effort to exploit the population: it was becoming impossible to muster any personnel or supplies in areas partially under allied control. The supply council suggested that this problem was rooted in both a shortage of cadres and the local people's dislike of the VC. The masses, according to the minutes, were "afflicted by fear—fear of hardships, difficulties, illnesses, lack of work and pay, the back and forth movement in weak areas, enemy terrorism—fear of the fierceness of war, fear of the protracted war." The council concluded that these problems had led to the failure of their program to provide medical and emotional support to soldiers.[59]

The documents captured after the 1966 campaign indicate a slow but steady deterioration in the combat capability of enemy units and an increasing disruption of the enemy's logistics. These problems, which emerged after the introduction of U.S. combat troops, formed a dangerous trend for communist military fortunes. The communist leadership had not yet developed an effective strategic and tactical response to U.S. intervention, and if this situation continued communist forces would eventually lack the capability to launch offensive operations of sufficient scope and intensity to affect directly the military balance in the war. Communist officials probably realized that, on balance, the war was stalemated and that allied operations were gaining offensive momentum. Without some sort of initiative to reverse this trend, they could only expect a worsening military future.

Reaction in North Vietnam

Although communist leaders waited to the end of the 1965 offensive to begin debating its outcome, arguments about the 1966 dry sea-

---

[59]"Within a Viet Cong Stronghold: Deliberations of the Supply Council, Chau Thanh District, Binh Duong Province, January 1967," *VDRN* doc. 4, pp. 1, 4.

son emerged soon after it began. Once again, the debate was between General Thanh and his supporters and his critics who backed General Giap's policy prescriptions. This time Thanh made serious concessions to his critics. By the summer of 1967, Thanh's conduct of the war was discredited. In fact, this new round in the debate was marked by a commentary, attributed to Cuu Long, transmitted in September 1966 by Liberation Radio in South Vietnam. Cuu Long took Thanh to task for again emphasizing main-force attacks and neglecting guerrilla operations. This critique of Thanh was repeated in an article published on 29 November 1966 in *Quan Doi Nhan Dan*. By publishing Cuu Long's critique during the 1966 campaign, the North Vietnamese leadership was apparently attempting to inform Thanh that he was failing to live up to the compromise over strategy reached on the eve of the 1966 dry season. Cuu Long accused him of improperly employing guerrilla forces in the ongoing campaign, the major complaint voiced about the 1965 campaign. According to Cuu Long, Thanh had failed to coordinate guerrilla, local, and main-force operations and instead used guerrilla units primarily to replace casualties in main-force units. He also noted that Thanh's policies had demoralized rank-and-file VC and had left the VC leadership confused about their role in the war. Instead of relying on "erroneous concepts such as the idea of depending on concentrated troops," according to Cuu Long, the war could best be prosecuted through the coordination of guerrilla, local, and main-force units: "If we fail to combine the three categories of troops, each category alone is not strong enough; if we fail to coordinate the three-pronged attacks, the armed struggle alone cannot bring into full play the power of the just cause of the masses."[60]

Without directly referring to Cuu Long's complaints, Thanh replied to his accusations in a commentary transmitted by Liberation Radio on 12 December 1966. The anonymous commentary stated that the offensive was progressing according to plan and that the concerns raised by Cuu Long were unfounded; guerrilla, local, and main-force operations were coordinated. In responding, however, Thanh failed to address many of the issues raised by Cuu Long's critique, such as the problems encountered in VC morale and leadership. Thanh was apparently unwilling to divert his attention from the dry-season campaign, which was beginning to pick up momentum.[61]

---

[60]Duiker, *Road to Power*, p. 251; Cuu Long quote from "Cuu Long on New Developments in the Guerrilla War in South Vietnam," *Quan Doi Nhan Dan* (Hanoi), 29 November 1966, in McGarvey, *Visions of Victory*, p. 112; see also pp. 101–113.
[61]"The Front's Correct Line Is the Strength and Faith of Our South Vietnamese Peo-

The Liberation Radio broadcast must have failed to satisfy Thanh's critics. On 22 December 1966, Radio Hanoi transmitted excerpts from Cuu Long's list of complaints. The commentary again noted that guerrillas could do more than just support the main forces and that they were responsible for one-third to two-fifths of enemy casualties during the past year. Guerrillas also were successful in countering the work of South Vietnamese intelligence agents. According to the commentary, evidence of the great potential of guerrilla warfare could be found in guerrilla accomplishments in urban warfare and in the ambushes of U.S. supply convoys. It is likely that the Radio Hanoi broadcast identified the way the North Vietnamese leadership hoped that Thanh would use VC guerrillas in the ongoing campaign.[62]

After this outburst of concern during the campaign, the debate over strategy rested until the close of the offensive. When it was renewed, communist leaders seemed to realize that military victory was temporarily beyond their grasp. The optimism that marked some of the past descriptions of the military situation was replaced by somber assessments. The idea of maintaining a military stalemate entered the debate for the first time. Communist leaders now seemed to believe that they should strive to prolong the war in order to wear down the allies, setting the stage for political initiatives. Apparently Giap's ideas about integrating guerrilla units, which would adopt the "independent fighting method," and main-force units, which would adopt the "coordinated fighting method," were now accepted as the preferred method for armed *dau tranh*.

The first evidence of this policy shift emerged in an article published in *Quan Doi Nhan Dan* in May. The author, General Thanh, abandoned his usual style of attacking anonymous critics and his advocacy of main-force attacks on allied units, staples of his strategic writings since the 1964 campaign. Instead he explained that the intensity of the fighting and the firepower of U.S. forces created difficulties during the 1966 campaign. Moreover, he did not claim, as he had in past analyses, that his forces could achieve military victory in the near future. Instead he suggested that the units under his command were capable of imposing a military stalemate on the allies. According to Thanh, "if we have to make more sacrifices and endure more hard-

---

ple," broadcast in Vietnamese to South Vietnam by Liberation Radio, 2330 GMT, 12 December 1966, in McGarvey, *Visions of Victory*, p. 16.

[62]Untitled broadcast in English by Radio Hanoi's Vietnam News Agency International Service, 1718 GMT, 22 December 1966, in McGarvey, *Visions of Victory*, pp. 16–17.

ships, and if we have to fight another five, ten, twenty years, or longer, we will fight resolutely."[63]

In a June article in *Quan Doi Nhan Dan*, Thanh, again under the pen name Truong Son, elaborated on the difficulties encountered in the 1966 campaign. The article, based on a discussion of the conclusions reached by the members of a strategy session, seemed to suggest that the communists realized that U.S. tactics and forces were highly effective during the previous campaign. In other words, the 1966 offensive, which had been based on a strategy advanced by Thanh, was defeated by the allies. Truong Son abandoned his usual advocacy of main-force attacks against allied units and instead suggested that guerrilla operations were the most promising way of prosecuting the war. He now claimed that guerrillas had gained worldwide attention by launching attacks on airbases and that they had managed to keep the allies off balance throughout the 1966 campaign. The article claimed that VC guerrillas were also successful in gathering intelligence and disrupting the ARVN pacification program. Guerrilla operations, according to the article, were the best way to prepare the way for main-force attacks: "Guerrilla warfare must be combined with concentrated fighting and vice-versa, for both have a decisive effect on the success of the armed struggle of our people's war at the present time."[64] Truong Son had abandoned his usual emphasis on main-force operations and instead advocated the armed *dau tranh* strategy championed by Giap.

By the summer of 1967, communist officials realized that the strategy adopted during the 1965 and 1966 winter-spring offensives had failed. VC and NVA units were suffering a gradual erosion of combat capability, caused by a decrease in troop morale, and the logistics system in the south was being slowly eliminated by allied search-and-destroy operations. Communist military assets were being depleted, but no progress toward victory was forthcoming. The communist leadership probably realized that, if current trends continued, they would eventually lack the resources to launch an offensive of sufficient scope and scale to affect significantly the outcome of the war.

The debate over strategy had run its course in the aftermath of the 1966 offensive. The ideas of General Thanh (often articulated under

[63]"General Nguyen Chi Thanh on the Victorious Dry-Season Campaign of 1966–67," *Quan Doi Nhan Dan* (Hanoi), 31 May 1967, in McGarvey, *Visions of Victory*, pp. 114–118.
[64]"Truong Son on the Lessons of NFLSV Victories," *Quan Doi Nhan Dan* (Hanoi), June 1967, in McGarvey, *Visions of Victory*, p. 146.

[49]

the pseudonym Truong Son) had been discredited by the failures of the 1965 and 1966 campaigns. Thanh was forced to admit failure and adopt the ideas of his critics. Although it took over two years of bitter debate and military failure, General Giap and his supporters succeeded in forcing the southern communists to agree to abandon main-force attacks on allied units and to return to the second stage of people's war. It was now up to Giap and his supporters to reverse the deteriorating position of NVA and VC units.

The communist debate over strategy also identified weaknesses in the allied war effort and underutilized communist strengths. Political instability in South Vietnam and a decline in the American public's support for the war were identified as major allied liabilities. The demands of coalition warfare on the allied side also seemed to be a potential area of exploitation. Experience had also shown that attacks on the allied logistics system sometimes produced spectacular results at little cost in men and resources. The failure to coordinate attacks among different types of units was seen as a major shortcoming of the 1965 and 1966 communist offensives. Communist leaders now accepted Giap's notion that coordinated attacks by NVA units and VC main-force and guerrilla units would allow them to overcome the superior firepower and mobility of allied units. Finally, the debate over strategy illustrates that the movement to unify Vietnam was made up of diverse forces and individuals, each with personal and professional concerns about the conduct of the war. The debate apparently became divisive as commanders staked their reputations and the lives of their troops on the accuracy of their assessments of the military situation. The concessions made by Thanh to his critics in the aftermath of the 1966 campaign had not eliminated these personal and professional concerns. Thus, any strategic or tactical initiative adopted by Giap and his supporters would have to take into account the needs and desires of this same disparate group of individuals and military organizations. To be successful, Giap's plan would have to maintain the consensus that had ended the divisive strategic debate within the communist heirarchy.

[2]

Plans, Preparations, and
Objectives of the Tet Offensive

Although there is disagreement about the causes and date of General Thanh's death, he apparently died sometime in the first half of 1967. Whatever its circumstances, his demise was a turning point in the debate over a response to U.S. intervention; opponents of Hanoi's prescriptions for the upcoming 1967 winter-spring offensive had lost their most prestigious spokesman. Vocal opposition to the strategy and tactics advocated by the North Vietnamese seems to have ended with Thanh's death. In fact, by this time, the switch in strategy had been solidified by personnel changes in the command structure. General Giap assumed overall command of the war effort, and Thanh's responsibilities were divided between at least two generals, Tran Do and Tran Va Tra. The available evidence also indicates that at least Tra agreed with Giap's views. Yet Thanh's death did little to alleviate the problems facing the communists in their effort to unite the country. North Vietnamese officials would still have to address these difficulties in any new initiative.[1]

This chapter focuses on the salient issues that faced the participants

[1]During the war, the communists claimed that General Thanh had died of a heart attack. General Westmoreland claims that Thanh died after being evacuated to Hanoi from chest wounds suffered in a B-52 raid over Cambodia in July 1967. Dave Richard Palmer agrees with Westmoreland about the timing and cause of Thanh's death. Robert Shaplen writes that Thanh died in early 1967 from wounds suffered in a B-52 raid in Tay Ninh province (Shaplen was probably unaware of the B-52 raids over Cambodia when he wrote his book). In contrast, Stanley Karnow claims that Thanh died of cancer in a Hanoi hospital during the summer of 1967. See Westmoreland, *Soldier*, p. 310; Palmer, *Summons*, p. 121; Shaplen, *Time out of Hand*, p. 397; and Karnow, *Vietnam*, p. 453. For a description of the effect of Thanh's death on the debate over strategy and tactics, see McGarvey, *Visions of Victory*, p. 23; and Thies, *When Governments Collide*, p. 344. For a discussion of the changes in the communist command after Thanh's death, see Lung, *General Offensives*, p. 17; and Karnow, *Vietnam*, p. 530.

in a July 1967 strategy session and on General Giap's suggestions for resolving these problems, published in a September 1967 article. Giap's role and status in the North Vietnamese politburo should not be exaggerated; other issues and personalities were important in the formulation of military and political strategy. But Giap was a prominent player, and his strategic prescriptions were apparently those implemented during the Tet offensive.

THE VIEW FROM HANOI

Although General Thanh's death facilitated the resolution of the debate over strategy, in an ironic twist his funeral also supplied the pretext for a meeting between North Vietnamese officials who ultimately adopted the prescriptions of his opponents. Events began to unfold in June 1967, when several North Vietnamese diplomats were quietly recalled to Hanoi. The North Vietnamese refused to comment about the meeting, and this silence fueled press reports that a major peace initiative was being developed. Speculation about the purpose of the meeting ceased, however, when Hanoi announced the death of Thanh on 6 July 1967. In the interim between the arrival of the diplomats in Hanoi and the funeral services, which took place on 7 July, the gathering communist dignitaries probably approved Giap's guidelines for the upcoming campaign.[2]

The Hanoi regime has never published a record of the July meeting, yet some evidence has emerged concerning the issues discussed there. Foremost among these issues was the failure of successive dry-season campaigns. NVA and VC units were experiencing a deterioration of combat and logistical capabilities. Search-and-destroy operations were reducing the momentum of communist offensives by hampering attempts to prepare the battlefield. Moreover, the allies were going on the offensive, increasing the proportion of the population and territory controlled by the Saigon regime; communist units in the south thus constituted a waning asset. If these trends continued, the communists would eventually lack the offensive capability needed to affect significantly the military situation. Balanced against these lia-

---

[2]For a description of the recall of North Vietnamese diplomats to Hanoi and the press speculation this provoked, see Oberdorfer, *Tet*, pp. 45–46. Richard Betts, Herbert Schandler, and W. W. Rostow all identify the July 1967 strategy session as the meeting in which the decision to launch the Tet offensive was made; see Betts, "Strategic Surprise for War Termination," p. 161; Schandler, *Unmaking of a President*, p. 66; and Rostow, *The Diffusion of Power* (New York, 1972), p. 460. For the dates of the announcement of Thanh's death and a description of his funeral, see Lung, *General Offensives*, p. 17; and Palmer, *Summons*, p. 166.

bilities, however, were allied weaknesses that could be exploited. The communists believed that American domestic opposition to the war would limit the increase in the U.S. effort in South Vietnam. A "neo-colonialist relationship" between the United States and South Vietnam was identified as a weakness in the opposing alliance. Dozens of vulnerable points in the allied logistics system also invited attack.

It is likely that domestic issues were also discussed. The U.S. bombing of North Vietnam caused extensive damage to its military installations, industrial base, and transportation network, even though it failed to affect critically Hanoi's capability or willingness to continue the war. The physical destruction caused by the raids was compounded by manpower dislocations. In response to the air attacks, the North Vietnamese had mobilized approximately 600,000 individuals for repair, dispersal, and transport programs and an estimated 145,000 people for active and passive air defense activities. The destruction and manpower dislocations caused a general disruption of the economy and shortages of consumer goods and food. The decline in indigenous production forced the North Vietnamese into the uncomfortable position of increased dependence on Soviet and Chinese aid.[3]

The bombing campaign also raised the possibility that the morale of the North Vietnamese population could suffer a precipitous decline. The repeated bombardment, especially by B-52 bombers, had a psychological impact far in excess of the actual death and destruction inflicted by the raids. In fact, the United States attempted to capitalize on the terror produced by B-52 raids by conducting a vigorous leaflet campaign over North Vietnam.[4]

Another domestic development the communists confronted was the growing number of North Vietnamese officials opposed to continued participation in the war. In fact, the officials at the July meeting may have reacted publicly to these peace proponents. On 22 July, an article entitled "The Anti-U.S. National-Salvation Fight Is Very Vio-

[3]Guenter Lewy, *America in Vietnam* (New York, 1978), pp. 338–392; "CINCPAC Message to JCS, January 1968, 1967 Progress Report [partial quote]," in Sharp, *Strategy for Defeat*, pp. 301–304; Sharp and Westmoreland, *Report*, pp. 53–54; *Command History 1967*, 1: 28–29, Hoopes, *Limits of Intervention*, pp. 75–91; and Thies, *When Governments Collide*, p. 218.

[4]Broyles, "The Road to Hill 10," p. 95; Karnow, *Vietnam*, p. 458; Truong Nhu Tang, David Chanoff, and Doan Van Toai, *A Viet Cong Memoir* (New York, 1985), pp. 167–169; *Command History 1967*, 1:28, 2:28–29, 657–664. An incident that illustrates North Vietnamese concern over civilian morale occurred in the 21–26 July meetings between North Vietnamese premier Pham Van Dong and two Frenchmen, Herbert Marcovich and Raymond Aubrac, who were acting as unofficial envoys for the United States. Pham Van Dong repeatedly complained about the bombing campaign and a possible escalation of the air war; see Thies, *When Governments Collide*, pp. 180–181, 218.

lent, but It Will Certainly Achieve Complete Victory" was published in *Quan Doi Nhan Dan.* The article, written by the deputy chief of the NVA's political department, Le Quang Dao, criticized officials who failed to recognize that "deadly and absolutely irreconcilable" differences existed between the United States and North Vietnam and instead believed that Hanoi should make concessions to obtain a negotiated settlement. The emergence of disillusioned officials who were urging a negotiated end to the fighting presented the collective leadership with a delicate problem. These officials had to be prevented from interfering in the upcoming winter-spring offensive.[5]

Participants at the July meeting discussed several international issues. They needed to develop an estimate of the likely U.S. reaction to the upcoming campaign. The North Vietnamese were especially concerned about the possibility of an invasion of their homeland. In a speech delivered in January 1967, Giap had addressed the possibility of invasion and what was needed to repel a U.S. landing in the north.[6]

The communists also had to assess the stability of the South Vietnamese regime. Buddhist unrest and the rebellion of ARVN units near the U.S. base at Da Nang in spring 1966 demonstrated that the Saigon government was still subjected to a variety of stresses. One of the apparent participants in the July meeting even admitted that the communists had just missed a golden opportunity by not taking advantage of the domestic unrest that spring. A letter sent by Le Duan to VC commanders in July 1967 contained an apology for failing to take "the initiative in inciting the masses to arise." Duan also noted, however, the experience had "taught us a lesson." The collective leadership apparently concluded that conditions were ripe for the emergence of a general uprising of the South Vietnamese population and the mutiny of ARVN units during the next campaign.[7]

The likelihood of continued Soviet and Chinese support during the upcoming offensive also had to be evaluated. Because of the destruction and dislocations created by the bombing in the north and the war in the south, the North Vietnamese were becoming increasingly de-

[5]Oberdorfer, *Tet,* p. 65; McGarvey, *Visions of Victory,* p. 22; Thomas Latimer, "Hanoi's Leaders and Their South Vietnam Policies, 1954–1968," (Ph.D. diss., Georgetown University, 1972), pp. 299–301, cited in Thies, *When Governments Collide,* p. 182; and Vien and Khuyen, *Reflections on the Vietnam War* p. 85.

[6]"General Vo Nguyen Giap on the Strategic Role of the Self-Defense Militia," transmitted by Radio Hanoi's Domestic Service, 1330 GMT, 3 April and 7 April 1967, in McGarvey, *Visions of Victory,* pp. 168–198.

[7]Karnow, *Vietnam,* pp. 446–449; see also Stanton, *Rise and Fall,* pp. 120–125. For a discussion of the NLF's unsuccessful effort to take advantage of domestic unrest in the spring of 1966, see Tang, Chanoff, and Toai, *Viet Cong Memoir,* pp. 103–107.

pendent on Soviet supplies of petroleum, oil, lubricants, and sophisticated weapons and Chinese light infantry weapons. But all was not well within the socialist bloc. The Chinese were in the midst of the cultural revolution and Sino-Soviet relations were deteriorating. Moreover, the Chinese leadership urged the North Vietnamese to wage a protracted war and to shun both negotiations and urban offensives; they could be expected to object to Giap's plan for the Tet offensive. The Soviets did not object to Hanoi's preference for urban attacks or, in principle, to negotiations with the United States. Thus, no matter which strategy was selected, an impression would be created that the Hanoi regime was taking sides in the Sino-Soviet dispute, making it more difficult for them to walk the fine line needed to secure Soviet and Chinese aid for the upcoming offensive.[8]

Further insight into the North Vietnamese assessment of the situation in the summer and fall of 1967 and their prescriptions for overcoming the impact of U.S. intervention is provided by an article published in *Nhan Dan* and *Quan Doi Nhan Dan* in mid-September 1967. In hindsight, the article, signed by General Giap and entitled "The Big Victory, the Great Task," provides a general description of the Tet offensive.[9] Giap based his analysis on a new interpretation of the situation. He claimed that the war was stalemated in favor of the communists: "Wanting a blitzkrieg, the U.S. imperialists have been forced to fight a protracted war . . . [which is] a big defeat for them." According to Giap, the United States adopted this strategy geared toward "winning a victory of strategic significance in a short period" in order to avoid domestic and international pressure against the war. Giap

---

[8]Following the Chinese detonation of a nuclear weapon in October 1964, Sino-Soviet relations deteriorated significantly. From 1965, both nations began to regard their mutual frontier as an area of potential hostilities, a fact reflected by the intermittent skirmishes along the border. For a discussion of the Sino-Soviet dispute during this period, see Rostow, *Diffusion of Power*, p. 370. For a discussion of the concerns of the North Vietnamese about the impact of the Sino-Soviet split on their ability to continue the war, see Shaplen, *Time out of Hand*, pp. 394–395. For a dicussion of the distrust that has existed between the Chinese and Vietnamese throughout history, see Bernard K. Gordon, "The Third Indochina Conflict," *Foreign Affairs* 65 (Fall 1986), 68. For a discussion of the Chinese and Soviet positions vis-à-vis Hanoi during this period, see Lomperis, *War Everyone Lost*, p. 75; and Karnow, *Vietnam*, p. 452.

[9]Vo Nguyen Giap, "The Big Victory, the Great Task," *Nhan Dan* and *Quan Doi Nhan Dan* (14–16 September, 1967), in McGarvey, *Visions of Victory*, pp. 199–251. For a discussion of Giap's September 1967 article, see Karnow, *Vietnam*, p. 535; Lewy, *America in Vietnam*, p. 67; Lomperis, *War Everyone Lost*, p. 151; Lung, *General Offensives*, p. 33; and Sharp and Westmoreland, *Report*, p. 135. In contrast to the interpretation presented here, Richard Betts argues that the publication of Giap's article was meant to deceive the allies by leading them to believe that the NVA and VC intended to conserve their forces and wage a protracted war of attrition, see Betts, "Strategic Surprise for War Termination" p. 161.

claimed that, as the war dragged on, "U.S. ruling circles" would be "increasingly opposed by the U.S. people" and "isolated in the international arena." In contrast, a protracted war worked in favor of communist interests: "the longer the South Vietnamese people fight, the stronger they become. The longer the enemy fights . . . the greater the difficulties he encounters." Giap was apparently attempting to reassure his colleagues and the forces under his command that the situation was not as bleak as it appeared: the allied failure to win quickly was a victory for the communists.[10]

Giap also provided a reassuring assessment of domestic developments within North Vietnam. He noted that civilians would continue to withstand the strain of the air war; civilian morale had not been seriously shaken by the bombing. Giap even claimed that the bombing had produced a rallying effect among civilians and that morale would not be broken if the United States escalated its air campaign in response to communist initiatives. According to Giap: "They ["U.S. imperialists"] may stage fierce strikes against our cities, villages, and populated areas, further intensify their strikes against our communication lines, step up their bombing and strafing of our dams and dikes, and strengthen their blockade of our coastal areas. Nevertheless, they definitely cannot shake our people's determination to . . . advance toward the reunification of the fatherland." Giap also noted that the threat posed by dissident officials had been contained: Intensified measures ensuring security and order had already been taken to guard against "the evil plotting of the reactionaries and spies."[11]

In Giap's view, the time had arrived to launch a major offensive that would accelerate favorable trends. A key innovation would be the use of not only NVA and VC main-force units and VC guerrillas but every instrument available to the communists for an all-out attack. Giap noted that these attacks should take place throughout South Vietnam and emphasized the importance of coordination against urban areas and allied bases in order to "directly hit the enemy in his deepest lair." Moreover, the attacks against urban areas would coincide with a general uprising among the southern population. Giap thus called for a coordinated offensive with every weapon in the communist arsenal: military struggle (*dau tranh vu trang*) undertaken by the VC and NVA; political struggle (*dau tranh chinh tri*) to promote domestic unrest; action among the military (*binh van*) to undermine the effectiveness of ARVN; diplomatic initiatives (*dich van*) to slow the U.S. response to

[10]Giap, "The Big Victory, the Great Task," in *Visions of Victory*, pp. 202, 213, 221–222.
[11]Ibid., pp. 205, 232, 241–242.

indications of an impending offensive; and action among the people (*dan van*) to bolster support for the coming offensive in communist controlled areas. The combination of these various weapons, according to Giap, would produce a force multiplier effect that would surmount the problems and exploit the opportunities confronting the communists.[12]

Crucial to Giap's proposal was the notion that conditions were ripe for a general uprising: "The people of all walks of life, including those who did not realize the true nature of the U.S. aggressors or who were fooled into following them, have now stood up to fight the enemy. This constitutes an advantage for the development and ultimate triumph of the . . . people's struggle." The South Vietnamese people and army were dissatisfied with the Saigon regime. For example, ARVN's poor military performance "brought about quarrels, conflicts, and discord among puppet authorities and army" creating a situation in which ARVN units were on the verge of revolt. The South Vietnamese were unhappy about the presence of foreign troops in their country: "Ever since U.S. troops invaded South Vietnam, the contradictions between the U.S. imperialists and the country-selling Vietnamese traitors and the Vietnamese people have become sharper and deeper." This dissatisfaction with the current state of affairs was also pronounced within the cities. According to Giap, "the political forces of the people in Southern cities and towns have developed more and more comprehensively, and will certainly intensify their political struggle and continuous attacks against the enemy's dens." Giap suggested that, with aid and encouragement, the South Vietnamese people and ARVN units would stage a mass uprising, thereby toppling the regime in Saigon. Attacking cities and arming the population would instigate the rebellion. ARVN units would "fall apart" under the combined pressure of "fighting and troop proselytizing." Giap wanted to attack directly the weakest link in the allied war effort. By striking at ARVN and the Saigon regime with a general uprising, he intended to eliminate the government presence among the southern population: "The puppet administration is the political buttress of the U.S. imperialists. . . . In view of this, our people in South Vietnam have combined their armed struggle with political struggle, to overthrow the puppet administration." In effect, Giap claimed that the South Vietnamese population and ARVN units would revolt, thereby eliminating Saigon's ability to prosecute the war.[13]

[12]Ibid., pp. 220–221.

[13]Ibid., pp. 202, 219–221, 226, 230–231. For a similar interpretation of Giap's belief that a general uprising could be instigated during the Tet offensive and for a discussion

Another innovation suggested by Giap was the incorporation of the element of surprise into the plans for the general offensive–general uprising. Top U.S. commanders, according to Giap, were particularly vulnerable to surprise attacks: "The U.S. generals are subjective and haughty, and have always been caught by surprise and defeated." Moreover, U.S. forces themselves fared little better in Giap's view: "The predominant characteristic of the war in South Vietnam is that U.S. troops have always been surprised, caught in the Liberation Armed Forces' trap, and wiped out." Behind the hyperbole, Giap was suggesting that the element of surprise would contribute to the success of the Tet campaign.[14]

How would the United States respond to this all-out attack? Giap recognized that the United States could invade North Vietnam, Laos, and Cambodia and escalate the bombing of the north. He claimed, however, that such a response was unlikely. Instead, the U.S. reaction would be limited to the deployment of an additional 50,000 troops by July 1968, the number of reinforcements that had already been scheduled for deployment by fall 1967. In general, the United States would not significantly escalate the war in response to the Tet offensive. Three factors would constrain it.

First, U.S. global commitments limited the resources that could be devoted to the war: "The U.S. imperialists must cope with the national liberation movement [in countries other than South Vietnam], with the socialist bloc, with the American people, and with other imperialist countries. The U.S. imperialists cannot mobilize all their forces for the war of aggression in Vietnam." According to Giap, the United States had already encountered difficulties in meeting General Westmoreland's troop requests. The Johnson administration was aware that only limited resources could be devoted to the conflict, claimed Giap, noting as evidence a trip made by Secretary of Defense McNamara to Saigon, purportedly to encourage Westmoreland to use U.S. forces more efficiently. Yet efforts to improve the U.S. tooth-to-tail ratio would ultimately fail, according to Giap, because logistical requirements would remain constant.[15]

Second, the U.S. strategy in Southeast Asia would limit its response to the campaign. American strategy, alternately referred to as "limited war" or "flexible response," was intended to prevent the pro-

---

of Giap's belief that ARVN units could be made to mutiny during the Tet offensive, see Palmer, *Summons*, p. 167.

[14]Giap, "The Big Victory, the Great Task," in *Visions of Victory*, pp. 213, 217.

[15]Ibid., pp. 237, 241–242.

gress of socialist peoples without interfering with other global commitments or precipitating a nuclear war:

> The U.S. imperialists . . . maintain that the strategy of flexible response, which envisions three types of war—the special war [U.S. advisory assistance to ARVN prior to 1965], local war, and total war—is the strategy most likely to help them avoid total passivity when they are not in a position to prosecute a nuclear war. . . . The U.S. imperialists must restrict the U.S. forces participating in a local war because otherwise their global strategy would be hampered and their influence throughout the world would diminish.

U.S. strategy, according to Giap, ensured that the geographic scope of the war and the military instruments used against the communists would be kept within relatively strict limits.[16]

A third factor that would limit the response to the offensive was domestic and international pressure on the Johnson administration. According to Giap, the United States was "increasingly isolated in the world" and was subjected to international protest against the war: "Progressive peoples throughout the world . . . have vehemently condemned the . . . aggression against Vietnam. . . . Many of the U.S. imperialists' satellite countries have shown themselves indifferent to the war of aggression in Vietnam; some of them have even officially protested against it." Giap also noted that the Johnson administration faced growing domestic unrest. To quell domestic opposition to the war and what Giap termed the "Negroes' boiling and widespread struggle," the administration had to limit the impact of the war on American society: "They must restrict their participation in order to avoid upsetting the political, economic, and social life of the United States. . . . They accept this restriction because they are convinced that they can achieve victory even if only a limited number of U.S. troops directly participate in a local war." Yet the administration could minimize the impact of the war, according to Giap, only by restricting its scope and intensity.[17]

Finally, Giap claimed that the Soviet Union and China would continue to send large quantities of aid during the 1967 winter-spring offensive. He suggested, however, that Soviet or Chinese aid should not be viewed as a panacea. The Vietnamese should count only on

---

[16]Ibid., p. 207.

[17]Ibid., pp. 206–207. For Giap's discussion of domestic protest against the war in the United States and growing racial unrest, see ibid., p. 240. For a similar interpretation of Giap's view of the domestic restraints limiting the U.S. response, see Palmer, *Summons*, p. 167.

their own resources to prosecute the war in the south: "No one can replace our people in carrying out the effort to wrest back independence and freedom for the Vietnamese fatherland. Only our people can decide their destiny."[18]

THE NORTH VIETNAMESE PLAN FOR THE TET OFFENSIVE

Although the actual Tet battle plan has never been revealed, the offensive reflected many of the ideas advanced by Giap and his supporters. It incorporated all communist assets, an idea championed by Giap since the summer of 1965. VC guerrilla attacks against the vulnerable points in the allied war effort, a tactic long advocated by Giap, were also used. Various aspects of the offensive were suggested at different times during the communist debate over strategy. It was during the Tet offensive, however, that the North Vietnamese integrated the strategic and tactical lessons learned after U.S. intervention into their own style of warfare.

Objectives

The primary objective of the Tet offensive was to win the war by instigating a general uprising. To achieve this goal, the communists intended to destroy ARVN and the administrative apparatus of the Saigon government. The communists had long believed that tensions between the South Vietnamese and U.S. governments constituted the major political problem facing the allies. They believed that the alliance would collapse under the pressure of a concentrated attack against its weakest member, South Vietnam. By eliminating the regime in Saigon and ARVN, the communists hoped to inflict a setback on the United States that would take years to overcome. Faced with the loss of its crucial ally and surrounded by a hostile population, U.S. forces would have to start from scratch in their effort to drive the communists from the country. Giap claimed that U.S. leaders would tire of this situation within a few years and seek a negotiated end to the conflict on communist terms.[19]

---

[18]Giap, "The Big Victory, the Great Task," in *Visions of Victory*, p. 223.

[19]For a similar interpretation of the objectives of the Tet offensive, see Lung, *General Offensives*, p. 26; Palmer, *Summons*, p. 176; and Sharp, *Strategy for Defeat*, p. 214. Norman Podhoretz, Harry Summers, and Fred C. Weyand identify another North Vietnamese objective during the Tet offensive: elimination of the VC in order to ensure that South Vietnam would be controlled by the North Vietnamese after the war; see Podhoretz, *Why We Were in Vietnam* (New York, 1982), p. 175; Summers, *On Strategy*, p. 96;

The Tet offensive was probably not intended to shift American public and elite opinion quickly against continued involvement in the war. Domestic opinion in the United States did, however, enter into the communist calculations about the wisdom of escalating the fighting in the south: Giap claimed that public opinion would help to constrain the U.S. response to Tet. Yet the American people, in Giap's view, would have to be exposed to a year or two of military stalemate before they would turn decisively against continued involvement in the war. In contrast, the communists probably hoped that the Tet offensive would produce a quick, unmistakable shift in South Vietnamese public opinion against the war, specifically, a general uprising. In retrospect, according to General Do, "we didn't achieve our main objective, which was to spur uprising throughout the south. Still, we inflicted heavy casualties on the Americans and their puppets. . . . As for making an impact in the United States, it had not been our intention—but it turned out be a fortunate result."[20] The quick impact of the offensive on American opinion was an unintended consequence of the campaign, although it was not an unwelcome development from the communist perspective.

Strategy

To achieve their Tet objectives, the communists implemented a strategy that incorporated two key initiatives: the coordination of all communist assets, and surprise. The integration of these initiatives into the campaign was intended to serve as a force multiplier that would allow the communists to escalate the war significantly without a concomitant increase in military resources; this was the ultimate innovation embodied in the Tet offensive.

Although participants in the debate over strategy sometimes noted that the coordinated attacks by NVA and VC main-force units and VC guerrillas would act as a major force multiplier, Giap took this argument one step farther in the plan for the Tet offensive. He called for not only the use of all communist military forces in a concerted attack but also the integration of every available political instrument into the

---

and Weyand, "Serving the People: The Basic Case for the United States Army," *CDRS Call*, May–June 1976, p. 5. In light of the military might arrayed against them, however, it is unlikely that the North Vietnamese would have intentionally sacrificed one of their best military assets for domestic political reasons.

[20]Tran Do, quoted by Karnow, *Vietnam*, p. 523. In contrast to the interpretation of the role of American public opinion in the communist strategy for the Tet offensive presented here, Podhoretz maintains that Tet was intended to influence American public opinion quickly; see *Why We Were in Vietnam*, p. 130.

campaign, including two political resources that had not been fully utilized. The first of these resources was diplomacy. The North Vietnamese used secret diplomatic exchanges, which took place intermittently with the Johnson administration and third parties, to deceive the allies about communist intentions. By softening their position in these exchanges, the North Vietnamese may have hoped to create a false sense of security among their enemies. A more forthcoming communist position was intended to sow dissension within the alliance. By ensuring that news of diplomatic progress was made public prior to the offensive, the communists attempted to make the South Vietnamese regime and population uneasy about U.S. willingness to continue to prosecute the war. Thus the communists intended to employ diplomacy not only to deceive U.S. decision makers but also to drive a wedge in the alliance at a time when allied solidarity was of crucial importance.[21] The second political resource to be tapped during the Tet campaign was the southern population. Giap claimed that the communists could harness the people's supposed hatred of the Saigon regime and the United States by instigating a general uprising, especially in the cities. VC attacks against key government installations, dissemination of propaganda, and provision of weapons to the population at the start of the offensive would spark the uprising. By fostering this revolt, the communists hoped to gain thousands of combatants, a new type of force that would strike at the allied rear and greatly contribute to the shock of the overall offensive.[22]

In addition to incorporating all assets in a coordinated attack, the communists hoped to surprise their opponents in terms of attack timing, scope, targets, and intensity. They apparently believed that the chaos produced by dozens of simultaneous surprise attacks would prevent the allies from quelling the general uprising before de facto communist control was established throughout the cities and large portions of the countryside.

To secure the objectives of the offensive, the communists adopted a three-phase strategy. The first phase lasted from about July 1967 to 31

[21]For a similar description of the motivations behind the softening of the North Vietnamese positions in talks with the United States, see Westmoreland, *Soldier*, p. 312; Karnow, *Vietnam*, p. 538; and Herring, *America's Longest War*, p. 185. Patrick McGarvey, however, claims that the North Vietnamese adopted a more forthcoming position in an effort to draw the United States "to the conference table in early January, and as the sessions were getting under way, present the world with the dramatic Tet assault—a Dien Bien Phu of sorts, which would place the United States in the weakest possible bargaining position"; see *Visions of Victory*, p. 55.

[22]Oberdorfer, *Tet*, p. 54; Shaplen, *Time out of Hand*, p. 391; Sharp, *Strategy for Defeat*, p. 214; and Palmer, *Summons*, p. 175. Bernard Brodie maintains that the North Vietnamese did not expect a general uprising during Tet; see "Tet Offensive," p. 333.

January 1968. During this time, the communists laid the diplomatic, logistical, organizational, political, and military groundwork for the conduct of the Tet attacks. Agreements with the Soviet Union and China were negotiated to ensure a continued flow of supplies during the campaign. The North Vietnamese also extended so-called peace feelers in secret third-party exchanges with the United States.[23]

Preparations were made to increase the movement of supplies and manpower along the Ho Chi Minh Trail, and weapon caches were positioned in southern cities. Organizational reforms were undertaken to increase command, control, and communication capabilities and the number of units available to commanders in the region around Saigon. Specialized sapper units were created for attacks against key urban installations. A motivational campaign was launched among cadres and military forces to ensure that they would be prepared to give their all during the offensive.[24]

Among the political initiatives was a disinformation campaign intended to sow dissension within the alliance. Similarly, a major propaganda campaign began to inform southerners that the conditions were ripe for the staging of a general uprising. In North Vietnam itself, those who advocated a negotiated end to the war were arrested to protect the element of surprise from compromise.[25]

Military initiatives also were undertaken during the initial phase. ARVN units and government facilities had to be deprived of prompt support from U.S. forces. To isolate ARVN and the government's administrative structure, the NVA launched attacks in sparsely populated areas along the DMZ and the western border of South Vietnam. The communists expected that U.S. commanders would not resist the opportunity to use their full firepower against NVA units and thus would remain in their usual operating areas far away from ARVN units and populated areas. The siege of the U.S. firebase at Khe Sanh, timed to preoccupy the U.S. command on the eve of the offensive, was the final initiative in the effort to keep U.S. forces separated from ARVN. This first phase, then, was designed to lay the groundwork for the wave of attacks and general uprising that would sweep South Vietnam during the second phase of the campaign. The communists

[23]Palmer, *Summons*, pp. 175–176; Herring, *America's Longest War*, pp. 184–185; and Shaplen, *Time out of Hand*, pp. 397–398.
[24]Sharp and Westmoreland, *Report*, p. 41; Shaplen, *Time out of Hand*, pp. 403, 410; Lung, *General Offensives*, pp. 28, 30, 34–35; and Karnow, *Vietnam*, pp. 514, 527–528. For an example of the literature distributed to VC soldiers, see "'The New Situation and Mission': A Viet Cong Training Document," *VDRN* doc. 20.
[25]Westmoreland, *Soldier*, pp. 311, 328; McGarvey, *Visions of Victory*, p. 50; Lung, *General Offensives*, p. 27; Oberdorfer, *Tet*, p. 65; and Thies, *When Governments Collide*, pp. 218–219.

hoped to keep allied units separated, leaving ARVN forces and cities open to direct attack.[26]

The second phase of the Tet offensive, which was probably to last from 31 January 1968 through early May 1968, was intended to instigate a general uprising and to destroy ARVN and the Saigon regime. During the opening hours of the offensive, the communists planned to attack at least 39 of South Vietnam's 44 provincial capitals, 5 of its 6 autonomous cities, and 71 of its 245 district capitals. In general, two types of targets were attacked: (1) administrative centers, ARVN headquarters and arsenals, and television and radio stations within the cities, and (2) ARVN units themselves. In addition to attacking ARVN forces to cause their disintegration, the communists adopted innovative methods to destroy entire ARVN units. Efforts were made to capture ARVN commanders and to force them to order their troops to lay down their weapons. VC guerrillas dressed in ARVN uniforms fired on ARVN troops and attempted to operate captured armored vehicles in an effort to fuel rumors about defections. ARVN soldiers were also urged by a propaganda campaign to join the communists, or at least to stop fighting and return to their homes.[27]

The second phase began the attempt to instigate a general uprising, especially in urban areas. The communists probably hoped that the uprising would be provoked by the presence of VC guerrillas in the cities, a vigorous propaganda campaign, and the sight of ARVN units reeling under attack, but they undertook special efforts to ensure its eruption. They attempted to attack jails and to arm prisoners. VC cadres, who had long remained underground in the cities, emerged from their hiding places and urged the people to revolt against the government. In case the general uprising failed to develop in some areas, the communists planned to attack the South Vietnamese naval headquarters near Saigon in order to capture ships to transport armed partisans to cities that had not yet revolted. Wherever the communists obtained even temporary control, they rounded up officials and officers in order to remove the rallying points for remaining government supporters.[28]

[26]Herring, *America's Longest War*, p. 185; Sharp and Westmoreland, *Report*, p. 135; Broyles, "The Road to Hill 10," p. 102; Palmer, *Summons*, p. 175; Summers, *On Strategy*, pp. 134–135; and Frances Fitzgerald, *Fire in the Lake: The Vietnamese and the Americans in Vietnam* (Boston, 1972), p. 392.

[27]Schandler, *Unmaking of a President*, p. 71; Shaplen, *Time out of Hand*, p. 415; Stanton, *Rise and Fall*, p. 245; and Lung, *General Offensives*, p. 29.

[28]Lung, *General Offensives*, p. 28; Stanton, *Rise and Fall*, p. 222; Shaplen, *Time out of Hand*, p. 408; Karnow, *Vietnam*, pp. 530–531; Lewy, *America in Vietnam*, pp. 274–275; and Keith W. Nolan, *Battle for Hue, Tet 1968* (Novato, Calif., 1983), p. 184. The VC also used the offensive to settle old scores against South Vietnamese government officials

The third phase of the offensive, which lasted from 5 May 1968 to February 1969, was intended to prevent allied forces from regaining their balance. This phase was itself divided into three waves of attacks: the first wave hit in two stages on 4 and 25 May 1968; the second began on 17 August 1968; and the third began on 22 February 1969. Because of the losses suffered in the previous phases of the offensive, the size and number of communist units participating in the attacks diminished over time. Moreover, the communists tended to rely on rocket and artillery attacks during the final phase, and little effort was made to enlist the aid of the South Vietnamese population in the attacks. In sum, the communists had planned to maintain military pressure on the allies after the second phase of the Tet offensive, but the failure of that second phase, in terms of objectives and casualties, eliminated much of the purpose and intensity of the third phase.[29]

THE COMMUNIST STRATEGY OF DECEPTION

Although there is still controversy about the communists' Tet objectives more than twenty years after the eruption of the offensive, one aspect of their 1967 campaign remains relatively unexamined. The communists' efforts to achieve surprise have been largely ignored in the literature on the Vietnam war. An examination of this strategy of deception illustrates the problems that confronted allied officers and intelligence analysts as they attempted to predict future communist behavior on the battlefield. With this hindsight, a compelling picture emerges of the communists' aspirations for the campaign and the difficult task facing intelligence analysts as they attempted to predict their opponent's behavior.

To obtain the element of surprise, the communists adopted a mix of deceptive strategies. Passive deception, which primarily relied on secrecy, was used to conceal preparations for the urban offensive and general uprising from allied intelligence analysts. Active deception, which largely took the form of offensive military action, drew allied attention away from the developing threat against the cities and kept U.S. units in their usual operating areas along the borders of South Vietnam. The North Vietnamese demonstrated the importance they placed on surprise by the risks they took. For example, they timed the

and traitors within their own ranks; see Tang, Chanoff, and Toai, *Viet Cong Memoir*, p. 110.
    [29]Lung, *General Offensives*, pp. 91–119; and Sharp and Westmoreland, *Report*, p. 166.

offensive to take advantage of the traditional truce and inevitable reduction in allied offensive operations and vigilance that occurred during the Tet holiday, even though they violated the most sacred Vietnamese holiday and risked provoking the hostility of the southern population. Ultimately, deceptive strategies, especially the efforts at passive deception, were so demanding that they overwhelmed the capabilities of the communist command structure. The attempt to maintain secrecy impaired the coordination of attacks throughout the country, and in the end the communists sacrificed coordination to maintain secrecy. The attack began prematurely in the northern provinces of South Vietnam.[30]

Early Passive Deception

Immediately after the strategy session held in Hanoi in July 1967, passive deception was all that was needed to maintain the security of the preparations under way for the phase-two attacks. Planning for the offensive was largely confined to senior officials. The NLF convened a secret congress sometime in August 1967, for example, to prepare a new political program to increase South Vietnamese support for their cause, but their program was not immediately disseminated to cadres. During this period, work on the offensive largely remained a paper exercise; access to operational plans, training materials, propaganda strategies, and logistical preparations could proceed on a strict need-to-know basis. At this point, many cadres could remain uninformed about the operational details of the campaign and still undertake activities in support of the Tet attacks. In August, for instance, the VC stepped up their use of female agents to elicit information about allied installations in Saigon, a key Tet target, but the agents were not told how the information they gathered would be used.[31]

---

[30]Sharp and Westmoreland, *Report*, p. 41. According to Lt. Gen. Daniel O. Graham, Tet truces had been generally respected by the communists for twenty years (Graham had overlooked the 1960 Tet offensive), and this contributed to the overall shock of the attack: "The fact is that the South Vietnamese really couldn't believe, despite how much evidence you poured in—or a lot of them couldn't believe—anybody would attack anybody during Tet"; see the testimony of Graham in House Select Committee on Intelligence, *U.S. Intelligence Agencies and Activities*, p. 1666. The gamble of provoking the animosity of the southern population by attacking during the holiday failed to pay off. According to Lung, "there was no doubt that in those areas under attack the urban people were irritated by what they considered a most treacherous act by the communists"; see *General Offensives*, p. 148. Shaplen also notes that the Tet attacks provoked the resentment of the South Vietnamese people; see *Time out of Hand*, p. 416.
[31]Oberdorfer, *Tet*, p. 60; and USMACV AC of S (Assistant Chief of Staff) J-2, *PERINTREP* (periodic intelligence report) August 1967, p. 12.

Other initiatives, which in hindsight take on tremendous significance, were treated in a matter-of-fact way by the communists. In September, Hanoi negotiated new military aid agreements with the Soviet Union and China to continue the flow of supplies during the offensive. As a result of these agreements, AK-47 assault rifles and B-40 rocket launchers—some still covered in packing grease when they fell into allied hands—became standard issue in VC units during the Tet attacks. The North Vietnamese even announced that they had signed a new "Agreement on China's Economic and Technical Assistance to Vietnam." By handling these agreements routinely the communists apparently attempted to reduce their importance in the minds of allied intelligence analysts.[32]

Another example of the activity undertaken during this period occurred at a meeting of COSVN sometime between late July and mid-August. VC commanders started logistical and organizational planning for the second phase of the offensive. Plans were made to strengthen the command and control network surrounding Saigon and communications stretching from the supply areas in Cambodia to Saigon. COSVN also reversed the practice of using VC soldiers as replacements in NVA units; NVA soldiers were now sent as replacements for VC units. Additionally, COSVN prepared materials to motivate their forces to lend full support to these logistical, organizational, and personnel initiatives. In fact, allied forces later captured various editions of training documents, dated 3 August 1967, which indicated that the agenda at the COSVN meeting, or some similar gathering, included the development of plans to make sure that cadres and military forces understood the objectives behind the offensive.[33]

A ten-page manuscript captured by allied forces in Tay Ninh province on 25 November 1967 provides insight into the preparation of cadres and soldiers. The training manual, entitled "Clearly Understand the New Situation and Mission: Take Advantage of Victories to Surge Forward and Completely Defeat the U.S. and Puppet Enemy" and dated 1 September 1967, was a typical reproduction of the 3 August study paper. The document, intended for "low-level cadres, Party members, and the sympathetic masses who are the target of the Party's development," provided a general outline of the strategy and objectives of the first two phases of the Tet offensive. In the initial

---

[32]Graham in House Select Committee on Intelligence, *U.S. Intelligence Agencies and Activities* p. 1652; U.S. Congress, Senate, *Stalemate in Vietnam*, report to the Committee on Foreign Relations United States Senate by Senator Joseph S. Clark on a study mission to South Vietnam, 90th Cong., 2d sess., 1968., p. 5; *Command History 1967*, 1:22, 113 n.11; and Lung, *General Offensives*, pp. 10, 24.

[33]Oberdorfer, *Tet*, pp. 57–58; and *VDRN* doc. 20.

phase, the goals were to "destroy a large part of the U.S. combat forces to render them incapable of carrying on the war and saving the puppet government and army from disintegration. Inflict heavy losses on the U.S. forces, both politically and militarily." Objectives in the second phase followed:

> Destroy and disintegrate the main body of the puppet army to such an extent that it ceases to be a force on which the U.S. imperialists can rely in pursuing their aggressive war. Wreck the puppet army to the point where it can no longer maintain the reactionary political regime of the U.S. henchmen in the South under any circumstances. . . . vigorously push forward our armed and political struggle, arouse the masses in the cities and rural areas temporarily under enemy control, use our political and military violent forces in the three-pronged attack, stand up forcefully to smash the enemy's oppressive machinery in order to create conditions for our march toward the seizure of state power for the people.

The document also explained how victory in these phases would culminate in a resounding defeat for the allies:

> These three tasks are related to one another and will have mutual effects. By destroying and wearing down many U.S. troops, we will cause the puppet troops to lose their morale increasingly and disintegrate. As the puppet troops are destroyed and disintegrated, the U.S. troops will find themselves in a more critical situation. As U.S. and puppet troops sustain losses and destruction, the enemy grip in the cities and rural areas under their temporary control will be loosened, and such a situation can give our people living in these areas a chance to rise up and attack the enemy. With the people in the cities and rural areas rising up to attack the enemy, the enemy rear base will become confused, the puppet army and regime will soon disintegrate, and the U.S. imperialists will get bogged down in an even more critically stalemated situation. Such a situation will enable our army and people to apply their all-out efforts to seize state power for the people.

In addition, the document identified some of the problems confronting the offensive. VC units were not at full strength and recruitment efforts were not making up this shortcoming. More effort was also needed to generate mass support for the communists: "The movement to gain popular participation in proselytizing is still very slow and has not been properly stepped up."[34]

Although the documents issued by senior communists during this

---

[34]*VDRN* doc. 20, pp. 1, 4–5, 8. For a discussion of this captured document, see Lung, *General Offensives*, p. 20; and Palmer, *Summons*, pp. 177–178.

period avoided references to operational details, the communists did risk disclosing their intentions by circulating these materials. But they had little choice in the matter. For the offensive to succeed, cadres and even junior officers had to know what was about to be required of them, a maximum effort. At a relatively early stage in the campaign, then, the need for secrecy came into conflict with the effort to launch a general offensive–general uprising. Publicity, not secrecy, was needed to inform communist forces and even the South Vietnamese population that the turning point in the war was on the horizon. The communists apparently attempted to overcome this dilemma by limiting the disclosure of operational details, but as the date for the Tet attacks approached, they would encounter increasing difficulties in maintaining secrecy.

Active Deception and Dich Van

During September, the communists continued to plan for the offensive. The VC began compiling lists of installations and officials slated for capture during the attack on Hue. On 28 September, COSVN dispatched an urgent message calling for stepped up political activities in the areas bordering Saigon and in the inner slums of the city. Toward the end of September, a motivational meeting, the "Second Congress of Heroes, Emulation Combatants, and Valiant Men of the South Vietnam People's Liberation Armed Forces," was held for outstanding VC soldiers in Binh Long province. By the end of the month, plans for the reorganization of the command and control network in the area around Saigon were completed. A Tet attack order that urged VC and NVA units to complete the "liberation of South Vietnam before the death of Uncle Ho" was issued by the end of September.[35]

At about this time, the North Vietnamese also decided to put their own house in order. The Hanoi regime eliminated many of its domestic opponents, those who advocated a negotiated end to the war. Over two hundred officials, including the superintendent of the party's School of Political Studies, the director of North Vietnam's intelligence agency, the deputy chairman of the State Science Committee, and the chief of the finance section of the Ministry of Light Industry, were arrested. The Standing Committee of the National Assembly enacted a secret decree designed to eliminate domestic opposition to the regime's war plans. Signed by Ho Chi Minh on 10 November and announced publicly on 10 March 1968, the decree pre-

[35]Karnow, *Vietnam*, pp. 154, 514, 530; Oberdorfer, *Tet*, p. 58; and Palmer, *Summons*, p. 166.

scribed death sentences, life prison terms, and lesser penalties for a long list of counterrevolutionary crimes.[36]

The communists also undertook several initiatives intended to sow dissension within the alliance and to undermine the political position of the South Vietnamese regime. The centerpiece of this *dich van* campaign emerged on 1 September. Liberation Radio transmitted a new NLF program intended to appeal to a wide segment of the southern population. The program not only promised freedom of the press, free elections, and free speech but also offered to welcome South Vietnamese officers and officials who defected to the communists.

Another *dich van* initiative launched during September came to be known as the "Buttercup affair." A VC agent named Sau Ha was captured by South Vietnamese authorities. During interrogation, Ha claimed that he had been authorized to open a negotiating channel with the United States. To back up his claim, Ha produced a letter authorizing him to discuss "prisoners and other matters" and a list of VC prisoners whose release was requested. In response, the U.S. administration pressured the Saigon regime to release some VC prisoners as a goodwill gesture and sent a letter to the communists through channels opened by Ha. In mid-October, the communists replied that negotiations were not possible unless the United States accepted the standard five-point plan for negotiations offered by the NLF. At this point, rumors that the United States was trying to reach a unilateral agreement with Hanoi began to circulate in Saigon. The rumors reached a peak on 30 November 1967 when South Vietnamese police chief Nguyen Ngoc Loan resigned in protest over the pressure to release VC prisoners. This communist initiative clearly succeeded in sowing dissension within the alliance.[37]

[36]Oberdorfer, *Tet*, p. 65; Thies, *When Governments Collide*, pp. 218–219; and Vien and Khuyen, *Reflections on the Vietnam War*, p. 85.
[37]Lung, *General Offensives*, pp. 26–32; Oberdorfer, *Tet*, pp. 60–65; Westmoreland, *Soldier*, pp. 311–312; and Lester A. Sobel, ed., *South Vietnam: U.S.–Communist Confrontation in Southeast Asia* (New York, 1969), 2:300–303. For an official U.S. interpretation of the Buttercup affair, see "Memo to the President from Rostow dated 1 December 1967" (doc. 33a) and "Cable from Bunker to Rostow 1 December 1967" (doc. 33c) in "Briefing Papers for Senior Advisors 1 December 1967," File: Meeting Notes Box 2, LBJ Library. In a 1988 interview with the author, W. W. Rostow noted that senior officials recognized at the time that the affair was probably an effort to sow dissension between the allies. The Johnson administration's commitment to a negotiated end to the war, according to Rostow, compelled them to investigate any apparent negotiating overture. The previously cited memo from Rostow to the president substantiates Rostow's 1988 interpretation of the incident. In contrast, Tang claims that the NLF was serious in its attempt to promote a prisoner exchange, but that South Vietnamese fears of secret negotiations between the NLF and the United States led them to execute the prisoners the NLF wanted returned. The executions caused the NLF to break off negotiations; see Tang, Chanoff, and Toai, *Viet Cong Memoir*, pp. 119–121.

The communists also initiated active deception to fix U.S. forces and attention on their usual operating areas along the border. This deception began to unfold in the form of repeated attacks against the U.S. Marine firebase at Con Thien near the DMZ. On 10 September, the 812th NVA Regiment staged a mass frontal assault on the perimeter of the 3d Battalion, 26th Marines. After repelling this initial assault with the aid of air and artillery support, the marines were subjected to repeated NVA ground attacks and artillery fire. Between 19 and 27 September the NVA fired over 3,077 artillery rounds at Con Thien. By the end of September the bombardment had tapered off, and on 4 October MACV declared that the siege of Con Thien had ended.[38]

This burst of active deception was probably intended to accompany a lapse, albeit necessary, in passive deception. Between 17 and 20 September, Radio Hanoi's domestic service broadcast General Giap's article, "The Big Victory, the Great Task." Indeed, one of the most mystifying events of this period is the North Vietnamese decision to make public Giap's analysis—revealing "practically a blueprint for the Tet offensive."[39] Apparently, the communists had to ensure that thousands of cadres in the south would realize and believe that the time was near for them to launch a general uprising in support of a general offensive. Written under the name of the foremost communist military leader and proclaimed to the world, publication of the article stood as a public commitment from the highest authority that the war-winning offensive would soon take place. Obviously, the communists were taking a calculated risk that U.S. analysts and their "country" experts (the South Vietnamese) would misinterpret the article or dismiss it as insignificant. In contrast, VC cadres, privy to secret communications and fluent in the jargon of the Vietnamese revolutionary, would immediately grasp its significance. The communists wanted to preserve the secrecy of the Tet attacks while making sure that the "man in the street" would play his part at the proper time. By timing the broadcast to coincide with the attack on Con Thien, the North Vietnamese might have hoped that the allies would mistakenly presume that the two incidents were related. In any event, that attack on Con Thien and the transmission of Giap's article created a pattern that would be repeated until Tet: lapses in passive deception accompanied by bursts of active deception.

[38]*Command History 1967*, 1:361–362; Stanton, *Rise and Fall*, p. 187; Karnow, *Vietnam*, p. 538; McGarvey, *Visions of Victory*, p. 48; Moyers S. Shore, *The Battle for Khe Sanh* (Washington, D.C., 1969), p. 21; and Lung, *General Offensives*, p. 8.

[39]Douglas Pike, Interview I, interviewed by Ted Gittinger, 4 June 1981, Oral History Collection, LBJ Library, p. 39. For the dates when Giap's article was transmitted by Radio Hanoi, see McGarvey, *Visions of Victory*, p. 199.

Active and Passive Deception Combined

In October, the communists started to develop tactical plans for the Tet attacks. Sometime during the month, senior VC commanders completed an outline of the plan for the attack on Saigon, briefed cadres at the regimental and company levels about the general objectives of the offensive, and began to train a VC unit to operate ARVN armored vehicles. By the third week of October, plans for the November attacks on Dak To—captured documents described the operation as a feint—were also completed.[40]

At this time the communists also took action to create the centerpiece of their passive deception campaign. On 19 October, the VC announced that they would observe a seven-day Tet truce, from 27 January to 3 February 1968 the longest cease-fire ever proposed by the communists. Because the holiday was so honored by all Vietnamese, it was fairly safe for the communists to assume that, unless they were unduly alarmed, ARVN units would be in a reduced state of readiness during the new year celebrations. A Tet truce was traditionally honored by belligerents, so many ARVN soldiers were likely to go on holiday leave during this time. Additionally, by 1968 the communists had established a pattern of non-aggressive activity during cease-fires, taking advantage of the reduction in U.S. bombing that often accompanied truces to surge supplies to their forces in the south. It is possible that the communists recognized that they had established this pattern of activity and supposed that the allies might expect them to resupply during this truce rather than launch a major offensive.[41]

A lapse in the communists' passive deception strategy also occurred between 20 and 22 October, when the Central Committee of the NLF issued an appeal for support for the upcoming winter-spring offensive. Once again, however, a burst of active deception quickly followed this attempt to publicize the gravity of the campaign. On 29 October, the communists renewed their effort to fix U.S. forces in their typical operating areas by attacking the district capital of Loc Ninh, located 115 kilometers north of Saigon near the Cambodian border. After overrunning Loc Ninh, the 273d VC Regiment attempted to hold it, absorbing hundreds of casualties when the allies

[40]Oberdorfer, *Tet*, p. 59; Lung, *General Offensives*, p. 33; and Westmoreland, *Soldier*, p. 239.
    [41]Lung, *General Offensives*, pp. 11, 148; Sharp and Westmoreland, *Report*, p. 157; Oberdorfer, *Tet*, pp. 70–71; and Schandler, *Unmaking of a President*, p. 66. For a discussion of North Vietnamese activity during the 1966 Christmas and New Year's truce and the 1967 Tet truce, see *Command History 1966*, pp. 30–31; and CINCPAC to JCS, 092007Z, Feb. 67, in *Command History 1967*, 1:494.

[72]

recaptured the city with the aid of massive air and artillery bombardment.[42]

During November, the communists continued to firm up their tactical plans. Sapper units, in particular the unit designated for the attack
on the Saigon radio station, began to train in earnest. Numerous documents were produced to inform lower-level cadres of their roles in
the Tet attacks. On 1 November, for example, the Provincial Standing
Committee of the PRP issued a directive describing the preparations
subordinate district committees were required to carry out in anticipa-
tion of the order to launch the Tet attacks. This document informed
party cadres that the "purpose of the revolutionary activities conducted for many years is mainly to support this phase, in this decisive
hour." It also told of the campaign's general strategy and objectives:

> The time is now more favorable [for an offensive] than ever before. This
> is to notify you that an offensive and uprising will take place in the very
> near future and we will mount stronger attacks on towns and cities, in
> coordination with the widespread [uprising] movement in the rural
> areas. The enemy will be thrown into utmost confusion. No matter how
> violently the enemy may react, he cannot avoid collapse. This is not only
> a golden opportunity to liberate hamlets and villages but also an oppor-
> tunity to liberate district seats, province capitals and South Viet-Nam as a
> whole.

Moreover, the PRP ordered cadres to help southerners, "friendly
agencies," and "all comrades [to] understand the situation and urge
them to score the most glorious achievements in this epoch-making
stage."[43]

Another directive, issued by a communist headquarters near My
Tho at about the same time as the 1 November PRP document, provided "guidelines for indoctrination of troops in the liberation of
towns and cities." This document instructed cadres and VC forces
about the importance of seizing their objectives within urban areas
and the difficulties they would encounter in the attacks:

> When there is an opportunity for the masses to rise up, we should pur-
> sue and attack the enemy fiercely. This is due to the fact that the enemy

---

[42]"Background Remarks," in "Rice Tassels and Potato Rows: Viet Cong Goals For
Production," *VDRN* doc. 17; Lung, *General Offensives*, pp. 9, 27; Karnow, *Vietnam*, p.
538; McGarvey, *Visions of Victory*, p. 48; Oberdorfer, *Tet*, p. 107; *Command History 1967*,
1:393–394; and Sobel, ed., *South Vietnam*, pp. 369–370.

[43]"'The Decisive Hour': Two Directives For Tet," *VDRN* doc. 28–29, pp. 3–4; and
Karnow, *Vietnam*, p. 527.

still has his armed force to resist against the masses. If we do not use our military force to neutralize the enemy force, the masses will not be able to gain victory through political activity alone. There will be little chance for success and much risk of being exposed to casualties. Therefore, cadre and troops should display high revolutionary spirit by fighting till the bitter end and keeping the enemy from reorganizing his forces to counterattack us.

This document also provides an important insight into the communists' perception of the urban population's mood and the likelihood that southerners would take advantage of the Tet attacks to stage a general uprising:

> Except for a number of reactionary personnel working for the enemy, malefactors, hoodlums, property owners and landlords whose interests are greatly influenced by the presence of the Americans and puppet government, the majority of the people have sympathy for and confidence in the Revolution. They are ready to stand up to liberate themselves, but this is still impossible since they are living in enemy controlled areas and are being misled by the psywar and propaganda machinery.[44]

Planning and dissemination of information about offensive orders continued during the second half of November. On 19 November, elements of the U.S. 101st Airborne Division captured a document that outlined the Tet attacks. In part, the document stated that "the time has come for a direct revolution and that the opportunity for a general offensive and general uprising is within reach." Ironically, this document, which has been labeled as the actual Tet attack order by many students of the war, was released at a press briefing on 5 January 1968 by the Joint United States Public Affairs Office in Saigon. The key paragraph of the document stated:

> Use very strong military attacks in coordination with the uprisings of the local population to take over towns and cities. Troops should flood the lowlands. They should move toward liberating the capital city [Saigon], take power and try to rally enemy brigades and regiments to our side one by one. Propaganda should be broadly disseminated among the population in general, and leaflets should be used to reach enemy officers and enlisted personnel. The above subject should be fully understood by cadre and troops. . . . do not specify times for implementation.[45]

---

[44]*VDRN* doc. 28–29, pp. 10–11.
[45]Document quoted in Oberdorfer, *Tet*, p. 118. On the release of the document, see Westmoreland, *Soldier*, pp. 313–314; and Palmer, *Summons*, pp. 178–179.

Another document, issued on 20 November by the Current Affairs Committee of the Women's Liberation Association of Binh Dinh province, contained an activity plan for December and January that listed the tasks assigned to female cadres in the Tet attacks. They were encouraged not only to "motivate their husbands, brothers and sons to join the army in order to kill the enemy and save our country" but also to "join the village and hamlet guerrilla forces." Additionally, the directive set the recruitment goals for female VC guerrillas: "By the end of December 1967, we must have met the prescribed quota, which means that female guerrillas should account for 50% or more of the guerrilla strength in the lowlands and 12% in the mountainous areas."[46]

Throughout November, the communists also continued their campaign of active deception by launching major attacks on the allied military complex at Dak To. The attacks on Dak To, located in Kontum province near the Cambodian border 450 kilometers north of Saigon, began on 4 November and lasted until 1 December. In the course of the fighting, the 174th NVA Regiment inflicted severe losses on the U.S. 4th Infantry Division and the U.S. 173d Airborne Brigade. Yet, in maintaining the pressure against allied positions, the NVA regiment lost an estimated 1,455 men after it was subjected to 151,000 rounds of artillery fire, 2,096 tactical air sorties, and 257 B-52 strikes. On 6 November, a U.S. unit captured a list of four objectives, issued by the B-3 (highlands) front command, which had been set for enemy units in the region around Dak To.[47] The list of objectives helps to explain the purpose behind the sacrifices made by the NVA in the battle of Dak To:

To annihilate a major U.S. element in order to force the enemy to deploy as many additional troops to the Western Highlands as possible and to destroy or disintegrate a large part of the Puppet Army.

To encourage units to improve, in combat, the technique of concentrated attacks in order to annihilate relatively large enemy units.

To destroy much of the enemy force, to liberate an important area and strengthen the base area, thus providing support for the political struggle movement.

[46]"Women in the Winter-Spring Campaign," *VDRN* doc. 24, p. 6.
[47]Stanton, *Rise and Fall*, pp. 171–178; Karnow, *Vietnam*, p. 538; Oberdorfer, *Tet*, p. 107; Lung, *General Offensives*, p. 9; *Command History 1967*, 1:378; and Sobel, ed., *South Vietnam*, pp. 370–371.

To effect close coordination with various battle areas throughout South Vietnam in order to achieve timely unity and stratagems.[48]

Dak To was attacked not only to fix U.S. forces in positions away from populated areas but also to allow NVA officers to perfect the tactics they would use in the Tet attacks.

The Climax of Deception, Khe Sanh

During December, planning and preparation for the Tet attacks took precedence over the military effort to draw U.S. attention away from the coastal areas. General Tran Van Tra left COSVN and moved to a forward headquarters near Saigon to supervise preparations and bolster troop morale. Urban terrorism also increased during December, a sign that highly motivated VC guerrillas had moved into position in southern cities.[49] On 1 December, the Military and Proselytizing Section of a district in Quang Ngai province issued the objectives of the propaganda program for its proselytizing units in the Tet attacks:

> Develop the insurrection within puppet forces. Accomplish at any price our mission of promoting military revolts in echelons ranging from platoon to company and of developing uprisings of puppet troops in district and key areas, with separated puppet officers aiding with our people and taking part in our people's fighting. Create and promote the anti-war movement to a degree that could cause obstructions to the enemy in the implementation of his great operation plans. Develop internal disagreements among the enemy, and strongly develop pacifist and neutralist tendencies so as to neutralize the enemy's fighting and limit to a maximum extent the enemy's effectiveness.[50]

Another document, issued by the Binh Dinh province PRP committee in early December, explained the origins and significance of the Tet attacks to the low-level cadres under its command: "In July 1967 a Resolution for a General Offensive and Uprising was adopted at the Political Bureau Congress. It was adopted after lengthy assessment of

[48]Document quoted in Oberdorfer, *Tet*, pp. 107–108. For a discussion of the document, see Betts, "Strategic Surprise for War Termination," p. 162; and Lung, *General Offensives*, p. 34.

[49]Oberdorfer, *Tet*, p. 59; Palmer, *Summons*, p. 178; and Michael Maclear, *The Ten Thousand Day War* (Toronto, 1981), p. 188. For a discussion of the techniques used by the VC to infiltrate Saigon, see Sharp and Westmoreland, *Report*, p. 158.

[50]"Sharpening the Third Prong: An Increase of Viet Cong Proselyting," VDRN doc. 18, p. 6.

the current political and military situation and with the realization that we possessed the capability for successes. . . . The General Offensive will occur only once every 1,000 years. . . . It will decide the fate of the country. . . . It will end the war. . . . It constitutes the wishes of both the Party and the people."[51]

During the second half of December, preparations for the Tet attacks gained increasing momentum. By 21 December, elements of the 325C NVA Division and the 304th NVA Division were beginning to concentrate around the U.S. Marine firebase at Khe Sanh. Located near the DMZ and the Laotian border, Khe Sanh was astride the "Santa Fe Trail," an extension of the Ho Chi Minh Trail used by NVA units in their trip to southern battlefields. At about the same time, Ho Chi Minh made his first public appearance in four months to lend his prestige to the developing campaign. Moreover, on 25 December, the commander of the VC 9th Division used the 24-hour Christmas truce to conduct a personal reconnaissance of Saigon.[52]

Even though the communists concentrated on preparing for the offensive during December, they also launched the main *dich van* (action among the enemy) initiative in their active deception strategy. On 29 December, the North Vietnamese undertook an ambitious diplomatic initiative. In a speech given at a diplomatic reception at the Mongolian embassy in Hanoi, North Vietnamese foreign minister Nguyen Duy Trinh modified the "Trinh formula" proposed on 28 January 1967, which concerned the initiation of negotiations with the United States. In the speech, transmitted by Radio Hanoi on 1 January 1968, Trinh stated that North Vietnam would (as opposed to "could") open negotiations with the United States after it stopped bombing the north. In reaction to this overture, the United States suspended bombing within five miles of the center of Hanoi on 3 January and extended the geographic scope of the suspension when a Romanian envoy carried the U.S. response to Hanoi in mid-January.[53]

During January, events unfolded rapidly. On 1 January, in addition to transmitting the new North Vietnamese position on the opening of negotiations, Radio Hanoi transmitted a poem written by Ho Chi Minh to dramatize the importance of the Tet attacks:

---

[51]Document quoted in Oberdorfer, *Tet*, p. 54.

[52]Shore, *Battle for Khe Sanh*, pp. 26–27, 29; Karnow, *Vietnam*, p. 539; McGarvey, *Visions of Victory*, p. 48; Sharp and Westmoreland, *Report*, p. 157; Palmer, *Summons*, pp. 167–168; Oberdorfer, *Tet*, pp. 59, 66; and Lung, *General Offensives*, p. 27.

[53]Thies, *When Governments Collide*, p. 198; McGarvey, *Visions of Victory*, p. 55; Karnow, *Vietnam*, p. 538; Oberdorfer, *Tet*, p. 68; Westmoreland, *Soldier*, p. 312; Betts, "Strategic Surprise for War Termination," p. 165; and Lung, *General Offensives*, p. 27.

[77]

> This spring far outshines previous springs.
> Of triumphs throughout the land come happy tidings.
> Forward! Total victory shall be ours![54]

During the night of 2 January, five NVA officers, including a regimental commander, an operations officer, and a communications officer, were killed as they conducted a foot reconnaissance of the Khe Sanh perimeter. The next day, in a clandestine broadcast from South Vietnam, Liberation Radio transmitted an appeal for an increase in agricultural production and food conservation in the south in order to "be ready to supply the battlefield." On 5 January, the U.S. 4th Infantry Division captured a document labeled "Urgent Combat Order Number One" which provided the details for the Tet attacks in Pleiku province. This document called for the attacks to begin "before the Tet holidays." On 15 January, the 4th Infantry Division also detected the movement of elements of the 174th NVA Regiment inside the Cambodian border. Artillery and air strikes, which were called in from the fifteenth to the start of the Tet attacks, prevented these units from crossing the South Vietnamese border in strength.[55]

Meanwhile, the siege of Khe Sanh began with a vengeance. The 325C and 304th NVA Divisions, which included six infantry and two artillery regiments, an unknown number of tanks, plus miscellaneous support and service units, had been consolidating around Khe Sanh. Additionally, two more NVA divisions, which served as a reserve, moved toward the firebase. By mid-January, NVA units had switched from reconnaissance operations and had begun to launch harassing raids along the Khe Sanh perimeter. At 1400 on 20 January, however, the defenders of Khe Sanh enjoyed a stroke of luck when NVA Lt. La Thanh Tonc surrendered to the marines. Lt. Tonc provided the marines with the NVA plan of attack on Khe Sanh, which was to begin that evening. The information was accurate: the first wave of attacks began on the night of 20 January and were followed by a major artillery bombardment the next night.[56]

Even after the siege of Khe Sanh had begun, the communists did

[54]Ho Chi Minh's poem is quoted in Karnow, *Vietnam*, p. 535; and Lung, *General Offensives*, p. 29.

[55]"Rice Tassels and Potato Rows: Viet Cong Goals for Production," *VDRN* doc. 17, p. 6; Shore, *Battle for Khe Sanh*, p. 29; Willard Pearson, *The War in the Northern Provinces* (Washington, D.C., 1975), p. 30; Westmoreland, *Soldier*, p. 317; Lung; *General Offensives*, p. 35; and Sharp and Westmoreland, *Report*, p. 160.

[56]Shore, *Battle for Khe Sanh*, pp. 33–39; Westmoreland, *Soldier*, p. 317; Karnow, *Vietnam*, p. 542; Maclear, *Ten Thousand Day War*, pp. 190–192; and Pearson, *War in the Northern Provinces*, pp. 29–31.

not abandon their efforts at passive deception. On 27 January, a spokesman for the NLF publicly appealed for the observance of the Tet truce and even hinted that the truce might be extended by the communists. This public initiative was soon followed, however, by the cancellation of leaves in all VC and NVA units. Moreover, by 28 January the final orders had been issued to all forces participating in the Tet attacks, and communist units were moving in force into the cities of the south.[57]

By late January the VC had taken up positions within the cities. On 28 January South Vietnamese security forces raided a meeting of eleven VC cadres in the suburbs of the coastal city of Qui Nhon. The cadres held two tape-recorded messages that called on the local population to take up arms and overthrow the government and also contained an announcement that "the forces struggling for peace and unification" had occupied Saigon, Hue, and Da Nang. That same night, in Cholon, the Chinese suburb of Saigon, about fourteen young recruits were met by three VC and provided with red arm bands and baskets of propaganda leaflets to be distributed throughout Cholon. A propaganda leaflet similar to those distributed in Cholon emphasized that the time had come for the general uprising:

THE TIME FOR ACTION HAS COME!

Courageously Surge Forward to Destroy the Americans and Puppets!
The bugle call of the Fatherland ordering the assault has
sounded over the mountains and rivers. Let the entire
army and people surge forward simultaneously to
destroy the enemy and liberate the country!
This is the time-opportunity to win total
victory. Be determined to smash the
entire puppet army and destroy
the entire puppet regime.
Hesitation is a sin against the Fatherland,
indecision is suicide.[58]

On 30 January, ARVN troops guarding the main gate of III Corps Tactical Zone headquarters in Bien Hoa killed a VC guerrilla who was lurking about the perimeter of the installation, and a group of VC sappers disguised as tourists were arrested as they attempted to rent a hotel room in Can Tho on the Mekong delta. Thus, the VC seem to

[57]Palmer, *Summons*, p. 184; Oberdorfer, *Tet*, p. 74; and Lung, *General Offensives*, p. 30.
[58]"'Time-Opportunity': The Uprising Appeal of Viet Cong Leaflets," VDRN doc. 22, p. 14.

have finished their preparations in the cities just hours before the start of the Tet attacks.[59]

Two other important actions were taken just before the Tet attacks. On 29 January, the people of North Vietnam celebrated the Tet holiday one day early. The reason provided by the government for moving the holiday forward one day was that the earth and sun were in an unusual and favorable conjunction a half hour before the beginning of the actual new year, making an earlier celebration more auspicious. And on the evening of 30 January, Radio Hanoi rebroadcast Ho Chi Minh's 1 January holiday poem. Enemy prisoners and defectors later revealed that the final line of the message, "Forward! Total victory shall be ours!" was actually a code that signaled that the time to launch the Tet attacks was at hand.[60]

During the night of 30 January, however, the North Vietnamese plan went awry. Five provincial capitals in the central highlands, Nha Trang, Ban Me Thout, Kontum, Pleiku, and Qui Nhon, and Da Nang in the north were attacked prematurely. At 2100 30 January a regional force unit captured a VC guerrilla on the Saigon defense perimeter. The prisoner quickly revealed that the Tet attacks would begin at 0300 31 January, and the information was accurate. The main wave of Tet attacks started on schedule.[61]

Appraising the Strategy of Deception

The deceptive strategy adopted by the communists had to overcome the dilemma inherent in the effort to gain the element of surprise for the general offensive–general uprising: publicity, not secrecy, was needed to instigate the urban revolt. The communists had

[59]Westmoreland, Soldier, p. 320; Lung, General Offensives, pp. 35, 37; and introductory remarks to VDRN doc. 22.

[60]Oberdorfer, Tet, pp. 67, 73; Palmer, Summons, p. 185; Westmoreland, Soldier, p. 312; and Lung, General Offensives, p. 29. By transmitting a coded attack message in the clear, the North Vietnamese followed a long tradition. The most famous example of this type of communication is the "East Wind Rain" message, the winds-code execute transmitted by the Japanese to ensure that their forces received the order to carry out the attack on Pearl Harbor. Another famous example was transmitted to the French resistance by the BBC on the eve of the Allied invasion of Normandy: "The long sobs of the violins of autumn wound my heart with a monotonous languor." In contrast to the allies in Vietnam, both the Americans before the attack on Pearl Harbor and the Germans before the Normandy invasion knew the meaning of the coded message. For a discussion of the "East Wind Rain" message, see Wohlstetter, Pearl Harbor, pp. 214–219; Samuel Eliot Morison, The Two-Ocean War (Boston, 1963), pp. 74–75; and Gordon W. Prange, At Dawn We Slept (New York, 1981), pp. 458–459. For a discussion of the coded message preceding the Normandy invasion, see David Kahn, Hitler's Spies (New York, 1978), pp. 504–505.

[61]Lung, General Offensives, p. 37.

to inform thousands of cadres and tens of thousands of city dwellers about the impending offensive while preserving secrecy. This dilemma is, however, only an extreme form of the problem inherent in any deception campaign. Regardless of the quality or sophistication of the deception, wise deception planners should assume that accurate indications of the main attack will reach the intended victim. The problem faced by the attacker is to make the main offensive appear less threatening than the diversionary attack, thereby misleading the victim about the real intentions and capabilities of the nation contemplating an offensive.

The communist strategy reflected the notion of interdependence between actions taken to inflate diversionary threats and those taken to minimize the apparent dangers posed by the main offensive. The border battles and the siege of Khe Sanh (active deception) seemed all the more threatening because of the secrecy (passive deception) used to reduce the apparent threat posed by the impending urban offensive. In the absence of passive deception to mask preparations for the urban attacks, allied intelligence organizations might have obtained information that indicated the development of two relatively equal threats, thereby decreasing the diversionary power of the active deception campaign. The passive deception undertaken by the communists could not prevent indications of the impending urban attacks from reaching allied intelligence organizations, but it did make the danger posed by NVA units along the borders and at Khe Sanh appear more threatening.

Conversely, when efforts to maintain secrecy had to be abandoned in order to inform cadres about the general uprising, active deception increased in intensity by maximizing the threat posed against the border areas. Major suspensions of the effort to maintain the secrecy about the urban attacks were matched by surges in offensive military activity. Bursts of active deception thus accompanied lapses in passive deception, reducing the apparent significance of information disseminated in preparation for the urban offensive.

The deceptive military attacks helped the communists overcome the dilemma of securing the element of surprise for the urban offensive, but they were extremely blunt and costly. As U.S. commanders pointed out at the time, the siege of Khe Sanh consumed more North Vietnamese than allied resources. Still, by paying an extremely heavy price, the communists were able to generate enough noise to overwhelm the signals leaked by the preparations for the impending urban offensive. The noise created by the border battles (Con Thien, Loc Ninh, and Dak To) and the siege of Khe Sanh was both quantitatively and qualitatively different from the signals generated by the

[81]

preparations for the urban offensive. Almost by definition, the eruption of a major military engagement appears more threatening than preparations for an offensive that may never materialize. Moreover, noise engendered by the "conventional" nature of the active deception campaign seemed far more threatening than the signals created by the "unconventional" portion of the Tet attacks, the effort to instigate a general uprising. For example, a clear description of the general offensive–general uprising received by allied intelligence on 27 January 1968 appears far less dangerous, in a conventional military sense, than the threat posed by the thousands of NVA soldiers surrounding Khe Sanh: "VC plan to attempt to launch political campaign in the city [Saigon] tonight by concentrating armed propagandists, dropping leaflets, displaying flags, setting up slogans, beating drums, and radio broadcasting. They are preparing to move into city an amount of weapons such as submachine guns and grenades to support mission they have. Further, they have instructions to annihilate Military Police."[62] From the U.S. perspective, the effort to prevent the VC from "beating drums" in downtown Saigon was a problem best handled by military police and not by the 82d Airborne.

In a fine example of the irony of deception, an error committed by the communists increased the effectiveness of their passive deception. The South Vietnamese did not overwhelmingly support the VC cause, so the effort to instigate a general uprising would end in failure. The source of this error can be linked to a breakdown in communication between junior cadre members and senior officials. In the aftermath of the offensive, captured junior officers admitted that they never expected the urban population in their area of operation to revolt. They claimed that they carried out their mission in the hope that their own assault would help start a general uprising in other areas. Senior communist officials apparently either ignored or never requested or received accurate estimates of the likelihood of a general uprising from their local commanders. Moreover, there is a distinct possibility that junior officers, in an effort to comply with directives from their superiors, simply overestimated VC strength in South Vietnam. One senior NVA officer, for instance, defected after discovering that the VC units he was supposed to command during the offensive existed only on paper. Senior communist officials would have readily accepted reports of widespread support for the communist cause and exaggerated estimates of VC strength because they tended to inter-

<hr>

[62]Item 56 2242, 24 January, Daily Journal Files, MACV J-2 Command Center, record group 334, accession number 70A0738, box number 2 of 11, National Records Center, Suitland, Maryland.

pret indications of anti-Americanism as evidence of approval of the VC.[63] This communist mistake added an element of unintended deception to the passive deception campaign. U.S. intelligence analysts and officers, who had a better understanding of the political sympathies of the South Vietnamese urban population than did senior communist officials, possessed dozens of captured documents that called for a general offensive–general uprising. They failed to realize, however, that the communist leadership had miscalculated. Because they possessed superior information about the status of their alliance, U.S. analysts believed that the call to instigate a general uprising was unrealistic and intended to inflate the apparent threat posed by a VC attack against urban areas. In other words, they usually treated captured documents that called for urban attacks and a revolt against the South Vietnamese government as part of an active deception campaign intended to draw U.S. attention and resources away from the developing threat along the border, especially at Khe Sanh.[64]

The Tet offensive was the first major communist initiative in response to U.S. intervention in the ground war. The decision to launch the offensive marked the end of the divisive debate over strategy and tactics that had hampered the communist prosecution of the war. During the 1967 winter-spring campaign, the communists abandoned the strategy of the 1964, 1965, and 1966 dry-season offensives. Instead, they planned to instigate a general uprising in their quest to end the war quickly. The communists believed that the United States would not devote the effort needed to overcome the setbacks created by the general offensive–general uprising and would seek a negotiated end to the war on communist terms.

Even though it is easy to overestimate the coherence of a deceptive strategy, it is safe to conclude that the communists implemented a mix of passive and active deceptive measures during the first stage of the Tet offensive. In adopting this deceptive strategy, however, they violated a fundamental principle of deception by allocating more resources to their diversionary initiatives than to the main offensive. They committed this error because they overestimated their political

---

[63]"2/6/68 Rostow Memo to LBJ" and "2/7/68 Rostow Memo to LBJ, with text of Cable Bunker to President," in *Vietnam: A Documentary Collection—Westmoreland v. CBS* (New York, 1985) exhibits 427, pp. 2–4; 696. Daniel O. Graham, Interview II, interviewed by Ted Gittinger, 8 November 1982, p. 16, and Douglas Pike, Interview I, interviewed by Ted Gittinger, 4 June 1981, p. 36, Oral History Collection, LBJ Library.

[64]For a discussion of the way U.S. officers and analysts interpreted the call to launch a general uprising, see House Select Committee on Intelligence, *U.S. Intelligence Agencies and Activities*, pp. 1996–1997.

and probably even their numerical strength in South Vietnam. Ultimately, this communist miscalculation aided the deception; it made calls to launch a general offensive–general uprising appear extremely unrealistic to allied intelligence analysts. For the allies to predict the Tet offensive, they would have to overcome probably the toughest problem that can confront intelligence analysts; they would have to recognize that the plan for the Tet offensive rested on a communist mistake.

During the first phase of the offensive, the communists were largely successful in implementing their deceptive strategy and in laying the groundwork for the Tet attacks. In comparison to the other two phases, the first was the most successful. Its overall success was marred only by failure in the final hours before the offensive, the effort to preserve the secrecy of the operation apparently interfered with the objective of achieving coordination. Some communist units jumped the gun and launched attacks about 24 hours before the offensive erupted throughout all of South Vietnam. Would the allies be able to respond in the time remaining?

PART II

THE ORIGINS OF SURPRISE

[3]

The Sources of
American Biases

To understand the American reaction to the communist deception that unfolded during the fall of 1967, it is necessary to describe the U.S. command's beliefs about the situation they faced. As the chapters in Part II show, these beliefs dominated American estimates of their opponent's intentions on the eve of the Tet offensive; information that contradicted these beliefs was largely ignored. The importance of American beliefs about "external" matters—about communist standard procedures and strategy—is readily apparent. But beliefs about "internal" matters—about allied strategy, the strength of the alliance, and future allied initiatives—also proved to be highly relevant. American beliefs about weaknesses in the alliance, as well as the general assessment of the ability of the allied command arrangements to respond to unexpected events, were of obvious importance because the communists intended to target ARVN and southern cities. Beliefs about communist behavior during truces were relevant because the offensive erupted during the Tet holiday, a time when a reduction in allied preparedness was usual. Beliefs about allied military fortunes and the likely communist assessment of their predicament were important because they governed expectations about the potential scope, purposes, and targets of a communist attack.

Some of the most significant American beliefs were drawn from information that only the allies possessed. U.S. estimates of the developing situation were influenced by knowledge of impending allied initiatives, plans that were supposedly secret, and by accurate information about the loyalties of the urban population, information that was misinterpreted by the architects of the Tet offensive. The Americans also employed particular facets of analogies drawn from the Battle of the Bulge, the siege at Dien Bien Phu, and the Chinese intervention in the Korean War, to guide their response to events.

THE COMMAND STRUCTURE

Although he was responsible for U.S. military operations inside South Vietnam and in the "extended battle zone," an area reaching just to the north of the DMZ, Gen. William Westmoreland, commander of MACV, did not control all U.S. units operating in North and South Vietnam. Westmoreland, who often reported directly to the Joint Chiefs of Staff, shared this responsibility with his immediate superior, Adm. U. S. Grant Sharp, commander in chief, Pacific (CINCPAC). As commander of a unified command, Sharp's area of responsibility stretched across the entire Pacific theater. From his headquarters in Hawaii, Sharp exercised control over both Seventh Fleet operations off the Vietnamese coast and Strategic Air Command (SAC) missions flown from Thailand and Guam. Thus he controlled three important aspects of the war effort: the air campaign against North Vietnam, air strikes and naval bombardment provided by elements of SAC and the Seventh Fleet against targets within South Vietnam, and reconnaissance missions flown over Vietnam by SAC aircraft. This command arrangement sometimes subjected forces to competing demands. SAC reconnaissance aircraft, for example, had to fulfill SAC missions before they could respond to MACV requests for intelligence sorties.[1]

[1]On U.S. command arrangements during the Vietnam War, see Summers, *On Strategy*, pp. 42–51; Douglas Kinnard, *The War Managers* (Hanover, N.H., 1977), pp. 29–32; Robert W. Komer, *Bureaucracy at War* (Boulder, Colo., 1986), pp. 13, 89; Sharp, *Strategy for Defeat*, especially pp. 269–271; Palmer, *25-Year War*, pp. 27–28; Robert L. Gallucci, *Neither Peace nor Honor* (Baltimore, 1975), pp. 87–105; Gelb, *Irony of Vietnam*, pp. 135–139; *Command History 1968*, 1:371–373; *Command History 1967*, 1:121–124; Staudenmaier, "Vietnam, Mao and Clausewitz," p. 88; Krepinevich, *Army*, p. 165; Sharp and Westmoreland, *Report*, pp. 101–103; Henry Brandon, *Anatomy of Error* (Boston, 1969), p. 29; Edward N. Luttwak, *The Pentagon and the Art of War* (New York, 1984), p. 41; Van Creveld, *Command in War*, pp. 241–242; Alain C. Enthoven and K. Wayne Smith, *How Much Is Enough?* (New York, 1971), p. 270; Schandler, *Unmaking of a President*, p. 41; Westmoreland, *Soldier*, pp. 75–76; Marvin Kalb and Ellie Abel, *Roots of Involvement: The U.S. in Asia, 1784–1971* (New York, 1971), pp. 209–213; Joseph A. McChristian, *The Role of Military Intelligence 1965–67* (Washington, D.C., 1974), pp. 97–98; and Julian J. Ewell and Ira A. Hunt, Jr., *Sharpening the Combat Edge: The Use of Analysis to Reinforce Military Judgment* (Washington, D.C., 1974), p. 5. In recent literature on command in war, the concept of command and control is referred to in a variety of ways, even though some authors admit that it is difficult to develop definitions for these terms: command, control, and communications (C^3); command, control, communications, and computers (C^4); command, control, communications, and intelligence (C^3I); and command, con-

Even within South Vietnam, Westmoreland did not reign supreme. He did not control operations conducted by several organizations, such as the Central Intelligence Agency (CIA), which played a direct part in the war. Moreover, the U.S. ambassador, not Westmoreland, was the ranking representative to the government of South Vietnam. The ambassador was also the senior member of the U.S. Mission Council—the top U.S. policy-coordinating body in the country—and was therefore nominally in charge of overall policy. As the ambassador's senior military adviser, Westmoreland was charged with coordinating military operations with U.S. political and economic policies. In theory, the Mission Council was supposed to oversee the allied prosecution of the war. In reality, it lacked the resources and organizational structure needed to unify the allied war effort.[2]

As commander of MACV, Westmoreland presided over a subunified command that served as the U.S. military headquarters in South Vietnam. At the heart of MACV was a large staff, including intelligence officers who provided Westmoreland with estimates of enemy intentions and capabilities and three "component" commanders, officers who commanded the units from their service engaged in South Vietnam: commanding general of the U.S. Army Vietnam (USARV); commander of U.S. Naval Forces, Vietnam; and commander of the Seventh Air Force.[3]

---

trol, communications, intelligence, and interoperability (C^3I^2). Van Creveld and Paul Bracken have abandoned these detailed terms on the grounds that they are redundant; see Van Creveld, *Command in War*, p. 1; and Paul Bracken, *The Command and Control of Nuclear Forces* (New Haven, Conn., 1983), p. 3. The Department of Defense defines command and control as "The exercise of authority and direction by a properly designated commander over assigned forces in the accomplishment of the mission. Command and control functions are performed through an arrangement of personnel, equipment, communications, facilities, and procedures which are employed by a commander in planning, directing, coordinating, and controlling forces and operations in the accomplishment of the mission"; see *Department of Defense Dictionary of Military and Associated Terms*, quoted in George E. Orr, *Combat Operations C³I: Fundamentals and Interactions* (Maxwell Air Force Base, Ala., 1983), p. 23.

[2]George S. Eckhardt, *Command and Control* (Washington, D.C., 1974), p. 48; Palmer, *25-Year War*, p. 30; Westmoreland, *Soldier*, pp. 75–76; McChristian, *Military Intelligence*, p. 106; Van Creveld, *Command in War*, p. 243; *Handbook for Military Support of Pacification* (Saigon, 1968), pp. 26–27; *Command History 1968*, 1:222–223; Komer, *Bureaucracy*, pp. 89–92; and *Command History 1967*, 3:1160–1162. The Mission Council was in part constituted by the commander of MACV, the CIA station chief in Saigon, and senior representatives from the United States Agency for International Development, the Office of the Special Assistant to the Ambassador, and the Joint United States Public Affairs Office. For sources that state that the CIA station chief was a member of the Mission Council, see "Transcript of Mike Wallace Interview with Walt Rostow 7/29/81," *Westmoreland v. CBS*, exhibit 14, p. 16; and Peer de Silva, *Sub Rosa* (New York, 1978), p. 221.

[3]Westmoreland, *Report*, p. 102; and *Command History 1967*, 1:124–127. At the time of the Tet offensive, Rear Adm. Kenneth L. Veth was serving as naval component com-

Westmoreland decided to serve as his own army component commander, for two reasons. For one, he stated that he could facilitate cooperation and coordination with his South Vietnamese counterpart, Gen. Cao Van Vien, the chairman of the Joint General Staff (JGS), by taking direct command of U.S. Army combat units. Westmoreland wanted MACV to mirror the command structure of the JGS, whereby General Vien, the overall commander of the Republic of Vietnam Armed Forces (RVNAF), served as his own ARVN component commander. Second, Westmoreland wanted to create a single field command, under the direction of an army general, to control U.S. ground operations throughout South Vietnam, but Admiral Sharp and members of the U.S. Marine Corps objected to this arrangement. Since Westmoreland, as commander of MACV, already possessed operational control over marine units, he decided to serve as army component commander, thereby providing a degree of unity to the U.S. military effort. Yet by serving as the army component commander, the position that would have the greatest impact on U.S. military operations within South Vietnam, Westmoreland reduced the amount of time he could devote to coordinating the allied military effort.[4]

The next rung in the chain of command for the conduct of U.S. military operations paralleled the South Vietnamese command structure before the buildup of U.S. forces. Organized into into five geographic areas, the South Vietnamese command structure was divided into four corps tactical zones (CTZs) and the Capital Military Region (CMR). Differences in the type of U.S. forces assigned to each of the four CTZs and their different missions produced variations in U.S. command arrangements. In I CTZ, which consisted of the five provinces just below the DMZ, U.S. forces were under the command of III Marine Amphibious Force (III MAF) headquarters located with I Corps headquarters at Da Nang. Because most of the U.S. forces in I Corps were marines, III MAF was under the command of Lt. Gen. Robert E. Cushman, USMC. In the weeks preceding the Tet offensive, however, Westmoreland moved several U.S. Army units into I CTZ, placing them under the control of a MACV forward command post on 25 January 1968. Commanded by Gen. Creighton W. Abrams, who arrived at the new headquarters near Hue on 13 February 1968, this command was responsible for U.S. Army combat operations in I

---

mander and Gen. William W. Momyer was serving as air force component commander; see Eckhardt, *Command and Control*, p. 91.

[4]Eckhardt, *Command and Control*, pp. 50–51; Palmer, *25-Year War*, pp. 33, 49; and Kinnard, *War Managers*, p. 58.

CTZ and, if necessary, for all U.S. forces in I CTZ. Abrams did not assume command of U.S. Marine units in I CTZ but instead chose the diplomatic approach and coordinated his activities with the commander of III MAF.[5]

In II and III CTZ, U.S. Army corps headquarters, designated Field Force, Vietnam (FFV), were established to command U.S. combat operations in these zones. In II CTZ, which comprised the twelve provinces of the central highlands, I FFV headquarters was located at Nha Trang in Khanh Hoa province, some distance from the II Corps headquarters at Pleiku. In III CTZ, consisting of the ten provinces surrounding Saigon and the CMR (Saigon and the district of Gia Dinh), II FFV served as headquarters and was located with III CTZ headquarters at Bien Hoa.[6]

The U.S. combat role in IV CTZ, which encompassed the sixteen provinces of the Mekong delta, was relatively limited. Thus, the adviser to the commander of IV Corps, Maj. Gen. George S. Eckhardt, who assumed command on 14 January 1968, was the senior U.S. officer in this region at the time of the Tet offensive. Eckhardt was not responsible, however, for the command of the U.S. Mobile Riverine Force, which consisted of elements drawn from the U.S. Navy's River Patrol Force (task force CTF 116) and the U.S. 9th Infantry Division. Instead, II FFV controlled army units conducting riverine operations through a designated subordinate headquarters, such as the 9th Infantry Division. Naval forces participating in riverine operations were controlled by the commander of U.S. naval forces at MACV. In effect,

---

[5]South Vietnamese CTZs were divided into division tactical areas, the area of tactical responsibility assigned to an ARVN infantry division. These areas often encompassed several provinces (or sectors), and in most cases the province chief, usually a field-grade ARVN officer, also served as the military sector commander. CTZ commanders, who held the rank of lieutenant general, were also military region governors and responsible for civil administration; thus, in political matters they reported directly to the president of South Vietnam, and in military matters they reported directly to the JGS. For a discussion of the organization of the South Vietnamese corps command structure, see Ngo Quang Truong, *RVNAF and U.S. Operational Cooperation and Coordination* (Washington, D.C., 1980), pp. 42–43; Palmer, *25-Year War*, p. 50; Westmoreland, *Soldier*, pp. 58, 345; Vien and Khuyen, *Reflections on the Vietnam War*, pp. 3–6; *Command History 1967*, 1:127–128; Eckhardt, *Command and Control*, pp. 55, 91; Shore, *Battle for Khe Sanh*, pp. 5, 132–133; *Command History 1968*, 1:217, 219; and Pearson, *War in the Northern Provinces*, pp. 66–68. Stanton gives 9 February 1968 as the day of Abrams's arrival; see *Rise and Fall*, p. 210.

[6]*Command History 1967*, 1:128; Truong, *RVNAF*, pp. 42–43, 49; Stanton, *Rise and Fall*, pp. 65–66; Palmer, *25-Year War*, p. 53; and Westmoreland, *Soldier*, p. 155. I FFV was under the command of Lt. Gen. William B. Rosson, and II FFV was under the command of Lt. Gen. Frederick Weyand at the time of the Tet offensive; see Eckhardt, *Command and Control*, pp. 53, 91.

army and navy units engaged in riverine operations were commanded separately.[7]

Coordinating Allied Operations

Various arrangements were devised to coordinate allied operations. Combat and support units provided by Australia, New Zealand, the Philippines, the Republic of China, and Thailand were controlled by the U.S. commander in the area in which they operated. The combat units supplied by the Republic of Korea, however, remained under the command of their own officers within the limits established by the Free World Military Assistance Council, composed of the commander of MACV, the commander of the Korean forces, and the chief of the JGS, who served as chairman.[8]

South Vietnamese military units were never under Westmoreland's direct command. Instead, the United States and South Vietnam instituted a command arrangement based on the concept of cooperation and coordination, described by one South Vietnamese general as "the principle of equal partnership and a harmonious division of tasks." The MACV staff, for example, included members of the JGS in its planning activities, but coordination was often undertaken on an ad hoc basis.[9] An important area of collaboration between MACV and JGS was the development of the annual combined campaign plan. The plan assigned the responsibility for offensive (search-and-destroy) operations to U.S. forces and the mission of pacification—

---

[7]Westmoreland, *Soldier*, p. 155; Eckhardt, *Command and Control*, pp. 57, 78–80, 91; and Sharp, *Strategy for Defeat*, p. 140.

[8]At the end of 1967, Free World Military Assistance Forces (FWMAF) totaled 59,450. The largest contingent, supplied by the Republic of Korea, totaled 47,829 and included 22 combat maneuver battalions; see *Command History 1968*, 1:345. For a description of the command arrangements governing these forces, see Eckhardt, *Command and Control*, pp. 46, 60; and Palmer, *25-Year War*, p. 50.

[9]Quotation from Truong, *RVNAF*, p. 19. According to Westmoreland, cooperation and coordination was practiced throughout the South Vietnamese and U.S. commands: "In the field our troops and the South Vietnamese fought side by side—from division level to the smallest unit—in close coordination and cooperation"; see Sharp and Westmoreland, *Report*, p. 104. For a South Vietnamese perspective on the quality of the relationship between U.S. and South Vietnamese advisers throughout the command hierarchy, see Stephen T. Hosmer, Konrad Kellen, and Brian M. Jenkins, *The Fall of South Vietnam* (New York, 1980), pp. 82–83. For an example of one method of implementing cooperation and coordination, the U.S. effort to assist the South Vietnamese in the area of pacification, see *Handbook for Military Support of Pacification*, pp. 34–41. The degree of cooperation and coordination between CTZ commanders and their U.S. counterparts varied. The commander of III MAF, for example, was briefed weekly by U.S. advisers to I Corps on developments affecting the South Vietnamese and met weekly with his South Vietnamese counterpart to discuss matters of mutual concern; see Pearson, *War in the Northern Provinces*, p. 105.

called "rural development" in 1967—to the South Vietnamese. Combined campaign plans did not, however, supply a plan for the overall allied prosecution of the war in the upcoming year. Instead, they were intended to help the South Vietnamese develop future strategy and to estimate the type and amount of U.S. assistance that would be required in the following year.[10]

Another important area of collaboration was the combined intelligence system, which was to utilize the Americans' advanced collection and analysis techniques and South Vietnamese experience and language skills. At the heart of this system were four combined intelligence centers staffed by South Vietnamese and Americans. The Combined Military Interrogation Center (CMIC) exploited information gleaned from interviews with prisoners of war, enemy suspects, and *Hoi Chanhs* (defectors referred to as ralliers during the war) and from interrogation reports forwarded by U.S. advisers. The Combined Document Exploitation Center (CDEC) analyzed captured enemy documents. Evaluations of captured enemy weapons, munitions, and equipment were produced by the Combined Material Exploitation Center (CMEC). Analysts at the Combined Intelligence Center, Vietnam (CICV) produced order-of-battle estimates, developed intelligence requirements, and carried out long-term analyses of enemy intentions and capabilities. CICV, under the joint direction of the MACV and JGS deputy chiefs of staff for intelligence (J-2), produced a wide variety of finished intelligence: daily intelligence summaries, monthly order-of-battle summaries, measurement of progress reports, monthly wrap-ups, periodic intelligence reports, and quarterly evaluations.[11] Although the combined intelligence system did not become fully operational until early 1967, it was capable of handling vast quantities of information well before the communist decision to launch the Tet offensive. In March 1967, for example, CDEC received 495,184 pages of captured documents and had determined that 58,667 pages were of intelligence value. During the same month, CMIC an-

[10]*Command History 1967*, 1:317–322; Westmoreland, *Soldier*, p. 252; Truong, *RVNAF*, pp. 22–23; and *Handbook for Military Support of Pacification*, pp. 5, 26.

[11]Eckhardt, *Command and Control*, p. 59; Sharp and Westmoreland, *Report*, p. 104; *Command History 1968*, 2:569–580; McChristian, *Military Intelligence*, pp. 12–64; Peter M. Dunn, "The American Army: The Vietnam War, 1965–1973," in *Armed Forces & Modern Counter-Insurgency*, ed. Ian F. W. Beckett and John Pimlott (London, 1985), p. 89; Truong, *RVNAF*, pp. 28, 30–36; and Bruce E. Jones, *War without Windows* (New York, 1987), pp. 83–84. The CIA also created its own Intelligence Coordination and Exploitation Program, which systematically exploited information on the VC, and the South Vietnamese maintained several independent intelligence-gathering organizations; see Thomas Powers, *The Man Who Kept the Secrets: Richard Helms and the CIA* (New York, 1979), p. 181; and Hoang Ngoc Lung, *Intelligence* (Washington, D.C., 1976), p. 37.

alyzed 928 interrogation reports turned in by U.S. advisers and published over 300 pieces of finished intelligence relating to prisoner interrogations.[12]

A small infrastructure existed for the coordination of U.S. and South Vietnamese military operations. In August 1967, for example, MACV had six liaison officers stationed on the JGS J-2 staff, and both the MACV and JGS J-2 staffs conducted weekly meetings. In addition, a combined intelligence staff, described by Joseph McChristian as a "prototype counterintelligence organization," was formed in November 1966 to help identify members of the VC infrastructure once they were captured.[13] Another command arrangement existed for the U.S. effort to advise the South Vietnamese. Westmoreland not only was responsible for the overall U.S. advisory effort but also acted as the chief adviser to the chairman of the JGS. In an effort to discharge this latter responsibility, he maintained close ties with General Vien and designated Brig. Gen. James L. Collins, Jr., as his personal representative and senior adviser to the JGS. Westmoreland delegated control of the navy and air force advisory units to their respective MACV component commanders. He also ordered MAF and FFV commanders to act as the senior advisers to ARVN corps commanders, while deputy senior advisers in I–III CTZ supervised the advisers in their areas of responsibility. Often this coordination was informal. One ad hoc arrangement established in I Corps on 6 September 1965, the I CORPS Joint Coordinating Council, was intended to "facilitate the coordination of Revolutionary Development [pacification] in the I Corps Tactical Zone/1st Region by minimizing duplication of effort and mutual interference between agencies engaged in or supporting the overall effort." The council, which had no directive authority or funds, was an informal gathering used by representatives of III MAF, I Corps Advisory Group, MACV, ARVN's I Corps headquarters, the embassy, and the U.S. pacification program to exchange information about developments in their areas of responsibility.[14]

Westmoreland retained operational control of U.S. Army advisers,

[12]CDEC and CMIC statistics from *PERINTREP*, March 1967, p. 29. Between July 1966 and May 1967, CDEC received over three million pages of enemy documents; see McChristian, *Military Intelligence*, p. 34. Van Creveld mistakenly claims that three million pages of documents were turned in to CDEC every month; see *Command in War*, p. 246.

[13]Truong, *RVNAF*, pp. 29, 128–134; *Command History 1967*, 1:383–385; and McChristian, *Military Intelligence*, pp. 71–78.

[14]Eckhardt, *Command and Control*, pp. 56–57, 73; *Handbook for Military Support of Pacification*, p. 31; Truong, *RVNAF*, p. 20; *Command History 1967*, 1:237–241; and "Statement of Mission, Composition and Functions, I Corps Joint Coordinating Council, 31 January, 1967," record group 319, accession number 71A4237, box number 10 of 15, folder number 6, National Records Center, Suitland, Maryland.

in itself a formidable task. By late 1967, the number of authorized army advisory positions had grown to over 9,000. Army advisers accompanied ARVN units down to the company level. Even though U.S. advisers usually operated with individual South Vietnamese units, they maintained separate communication channels with their American superiors; this redundancy often complicated their efforts. ARVN units, for example, could call in their own reinforcements and artillery support, but their advisers had to request helicopter transport of ARVN reinforcements or U.S. artillery and air strikes through U.S. communication channels.[15]

Another command arrangement helped the South Vietnamese carry out their pacification mission. In May 1967, Westmoreland was placed in charge of the U.S. pacification effort. He delegated this responsibility to Robert Komer, who as special assistant to the president held the rank of ambassador. Komer served as Westmoreland's deputy for civil operations and rural development support (CORDS) and presided over a combined U.S. military and civilian operation. He created a single U.S. pacification team for each province and established CORDS staff offices at FFV and MAF headquarters to create a direct link between CORDS officials, provincial senior advisers, and U.S. commanders to coordinate military operations undertaken to support pacification. In effect, the CORDS system constituted a second chain of command in the U.S. advisory effort. On the one hand, CORDS exercised control over U.S. civil and military advisory efforts pertaining to pacification. U.S. advisers assigned to South Vietnamese regional force and popular force units intended to protect villages, for example, were placed under Komer's operational control. On the other hand, Westmoreland exercised control over army advisers assigned to regular ARVN units.[16]

Weaknesses in the Allied Command Structure

The allied command structure was cumbersome and fractionated. There were separate command channels for the control of U.S. combat units, ARVN units, other allied units, the advisory effort, and the pacification campaign, leading to a wasteful duplication of effort. The massive amount of information that flowed between various head-

[15]*Command History 1967*, 1:224–226; and Harvey Meyerson, *Vinh Long* (Boston, 1970), pp. 50–51.

[16]Komer, *Bureaucracy*, pp. 118–120; Eckhardt, *Command and Control*, pp. 69–73; Kinnard, *War Managers*, pp. 104–106; Westmoreland, *Soldier*, pp. 215–216; Lewy, *America in Vietnam*, pp. 123–126; *Handbook for Military Support of Pacification*, pp. 27–31; and *Command History 1967*, 2:587–589.

quarters threatened to overwhelm communication facilities. Moreover, when U.S. commanders attempted to overcome these difficulties by giving routine messages high priority, they only made matters worse. The ever-increasing volume of high-priority messages slowed the transmission speed of the entire communication system. Even though communication capabilities improved throughout the war—for instance, a priority channel codenamed Red Rocket was created to provide communications between the president, the secretary of defense, the Joint Chiefs of Staff, and divisional commanders in Vietnam—they never kept pace with increasing demand.[17]

The very existence of dozens of headquarters and liaison offices, each constantly issuing requests for information, further burdened command arrangements and communication facilities. To meet these requests, many of the reports issued by CICV repeated the same information, but in the different formats required by various headquarters. Moreover, since most of the information in this blizzard of paperwork was classified, the need for secure handling facilities spread throughout the command, further adding to administrative burdens. The flow of paper reached such proportions that the Joint Chiefs at one time attempted to restrict the amount of paper supplied to MACV to prevent commanders from being overwhelmed by paperwork.[18]

The command structure did not reflect the principle of unity of command. No one below presidential level was primarily concerned with the overall alliance effort to prosecute the war. Westmoreland was in a good position to monitor the conduct of the whole war effort, but he turned away from this responsibility, placing greater emphasis on personally commanding U.S. combat units and advisers than on supervising the alliance. This task, which obviously demanded a tremendous amount of time and energy, detracted from Westmoreland's ability to supervise the overall war effort.[19]

Informal efforts to unite South Vietnamese and U.S. military operations—the policy of coordination and cooperation—were less than successful. Coordination was often abandoned during important operations; each side surprised the other with military initiatives. Without any warning, for example, ARVN reorganized its command structure around Saigon during 1966, with no explanation. To prevent a breach of security, U.S. officers never informed ARVN about prepara-

[17]Van Creveld, *Command in War*, pp. 238–239; Pearson, *War in the Northern Provinces*, p. 102; *Command History 1967*, 2:775–790; and *Command History 1968*, 2:727.

[18]Luttwak, *Pentagon*, pp. 28–29; Jones, *War without Windows*, p. 84; and Van Creveld, *Command in War*, pp. 244, 249.

[19]Komer, *Bureaucracy*, pp. 82–97; and Phillip Davidson, Oral History I, p. 75, LBJ Library.

tions for the largest operation undertaken up to that point during the war, Junction City.[20]

The combined intelligence system never really functioned as an integrated operation. The allies often withheld important information from each other, and intelligence assets were not evenly distributed between allied units. Korean units rarely shared captured documents. Some ARVN officers preferred to present important pieces of intelligence to South Vietnamese politicians rather than to intelligence personnel. The South Vietnamese National Police Force and Central Intelligence Organization sometimes failed to share important information with ARVN officers. ARVN units often lacked intelligence support for combat operations. U.S. commanders also withheld a good deal of information from their ARVN counterparts. South Vietnamese analysts at the CICV did not have access to information collected with sophisticated signals intelligence systems, information that was also withheld from units in the field.[21]

Divisions in the command structure were on occasion directly responsible for the "accidental delivery of ordnance" against allied units. On 2 March 1967, a B-52 strike authorized by III MAF hit an RVN police field force compound near the DMZ. The strike, which resulted in 43 friendly casualties, was cleared by representatives of the 3d Marine Division, MACV, the I Corps Advisory Group, and the 1st ARVN Division. Everyone involved in the strike authorization believed reports turned in at the end of previous U.S. and South Vietnamese operations indicating that the area had been cleared of civilians and friendly forces. Apparently, the strike planners had no way of checking on the whereabouts of RVN police units.[22]

The weaknesses in the allied command structure were deficiencies that could be exploited by the communists. Because command arrangements were cumbersome, important information sometimes

---

[20]On 7 June 1966, the CMR was reorganized and renamed the Capital Military District (CMD). According to the 1966 MACV command history, "the reason for the change was not entirely clear, but it appeared to have been made for political reasons. The change was a unilateral GVN decision and US personnel were not informed until after its completion"; see *Command History 1966*, p. 122. For a discussion of the U.S. failure to inform ARVN about Junction City, see Truong, *RVNAF*, p. 26; and Dunn, "American Army," p. 90.

[21]Lung, *General Offensives*, pp. 40–41; Truong, *RVNAF*, pp. 70–71; Jones, *War without Windows*, p. 136; Davidson, Oral History I, p. 23; "Transcript of George Crile Interview with Russell Cooley 4/9/81," "Letter Number 73 from James Meacham to Wife," and "5/24/67 Draft Adams Memo on Captured Viet Cong Documents," in *Westmoreland v. CBS*, exhibits 11, pp. 6–7; 214CC, p. 1; 578A, p. 3. See also Palmer, *25-Year War*, pp. 52, 63, 73; and Glenn E. Helm, "The Tet 1968 Offensive: A Failure of Allied Intelligence," M.A. thesis, Arizona State University, December 1989, pp. 128–130.

[22]Krepinevich, *Army*, p. 20; and *Command History 1967*, 1:456–457.

bogged down in transmission to the field commanders who could put it to good use. On 30 January 1968, for example, a radio intercept station at the Phu Bai combat base south of Hue picked up radio traffic that indicated an imminent attack on Hue. Following standard operating procedures, the intercepts were relayed to Da Nang for analysis. Transmitted through several command layers, the results of this analysis did not reach the MACV compound until it had already been brought under fire. In a sense, modern communication equipment created the illusion that the command system was a finely honed instrument that could respond quickly to orders issued by senior officers. In reality, the communications systems, often overburdened by ever-increasing amounts of routine traffic, could not bridge the gap rapidly between the separate command structures maintained by the allies, leading to a sluggish response to enemy initiatives.[23]

The many divisions in the allied command structure also created a vulnerability. The communists could be expected to engage in the usual military practice of using the seams between administrative areas, the points at which the authority of one commander began and another ended, as avenues of attack. The fact that different allied contingents often operated in the same geographic areas only compounded the problem, increasing the possibility that the communists could shatter allied unity by attacking its weakest member, the South Vietnamese. In fact, the seams that divided the alliance appeared at its most senior levels. Given the lack of unity of command, no one was specifically charged with identifying communist initiatives that threatened all members of the alliance.

Beliefs about the Command Problem

When the communists surveyed the military situation in South Vietnam before their decision to launch the Tet offensive, they identified the allied command structure as a weakness. The slow allied reaction to communist initiatives and the divisions between ARVN and U.S. forces were liabilities that could be exploited. The communists were receptive to indications of significant divisions within the opposing alliance because they believed that there was an inherent tension in joint military endeavors undertaken by "imperialists" and their "puppets." Because of this inherent conflict, the communists were quick to accept evidence of temporary or chronic allied military or

[23]Westmoreland, *Soldier*, p. 329; Oberdorfer, *Tet*, p. 209; Nolan, *Battle for Hue*, p. 2; and Maclear, *Ten Thousand Day War*, p. 205.

political problems as manifestations of operational disunity. They correctly concluded that South Vietnamese units and government installations could be singled out and subjected to direct attack.

Before the Tet offensive, there were available indications that the communists had identified problems within the alliance. A commentary broadcast by Radio Hanoi in June 1966 provided a description of command relationships in the alliance that mirrored the analysis contained in secret communist communications: "The two forces of master and servant do not have confidence in each other, do not cooperate with each other, so that though their numerical strength is great, it cannot be merged into one unified bloc." U.S. commanders also had evidence that the communists exploited weaknesses in command arrangements. The VC jammed radio links to U.S. advisers, for instance, while ignoring ARVN radio communications, to prevent U.S. air and artillery support from reaching ARVN units under attack.[24]

Even though U.S. commanders had information suggesting that the enemy intended to exploit weaknesses in command arrangements, they did not pay particular attention to this information before the Tet offensive. They were well aware of problems within the alliance, but the weakness in the command structure, the external vulnerabilities that could be exploited by the enemy, were not salient to them. Instead, they believed that other problems—interservice disputes and the need to prevent command reorganizations that would offend South Vietnamese sensitivities—were the main issues confronting the alliance.

Interservice disputes concerning U.S. command arrangements emerged at least three times before the Tet offensive. At the core of this struggle was the issue of whether MACV should be organized as a specified command (in which a single service controlled all forces operating in the country) or as a unified command (whereby component commanders controlled the forces supplied by their services). The debate started during the creation of MACV and influenced the decision of 8 February 1962 to designate its headquarters as a subordinate unified command under CINCPAC. In the summer of 1964, the debate was reopened when Gen. Paul D. Harkins, the departing

---

[24]Quotation from "Truong Son on the 1965–66 Dry Season," broadcast by Radio Hanoi's domestic service to South Vietnam, 4–7 July 1966, in McGarvey, *Visions of Victory*, p. 76. For a similar analysis contained in secret communist communications, see "Sharpening the Third Prong: An Increase in Viet Cong Proselyting," *VDRN* doc. 18, p. 6. During an attack in IV CTZ during May 1967, the VC jammed an adviser's transmissions while the unit he was assigned to was attacked; see *PERINTREP*, May 1967, p. 12.

MACV commander, suggested that MACV be redesignated as a specified command under army control. In early 1967, the issue again came to the fore when Gen. Harold K. Johnson, the army chief of staff, suggested that Westmoreland stop serving as his own army component commander. The air force supported General Johnson's move in the hope that the reorganization would result in the appointment of an air force officer as deputy commander of MACV.[25]

This interservice rivalry often affected the war effort, especially the air war over South Vietnam. In 1962, for example, the air force gained operational control of the light transport aircraft flown by the army. In early 1965, the air force prevented the army from operating Mohawk (light transport) aircraft in a ground attack role but failed in its effort to prevent the army from using helicopter gunships. On the eve of the Tet offensive, the most divisive debate over command of the air war erupted when Westmoreland attempted to place marine air units under the operational control of air force tactical air control centers to increase the air support available to army units transferred to I CTZ and to facilitate air operations supporting Khe Sanh.[26]

In addition to interservice rivalry, U.S. officers were often preoccupied with controversies sparked by efforts to place South Vietnamese and Korean forces under Westmoreland's command. The creation of a joint command was initially championed by Westmoreland. He hoped to replicate command arrangements implemented during the Korean War whereby U.S. officers retained operational control of South Korean forces. This arrangement not only facilitated allied operations but also allowed U.S. commanders to weed out incompetent Korean officers. The South Vietnamese took a dim view of the proposal because it threatened to eliminate their traditional criterion for promotion, political patronage. By May 1965, after the Republic of Korea also objected to the idea, the initiative was dropped. Westmoreland justified this decision by citing South Vietnamese concerns that the creation of a joint command, similar to the command ar-

[25]Luttwak, *Pentagon*, p. 27; Eckhardt, *Command and Control*, pp. 26–28, 38–41; Palmer, *25-Year War*, p. 49; and Kinnard, *War Managers*, p. 60.
[26]Eckhardt, *Command and Control*, pp. 37–38, 75; John J. Tolson, *Airmobility 1961–1971* (Washington, D.C., 1973), pp. 10–12; Palmer, *25-Year War*, pp. 27–28, 160–161; Kinnard, *War Managers*, pp. 59–60, 62; *Command History 1968*, 1:379, 433–440; Bernard C. Nalty, *Air Power and the Fight for Khe Sanh* (Washington, D.C., 1973), pp. 68–80; Westmoreland, *Soldier*, pp. 342–345; Pearson, *War in the Northern Provinces*, pp. 71–72; Thies, *When Governments Collide*, pp. 320–321; and Stanton, *Rise and Fall*, p. 256. The CIA and the air force battled over control of reconnaissance along the Ho Chi Minh Trail, and the CIA and MACV also fought for control of the pacification effort; see John Ranelagh, *The Agency: The Rise and Decline of the CIA* (New York, 1987), pp. 442–445.

rangements established by the French during the Indochina war, would leave them open to communist charges that they were serving as puppets of the U.S. neo-colonialist imperialists.[27]

Because a joint command would obviously increase military effectiveness, the idea of placing South Vietnamese and Korean forces under U.S. command did not die with Westmoreland's decision not to implement the initiative in 1965. A study completed by the army in March 1966 entitled "Program for the Pacification and Long-Term Development of South Vietnam" called for the United States to control a wide range of South Vietnamese civil and military activities. Westmoreland objected to the proposal, according to the MACV command history, claiming that it was important "to avoid conditions which would cause RVN officials to be branded as U.S. puppets." In fact, Westmoreland attempted to suppress the study; army officers were not allowed to discuss its existence outside the Department of Defense. In April 1967, Robert Komer also suggested that, if control of South Korean units was out of the question, MACV should at least assume command of ARVN.[28]

Even after the Tet offensive, when it had become apparent that the communists had exploited a divided command structure by focusing their attacks on ARVN, Westmoreland rejected Secretary of Defense McNamara's suggestion for strengthening U.S. control of allied units. He justified his decision on the grounds that "the implementation of a combined command arrangement with a US officer in command could well result in increased Communist claims of US neo-colonialism. Parallels could be drawn with the immediate postwar relation-

---

[27]Krepinevich, *Army*, pp. 194–195; Kinnard, *War Managers*, pp. 56, 92; Summers, *On Strategy*, pp. 166–167; Komer, *Bureaucracy*, pp. 97–98, 100–101; Vien and Khuyen, *Reflections on the Vietnam War*, pp. 53–54; Lewy, *America in Vietnam*, pp. 121–122; Eckhardt, *Command and Control*, pp. 59, 61; Truong, *RVNAF*, pp. 18–19; Sharp and Westmoreland, *Report*, p. 104; and Hosmer, Kellen, and Jenkins, *Fall of South Vietnam*, p. 71. The South Vietnamese often relied on the "colonial" issue in their arguments against various U.S. initiatives. For example, in a memo to Ambassador Lodge, Edward Lansdale reported that the South Vietnamese minister of rural development objected to a proposed deployment of U.S. combat troops to the delta because he felt "very strongly that there might be some popular reaction set against the US, once American forces get operating in so heavily populated an area as there is in IV Corps"; see *Command History 1966*, pp. 139, 141. For Westmoreland's argument that the command arrangement never seriously impeded the allied war effort, see Westmoreland, *Soldier*, pp. 133–134. For the argument that on balance the benefits of placing the South Vietnamese under U.S. control would have outweighed the drawbacks, see Palmer, *25-Year War*, p. 52.

[28]Westmoreland in *Command History 1966*, p. 511; see also pp. 510–512; Krepinevich, *Army*, pp. 180–182, 187; Komer, *Bureaucracy*, p. 102; and Lewy, *America in Vietnam*, p. 122. Neil Sheehan has also described Gen. Robert York's efforts in early 1966 to convince Westmoreland to form a joint command; see *Bright Shining Lie*, pp. 554–556.

ship between the French and Bao Dai." Westmoreland also rejected the proposal to place Korean units under his operational control, claiming that the Koreans would attempt to extract a costly quid pro quo from their ally: they would demand that U.S. units in South Korea be placed under the operational control of Korean commanders. In the end, Westmoreland claimed that "he had the advantages of a unified command without the disadvantages."[29]

Because U.S. officers were so deeply involved in the internal matters of interservice rivalry and command reorganization, they failed to realize that the command structure suffered from external vulnerabilities. In a sense, these internal problems demanded immediate attention, while external problems failed to generate pressing bureaucratic pressures for reform. Even though they were aware that the communists recognized and intended to exacerbate tensions within the alliance, U.S. officers usually dismissed these types of initiatives as enemy propaganda. In effect, they believed that problems with the command structure were an internal matter, and this belief caused them to miss indications that the enemy intended to exploit command vulnerabilities during the offensive.[30]

BELIEFS ABOUT ENEMY STRATEGY BEFORE THE TET OFFENSIVE

Although U.S. intelligence analysts and officers developed several subtle descriptions of enemy strategy and tactics between 1964 and June 1967, a few generalizations can be made about the substance of their analyses. These interpretations of communist strategy were often conducted within the framework of the three-phase strategy of people's war. According to the 1966 MACV command history, "the enemy's long-range plan of military strategy had three phases. The first phase called for the creation of a political organization and a guerrilla capability, and the initiation of guerrilla warfare. The second phase called for the establishment of larger bases from which a 'strategic mobility' effort could be launched. The third phase called for the

---

[29]Quotations from *Command History 1968*, 2:222. Westmoreland repeated this observation in 1985; see William C. Westmoreland, Oral History II, interviewed by Charles B. MacDonald, 25 July 1985, p. 6, LBJ Library.

[30]The June 1967 *PERINTREP*, p. 33, noted the emphasis the communists placed on the divisions within the alliance: "One of the most frequent themes appearing in NVN/VC propaganda is that of 'GVN Internal Problems.' Enemy propagandists aim at a clearly defined objective: The driving of a wedge between the U.S. and GVN and the people. Since virtually every major undertaking of the GVN poses a potential exploitable situation, the enemy is always ready to create mistrust through subtle hints and speculations."

initiation of the final large-scale attacks that would annihilate the opposing forces."[31]

U.S. intelligence analysts focused on the military aspects of people's war, even though they recognized that an unsophisticated application of this framework could lead to oversimplified analyses. As the war progressed, analysts who followed the communist debate over strategy realized that each of the three phases of people's war embodied a degree of flexibility of tactics, forces, and objectives. In contrast, ARVN analysts' rigid application of the three-phase framework had a detrimental impact on their estimates of enemy intentions.[32] In the U.S. analysts' view, the deployment of U.S. combat units to Vietnam prevented the communists from moving into the final phase of people's war. They generally suggested that the enemy was stuck between the second phase, characterized by an emphasis on strategic mobility, and the opening round of the final phase, characterized by local counteroffensives. Westmoreland, however, is an exception to this generalization. He has claimed that he always believed that the enemy had reached the third phase of people's war. During a commanders' conference on 27 June 1966, for example, Westmoreland stated that the enemy was fully committed to phase-three operations and either could not or would not revert to a less advanced phase. Yet Westmoreland was apparently confused about the characteristics of each phase of people's war; he justified his description of communist strategy by characterizing enemy operations in terms of strategic mobility, a characteristic of the second phase. In any event, most analysts believed that the enemy had decided to switch from phase two to phase three in 1964.[33]

[31]*Command History 1966*, p. 19.

[32]*Command History 1967*, 1:70, 74; and Combined Intelligence Center Vietnam (CICV), *Strategy since 1954*, Study 67–037 (Headquarters, USMACV, 29 June 1967), pp. 27–34. ARVN analysts believed that the enemy was in the second phase of people's war and was even on the verge of reverting to the first phase before the Tet offensive. They argued that, since the communists followed the precepts of people's war, they would not attempt a "win-the-war" offensive while in phase one or two; see Lung, *General Offensives*, p. 39.

[33]*Command History 1966*, pp. 16–21, 58–60, 346–347; Westmoreland, *Soldier*, p. 194; and "The Vietnamese Communists' Will to Persist" (CIA memorandum: 28 August 1966), in *Westmoreland v. CBS*, exhibit 217, p. 7. CICV analysts described mobile warfare (strategic mobility) as initiating "the period of 'equilibrium' [phase two] for the Communist insurgents. Starting with the small guerrilla units in stage one, larger units are gradually formed and fighting evolves from guerrilla action to employment of forces using the principle of regular warfare, though not yet in fixed or 'positional' engagements. . . . Mobile warfare is gradually upgraded and, as mobile warfare swings the equilibrium of strength to the insurgents, the stage is set for phase three, the 'general counteroffensive'. Local counteroffensive operations, which herald the initiation of phase three . . . are begun when the growth of the units into regiments and divisions has been accomplished"; see CICV, *Strategy since 1954*, pp. 13–14.

By March 1967, however, MACV J-2 was convinced that the enemy had abandoned all hope of defeating the allies by launching a massive conventional attack, a classic phase-three operation. A CICV study written in June 1967, for example, claimed: "Positional warfare in set-piece battles for 'liberated areas' is necessary for final victory in the precepts of Mao's 'Three-Phase' doctrine. For the VC/NVA forces in South Vietnam the final step in Mao's thesis is probably not feasible. More specifically, as long as the US forces are committed in Vietnam an overall insurgent military victory is not possible."[34]

Intelligence analysts did not suggest, however, that the communist inability to reach the third phase of people's war would result in the abandonment of their goal of forcefully unifying Vietnam.[35] They claimed that the communists had identified an alternative strategy for the realization of their goal. Instead of confronting the firepower of allied forces by launching a major offensive, the communists would attempt to conduct an extended war of attrition. By falling back to phase-two operations and emphasizing guerrilla operations, the enemy intended to weaken the allies gradually, wreck the pacification program, and exploit worldwide peace movements. According to analysts, the enemy believed that the high cost in blood and treasure, international pressure, and domestic dissension would inevitably force the United States to withdraw its forces. Writing in June 1967, CICV analysts claimed that "there is little reason to think that Ho Chi Minh and the leadership in Hanoi feel that the outcome of the war will be any different politically from the French-Indochina War. Political factors may overcome the weaknesses of the military stance of the VC/NVA forces. Eventual war weariness may undermine the support of the United States government just as it did the French government."[36]

[34]CICV, *Strategy since 1954*, p. 29. This view was also shared by senior administration officials; see "Rostow Memorandum to President," 22 July 1967, doc. 22, NSF Aides File Memos to the President, W. Rostow, vol. 35, DSDUF Vietnam Box 3, and Henry Owen, "Memorandum Subject 1864–1967" (including cover note from Rostow to President), doc. 174, NSF Memos to the President, W. Rostow, vol. 24, DSDUF Vietnam Box 2, LBJ Library.

[35]*Command History 1967*, 1:73. During January 1967, CIA analysts noted that the communists had recently begun to reexamine their strategy and tactics, "probably because they now recognize that an outright military victory is impossible"; see "Memo 1/9/67, from Office of National Estimates to Director," in *Westmoreland v. CBS*, exhibit 225, p. 5.

[36]CICV, *Strategy since 1954*, p. 34. In his 1967 command guidance issued to field commanders, Westmoreland claimed that "the VC/NVA forces no longer have the capability of achieving a military victory. We must make 1967 the year during which it will become evident to the enemy and the world that we can and will achieve our military objectives"; see message from COMUSMACV, 241227Z, Jan. 1967, in *Command History 1967*, 1:326. CICV analysts made a similar claim in February 1967: "While the enemy

At about the same time, CICV analysts obtained evidence of a so-phisticated enemy capability to monitor the contents of media reports on the war. An English language propaganda booklet obtained in April 1967, for example, combined commentary espousing familiar communist themes with political cartoons gleaned from the American press. The analysts were not particularly concerned with the impact of this propaganda on U.S. troops, but they noted that the booklet demonstrated that the enemy could monitor and employ media cov-erage of the war for its own purposes. Thus, analysts claimed, the enemy had decided that victory could be attained through the imple-mentation of an attrition strategy intended to maximize the political impact of the war in the United States.[37]

By June 1967, U.S. analysts and officers also believed they had identified the strategy implemented by the communists between 1965 and June 1967. The strategy, nestled within the second phase of peo-ple's war, emphasized strategic mobility. Intended to overcome the superior tactical mobility enjoyed by allied forces, strategic mobility resulted in the deployment of NVA divisions along the border areas of South Vietnam. By mid-1967, two of these fronts had been identi-fied: one stretching along the DMZ into Laos, the other along the Cambodian border on the Kontum–Pleiku axis. These NVA units were assumed to pose the threat of a conventional invasion and to tie down allied forces in a costly battle of attrition. As allied forces moved away from populated coastal areas, VC main-force and guer-rilla attacks against ARVN units engaged in pacification would be fa-cilitated. And by posing multiple threats in widely separated areas, the communists were supposed to be able to tie down allied units, allowing them to attack allied targets at times and places of their own choosing.[38]

The concept of strategic mobility presented intelligence analysts with a difficult problem—that of determining which region of South Vietnam would be the next target. Moreover, if allied units became overly concentrated in one region, this would invite attack in other

---

probably no longer believes that he can evict the FWMAF from SVN, he may well consider it likely that he can wear them down to the point of quitting. The enemy considers it possible that if he can continue to harass and attrit the FWMAF, their governments and peoples will eventually become exasperated with the prolongation of the war and recall their forces"; see *PERINTREP*, February 1967, p. 41.

[37]*Command History 1967*, 1:73. CIA analysts made a similar point in January 1967; see *Westmoreland v. CBS*, exhibit 225, p. 5. The CIA reiterated this point again in June 1967; see "5/23/67, Central Intelligence Agency, 'The Vietnam Situation: An Analysis and Estimate'," in *Westmoreland v. CBS*, exhibit 237, p. 3. For the implications drawn by CICV analysts from the captured document, see *PERINTREP*, May 1967, p. 34.

[38]*Command History 1966*, pp. 19–20; and *Command History 1967*, 1:70–73.

regions. By June 1966, Westmoreland recognized this problem. He stated that the allies had to react rapidly to enemy initiatives and defeat communist offensive thrusts quickly to minimize the time the allies were vulnerable to attack in other areas.[39]

Westmoreland even recognized that an element of deception was contained in the concept of strategic mobility. In early 1966, he claimed that the enemy was trying to lure American forces toward the DMZ and away from the U.S. units protecting Saigon, which was the enemy's preferred objective. A similar enemy effort also was identified in early 1967.[40] Still, the belief that the communists had given up on third-phase attacks led U.S. analysts to draw mistaken inferences from their understanding of strategic mobility. Even though they realized that the 1967 winter-spring offensive might embody some form of deception, they incorrectly thought that the main thrust would come in the border regions, the only area where the communists seemed to possess significant military capability. Because the communists supposedly realized that conventional victory was beyond their grasp, analysts did not place much credence in information that indicated a communist attack of southern cities, an effort viewed as hopeless because of a lack of resources. Such information was dismissed as propaganda, intended to bolster the troops involved in a suicidal diversion of U.S. units away from the main communist attack that would take place along the borders of South Vietnam.

BELIEFS ABOUT ENEMY ACTIVITY DURING TRUCES

According to the interim report of the official U.S. government investigation into the performance of intelligence organizations before the Tet offensive, "few US or GVN officials believed the enemy would attack during Tet, nor did the Vietnamese public."[41] Many students of the war concur in this observation. The origins of this belief can be traced to two sources. U.S. officers realized the importance the South Vietnamese placed on the Tet holiday, which symbolized "solidarity of the Vietnamese people."[42] Enemy attacks during the Tet holiday would hurt the communist cause because they would be deeply resented by the South Vietnamese. "I frankly did not think they would

---

[39]*Command History 1966*, pp. 3, 347; *Command History 1967*, 1:73.
[40]Pearson, *War in the Northern Provinces*, p. 8; Sharp and Westmoreland, *Report*, p. 116; and *Command History 1967*, 1:330.
[41]House Select Committee on Intelligence, *U.S. Intelligence Agencies and Activities*, p. 1995.
[42]*Ibid.*

assume the psychological disadvantage of hitting at Tet itself," Westmoreland stated in 1972, "so I thought it would be before or after Tet."[43] Additionally, enemy behavior during earlier holiday stand-downs had been closely monitored. Before the 1968 Tet truce, analysts and commanders had identified a pattern in enemy behavior that suggested that the 1967 winter-spring offensive would begin at the close of the Tet holiday.[44]

In 1966 and 1967, the allies agreed to various truces during the Christmas, New Year, and Tet holidays and on Buddha's birthday. These holiday stand-downs, which often entailed a temporary curtailment of the bombing campaign over North Vietnam, were never popular with senior U.S. commanders. In the months before the 1967 Tet holiday, for example, the Joint Chiefs of Staff, Admiral Sharp, and General Westmoreland recommended that the allies avoid participation in a Tet truce. They argued that the enemy benefited more from truces than the allies and that stand-downs ultimately resulted in increased friendly casualties. To bolster their arguments, senior commanders paid special attention to enemy activity during holiday truces.[45] During the 1966 Christmas and New Year stand-downs, an overall trend in enemy activity developed that would remain unbroken until the 1968 Tet truce. The primary task undertaken by the enemy was a major resupply effort. During the 48-hour Christmas stand-down, for example, aircraft engaged in Operation Sea Dragon (armed reconnaissance over the coastal waterways of North Vietnam) observed more traffic than had been cited over the previous two months.[46] Traffic analysis revealed that this enemy effort could have resulted in the movement of over 10,000 tons of cargo to within 16 kilometers of the DMZ. The communists also took advantage of both truces to carry out troop movements that would have been impossible under normal combat conditions. In support of this observation, Westmoreland pointed to a 27 December incident in which a U.S. artillery battery was overrun in Binh Dinh province. Westmoreland

[43]Westmoreland quoted in Schandler, *Unmaking of a President*, p. 75.
[44]"Prepared Statement of William E. Colby, Director, Central Intelligence Agency," in House Select Committee on Intelligence, *U.S. Intelligence Agencies and Activities*, p. 1693; Palmer, *25-Year War*, p. 78; Shaplen, *Time out of Hand*, p. 403; Palmer, *Summons*, p. 183; Lung, *General Offensives*, p. 43; Betts, "Strategic Surprise for War Termination," p. 162; Oberdorfer, *Tet*, p. 70; and Daniel O. Graham's testimony in House Select Committee on Intelligence, *U.S. Intelligence Agencies and Activities*, p. 1666.
[45]*Command History 1968*, 1:375; and Sharp, *Strategy for Defeat*, p. 145.
[46]*Command History 1966*, p. 30–31. Operation Sea Dragon, initiated in October 1966, involved the use of Seventh Fleet ships and aircraft to attack any waterborne logistic craft in the coastal water of North Vietnam between the DMZ and the 18th parallel; see *Command History 1967*, 1:492.

maintained that the Christmas cease-fire had provided the communists with the opportunity to mass for this attack. Apparently, the communists gave the least emphasis to initiating attacks during these truces.

The Tet cease-fire followed on the heels of the Christmas and New Year truces, and both Sharp and Westmoreland believed that the enemy would again undertake a major resupply effort. Although their request to fire on the targets detected by Operation Sea Dragon during the truce was denied by the Johnson administration, they planned to increase U.S. reconnaissance during the cease-fire. Both Sharp and Westmoreland hoped that by providing a clear picture of the enemy supply effort they could strengthen their arguments for an early curtailment of the bombing pause. In a further effort to circumvent the upcoming Tet truce, Sharp proposed the selective mining of North Vietnamese inland and territorial waters, noting that mines set before the truce would yield extra dividends by catching the high-density traffic predicted for the Tet period.[47]

The four-day Tet truce began at 0800 8 February 1967 and, as Sharp and Westmoreland expected, the North Vietnamese logistic effort increased immediately. On 9 February, Sharp provided the Joint Chiefs with his early assessment of enemy activity.

> We are now watching the results of our interdiction efforts being overcome and pressure being taken off Hanoi as a result of a stand-down in which NVN [North Vietnam] is the only one to gain any advantage. Once these large quantities of material are in the hands of our enemy, who obviously is in dire need of them, they cannot but contribute substantially to the loss of more American lives. . . . These actions are not those one would expect from an enemy on the verge of suing for peace. . . . I urgently request authority to attack this traffic with air and naval forces which are now in position to stop [it] immediately.[48]

Even though Sharp's message was partially intended to serve as a warning about the discussions then going on between Soviet premier Aleksei Kosygin and British prime minister Harold Wilson, it did not

[47]*Command History 1967*, 1:493; and Thies, *When Governments Collide*, p. 159.
[48]CINCPAC to JCS, 092007Z, Feb. 1967, in *Command History 1967*, 1:494. Although Sharp might have been a little premature in his prediction of dire consequences, his estimate of the scope of the enemy logistical effort was confirmed in an intelligence summary provided by Westmoreland on 10 February: "During the daylight hours on 9 February, at least 300 waterborne logistics craft were sighted, many over 100 feet in length. . . . During the first 24 hours of the Tet stand-down, more than 500 trucks were reported in the Mu Gia Pass area. . . . In addition, there was at least one truck per mile along Routes 1A and 100 south from the ferry. This would total 45 to 50 trucks moving towards the DMZ area"; COMUSMACV to CINCPAC, 100835Z, Feb. 1967, in *Command History 1967*, 1:494–495.

overestimate the scope of the enemy logistic effort. During the Tet cease-fire, Westmoreland reported that over 2,200 trucks and 702 cargo vessels were spotted. Intelligence analysts estimated that, within the first sixty hours of the truce, the enemy had moved 36,000 tons of supplies into positions just north of the DMZ.[49]

CICV analysts noted that the communists also used the 1967 Tet cease-fire to rest and resupply units in the areas south of the DMZ. At the close of these resupply operations, the enemy began moving units into position to resume previous activities, in some instances at increased levels. After the end of the Tet truce, the enemy initiated offensive operations in II CTZ on 14 February. In III and IV CTZ, enemy activity decreased during the truce and resumed previous levels at its conclusion.[50]

By the end of the 1967 Tet truce, the communists had established a pattern of cease-fire activity that was repeated during the truces declared in 1967 for Buddha's birthday (23 May), Christmas, and New Year's Day. Yet after the 1967 Tet holiday the allies were less willing to give the communists a free-ride during truce periods. Only limited restrictions were placed on the interdiction campaign during Buddha's birthday, but the communists still attempted to carry out increased logistical efforts. It is possible, moreover, that the communists recognized that their truce behavior had established a pattern of activity that might lull their enemy into believing that they would always use cease-fires for resupply purposes. The North Vietnamese,

[49]Sharp's request for the termination of the truce was denied and the cease-fire was even extended until Kosygin departed London on 12 February. The Joint Chiefs granted authority to resume the air campaign against North Vietnam on 13 February; see *Command History 1967*, 1:495–496. Ironically, the U.S. "Phase A–Phase B" proposal for the cessation of North Vietnamese infiltration of South Vietnam after a U.S. bombing halt in the north was under consideration during the negotiations between Kosygin and Wilson. Members of the Johnson administration apparently believed that the enemy's behavior during the Tet truce, in which a surge in infiltration was the response to a U.S. bombing halt, provided a clear indication of the enemy's response to the proposal. For a discussion of these exchanges, see Karnow, *Vietnam*, pp. 494–496; Maclear, *Ten Thousand Day War*, p. 206; Brandon, *Anatomy of Error*, pp. 82–99; Thies, *When Governments Collide*, pp. 159–165; and Lyndon Baines Johnson, *The Vantage Point* (New York, 1971), pp. 252–255. For American estimates of total tonnage moved toward the DMZ by the enemy during the Tet truce, see *Command History 1967*, 1:496. The February 1967, *PERINTREP*, p. 1, provides a different estimate of the enemy logistical effort along the DMZ: "North Vietnam took full advantage of the Tet stand-down 8–10 February, to move supplies and possibly troops into southern MR [military region] IV and the DMZ area of NVN. It is estimated that NVN moved 22,300–25,100 tons of supplies into the area of NVN below 18 degrees north. 18,000 tons were moved by water craft and some 4,300–7,000 tons by truck. The NVN resupply operations during the Tet stand-down were obviously the result of extensive planning and coordination. The large number of water craft and vehicles sighted during Tet was in marked contrast to the small number of waterborne and vehicular sightings during normal ROLLING THUNDER and SEA DRAGON operations."
[50]*PERINTREP*, February 1967, pp. 7–12.

not the allies, proposed Christmas, New Year, and Tet cease-fires on 18 November 1967. U.S. officials reduced the duration of the proposed cease-fires to 24 hours for Christmas and 36 hours for New Year's to limit the enemy's resupply effort. Sharp and Westmoreland were also authorized to renew the interdiction campaign, which was temporarily terminated during these truce periods, if surges in logistical activity were observed. The short duration of the truces apparently militated against a termination of the cease-fires. By the time commanders had evidence of increased logistical efforts the truces were over.[51]

In effect, two beliefs influenced U.S. commanders' perceptions of the likelihood of communist attacks during the Tet truce. First, they believed that the South Vietnamese population would take an exceedingly dim view of a communist violation of the Tet truce. The Vietnamese were thought to consider Tet sacred, and the communists were expected to realize that a major attack during this period would ultimately rebound to their detriment. Speaking years after the offensive, General Wheeler noted, "I would say that no one really expected the enemy to launch the attack because . . . this is a very sacred time to all the Vietnamese, North and South." The second belief was drawn from past enemy behavior during holiday truces. Even though the enemy engaged in a wide variety of activity during truce periods, the Americans noted that the primary communist objective was to take advantage of the temporary termination of the interdiction campaign to conduct intensified resupply activities. Writing in the aftermath of the Tet offensive, CICV analysts remarked, "Although the enemy has, during past truces, initiated some harassing-type actions, the Tet attacks mark the first time that he has deliberately used a truce period to gain the advantage of surprise on a country-wide basis."[52]

Believing that the South Vietnamese populace would find a broken Tet truce reprehensible, and assuming that such a truce would be used, as usual, for resupply, U.S. commanders came to a natural conclusion: if the winter-spring offensive did not materialize before the Tet holiday, it would probably come at the conclusion of the Tet cease-fire. They believed that it made more sense for the communists to avoid arousing the hostility of the South Vietnamese population by not attacking during Tet. It also made good sense to use the Tet truce to

[51]Sharp and Westmoreland, *Report*, pp. 41, 43; *Command History 1967*, 1:354–356; and *The Pentagon Papers, Senator Gravel Edition* (Boston, 1971), 4:187.
[52]Earle G. Wheeler, Oral History II, interviewed by Dorothy Pierce McSweeney, 7 May 1970, pp. 1–2, LBJ Library; and *PERINTREP*, January 1968, p. 4.

conduct a last-minute resupply effort before the upcoming offensive. Recent enemy behavior during truces was far more conspicuous than the fact that throughout their history the Vietnamese had launched surprise attacks against invaders during the Tet holidays. Ironically, Westmoreland himself displayed in his living quarters a statue of Quang Trung, the leader of one of the more successful Tet attacks that surprised the Chinese in 1789.[53]

BELIEFS ORIGINATING IN U.S. STRATEGY

Although Westmoreland ultimately proposed a four-phase strategy after the Tet offensive, in 1965 he adopted a three-phase strategy. In phase one, which was implemented throughout 1965, U.S. forces established and defended base areas within South Vietnam and launched spoiling attacks to deny the communists a quick victory during the buildup, for example in the battle of the Ia Drang valley. By mid-1966, Westmoreland began implementing the second phase of his strategy. A division of labor emerged between the allies. U.S. forces concentrated on search-and-destroy operations and ARVN focused on pacification. U.S. units engaged in sustained offensive operations against enemy base camps within South Vietnam, an action that sometimes forced enemy units to face superior firepower. In phase three, U.S. units would eliminate the threat posed to South Vietnam by enemy main-force units by either pushing them back across the borders of the country, destroying them, or forcing them to disperse into small groups. In phase four, U.S. troops would move into North Vietnam, Cambodia, and Laos before withdrawing altogether. By late 1967, U.S. commanders believed that they had reached the third phase in this strategy.[54]

[53]Oberdorfer, *Tet*, p. 71.
[54]*Pentagon Papers, Gravel*, 4:296–297; Westmoreland, *Soldier*, pp. 145–146; Karnow, *Vietnam*, p. 435; Maclear, *Ten Thousand Day War*, pp. 153–154; Krepinevich, *Army*, p. 151; Nalty, *Air Power*, p. 3; Sharp and Westmoreland, *Report*, pp. 131–132; Palmer, *Summons*, pp. 91–103; Stanton, *Rise and Fall*, pp. 56–61; and Tolson, *Airmobility*, pp. 73–83. 1966 was a transitional year for U.S. strategy; Westmoreland has claimed that he focused on securing the U.S. buildup while increasing the scope and intensity of offensive operations; see "Letter from Westmoreland to E. H. Simmons, 27 May 1978," in *Westmoreland v. CBS*, exhibit 215B, p. 1. In meetings with the president, Joint Chiefs of Staff, secretary of defense, and the Senate and House Armed Services committees in November 1967, Westmoreland stated that the U.S. could begin withdrawing its troops and turning over the defense of South Vietnam to ARVN "in approximately two years." This would indicate that the United States had either entered or was about to enter the third phase of Westmoreland's strategy; see "Notes for Talk with the President" (November 1967), in *Westmoreland v. CBS*, exhibit 283, p. 4. Although no firm

Westmoreland's strategy was intended to secure two objectives. First, his ground forces were to serve as a shield, cutting off the infiltration of men and supplies into South Vietnam and blocking North Vietnamese invasion routes into the country. Behind this shield, ARVN forces and other allied units engaged in pacification could perform their tasks relatively free from the threat posed by main-force units operating near the border. In August 1966, for example, Westmoreland stated in a cable to Sharp that "the growing strength of US/ Free World Forces will provide the shield that will permit ARVN to shift its weight of effort to an extent not heretofore feasible to direct support of Revolutionary Development."[55] A geographic subdivision of CTZs that reflected the plan of a shield for pacification was also developed. U.S. units were to prevent enemy forces from penetrating through border surveillance zones, allowing the pacification effort to continue in clearing, consolidation, and secure zones. The ultimate objective behind the shield strategy was to push communist main-force units away from populated areas and to force their withdrawal from South Vietnam.[56]

The second objective of U.S. strategy was to kill large numbers of communist troops. In fact, the attrition of enemy forces was often referred to by senior officers as the cornerstone of U.S. strategy in the ground war. To "attrit, by year's end, VC/NVA forces at a rate as high as their capability to put men into the field" was set as a primary military goal during the February 1966 Honolulu conference.[57] In his

---

course of action was embodied in the fourth phase, various ideas were advanced both before and after the Tet offensive: launching ground operations to sever the Ho Chi Minh Trail; raiding enemy border sanctuaries in Laos and Cambodia; or invading North Vietnam to destroy enemy bases immediately north of the DMZ; see Westmoreland, *Soldier*, pp. 354–355; Davidson, Oral History I, pp. 34–35; "Notes on [Westmoreland's] Discussions with the President, 27 April 1967" and "5/26/67 Cable from Wheeler to Sharp," in *Westmoreland v. CBS*, exhibits 1400A, p. 1; 1429, pp. 1–2; and Bob Brewin and Sydney Shaw, *Vietnam on Trial: Westmoreland vs. CBS* (New York, 1987), pp. 132, 136. The third initiative, which grew out of contingency planning undertaken in response to the enemy buildup along the DMZ before the Tet campaign (Operation Pacific Grove, CTF 76 Oplan 123–68), apparently would have served as the core of the fourth phase of U.S. strategy; see *Command History 1968*, 2:781–782.

[55]COMUSMACV to CINCPAC, 260242Z, Aug. 1966, in *Command History 1967*, 1:323.

[56]The best description of the objectives of U.S. strategy, which emphasizes the need for U.S. forces to act as a shield for South Vietnam (a shield against China as well as North Vietnam), is a June 1966 CINCPAC strategy directive; see *Command History 1966*, p. 345; see also CINCPAC to COMUSMACV, 280050Z, Sept. 1966, in *Command History 1967*, 1:313–316; Stanton, *Rise and Fall*, pp. 83, 134; Komer, *Bureaucracy*, p. 57, Kinnard, *War Managers*, pp. 39–40; Palmer, *25-Year War*, p. 65; and Truong, *RVNAF*, pp. 72–76.

[57]"1966 Program to Increase the Effectiveness of Military Operations and Anticipated Results Thereof" (drafted by William Bundy and John McNaughton), in *Westmoreland v. CBS*, exhibit 215D. For a description of the importance of this memo in terms of the U.S. ground strategy for the war, see "Letter from Westmoreland to E.H. Simmons, 27

guidance to subordinate commanders for 1967, Westmoreland also stated that he intended to mount a "general offensive" designed in part to "decimate enemy forces, destroy his base areas and disrupt the VC infrastructure."[58] Westmoreland hoped that, against superior firepower and mobility, enemy main-force units would be gradually worn down until they no longer posed a threat. Alternatively, he thought that enough casualties might eventually convince the North Vietnamese that they could not win the war.[59]

By 1967, U.S. commanders and intelligence analysts placed increasing emphasis on both the conduct of military operations in the border areas of South Vietnam and enemy activity in these regions. The reason for this emphasis is clear: it was dictated by the shield objective— to prevent enemy infiltration and to push enemy main-force units out of the country. As the strategy succeeded, U.S. units operated farther and farther away from populated areas. Operations Cedar Falls and Junction City in early 1967, for example, were judged successful because they forced VC divisions out of their sanctuaries in the Iron Triangle, located a few kilometers northwest of Saigon, and War Zone C and into Cambodia. Moreover, because infiltration and the number of NVA divisions were greatest along the DMZ, protecting this area was given the highest priority by Westmoreland. Contingency planning to defeat a possible invasion of I CTZ was an ongoing concern throughout the war. As early as October 1966, Westmoreland created a marine reserve force, located on amphibious vessels, to guard against an NVA invasion across the DMZ. During the buildup in 1966 and early 1967, the initial deployment of U.S. units was often governed by the level of enemy activity along the border. By late 1966, Westmoreland began to transfer units to I CTZ, and he continued to do so until well after the conclusion of the Tet offensive.[60]

The attrition objective embodied in U.S. strategy could also be best pursued in the border regions, especially in I CTZ. The high concentration of NVA units in the area provided several lucrative targets. Relaxed rules of engagement in this area also allowed U.S. units to

---

May 1978," in *Westmoreland v. CBS*, exhibit 215B, p. 3; and Westmoreland, *Soldier*, pp. 160–161.

[58]Message from COMUSMACV, 241227Z, Jan. 1967, in *Command History 1967*, 1:326.

[59]Komer, *Bureaucracy*, pp. 56–58; Kinnard, *War Managers*, pp. 42–43; Lewy, *America in Vietnam*, pp. 51–52; Westmoreland, *Soldier*, pp. 149–150; Ewell and Hunt, *Sharpening the Combat Edge*, pp. 225–227; Palmer, *Summons*, pp. 116–117; Krepinevich, *Army*, pp. 164–168; Herring, *America's Longest War*, p. 151; and *Westmoreland v. CBS*, exhibit 14, pp. 8–9.

[60]*Command History 1967*, 1:4, 385–390, 2:1027; *Command History 1966*, pp. 79, 125, 419; Stanton, *Rise and Fall*, pp. 205–207; Robert Thompson, *No Exit from Vietnam* (New York, 1969), pp. 100–101; and Truong, *RVNAF*, p. 135.

use their superior firepower freely.[61] The importance placed on operations along the DMZ also manifested itself in CICV analysts' emphasis on estimates of enemy main-force units, especially NVA units; they were willing to tolerate wrangling over estimates of the strength of VC self-defense forces (part-time guerrillas) to protect their estimates of NVA strength from what they believed to be outside interference.[62]

By mid-1967, then, U.S. units were concentrating along the border regions of South Vietnam, especially along the DMZ. Because strategy and troop deployments were focused on these areas, analysts and commanders believed that the enemy main-force units opposing U.S. units in this region constituted the greatest threat to the allied war effort. Simply put, they believed that the main thrust of the 1967 winter-spring offensive would come where the greatest number of NVA units were in close contact with U.S. forces, along the DMZ. They also believed that U.S. units, because of their mission and capabilities, posed the primary threat to the communists and would therefore constitute the main target of an enemy offensive. There was a strict division between the offensive mission assigned to U.S. units, the search-and-destroy operations, and the defensive mission assigned to ARVN, pacification. A September 1966 CINCPAC directive to Westmoreland, for example, stated that the mission assigned to U.S. units was "to seek out and destroy communist forces and infrastructure by expanded offensive military operations. . . . Enemy forces will be broken up into small bands whose chief concern will be their own existence."[63] By mid-1967, search-and-destroy missions accounted for 75 percent of the operations conducted by U.S. units.[64] In contrast, the 1967 combined campaign plan, issued in November 1966, assigned a different mission to ARVN:

[61]Westmoreland, *Soldier*, pp. 150, 315. Although the rules of engagement followed by U.S. forces in all areas of South Vietnam were often not clearly understood by the troops, they were least restrictive near the DMZ; see Kinnard, *War Managers*, pp. 51–53; Lewy, *America in Vietnam*, 233–237; and *Command History 1967*, 1:352–353.

[62]Renata Adler, *Reckless Disregard* (New York, 1986), p. 113; Krepinevich, *Army*, p. 229; and Komer, *Bureaucracy*, p. 61.

[63]CINCPAC to COMUSMACV, 280050Z, Sept. 1966, in *Command History 1967*, 1:312.

[64]*Handbook for Military Support of Pacification*, pp. 33, 42; Lewy, *America in Vietnam*, p. 57; Lung, *General Offensives*, p. 7; Maclear, *Ten Thousand Day War*, p. 156; Herring, *America's Longest War*, p. 151; Gelb, *Irony of Vietnam*, pp. 133–135; Gallucci, *Neither Peace nor Honor*, pp. 106–115; Kinnard, *War Managers*, pp. 39–40; Sharp and Westmoreland, *Report*, p. 117; and Krepinevich, *Army*, p. 183. Harry Summers, in insisting that U.S. forces concentrated on supporting ARVN in its counterinsurgency role, takes an exceptional position on the distinction between the missions assigned to ARVN and U.S. units; see *On Strategy*, p. 173.

1. On a priority basis, dispose forces and conduct operations to provide security for populated areas with priority to the National Priority area within the respective CTZ and protect civil elements engaged in RD [rural development] activities.

2. Conduct an active defense of all provincial capitals, district towns, logistic and operational bases, and other significant political and economic centers with particular emphasis on those locations identified as areas requiring special defense. This defense would be characterized by saturation day and night patrolling, ambushes and other anti-guerrilla tactics to supplement the static defense of the area.[65]

There were several reasons for this division of labor between the allies. Familiarity with their own language and society made ARVN units the logical choice for the pacification mission. U.S. commanders also were sensitive to South Vietnamese concerns that a large U.S. presence in populated areas would increase anti-American sentiment among the people. At the same time, the superior maneuverability and firepower of U.S. units seemed to make them the obvious candidates for offensive operations. Army officers were eager to use their units in large-scale search-and-destroy operations that utilized their capabilities for fighting a high-intensity conventional conflict. Because the force structure, doctrine, and mission of the U.S. Army were geared toward conventional military operations, rather than toward counterinsurgency or pacification operations, army commanders were happy to delegate the pacification mission to their ARVN counterparts. According to Townsend Hoopes, Westmoreland "relished the challenge of searching out and destroying the NVN regular forces, but was essentially indifferent to the fighting capabilities of the ARVN, asking only that it get out of his way."[66]

U.S. Army commanders believed that the search-and-destroy operations were the most important missions in the allied war effort. Pacification, which they believed was defensive in nature, was considered relatively unimportant. Moreover, even other army missions paled in comparison. The army advisory effort, for instance, receded

[65]For a summary of the ARVN mission in the 1967 combined campaign plan, see *Command History 1967*, 1:320–321.

[66]Quotation from Townsend Hoopes, *Limits of Intervention*, p. 63. See Westmoreland, *Soldier*, p. 146; Truong, *RVNAF*, p. 7; *Command History 1966*, pp. 640–646; *Command History 1968*, 2:803–805; *Command History 1967*, 2:1046–1054; Lewy, *America in Vietnam*, p. 51; Herring, *America's Longest War*, pp. 150–151; Thompson, *No Exit from Vietnam*, p. 100; Komer, *Bureaucracy*, pp. 160–161; Stanton, *Rise and Fall*, p. 81; Dunn, "American Army," p. 85; Bernard Brodie, *War and Politics* (New York, 1973), pp. 188–189; and Krepinevich, *Army*, passim.

in importance. Officers even attempted to avoid advisory duty out of a belief that it would be detrimental to their careers. Army officers believed that U.S. combat units constituted the "first team," entrusted with the most important mission because of their superior firepower, mobility, and fighting spirit.[67]

In contrast, the U.S. military had a low opinion of ARVN capabilities. The high desertion rates that afflicted most ARVN formations and the chronic underutilization of some units were thought to testify to ARVN's general lack of fighting prowess. U.S. commanders also attributed the poor performance often turned in by ARVN to the quality of its officer corps, considered to be at best incompetent and at worst hopelessly corrupt. In fact, decisions made by Westmoreland to delegate important missions to ARVN were usually driven by his concerns about South Vietnamese prestige. For example, on 14 December 1967, at the conclusion of Operation Fairfax which was intended to eliminate the VC presence around Saigon, the U.S. 199th Light Infantry Brigade turned over responsibility for guarding the approaches to the city to the ARVN 5th Ranger Group. Westmoreland, who wanted the South Vietnamese to defend their own capital, apparently believed that the 380-day operation had reduced the enemy presence in the vicinity of Saigon to a level that could be handled by ARVN. Moreover, on 27 January 1968, well after the siege of Khe Sanh had started, the 37th ARVN Ranger Battalion was moved to the firebase. It was recognized at the time that the deployment of the ARVN battalion was a symbolic gesture undertaken at the urging of Westmoreland.[68]

Even though it seems equally plausible that the communists would strike at the weakest member of the alliance, not at the strongest, Americans tended to believe that they would attack U.S. units because they posed the greatest threat. In other words, Americans

[67]Krepinevich, *Army*, pp. 168–169, 207–210; Stanton, *Rise and Fall*, p. 82; Palmer, *25-Year War*, p. 179; Thompson, *No Exit from Vietnam*, pp. 149–150; Komer, *Bureaucracy*, p. 124; Lewy, *America in Vietnam*, p. 119; Kinnard, *War Managers*, p. 89; and Truong, *RVNAF*, p. 163.

[68]Lewy, *America in Vietnam*, p. 163; Truong, *RVNAF*, pp. 128–134, 150; Senate Committee on Foreign Relations, *Stalemate in Vietnam*, pp. 9–11; *Command History 1967*, 1:169, 173–177, 383–385; Stanton, *Rise and Fall*, pp. 82–83, 143–144, 249; Herring, *America's Longest War*, pp. 162–163; Palmer, *25-Year War*, p. 56; Maclear, *Ten Thousand Day War*, p. 149; Hosmer, Kellen, and Jenkins, *Fall of South Vietnam*, pp. 74–76; McChristian, *Military Intelligence*, pp. 78–79; Brodie, *War and Politics*, pp. 165–197; Sharp and Westmoreland, *Report*, pp. 140–141, 283, 339; Oberdorfer, *Tet*, p. 8; Westmoreland, *Soldier*, p. 207; Lung, *General Offensives*, p. 11; and Krepinevich, *Army*, p. 194. Kinnard notes, however, that U.S. generals considered one ARVN officer, Lt. Gen. Ngo Quang Truong, as highly competent; see *War Managers*, p. 86. The ARVN battalion deployed to Khe Sanh was even under strength when it arrived; Shore, *Battle for Khe Sanh*, p. 51.

seemed to believe that it made military sense for the communists to attempt to damage the strongest allied units; they could not reduce allied offensive power significantly by attacking ARVN, which was assigned a defensive mission. A preferred strategy influenced their beliefs; the Americans apparently did not anticipate that the communists would attempt to exploit allied weaknesses and not directly confront allied strengths.

Another belief that originated in U.S. strategy, one widely shared by commanders and intelligence officers at MACV, was that Westmoreland's strategy was working. Indeed, there is agreement among students of the war that a feeling of optimism prevailed in Saigon and Washington during the fall of 1967. Even though there was ample evidence that the shield objective was slowly being realized by mid-1967—Westmoreland noted in July that "we have pushed the enemy further and further back into the jungles"—this optimism primarily flowed from a belief that the attrition objectives were being fulfilled.[69] When the objective of killing VC/NVA troops at "a rate as high as their capability to put men into the field" was established at the February 1966 Honolulu conference, analysts were presented with the problem of determining when this objective had been realized. Ultimately, they relied on two types of evidence to measure progress in meeting the attrition objective: they watched the morale of enemy combat units and developments in communist personnel replacement policies, and they monitored the ratio of enemy losses to the rate of North Vietnamese infiltration and VC recruitment in South Vietnam, a practice that relied on the infamous and unreliable "body count." The point at which enemy losses were equal to the number of replacements available was termed the "crossover point," a juncture at which the attrition objective would be fulfilled. By mid-1967, analysts at MACV concluded that this objective had been realized.[70]

[69]Westmoreland quoted in "7/13/67 WCW/LBJ Press Conference," in *Westmoreland v. CBS*, 409A, p. 2. See Gelb, *Irony of Vietnam*, pp. 315–371; Summers, *On Strategy*, pp. 154–155; Palmer, *Summons*, p. 203; Oberdorfer, *Tet*, p. 99; Karnow, *Vietnam*, p. 543; Kinnard, *War Managers*, p. 76; Betts, "Strategic Surprise for War Termination," pp. 159, 161; Stanton, *Rise and Fall*, p. 140; and Lung, *General Offensives*, p. 8. Members of the CIA and Secretary of Defense McNamara were not as optimistic as MACV; see Laqueur, *World of Secrets*, p. 182; Schandler, *Unmaking of a President*, pp. 64–65; Johnson, *Vantage Point*, pp. 372–378; and "Criles Notes on Robert McNamara" (off-the-record meeting 16 June 1981), in *Westmoreland v. CBS*, exhibit 33, p. 2.

[70]*Westmoreland v. CBS*, exhibit 215D; Krepinevich, *Army*, pp. 202–205; Palmer, *25-Year War*, pp. 164–165; Herring, *America's Longest War*, pp. 153–154; Lewy, *America in Vietnam*, pp. 78–82; Lomperis, *War Everyone Lost*, pp. 70–71; and Kinnard, *War Managers*, pp. 72–75. For a defense of the body count, see Ewell and Hunt, *Sharpening the Combat Edge*, pp. 227–228. For a definition of the crossover point, see Graham's testimony in House Select Committee on Intelligence, *U.S. Intelligence Agencies and Activities*, p. 1683.

An early indication of the realization of the attrition objective was provided by an August 1966 CIA report entitled "The Vietnamese Communists Will to Persist." Not only were VC forces suffering morale problems, according to the study, they were also experiencing difficulty replacing losses and had begun to use North Vietnamese soldiers as replacements in VC units. The CIA also predicted that the presence of North Vietnamese among VC units dominated by southerners would lead to tensions between the two groups. Once these trends were identified in the CIA report, analysts and officers continued to compile evidence to demonstrate their acceleration and, by implication, the increasing impact of the attrition strategy. A rise in the number of enemy deserters and defectors in late 1966, for example, was seen as evidence of a further deterioration in enemy morale. In February 1967, CICV analysts identified an enemy effort to counteract the allied defection program as a clear sign that the enemy was concerned about deteriorating morale and defections. CICV analysts reported in April 1967 that critical morale problems existed in some enemy units. They claimed that the enemy was even considering the deactivation of the VC V25 Battalion because of morale problems caused by heavy losses, the death of the battalion commander, and the need for replacements in other VC units. The commander of III MAF also called attention to the manpower problem faced by VC units in I CTZ during June 1967 when he reported that in some areas of South Vietnam women consitituted 29 percent of the VC guerrilla force.[71]

Numerical measurements formed the most important indicator of progress in the attrition strategy. Here the notion of a crossover point was crucial. Even though Admiral Sharp stated in July 1966 that the attrition goal established at the Honolulu conference could not be achieved during 1966, Ambassador Lodge claimed on 31 August 1966 that the crossover point had been reached. In support of his argument that U.S. forces should take on a greater share of the pacification effort, Lodge claimed that Westmoreland had stated that the U.S. had "reached a crossover point where the rate of enemy losses equals the rate of infiltration." In a 28 February 1967 memorandum to the president, Robert Komer asserted that allied forces had reached the crossover point. During the Guam conference of 20–21 March 1967, Westmoreland was less sanguine about reaching the crossover point. He did, however, claim that the enemy's losses would soon exceed infiltration and replacement rates.[72]

---

[71]*Westmoreland v. CBS*, exhibits 217, pp. 5, 13; 224; *PERINTREP*, February 1967, p. 34; April 1967, p. A-29; and *Command History 1967*, 1:53.
[72]*Pentagon Papers, Gravel*, 4:322, 390; *Pentagon Papers, Times*, p. 555. CINCPAC did not

Starting in April 1967, U.S. officers and CICV analysts began to assert that the crossover point had been attained. In a 28 April meeting with the president, Westmoreland stated that the crossover point had been reached in areas other than the two northern provinces. In June 1967, MACV analysts claimed that the crossover point had been reached throughout South Vietnam. In the "Crossover Memo of June 1967," Col. Daniel Graham, an analyst in the order-of-battle section at MACV J-2, stated that the monthly infiltration rate had dropped to 6,000–7,000 men per month, and that VC recruitment had dropped to 3,500 per month. At these rates, the enemy was losing men faster than they could be replaced. Graham's memo formed the basis of the June measurement of progress report, which stated that the crossover point had been reached. In contrast, during May 1967, CIA analysts stated that the crossover point had not yet been attained.[73]

In effect, by June 1967 U.S. commanders believed that they had reached the crossover point, thereby fulfilling the attrition goals established in February 1966. By definition, the attrition objective had been realized; by implication, the allies were now starting to win the war. And once the crossover point had been reached, it was seemingly assumed that the communists could never tip the infiltration–loss ratio again in their favor (as we see in the following chapters). The conclusion that the crossover point had been attained not only created an atmosphere of optimism in Saigon and Washington but also made commanders and analysts very slow to call attention to evidence of increased enemy infiltration prior to the Tet offensive.[74]

---

think that this goal could be achieved in 1966 because of the enemy's demonstrated ability to increase its forces despite losses; see message from CINCPAC 112330Z, Jul. 1966, in *Command History 1966*, p. 347.

[73]*Pentagon Papers, Times*, p. 568; Thies, *When Governments Collide*, pp. 172–173; "Adams' William Westmoreland Chronology," "Adams' James Meacham Chronology," and "Monograph by Allen 'Indochina Wars—1950–1975'," in *Westmoreland v. CBS*, exhibits 64, pp. 11–12; 58, p. 39; 313, p. 313; see also Daniel O. Graham's testimony in House Select Committee on Intelligence, *U.S. Intelligence Agencies and Activities*, p. 1682; Daniel Graham, Oral History I, 24 May 1982, pp. 7–9, Oral History II, 8 November 1982, pp. 5–6, LBJ Library; and Kinnard *War Managers*, pp. 69–70. The MACV measurement of progress report was issued on a monthly basis by MACV J-3 and was based on selected data on VC personnel and weapons losses; VC initiated incidents; the number of defectors by CTZ; and order of battle data on combat, support, irregular, and political personnel by CTZ. This report was distributed to national agencies, higher and lateral commands, subordinate MACV commands, and others; see "Report of the Honolulu Conference to Standardize Methods for Developing and Presenting Statistics on Order of Battle, Infiltration Trends and Estimates," in *Westmoreland v. CBS*, exhibit 227, p. C-4. For the May 1967 CIA claim that the crossover point had not yet been reached, see *Westmoreland v. CBS*, exhibit 237, p. 7.

[74]U.S. commanders and analysts continued to believe that they had reached the crossover point until the Tet offensive, see Senate Committee on Foreign Relations, *Stalemate in Vietnam*, p. 9.

Beliefs Based on Superior Allied Information

In comparison to their communist adversaries, U.S. intelligence analysts and officers possessed superior information about the priorities of allied military initiatives and the political situation in South Vietnam. During the fall of 1967, Americans were busily constructing an antiinfiltration barrier across South Vietnam and Laos. Construction timetables and the technology used in the barrier were highly classified. Americans also possessed an accurate assessment of the sympathies of most of the South Vietnamese urban population. But this superior information was misused in efforts to anticipate the main enemy thrust of the 1967 winter-spring campaign. U.S. analysts and officers tended to interpret enemy behavior and informtion about communist intentions using the information they alone possessed about the status of the allied war effort.

The Barrier

The infiltration of men and supplies from North Vietnam through Laos and across the DMZ was a problem for the allies throughout the war. By early 1966, approximately fifteen battalion-equivalents per month were entering South Vietnam, an increase from about two per month in late 1964. As early as April 1965, a U.S. Army study had examined the requirements needed to seal off South Vietnam. The study, commissioned by General Johnson, the army chief of staff, reported that the project would require over three army divisions, 18,000 engineer troops, and large numbers of indigenous laborers. Even then, the communists might circumvent this seal by pushing their infiltration routes farther to the west into Thailand. Enthusiasm for the barrier concept was cooled by this initial study, but the findings of the Jason Summer Study Group released in September 1965 increased interest in the idea. The Jason Group reported that bombing North Vietnam had little effect on infiltration and that an antiinfiltration barrier would be more effective in blocking the flow of men and material into South Vietnam. The barrier system proposed by the Jason Group was ultimately adopted, but only after several other systems were considered.[75]

[75]"Annex A—The Anti-infiltration Barrier," in *Command History 1967*, 3:1070; Krepinevich, *Army*, pp. 144–145; Komer, *Bureaucracy*, p. 53; Mark Clodfelter, *The Limits of Air Power: The American Bombing of North Vietnam* (New York, 1989), pp. 99–100; and *Pentagon Papers, Gravel*, 4:335. The Jason Group was made up of scientists from the academic community in Cambridge, Mass.; see Gregg Herken, *Counsels of War* (New York, 1985), pp. 60–61, 210–212.

During 1966, Westmoreland and Sharp were asked to comment on several barrier proposals. In March 1966, the Joint Chiefs of Staff asked for Sharp's views on constructing a barrier from the South China Sea to Thailand. Deputy Ambassador Porter asked Westmoreland in April 1966 to comment on a plan to construct a barrier from Saigon west through Hau Nghia province to the nearest point along the Cambodian border. In September, the Joint Chiefs asked Sharp and Westmoreland about the creation of an air-supported barrier system across infiltration routes in Laos and the DMZ. In response to each of these proposals, Westmoreland and Sharp expressed strong reservations. They stated repeatedly that the construction and garrisoning of a barrier would consume an inordinate amount of manpower and material, overburden logistical capabilities, and tie down large numbers of U.S. units in static defensive positions, providing the enemy a free reign throughout the rest of South Vietnam.[76]

The barrier project gained momentum after Secretary of Defense McNamara created Joint Task Force 728, headed by Lt. Gen. Alfred D. Starbird. The task force's mission was to "provide an infiltration interdiction system, to stop (or at a minimum to substantially reduce) the flow of men and supplies from North to South Vietnam."[77] In an October 1966 meeting in South Vietnam, Westmoreland told McNamara that he would support the construction of a ground barrier across South Vietnam and an air-supported barrier across Laos on the condition that forces beyond those needed for other MACV requirements be provided for barrier construction and manning. When the Joint Chiefs of Staff informed Sharp and Westmoreland in November 1966 that additional forces for the barrier (Project Practice Nine) would not be forthcoming, Westmoreland lodged his last complaint against the endeavor: "I am unable to concur in meeting all Practice Nine requirements from approved in-country assets alone. I consider it essential that an inflexible time schedule be avoided, that a realistic approach be taken toward construction of a physical barrier consistent with the overall MACV mission, and that freedom of action by the commander in the field be preserved."[78]

By the end of the year, the Starbird task force and MACV were busy developing plans for a barrier stretching along the DMZ and through Laos. On 26 January 1967, Westmoreland completed the MACV Practice Nine requirements plan. The planned barrier submitted to the Joint Chiefs in February would consist of a series of

---

[76]"Annex A—The Anti-infiltration Barrier," in *Command History 1967*, 3:1071–1073.
[77]SECDEF to DIR JTF 728, 15 Sept. 1966, in *Command History 1967*, 3:1073.
[78]COMUSMACV to CINCPAC, 211315Z, Nov. 1966, in *Command History 1967*, 3:1075.

strong points and fortified bases along the DMZ that would be constructed and manned by combat troops. These fortifications would occupy key terrain features and serve as both patrol and fire support bases. Barbed wire and mine field obstacles would be laid in front of the strong points to channel enemy movements. A network of seismic, infrared, and acoustic detectors, xenon searchlights, and ground radar would be employed to conduct surveillance of likely infiltration routes. After all civilians had been removed from the vicinity of this obstacle system, artillery and naval gunfire could quickly attack enemy concentrations.[79]

On 11 March, Westmoreland published the MACV Practice Nine air-supported antiinfiltration plan, which was intended to limit infiltration in an area extending west of the strong point obstacle system through Laos to the Thai border. The plan described the second component of the barrier (eventually given the codename Muscle Shoals): an antivehicular system (eventually given the codename Mud River) and an antipersonnel system (eventually given the codename Dump Truck). Air-emplaced acoustic sensors would be dropped along potential vehicular routes. Air-delivered mines would be used to damage vehicles and halt enemy traffic detected in areas that could be easily attacked. Troop movements would be detected and impeded by air-implanted seismic and acoustic sensors and two types of Gravel minelets. The larger version of the minelet would cause severe injury, thereby impeding and channeling enemy infiltration. The smaller minelet would cause a loud explosion that would be detected by acoustic sensors in the area; large enemy troop concentrations could then be attacked by air.[80]

By the end of April 1967, the barrier had progressed significantly. Direct supervision of barrier construction was turned over to III MAF, and U.S. Marine and ARVN units had actually started to work on the project. A list of materials needed for barrier construction and a schedule for their delivery was completed by mid-April. Military and political representatives of the Saigon regime were informed about the construction of the strong point obstacle system on 17 March, but they were not told about the air-supported antiinfiltration barrier that was to be created in Laos. In terms of secrecy, the decision not to inform the South Vietnamese about the extension of the barrier into Laos was appropriate. During a press conference at the Bien Hoa air-

[79]"Annex A—The Anti-infiltration Barrier," in *Command History 1967*, 3:1073–1077, 1090–1091; Pearson, *War in the Northern Provinces*, pp. 21–24; Brewin and Shaw, *Vietnam on Trial*, pp. 139–146; and Ewell and Hunt, *Sharpening the Combat Edge*, p. 97.
[80]"Annex A—The Anti-infiltration Barrier," in *Command History 1967*, 3:1078, 1103–1107; and Nalty, *Air Power*, pp. 90–94.

base on 15 April 1967, Premier Ky stated that the allies intended to build a defense perimeter south of the DMZ. Ky's statement probably constituted the first public admission that the barrier was actually being constructed. By the time of Secretary of Defense McNamara's trip to Saigon in July, barrier construction had gained significant momentum. Westmoreland and the commander of III MAF had overcome a major obstacle: the floodplain east of Gio Linh. Vegetation around the strong points of Gio Linh and Con Thien had been cleared out to a radius of 500 meters, and a 600-meter-wide strip had been cleared between the two strong points and eastward to the floodplain. At the same time, roads connecting the strong points were being built, and Routes 1, 9, and 561 were upgraded. McNamara was told that the installation of obstacles in the strip between Gio Linh and Con Thien would begin during September, and that the barrier between Con Thien and the floodplain would probably be operational by 1 November. Work on the Muscle Shoals portion of the barrier was also well under way. Aircraft for sensor delivery and monitoring and helicopters for the implacement of more delicate components were being readied to conduct initial operations by 1 November. Airbases and navigational aids in Thailand were upgraded to support air operations. Plans for the creation of thirty-four Prairie Fire Spike teams, composed of three U.S. NCOs and nine indigenous personnel, had been formulated. Operating along likely infiltration routes, these teams would monitor infiltration, call in air strikes, and detect penetrations of the system. It was also hoped that they could emplace about fifty sensors per month with pinpoint accuracy.[81]

As the following chapters show, plans for the November completion of the strong point obstacle system were ruined by enemy activity during the late summer and early fall of 1967. Because of the importance they placed on the barrier, U.S. officials interpreted this enemy activity as a deliberate effort to prevent the completion of the Practice Nine project. Alternative explanations—that the communists were pursuing their strategy of strategic mobility by attempting to lure U.S. forces away from the cities of the south, for example—went unexamined. Moreover, even though increased enemy activity undermined completion of the project, Westmoreland apparently believed that the work already completed on the system improved U.S. defenses along the DMZ—in other words, that he was relatively well prepared to meet a major attack against the outposts dotting the partially completed portions of the barrier. Again, then, U.S. com-

[81]"Annex A—The Anti-infiltration Barrier," in *Command History 1967*, 3:1087–1094, 1106–1108.

manders expected the main thrust of the 1967 winter-spring offensive to be directed against an allied military initiative they considered to be important and relatively well prepared.

The South Vietnamese Urban Population

The question of whether the communists believed their own propaganda plagued intelligence analysts throughout the war. The problem was made all the more difficult by evidence that indicated that communist propaganda accurately reflected the enemy's plans and objectives. In plans recorded in captured enemy notebooks and documents, for example, communist commanders called for an increase in the strength of VC guerrillas and self-defense forces to about 300,000 in 1965 and 1966. Although General McChristian, the MACV J-2 at the time, dismissed these plans as internal propaganda, he did note that the communist figure of 180,000 for the current strength of the VC guerrilla and self-defense forces was close to the 198,000 estimated by the CICV. Intelligence analysts also realized that the communists were careful in selecting the themes they chose to emphasize. In August 1966, CIA analysts pointed out that, even though North Vietnamese optimism about their prospects peaked in 1965, they still refrained in their statements from tying victory to a definite calendar date. Finally, analysts recognized that the communists put tremendous effort into their propaganda activities. The exploits of VC armed propaganda teams, which combined coercion with simple dramatic sketches, were well known. In fact, these VC propaganda teams apparently served as a model for allied Go Team, County Fair, and Hamlet Festival operations in which allied personnel entered a hamlet and provided food, agricultural information, entertainment, medical care, and propaganda while at the same time interrogating suspects and recruiting potential informants.[82]

The conduct and content of allied propaganda could also have provided intelligence analysts with some insights into the relationship between enemy propaganda and actual communist plans and objectives. Analysts were highly familiar with allied propaganda because they often helped to identify areas of enemy weakness and to formulate propaganda themes. The allies worked hard on these psychological warfare activities: by 1967 they could produce 400 million propaganda leaflets per month. Of particular interest is an unusually large

---

[82]*Westmoreland v. CBS*, exhibits 229; 217, p. 7; Pike, *Viet Cong*, pp. 126–132; *PERIN-TREP*, May 1967, p. 37; and *Handbook for Military Support of Pacification*, pp. 51–52, B1–B3.

propaganda campaign undertaken in January 1967; 59 million leaflets were dropped over North Vietnam and the Ho Chi Minh Trail. The purpose of the operation was to test the effectiveness of allied propaganda against a suspected enemy weakness, the morale of infiltrators experiencing the rigors of the trail for the first time. In the wake of the campaign, defector and POW interrogations revealed that the propaganda did have a detrimental effect on NVA morale. One leaflet in particular, "A North Vietnamese Soldier's Poem to His Mother," was especially effective. Analysts could have noted that the poem reflected their beliefs about the rigors faced by infiltrators and was effective because it accurately identified an enemy weakness and exploited it in a way that deeply affected NVA soldiers.[83]

The enemy's habitual public exaggeration of the number of casualties and defeats inflicted on allied forces greatly complicated intelligence analyses of fact and fantasy in communist propaganda. In the first nine months of 1966, for example, VC propaganda claimed that 88,000 Americans had been killed, even though this figure was over one-quarter of the 311,000 U.S. troops in South Vietnam at the time. After Operation Junction City, the communists claimed that 13,500 allied troops had been killed; 282 allied soldiers actually died during the operation. The North Vietnamese claimed that 3,500 allied troops had been killed, wounded, or captured in the battle of Dak To and that the "U.S. Para Brigade 173" had been put out of action. In reality, by the end of November 1967, 362 allied soldiers had been killed in the fighting around Dak To. Did these exaggerated claims, which were also reflected in secret enemy documents captured by the allies, represent actual communist perceptions of developments in the south?[84] On the one hand, the nonexistent casualties and victories could be an effort to insulate the North Vietnamese population and southern cadres from the truth about the decline in communist military fortunes. On the other hand, it was possible that the North Vietnamese had fallen victim to erroneous casualty and victory reports turned in by communist commanders and cadres in South Vietnam. CICV analysts captured this problem in a June 1967 report: "The North Vietnamese government leans heavily on the psychological ad-

[83]*Command History 1967*, 2:633, 657, 659; and *Westmoreland v. CBS*, exhibit 217, p. V1–7.

[84]Pike, *Viet Cong*, pp. 103–104; *Command History 1967*, 2:655; *Command History 1967*, 1:379, 390; "The P.L.A.F. Control Tan Canh Urban Centre, Overrun the Puppet 'Special Forces' Base Camp, and Pound Nearly All Enemy's Bases in Dak To Region," *Vietnam Courier*, 4 December 1967, pp. 1, 7. The U.S. 4th Infantry Division and the 173d Airborne Brigade did, however, suffer serious casualties in the fighting around Dak To; see Stanton, *Rise and Fall*, p. 178.

vantage it can derive through the use of inflated statistics, war crimes charges, and boasts of victory. . . . Inflated reports of U.S. plane losses and the alleged result of dedication to the anti-U.S. national survival struggle serve to bolster the morale of the people. The number of U.S. planes downed, although grossly exaggerated in enemy broadcasts, is undoubtedly a factor accounting for any optimism the enemy might have in the air war."[85]

Even though analysts recognized that the communist leadership might believe some of the exaggerated claims made in their propaganda, they never attempted to explore fully this phenomenon. Perhaps commanders and analysts were unwilling to call into question the validity of some of the methods they used to measure progress in the war. The body count, for example, would not have stood up to close scrutiny. Moreover, by mid-1967, U.S. analysts and commanders believed that they were winning the war. To entertain seriously the possibility that the communist leadership still believed that they were winning the war would have increased the difficulty of predicting enemy activity. Instead of predicting how the communists would react to allied initiatives, analysts would again have to anticipate the offensive operations of opponents who did not believe that they had lost the initiative. By raising the possibility that the communists still believed that they were winning the war, the analysts would have raised questions about the accuracy of indicators that demonstrated that the allies were prevailing in the struggle. Analysts and commanders might be called before their superiors to explain how the enemy could still believe that they were winning the war, given that the agreed measures of progress indicated otherwise.[86]

In hindsight it is apparent that communist calls for a general upris-

---

[85]Quotation from *PERINTREP*, June 1967, p. 32. For a discussion of the difficulties posed by the inflated claims made in enemy propaganda, see *Command History 1967*, 1:653–654. In an August 1966 report, CIA analysts also referred in passing to the problem of inflated claims; see *Westmoreland v. CBS*, exhibit 217, p. ix-5.

[86]A March 1967 incident illustrates some of the problems that might have been raised by a thorough examination of communist perceptions of their own propaganda. Throughout 1966, the measures used by MACV showed a steady decrease in the number of large-scale enemy-initiated incidents. Improvements in intelligence techniques in early 1967 led MACV analysts to revise the way they counted large-scale enemy-initiated incidents. After nearly a year of reporting that large-scale attacks were decreasing in number, analysts reported that the number of incidents had been slowly increasing throughout 1966 and that there had been a sharp increase in the number of incidents in January 1967. This conclusion prompted a sharp response from Gen. Earle G. Wheeler, chairman of the Joint Chiefs of Staff: "I cannot go to the President and tell him that, contrary to my reports and those of the other Chiefs as to progress of the war in which we have laid great stress upon the thesis you have seized the initiative from the enemy, the situation is such that we are not sure who has the initiative"; see "Cable, 3/11/67 from Wheeler to Westmoreland," in *Westmoreland v. CBS*, exhibit 233, p. 5.

ing issued before the Tet offensive were not propaganda. The North Vietnamese leadership believed that conditions in South Vietnamese urban areas were ripe for a popular revolt against the Saigon regime. Since the concept of the general uprising, the Vietnamese contribution to the strategy of people's war, was crucial in their strategy, the North Vietnamese were receptive to reports that the south was ready to revolt. Thus the Hanoi leadership fell victim to the exaggerated reports of success turned in by cadres and commanders fighting in the south. "They [the communists] obviously expected a massive uprising to accompany their Tet offensive," according to Col. Daniel Graham, "Perhaps they . . . were taken in by VC documents inflating their strength."[87]

Still, intelligence analysts and commanders dismissed calls for a general uprising during the Tet holidays as propaganda. "Commanders and intelligence officers," according to U.S. government investigators, "saw his [the enemy's] generalized calls for a 'general uprising' as merely exhortatory, and not as a blueprint for what was to follow." U.S. commanders and analysts had many sources of information about the southern population, not the least of which were the contacts with their ARVN counterparts, and this accurate information indicated that the South Vietnamese population would not revolt in support of the communists. They also believed that the communists had lost the offensive capability needed for such an endeavor to stand even a marginal chance of success. The combination of accurate information about public sentiment in the south and the belief that the communists lacked the military capability to spark a general uprising led analysts and commanders to estimate that an attack on southern cities was extremely unlikely. General Davidson, MACV J-2 at the time of the Tet offensive, told Westmoreland, "Even had I known exactly what was to take place, it was so preposterous that I probably would have been unable to sell it to anybody."[88]

[87]Graham quotation from House Select Committee on Intelligence, *U.S. Intelligence Agencies and Activities*, p. 1655. Graham also detailed instances of communist exaggerations: "There was a strong tendency in all VC documents to their superiors to overstate success. For instance, VC commanders would report numbers of U.S. and Allied armored personnel carriers destroyed in districts and provinces where we had no armored personnel carriers"; see p. 1654. For assertions that the North Vietnamese fell victim to the exaggerated reports turned in by cadres and commanders in the south, see Lomperis, *War Everyone Lost*, pp. 80–81; Vien and Khuyen, *Reflections on the Vietnam War*, p. 86; Race, *War Comes to Long An*, p. 270; and Lung, *General Offensives*, p. 156. North Vietnamese leaders were actually more optimistic about the current military situation and the prospects for eventual victory then their southern counterparts; see Pike, *Viet Cong*, p. 326.

[88]House Select Committee on Intelligence, *U.S. Intelligence Agencies and Activities*, 1996–1997; Sharp and Westmoreland, *Report*, p. 135; Palmer, *25-Year War*, pp. 77–78;

[127]

Although an accurate prediction of the Tet attacks on the cities of the south was written by Joseph Hovey, a CIA analyst stationed in Saigon, even Hovey and his CIA colleagues found their own analysis hard to believe. Commenting on his report, which was passed on to Westmoreland and eventually to President Johnson on 15 December 1967, Hovey stated: "We received a request from the special assistant to the President, Mr. Rostow, asking what these reports of an impending attack meant. What was behind them? Now, within the station there was a great deal of uncertainty about this because we couldn't really believe that the enemy was serious when they were talking about this." Skepticism also was pervasive at the White House. According to Brig. Gen. Robert Ginsburgh, who assisted Walt Rostow in providing intelligence to President Johnson before and during the Tet offensive, "We probably did not pay sufficient credence to . . . the element of their campagn which talked about an uprising in the cities. We paid less attention . . . than we should have probably because it didn't look like such a campaign would be effective."[89]

In sum, intelligence analysts and commanders had accurate information about the enemy's Tet objectives, but these objectives appeared unrealistic in light of information about the mood of the South Vietnamese population and allied beliefs about the status of communist forces. A failure to anticipate the possibility of enemy miscalculation had confounded intelligence analysts. As a result, they dismissed communist calls for a general uprising as propaganda. In a sense, then, the calls for a general uprising detected by the allies inadvertently contributed to the deception campaign launched by the communists before the offensive.[90]

---

and Betts, "Strategic Surprise for War Termination," p. 161. American commanders and intelligence analysts often turned to the estimates of enemy intentions produced by their South Vietnamese counterparts, their in-house experts on the enemy. In fact, South Vietnamese behavior was sometimes used to explain enemy behavior. In an April 1967 memorandum to Robert Komer, George Carver stated that the VC and ARVN desertion problems stemmed from similar causes; see *Westmoreland v. CBS*, exhibit 235, p. 2. In any event, many in ARVN intelligence did not believe or act as if the communists would attack the cities of the south in an effort to spark a general uprising; see Lung, *General Offensives*, pp. 37–38. Davidson quoted in Westmoreland, *Soldier*, p. 321.

[89]Quote from "Joseph Hovey Interview Transcript" (with George Crile, 27 January 1981), in *Westmoreland v. CBS*, exhibit 3, p. 8; see also exhibit 34C, p. 1; and Betts, "Strategic Surprise for War Termination," p. 162. Ginsburgh quoted in Nalty, *Air Power*, p. 29.

[90]For a similar incident, see Raymond Garthoff, *Reflections on the Cuban Missile Crisis* (Washington, D.C., 1989), p. 157.

As officers and analysts received information about the impending 1967 winter-spring campaign, they compared the developing situation to previous military events in an effort to estimate the likely course of the upcoming offensive. Three incidents were used at various times to describe the 1967 situation: the Battle of the Bulge, the siege at Dien Bien Phu; and the Chinese intervention in the Korean war.

The Battle of the Bulge

The Battle of the Bulge was used for the first time by an American to explain the situation facing the allies in Vietnam in late 1967. Gen. Earle G. Wheeler, chairman of the Joint Chiefs of Staff, told the Detroit Economic Club, on 18 December "As far as the future is concerned . . . I must point out that the North Vietnamese are not yet at the end of their military rope. Although North Vietnam—as well as the Vietcong—is feeling a manpower pinch, they still have the ability to send additional troops to the south. Thus, there is still some heavy fighting ahead—it is entirely possible that there may be a communist thrust similar to the desperate effort of the Germans in the Battle of the Bulge in World War II."[91]

The analogy itself was drawn from the 16 December 1944 German attack in the Ardennes, an event that was indelibly imprinted in the minds of the senior U.S. Army commanders in Vietnam. Westmoreland, for example, was serving with the 9th Infantry Division, part of the U.S. First Army that bore the brunt of the offensive. General Creighton Abrams, deputy commander of MACV, was in command of the armored column that relieved the encircled 101st Airborne Division that was guarding the key crossroads near the town of Bastogne.[92]

It is easy to reconstruct the analogy as it would have appeared to U.S. commanders on the eve of the Tet offensive. Following the Nor-

[91]Wheeler, 18 December 1967 address to Detroit Economic Club quoted in Peter Braestrup, *Big Story* (Boulder, Colo., 1977), 1:60.

[92]Westmoreland served on the northern "shoulder" of the German salient; see Westmoreland, *Soldier*, pp. 18–19; and Hugh M. Cole, *The Ardennes: Battle of the Bulge* (Washington, D.C., 1965), p. 134. Abrams was in command of the 37th Tank Battalion of the 4th Armored Division; see John S. D. Eisenhower, *The Bitter Woods* (New York, 1969), p. 342. For analyses that compare the Tet offensive to the Battle of the Bulge, see Karnow, *Vietnam*, p. 535; and Pearson, *War in the Northern Provinces*, p. 96. For arguments that the Ardennes and Tet offensives are not similar, see Herring, *America's Longest War*, p. 184; and Brodie, "Tet Offensive," pp. 332–333.

mandy invasion, Nazi forces had been pushed back to the German border. Surveying the situation in early December 1944, allied commanders and intelligence analysts believed that the Nazi war machine had lost its offensive capability. German forces had suffered terrific losses in men and equipment and were encountering growing morale, desertion, and manpower problems. In the weeks preceding the Ardennes offensive, allied officers did voice concerns about one area of their line: the VIII Corps sector under the control of the U.S. First Army. Since it was the quietest portion of the front, the area was used to train and rest units. On 16 December, the 140-kilometer sector along the Ardennes forest was held by two recently arrived infantry divisions, a newly arrived armored division, and two veteran divisions recuperating after heavy fighting. Concerns about the Ardennes sector, however, paled in comparison to the offensive-mindedness of intelligence analysts and commanders as they prepared for dual thrusts into Germany. The purpose of the Germans' Ardennes offensive was to drive a wedge between allied forces, to capture the port of Antwerp, a key allied logistics facility, and to wreck the alliance by destroying British and Canadian forces, the weaker members of the alliance, to the north of the salient created by the German attack. The Germans began forming the nucleus of an assault army in September 1944. By paying meticulous attention to secrecy and deception, nineteen German divisions avoided detection as they moved into positions opposite VIII Corps. The offensive caught the allied command by complete surprise. VIII Corps crumbled before the Nazi onslaught, a development that was partially concealed from the public by censorship. At its height, the German offensive, aided by inclement weather that temporarily grounded allied air forces, drove an approximately 65-kilometer-wide wedge 100 kilometers behind the VIII Corps line.[93]

In the end, the allies rallied to meet the situation. The combination of fierce fighting and air power contained and then eliminated the salient in the allied line. The Ardennes offensive surprised allied commanders because it was daring in light of actual German resources; the paucity of German resources in turn doomed the initiative to failure. Even though some historians have argued that the Ardennes offensive lengthened the war by a few weeks, it is possible that the

---

[93]Cole, *Ardennes*, passim; Eisenhower, *Bitter Woods*, passim; Hanson Baldwin, *Battles Lost and Won* (New York, 1966), pp. 315–367; David Eisenhower, *Eisenhower at War, 1943–1945* (New York, 1987), pp. 554–661; Omar N. Bradley, *A Soldier's Story* (New York, 1951), pp. 447–495; and Dwight D. Eisenhower, *Crusade in Europe* (New York, 1948), pp. 337–365.

irreplaceable losses suffered by the Germans during the battle actually shortened the war.

Comparing the Battle of the Bulge to the situation in Vietnam in late 1967 should have been, on balance, more of a help than a hindrance to allied commanders. Both offensives were prompted by the opponent's realization that the capacity to influence the war through offensive action was rapidly waning and that only an all-out attack could reverse the situation. Before the Ardennes offensive, the allies believed that the Germans had lost the initiative. They were subsequently surprised by the scope of the offensive, the product of weeks of German effort to generate forces. This could have served as a warning to those who believed that the communists had also lost the initiative in 1967. The observed decrease in communist activity could have been interpreted as evidence of an enemy effort to generate forces for an upcoming offensive. Moreover, German secrecy and deception had facilitated the surprise inflicted on the allies, and the same possibility could have been clear in Vietnam. And, the Germans struck not only at a weak point in the allied line but also along the seam that divided U.S. and Anglo-Canadian forces. The Ardennes analogy could have alerted the allies to the possibility that the main enemy blow would fall not against the relatively well-prepared defensive positions along the DMZ but instead against the weakest member of the alliance, the South Vietnamese. U.S. commanders might also have noted that censorship no longer shielded the American public from the grim initial setbacks that often follow a major enemy offensive. Finally, the Ardennes analogy illustrated that desperate opponents can achieve surprise by reaching for overly ambitious objectives, even though they may fail in the effort.

Although most U.S. officers began to draw specific analogies to the Battle of the Bulge only after the Tet attacks, they did describe the situation before the offensive in terms reminiscent of the Ardennes offensive. They selectively applied the analogy, however, by emphasizing the fact that the communists had lost the initiative and might attempt to launch an all-out offensive with their remaining forces in order to stop the further deterioration of their military position. In a 20 December cable to General Wheeler, for example, Westmoreland stated:

> The enemy has already made a crucial decision concerning the conduct of the war. In late September, the enemy decided that prolongation of his past policies for conducting the war would lead to his defeat, and that he would have to make a major effort to reverse this downward trend. The

enemy was forced to this grave decision by the deterioration of his position over the last six months, and a realization that the trends were running against him. . . . His decision therefore was to undertake an intensified countrywide effort, perhaps a maximum effort, over a relatively short period.

Westmoreland's remark apparently reached the president, who told the Australian cabinet on 21 December and even the pope on 23 December that the North Vietnamese were under great pressure and would employ "kamikaze" tactics to gain a victory. Even though Johnson described the situation with a different analogy, he highlighted the suicidal desperation that motivated communist behavior, the aspect of the Battle of the Bulge emphasized by senior officers.[94]

Wheeler and Westmoreland probably focused on this feature of the Battle of the Bulge because it complemented their belief that the enemy's military situation was deteriorating. The analogy was able to reconcile indications of increasing enemy activity with the belief that the communists were in dire straits. A "go-for-broke" offensive would mark the beginning of the end for communist forces, just as it started the final collapse of the Nazi war machine. A recognition of the more unpleasant aspects of the analogy, however, would have better served the allied cause. But the unpleasant aspects were ignored because they contradicted beliefs about the absence of allied vulnerabilities that could be exploited by the communists. References to the Ardennes offensive were soon superseded by a Dien Bien Phu analogy, which was applied directly to the situation at Khe Sanh. Yet, in the aftermath of the first wave of the Tet attacks, Westmoreland again began to rely on some of the more favorable aspects of the Ardennes analogy to describe the Tet attacks.[95]

[94]Westmoreland cable to Wheeler quoted in Braestrup, *Big Story*, 1:61. Westmoreland believes that his 20 December cable influenced Johnson's remarks to the Australian cabinet; see Westmoreland, *Soldier*, p. 314. General Davidson, MACV J-2, seconds Westmoreland's observation; see Davidson, Oral History I, p. 41. Walt Rostow, in an interview with the author on 7 January 1988, indicated that Johnson, in using the phrase "kamikaze attacks," was suggesting that the communists intended to risk all in a major offensive. Years after the war, Oberdorfer noted that the term "go for broke" was used to describe enemy intentions on the eve of the offensive; see Don Oberdorfer, Oral History II, interviewed by Ted Gittinger, 17 September 1981, p. 10, LBJ Library. For Johnson's remarks, see Johnson, *Vantage Point*, p. 379; "President's Meeting with Pope" (Dec. 23, 1967) from J. Valenti's Notes, Doc. 39, Meeting Notes File Box 2, Folder: 23 December 67 Meeting with the Pope, LBJ Library; and Larry Berman, *Lyndon Johnson's War* (New York, 1989), pp. 124–137.

[95]In an interview with an Associated Press correspondent on 25 February 1968, Westmoreland stated, "I liken the recent Tet offensive by the leadership in Hanoi to the Battle of the Bulge in World War II. By committing a large share of his communist forces to a major offensive, he achieved some tactical surprise." In a background brief-

Dien Bien Phu

Unlike the Battle of the Bulge, Dien Bien Phu exerted a powerful influence on intelligence analysts and commanders more than a year before the onset of the Tet attacks. Intelligence analysts believed that, given General Giap's earlier victory and the devastating impact it had on French public opinion, the North Vietnamese would attempt to inflict another "Dien Bien Phu" on the United States. U.S. commanders did not, however, recoil from the prospect of engaging the communists in a set piece battle. In a sense, this is surprising. In contrast to the Battle of the Bulge, Dien Bien Phu did not have a "happy ending" for Giap's opponents. Yet U.S. commanders hoped that the communists would attempt to repeat their earlier victory, thereby allowing U.S. firepower to be fully utilized. As the siege of Khe Sanh materialized on the eve of the Tet offensive, it appeared that these hopes would finally be fulfilled.

The basic points of the analogy can be summarized simply. In a parachute assault on 20 November 1953, General Navarre's forces quickly overcame weak Vietminh resistance at an abandoned French airstrip in the northwest corner of Vietnam. Navarre had decided to reoccupy the airstrip in order to create a *Base Aero-Terrestre* (airhead) to counter Vietminh pressure on northern Laos, and he eventually built up the strength of the garrison at Dien Bien Phu to about 17,000 men. Soon after General Giap's assault on Dien Bien Phu in March 1954, it became apparent that the French had made several errors that would doom the garrison. They had failed to occupy the outlying heights surrounding the valley out of a mistaken belief that the Vietminh lacked artillery of sufficient caliber to reach the French positions. The French soon found themselves outgunned by Chinese-supplied artillery. The garrison at Dien Bien Phu quickly lost the artillery duel, effectively curtailing its resupply by air. Outgunned, surrounded by approximately 70,000 Vietminh, and confronted with a lack of logistical and air support, the garrison surrendered on 8 May. Even though the French suffered thousands of casualties and a major tactical defeat, the French Expeditionary Force still retained its combat

---

ing to reporters on 6 March 1968, Westmoreland stated, "In some way the best analogy that comes to my mind from history, as I reviewed the events of the last several weeks, is that of the Battle of the Bulge. . . . The Germans achieved surprise at that time; to counter their successes required major redeployment of U.S. forces and reactions. Many of you were there. So was I. . . . It was about seven weeks later before things were back to normal. We're on our sixth week now and things are getting back to normal in this country"; see Braestrup, *Big Story*, 2:155, 208.

capability. But French public opinion, stung by the suffering of the garrison, turned away from a continuation of the war, a decision that was formalized by the 1954 Geneva Accords.[96]

Although the events at Dien Bien Phu painted a gloomy picture of the outcome of a siege of a major U.S. base, analysts seized on the analogy because it fit well with their beliefs about enemy strategy. Analysts believed that the communists had realized by mid-1966 that a strategic victory was beyond their grasp, but they were still expected to draw on their experience in the Indochina war. In particular, analysts claimed that the communists would use Dien Bien Phu to guide their strategy, as suggested in this August 1966 CIA report:

> Present Vietnamese Communist strategy is appreciably influenced by the 1946–1954 struggle in which the Communist-controlled Viet Minh forced the French to withdraw from Vietnam. In Communist eyes, probably the most significant feature of this earlier successful campaign was the fact it was won without inflicting a strategic defeat on the French Military Force (The battle of Dienbienphu was a major tactical—rather than strategic— reverse for the French. It certainly did not destroy the French Expeditionary Corps as an effective military entity.). During their nine-year struggle, the Communists successfully used military pressure as a political abrasive. They worked more on French will than on French strategic capabilities and eventually succeeded in making the struggle a politically unsaleable commodity in metropolitan France.[97]

By mid-1967, CIA analysts were stating that the enemy was attempting to apply the lesson drawn from the siege of Dien Bien Phu to their current situation. A CIA analysis disseminated in May 1967 which describes how the communists would apply the Dien Bien Phu analogy is worth quoting at length:

> In evolving its strategy, Hanoi has rationalized it within the context of the dogma which led to its victory over the French. Indeed the nature of the plans for the current spring-summer campaign bear the earmarks of General Giap's 1953–54 campaign against the French. From Hanoi's point of view, the circumstances of 1966–67 bear a striking similarity to those of the earlier period. Then General Navarre had brought a new offensive spirit to the French Expeditionary Corps. He relegated ARVN [sic] to the task of pacification, using ARVN [sic] units to replace those of the Expe-

---

[96]Bernard B. Fall, *Street without Joy* (New York, 1972), pp. 312–330; and *Hell in a Very Small Place: The Siege of Dien Bien Phu* (New York, 1985), passim; Betts, "Strategic Surprise for War Termination," pp. 153–158; Lomperis, *War Everyone Lost*, pp. 43–46; and Giap, *People's War*, pp. 153–188.

[97]*Westmoreland v. CBS*, exhibit 217, p. 8.

ditionary Corps in static missions, and grouping the latter to form an unprecedentedly large general reserve whose mission was to engage the Viet Minh's main battle force. Navarre used his mobile force in a number of dramatic raids into Viet Minh base areas—including the seizure of Dien Bien Phu—and creating an atmosphere of confidence in ultimate French success. He also planned—and launched—a major offensive in the south designed to roll up the Viet Minh and pacify Phu Yen and Binh Dinh provinces. But Giap countered with a series of thrusts which caused the French to deploy most of their general reserve to protect previously unthreatened areas, so that the French were left with inadequate reserves to deal with the main Viet Minh effort when it developed at Dien Bien Phu. All of these main force operations were accompanied by intensified guerrilla warfare throughout the country aimed at immobilizing the maximum number of French-Vietnamese troops to protect pacified areas and bases. The strategy succeeded before, and Hanoi apparently believes that it will again.[98]

The CIA's use of the Dien Bien Phu analogy is interesting because it did not dwell on the tactical mistakes made by the French garrison. Instead, it placed Dien Bien Phu in its overall strategic context by noting that Giap launched diversionary attacks throughout the country in support of the main effort against the French base. In contrast, U.S. commanders applied the analogy by focusing on the tactical situation faced by the French. Commanders were sensitive to the possibility that the communists would attempt to repeat their success at Dien Bien Phu, but they focused on the tactical problems of siege warfare and paid little attention to the diversionary efforts undertaken by Giap against the French. They also did not anticipate that the communists might attempt something other than a siege of a major base to deliver a political shock to the allies. As later chapters show, these commanders were convinced that the enemy intended to lay siege to Khe Sanh—a strong point in the antiinfiltration barrier—to inflict a "Dien Bien Phu" on the United States. The similarities between the communist efforts against the French and against the Americans at Khe Sanh were in fact remarkable. For example, the NVA 304th Division, which was present at Dien Bien Phu, was detected in the vicinity of Khe Sanh. U.S. commanders became quite preoccupied with their efforts to defeat the North Vietnamese attempt to overrun the U.S. garrison on the eve of the Tet offensive.[99]

---

[98]Ibid., exhibit 237, pp. 12–13.

[99]The NVA 304th Division was detected in the vicinity of Khe Sanh on 23 January 1968; see *PERINTREP*, January 1968, p. 5; and Oberdorfer, *Tet*, pp. 109–110. For repre-

Chinese Intervention in the Korean War

The Chinese intervention in Korea in 1950 was a stark reminder to the Johnson administration of what could befall the allies if escalation of the war provoked a major Chinese military response. U.S. commanders and analysts, however, did not believe that the Chinese were preparing to intervene in the conflict in late 1967. Instead, in the days preceding the Tet offensive, they tended to use the Korean analogy to interpret hostile North Korean actions. On the eve of the Tet offensive, some U.S. commanders considered the distinct possibility that other communist states would launch attacks in support of the 1967 winter-spring offensive.[100]

The intervention in Korea is probably the best known of the three incidents used by Americans in Vietnam to estimate their opponent's behavior. After General MacArthur's successful landing on 15 September 1950 at Inchon, U.N. forces routed North Korean units and moved north toward the 38th parallel. Encouraged by the collapse of the North Koreans, the Truman administration permitted MacArthur's forces to advance beyond the 38th parallel to destroy remaining North Korean units and unify Korea. Chinese premier Chou Enlai had already issued warnings through Indian intermediaries that the Chinese would intervene in the conflict if U.N. forces crossed the 38th parallel. The Truman administration and MacArthur did not respond to these warnings, and on 28 October the Chinese entered the conflict decisively, routing Eighth Army units near the Yalu River. Fighting stalemated approximately along the 38th parallel until an armistice was signed on 27 July 1953. The Chinese intervention greatly increased the political and human costs of U.S. involvement in the Korean War.[101]

---

sentative arguments that Westmoreland equated Khe Sanh with Dien Bien Phu, see Pearson, *War in the Northern Provinces*, pp. 94–96; Betts, "Strategic Surprise for War Termination," p. 160; Lewy, *America in Vietnam*, pp. 127–128; and Fitzgerald, *Fire in the Lake*, p. 391.

[100]For representative descriptions of how the Korean analogy influenced the U.S. escalation and conduct of the war in Vietnam, see Sharp, *Strategy for Defeat*, p. 4; Dennis M. Drew, *Rolling Thunder 1965: Anatomy of a Failure*, Cadre Paper AU-ARI-CP-86-3 (Maxwell Air Force Base, 1986), pp. 8–10; Kinnard, *War Managers*, pp. 24–26; Kahin, *Intervention*, pp. 338–341; Lewy, *America in Vietnam*, pp. 392–393; Gelb, *Irony of Vietnam*, pp. 264–265; and Maclear, *Ten Thousand Day War*, p. 169.

[101]Dean Acheson, *Present at the Creation* (New York, 1969), pp. 403–425, 444–455, 461–462; Robert Leckie, *Conflict: The History of the Korean War, 1950–53* (New York, 1962), pp. 125–206; Harry S. Truman, *Years of Trial and Hope* (New York, 1956), pp. 349–386; Betts, *Surprise Attack*, pp. 51–62; Tang Tsou, *America's Failure in China* (Chicago, 1963), pp. 555–591; W. W. Rostow, *The United States in the World Arena* (New York, 1960), pp.

In the months preceding the Tet offensive, civilian and military analysts claimed that it was unlikely that the Chinese would intervene. CICV analysts identified China's preoccupation with the cultural revolution and Hanoi's fears that Chinese intervention would threaten North Vietnamese sovereignty as factors that militated against Chinese involvement. During 1966 and 1967, CIA analysts also thought that there were few indications of Chinese preparations to intervene. They did point to the presence of North Korean "volunteers" in the North Vietnamese air force and the occasional efforts of Chinese fighter aircraft to challenge U.S. aircraft over North Vietnam, but they claimed that these communist initiatives were intended simply to test the U.S. reaction to communist "volunteers" in the war. The CIA repeatedly claimed that, if the U.S. conducted ground operations in the northern portion of North Vietnam or if the regime in Hanoi was on the verge of collapse, China would mimic its behavior during the Korean War by first issuing warnings before intervening. The scope and intensity of the U.S. military effort in 1967 or even the conduct of military operations just north of the DMZ, according to the CIA analysts, would not provoke a Chinese military response.[102]

Although the allies did not believe that China would intervene in support of the 1967 winter-spring offensive, the Korean analogy sensitized them to the possibility that other communist countries might take action on behalf of Hanoi. During the last week in January 1968, officials in Washington and Saigon began to interpret international developments as evidence that other communist nations might launch a coordinated political-military offensive. In late 1967, intelligence reports indicated that another "Berlin crisis" was developing. A navigational beacon used in the air campaign over North Vietnam was overrun in the weeks preceding the Tet offensive by communist forces in Laos. North Korea seized the U.S. intelligence ship *Pueblo* on 23 January 1968, and a few days later a North Korean assassination squad attempted to storm the residence of the South Korean president. Even though a Korean analogy was not explicit in descriptions of the situation facing the allies, before the 1967 offensive analysts feared that the communists were about to undertake a major escalation of the war by launching attacks or political initiatives in other regions to support the upcoming communist campaign. The Americans still did not believe

---

230–243; Robert Endicott Osgood, *Limited War: The Challenge to American Strategy* (Chicago, 1957), pp. 163–193; and J. Lawton Collins, *War in Peacetime: The History and Lessons of Korea* (Boston, 1969), passim.
[102]*PERINTREP*, March 1967, pp. 3, 5; April 1967, pp. 3–4; October 1967, pp. 11; and November 1967, pp. 11–12; *Westmoreland v. CBS*, exhibits 217, p. 9; 237, pt. VII, pp. 1–3.

that the Chinese were preparing to intervene in the war, but the Korean analogy made them sensitive to developments that indicated that other communist nations might aid the North Vietnamese. The belief that the North Vietnamese were weakening facilitated the application of the Korean analogy to the situation facing the allies: other communist nations might aid North Vietnam in its "go-for-broke" offensive.[103]

How did the beliefs embraced by U.S. policymakers and analysts shape their estimates of the situation they faced in Vietnam? Because they believed that the communists recognized that they could no longer achieve a strategic military victory, they figured that the enemy's military strategy was now geared toward eliminating American and international public support for the allied war effort. In other words, they expected that future enemy initiatives would have limited objectives in line with their limited resources. If an attack developed, it would be geared toward some strategically insignificant but spectacular allied setback. Reinforcing this belief about communist strategy was the belief that U.S. units had achieved their shield and attrition objectives, further limiting communist options. ARVN and southern cities were safe behind the shield provided by U.S. units. Furthermore, accurate allied assessments of the political climate in southern cities made communist efforts to instigate a general uprising, using the limited forces still operating behind the shield, appear highly unrealistic.

The belief that allied command arrangements did not create external vulnerabilities and the belief that U.S. units, because of their capabilities and mission, constituted the primary threat to the enemy's war effort, led analysts to expect the communists to reduce the threat posed by U.S. units. In a sense, an element of preferred strategy entered U.S. estimates at this juncture: it was believed that the communists would attack the units that were in relatively well-prepared defensive positions along the DMZ. Here the border battles and the siege of Khe Sanh loomed large in the minds of Americans. These communist initiatives were seen not only as a response to the construction of the barrier—in a bizarre twist, even as a response to preparations to start barrier operations over Laos, preparations that supposedly remained secret from the communists—but also as an effort to inflict a spectacular setback on the allies. The siege of Khe Sanh

---

[103]Oberdorfer, *Tet*, p. 163; Westmoreland quoted in "Adams' Notes on William Westmoreland," in *Westmoreland v. CBS*, exhibit 191, p. 31; see also Johnson, *Vantage Point*, p. 385; and Rostow, *Diffusion of Power*, pp. 410–411.

was interpreted as a communist attempt to repeat the earlier success at Dien Bien Phu—to inflict a psychological defeat on the allies.

Because of previous communist behavior during truces, the enemy was expected to use the Tet holiday to surge supplies toward southern battlefields. Because it made military sense to use the truce for logistical purposes, and because the communists would have to pay a significant political price by violating the Tet holidays, the allies believed that, if the communists' annual winter-spring offensive did not materialize before Tet, it would wait until after the holidays.

In sum, the centerpiece of the 1967 winter-spring offensive was expected to unfold after the Tet holidays in a conventional assault against Khe Sanh. The siege of the firebase would be supported by communist diversionary efforts behind the shield provided by U.S. forces, but it was imperative that these diversions not draw resources away from Khe Sanh and the communist efforts there to inflict a psychological setback against the alliance.

[4]

Missing the Signals:
July–November 1967

The five months following the 7 July 1967 North Vietnamese decision to launch the Tet offensive are extremely important in the history of U.S. responses to signals of impending attack. During this time, the communists generated numerous signals related to their preparations for the attacks. The American interpretation of these signals was, however, influenced in a variety of ways by preestablished beliefs about allied and communist military fortunes. Even though many analysts realized by the end of November that the enemy was engaged in several forms of atypical activity, their overall estimate of the situation changed little during the period under consideration.

In contrast, by the end of November analysts assigned to the CIA station in Saigon drafted an accurate estimate of the strategy, scope, targets, and timing of the Tet offensive. This analysis demonstrates that allied intelligence possessed the information needed to describe accurately the 1967 winter-spring campaign more than two months before the Tet attacks; it also shows that individuals who were less affected by the prevailing beliefs succeeded in accurately describing the situation facing the allies.

Because this chapter covers such a long period, it is organized thematically to trace the gradual changes in the U.S. response to developing events. In the next chapter, the narrative is organized more along chronological lines to follow the flurry of rapidly unfolding developments during the two months preceding the offensive. The division of the story into these two parts also reflects the fact that after November, the U.S. command generally recognized that they were facing a major offensive. This chapter describes the events that led to this conclusion. Chapter 5 describes the U.S. response to the impending offensive.

MILITARY DEVELOPMENTS

During July fighting was relatively light throughout most of South Vietnam. The communists staged only six large-scale attacks, two in I CTZ and four in III CTZ. There were, however, two exceptions to this relatively low level of enemy activity. In what MACV analysts described as an effort to relieve allied pressure against VC guerrilla units operating in populated coastal areas, enemy main-force units continued offensive operations against U.S. forces in the western highlands (II CTZ). Even heavier fighting erupted when aerial reconnaissance spotted a major enemy force moving toward Con Thien, one of the strong points in the barrier under construction along the DMZ. Between 5 and 14 July, an artillery duel between North Vietnamese and U.S. forces raged around Con Thien, and U.S. Marine units called in air strikes to support ground operations intended to drive the NVA away from the base. During the battle, Con Thien and the nearby strong point of Gio Linh were subjected to the largest communist rocket and artillery bombardment of the war to that date. By the time the fighting temporarily died down on 14 July, over one thousand North Vietnamese had been killed in the fighting around the base.[1]

In August the level of combat varied by area. The NVA generally avoided allied units, leading to a reduction in activity along the DMZ, while VC activity increased. In I CTZ, fighting tapered off when NVA units disengaged after the July attack on Con Thien, but work on the barrier was slowed by enemy harassment. A communist attack also succeeded in freeing over one thousand prisoners from the Quang Ngai province jail in I CTZ. The only significant large scale attack launched during August was staged against the Le Chen special forces camp in III CTZ. U.S. analysts also identified indications that the communists were gearing up for offensive operations near Dak To (in the western highlands in II CTZ where U.S. units formed a shield along the Cambodian border), but no contact was made with enemy units. In contrast, there was a rise in VC terrorism, sabotage, and attacks against allied lines of communication.[2]

---

[1] *PERINTREP* July 1967, pp. 7, A-32; Gary L. Telfer, Lane Rogers, and V. Keith Fleming, Jr., *U.S. Marines in Vietnam Fighting the North Vietnamese 1967* (Washington, D.C., 1984), pp. 96–104; *Command History 1967*, 1:360–361; Stanton, *Rise and Fall*, p. 186; and Nalty, *Air Power*, p. 38. A "large-scale attack" was an enemy-initiated incident involving a force at least of battalion size; see *PERINTREP*, February 1967, p.viii.

[2] *PERINTREP*, August 1967, pp. 2–5, 16; "9/6/67 General Westmoreland's Military Assessment for August 1967," *Westmoreland v. CBS*, exhibit 828; Command History *1967*, 1:361, 374–375; 2:992. For the definitions of terrorism and sabotage used by MACV analysts, see *PERINTREP*, February 1967, p. ix.

Although commanders and analysts offered different explanations for the decrease in activity along the DMZ and the increase of guerrilla attacks and indications of an impending attack in the western highlands, all explanations were easily accommodated by beliefs about the allied and communist military status. General Wheeler, meeting with President Johnson on 18 August, stated that NVA units moved away from the DMZ because they had to rest and refit after the heavy casualties suffered in July; in other words, Westmoreland's shield strategy had worked. Enemy offensive preparations in the western highlands (Dak To) and the sharp jump in VC terrorist attacks in August were explained differently. The enemy was attempting to disrupt the South Vietnamese presidential elections scheduled for September. Terrorist activity was intended to reduce voter turnout, and the communists hoped to inflict a tactical defeat on the allies in the western highlands in order to embarrass the South Vietnamese government on the eve of the elections. Both increases and decreases in enemy activity were explained as responses to allied initiatives, a reflection of the belief that the communists recognized that they were now on the defensive.[3]

This interpretation of the rise in VC terrorist incidents in August and the movement of NVA units away from the DMZ seems correct, but it was wrong to suggest that the buildup around Dak To was a response to an allied initiative (i.e., September elections). Enemy activity around Dak To was part of the communist effort to fix U.S. units in their usual operating areas and to divert additional forces away from the populated areas of South Vietnam. The tendency to explain communist actions as a response to allied initiatives, or to fail to account for activity that could not be explained readily in this manner (the attacks on the Quang Ngai province jail), would continue to be detrimental to U.S. interpretations of information until the Tet offensive. In any event, commanders and analysts still found little cause for alarm on the battlefield. Army chief of staff Johnson told reporters during a trip to South Vietnam in August that there was "a smell of success in every major area of the war."[4]

[3]"8/18/67 Notes of Meeting with Rusk, McNamara, Wheeler, Rostow in Cabinet Room, from Jim Jones to the President," *Westmoreland v. CBS*, exhibit 249; see also exhibit 828; and *PERINTREP*, August 1967, pp. 2–5.
[4]General Johnson quoted in *Pentagon Papers, Gravel*, 4:527. Johnson's statement mirrored Westmoreland's 1 August assessment of the situation: "It has become apparent that a vocal segment of the news profession is equating a lack of major combat operations such as Cedar Falls and Junction City with a stalemate at best, or a loss of the initiative on our part at worst. Nothing could be farther from the truth, of course. If the enemy was exercising even modest initiative the more than 30 large operations under way and more than 5,000 small units actions undertaken each day would have more success in finding him. Enemy units can feed and supply themselves enough for about

The communists launched five large-scale attacks against ARVN units in September, the largest again in the vicinity of the barrier outpost at Con Thien. After the lull in August, major fighting developed during the first half of September as U.S. Marine units defeated NVA attacks and preempted others. With the onset of the northeast monsoon at the end of September, enemy ground pressure against the base eased, but artillery attacks increased. During the week of 19–27 September, Con Thien was subjected to the heaviest sustained bombardment of the war to that date. More than three thousand mortar, artillery, and rocket rounds hit the position.[5]

In response to enemy pressure against Con Thien, Westmoreland organized Operation Neutralize, which lasted from 12 September to 1 November. Intended to eliminate NVA artillery along the DMZ, the operation coordinated airstrikes launched by Task Force 77, the Seventh Air Force, and Guam-based B-52s. Bad weather, however, hampered the conduct of Neutralize, and the operation's objectives were not completely achieved. Still, the effort to coordinate air strikes in support of Con Thien was by no means a total failure. U.S. commanders were pleased that Operation Neutralize prevented the North Vietnamese from concentrating troops, supplies, and artillery for a massed assault against the outpost. The B-52 strikes were judged to be effective in destroying fortified enemy positions. Moreover, the U.S. command was quick to assimilate lessons offered by the effort to use massed airpower in support of a static defense. When a B-52 accidentally dropped its bomb load within a 3-kilometer safety zone around Con Thien, the bombs caused no American casualties but produced many secondary explosions. It became clear that the enemy was taking advantage of the safety zone, so standard operating procedures changed: B-52s were now allowed to drop bomb loads closer to defensive positions. To further improve the performance of U.S. units, Westmoreland also ordered a study of the ground tactics of both sides in the battle of Con Thien.[6]

---

one day of action in 30. The enemy strategy is smart and economical, but basically defensive. He accepts major combat occasionally along the DMZ or in the highlands were he has both sanctuary and short lines of communications. Elsewhere he reacts against Revolutionary Development [pacification operations] and growing civilian commerce by attacking RD operations and sabotaging LOCs. His only real initiative is expressed in long-range attacks against our base areas. These are expensive to him in relation to the publicity he gets"; Cable, Westmoreland to Wheeler, 1 August 1967, pp. 1–2, doc. 6B, DSDUF Vietnam Box 4, Folder: NSF Country File Vietnam Memos to the President, LBJ Library.

[5]*PERINTREP*, September 1967, p. 12; Telfer et al., *U.S. Marines*, pp. 132–134; *Command History 1967*, 1:361; Pearson, *War in the Northern Provinces*, p. 18; and Stanton, *Rise and Fall*, p. 187.

[6]*Command History 1967*, 1:452–453; Nalty, *Air Power*, pp. 15, 62, 82–83; Shore, *Battle for Khe Sanh*, p. 104; and Westmoreland, *Soldier*, p. 271.

The diversionary attacks against Con Thien had an important impact on U.S. strategy. The innovative response to the attacks, Operation Neutralize, was a useful exercise in massed airpower. The North Vietnamese would eventually pay a heavy price for providing the Americans with this opportunity; they would confront a better prepared opponent when they attempted to mount another sustained attack against a barrier outpost, Khe Sanh. But the attack against Con Thien also yielded dividends to the communists by increasing American confidence in massed airpower. The conviction that massed air attacks could effectively support static defensive positions was a critical factor in the eventual U.S. decision to defend Khe Sanh. Despite heavy losses, then, the divisionary attacks launched against Con Thien were successful because they increased U.S. willingness to engage in siege warfare along the DMZ.[7]

Enemy activity dropped off in III and IV CTZ after a sharp increase in early September. MACV analysts attributed the temporary September increase in activity to VC attempts to disrupt the elections; the VC campaign was again interpreted as a response to allied initiatives. In the western highlands of II CTZ, however, U.S. commanders saw numerous indications of an increase in enemy activity. MACV analysts correctly interpreted this information as preparations for an offensive within the B-3 front command area, but they did not offer an explanation—or repeat their earlier analysis linking this action to the September elections—for the NVA decision to attack the U.S. units serving as a shield in this area.[8]

Although enemy pressure against Con Thien eased by the beginning of October, work on the barrier was slowed by bad weather and enemy harassment. Heavy fighting did, however, erupt in northern III CTZ near the Cambodian border. On 27 October, the NVA 88th Regiment attacked the command post of the 3d Battalion, 9th ARVN Infantry Regiment that was located 4 kilometers south of Song Be. The ARVN soldiers, outnumbered four to one, prevented the attackers from penetrating the perimeter of their compound, and by dawn the North Vietnamese had withdrawn into the jungle. The next major attack began on 29 October, when elements of the 272d and 273d VC Regiments and the NVA 165th Regiment attacked the town of Loc Ninh, which was defended by three civilian irregular defense group (CIDG) companies, a regional force company, and a popular force platoon. The VC succeeded in penetrating the town's defenses, although they were eventually repulsed when reinforcements from

[7]Nalty, *Air Power*, pp. 83–84.
[8]*PERINTREP*, September 1967, pp. 3–4.

other CIDG companies and the 5th ARVN Division arrived. Attacks against Loc Ninh and nearby allied installations continued for the next few days, reaching a peak on 31 October when a CIDG camp 2 kilometers southwest of the town was attacked by about 1,500 VC. Once again, the CIDG units succeeded in driving off the attackers. During the three days of fighting around Loc Ninh, ARVN forces and U.S. units engaged in search-and-destroy operations reportedly killing over 800 VC in the area at a cost of 50 allied casualties.[9]

Another significant development occurred in III CTZ during October. Allied units captured two large weapons caches just east of Saigon. Senior U.S. officials were apparently surprised by the number and types of weapons captured. One of the supply dumps, controlled by VC Rear Services Group 84, yielded 75-mm howitzers, 57-mm recoilless rifles, 60-mm and 83-mm mortars, 199 machine guns, about one thousand small arms, and large quantities of ammunition and medical supplies.[10]

Throughout the rest of South Vietnam there was an increase in enemy activity directed against units and individuals involved in pacification. MACV analysts also reported a further increase in enemy activity in the border areas of II CTZ. Westmoreland noted in his monthly military assessment that there was a "shadow of major enemy forces stirring in the Western Highlands." Enemy units subordinate to the B-3 front headquarters conducted rocket, mortar, and some ground attacks against several allied installations and towns in Pleiku and Darlac provinces. "In the Western Highlands and Kontum Province," according to Westmoreland's October report, "ominous signs persist of an offensive buildup by elements of the B-3 front."[11]

The communists launched seven large-scale attacks during November, but the most severe fighting was along the Cambodian border in Kontum province (II CTZ) near Dak To. Between 3 and 13 November, allied units repeatedly attacked the NVA 32d and 66th Regiments that had taken up positions west and southwest of the town. On 13

---

[9]*Command History 1967*, 1:392–394; *PERINTREP*, October 1967, pp. 2, 4; November 1967, p. 4; Lung, *General Offensives*, p. 9; Stanton, *Rise and Fall*, p. 139; Westmoreland, *Soldier*, pp. 236–237; and "11/12/67, General Westmoreland's Monthly Military Assessment for the Month of October," *Westmoreland v. CBS*, exhibit 830B, pp. 9–10. Although the mission of civilian irregular defense groups changed during the war, during the fall of 1967 they conducted unconventional warfare operations against the VC. The CIDG units were comprised of U.S. Army Special Forces personnel and individuals drawn from the local population; see Krepinevich, *Army*, pp. 69–75.

[10]"10/18/67 Bunker Cable to LBJ, No. 25" in *Westmoreland v. CBS*, exhibit 846C, p. 6; and *PERINTREP*, October 1967, p. 4.

[11]Quotes from *Westmoreland v. CBS*, exhibit 830B, pp. 5, 7. For additional discussion of developments throughout South Vietnam, see *PERINTREP*, October 1967, pp. 3–5.

November, fighting in the area intensified when the NVA 24th Regiment attacked Dak To from the northwest. Communist forces destroyed ammunition storage facilities and two C-130s on the fifteenth. By the seventeenth, allied units became engaged in heavy fighting to the southwest and northeast of the city. After five days of fighting, the U.S. 173d Airborne Brigade suffered heavy casualties but succeeded in capturing Hill 875, located southwest of the city, from the NVA 174th Regiment, while ARVN units remained engaged northeast of Dak To. Fighting in the area had tapered off to occasional enemy sniper and mortar fire by the end of November. At least 362 allied troops and about 1,600 North Vietnamese soldiers were killed during the month-long series of battles.[12]

There was also an increase in enemy activity in both III and IV CTZ during November. In the areas along the Cambodia border in III CTZ, VC and NVA units launched several attacks, including a renewed assault on Song Be, offered stiff resistance to U.S. attacks against base camps in the area, and repositioned forces. The attacks in IV CTZ were largely coordinated assaults on district towns and ARVN night defensive positions and efforts to interdict National Highway 4. Given their beliefs about the decline of communist military fortunes, especially of communist forces still operating behind the shield, this increase in activity apparently fulfilled analysts' expectations about the gravity of the 1967 winter-spring campaign in IV CTZ. Analysts believed that the enemy would continue to use its improved ability to coordinate attacks in an effort to achieve what they considered to be the main objective of the campaign in the delta, the disruption of the pacification program. In contrast, enemy activity in I CTZ remained at low levels. NVA units had moved away from the DMZ throughout most of the month, although there were indications that by the end of November elements of the NVA 90th and 803d Regiments had moved into the vicinity of Con Thien. North Vietnamese forces also launched four "attacks by fire" against U.S. units operating in the vicinity of Khe Sanh.[13]

In sum, between July and November 1967 the communist strategy of deception unfolded in the attacks against Con Thien and in a series

---

[12]*PERINTREP*, November 1967, pp. 2–3, 14; *Command History 1967*, 1:378–379; Westmoreland, *Soldier*, p. 238; Stanton, *Rise and Fall*, pp. 171–178; Lung, *General Offensives*, p. 9; and "12/16/67 General Westmoreland's Monthly Military Assessment for November 1967," in *Westmoreland v. CBS*, exhibit 831, pp. 6–7. Elements of the U.S. 4th Infantry Division, the U.S. 1st Cavalry Division, and seven South Vietnamese battalions in addition to the 173d Airborne Division were engaged in the fighting; see Sharp and Westmoreland, *Report*, pp. 155–156.

[13]*PERINTREP*, November 1967, pp. 1–2, 4–5; *Command History 1967*, 1:363–364; and *Westmoreland v. CBS*, exhibit 831, pp. 4, 15–18.

of assaults against Song Be, Loc Ninh, and Dak To. Collectively known as the border battles, this increase in communist military action was generally viewed as a sign of success: main-force communist units were venting their fury against the shield formed by U.S. units. There seemed little to be alarmed about, and U.S. commanders actually appreciated the opportunity to direct the full force of their firepower against main-force NVA and VC units that had finally stood their ground. Behind the shield, the increase in VC activity was also described as a response to an allied initiative, the South Vietnamese elections. Indeed, even the November increase in VC attacks against the pacification effort was not interpreted as particularly threatening. A winter-spring offensive was expected, and the moderate—when compared to the Tet attacks—increase in VC activity met analysts' expectations about the capabilities of the weakened units operating behind the shield. The sacrifices made by the communists during the border battles were thus worthwhile because they increased the allied preoccupation with events along the borders.

SIGNALS

U.S. analysts apparently failed to attach any special significance to the most important signal emerging during July, the meeting of North Vietnamese dignitaries in Hanoi. Even though the western press reported the meeting, the MACV monthly intelligence summary did not mention the gathering, and Defense Department spokesmen refused to speculate publicly about its significance. Americans apparently attached special importance to the meeting only after the offensive. Douglas Pike, in an article written in February 1968 for a nonclassified journal, was one of the first to claim that the decision to launch the offensive was made during the summer of 1967 and that preparations for the Tet attacks started in July 1967, suggesting that either documents or prisoners captured during the offensive provided Americans their first information about the significance of the meeting.[14]

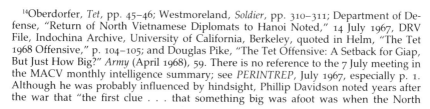

[14]Oberdorfer, *Tet*, pp. 45–46; Westmoreland, *Soldier*, pp. 310–311; Department of Defense, "Return of North Vietnamese Diplomats to Hanoi Noted," 14 July 1967, DRV File, Indochina Archive, University of California, Berkeley, quoted in Helm, "The Tet 1968 Offensive," p. 104–105; and Douglas Pike, "The Tet Offensive: A Setback for Giap, But Just How Big?" *Army* (April 1968), 59. There is no reference to the 7 July meeting in the MACV monthly intelligence summary; see *PERINTREP*, July 1967, especially p. 1. Although he was probably influenced by hindsight, Phillip Davidson noted years after the war that "the first clue . . . that something big was afoot was when the North

In contrast, CIA analysts noted that the VC in An Giang province had apparently launched a *dong khoi* (move out all forces) campaign. Even though the details of the campaign remained obscure, the CIA suggested that the program would place all VC units under a military command and was intended to make cadres work harder for the success of the fall-winter campaign. The CIA even noted that the VC were showing more interest in urban operations; in Kien Hoa province a "resigned-to-death" class was held to train VC to launch suicide attacks against government installations. The MACV monthly intelligence summary reported several other developments that in hindsight also appear to be preparations for the offensive, but at the time they could be viewed only as relatively normal enemy activities. Analysts noted that the enemy's B-3 front headquarters (in western II CTZ) continued to augment its command structure, an initiative possibly undertaken in preparation for the border battles. The VC were improving their sapper capability in I CTZ, possibly in preparation for the Tet attacks, by increasing the size of sapper units. The summary also provided the details of the intelligence requirements issued by the VC Western Region Committee. The collection effort, which was to be implemented no later than 15 May 1967, ordered VC cell leaders in urban areas to ascertain the strength of all South Vietnamese forces in the immediate vicinity, develop reliable means to transmit this information, and urge individuals loyal to the VC cause to enlist in ARVN for duty in headquarters and supply depots. The fact that these intelligence requirements—issued before the decision to launch the offensive—could have helped to prepare for the Tet attacks illustrates an important point. The enemy normally undertook activities that were similar to the preparations for the offensive; it would take some time before these efforts reached a level at which they could be noticed by analysts.[15]

During August, American analysts still possessed little evidence to indicate that the enemy had decided to launch a major offensive, but in hindsight the information obtained by MACV does indicate that the North Vietnamese had begun preparations. On 5 August, the North Vietnamese and representatives of the People's Republic of

---

Vietnamese called their ambassadors home. They'd done this, to the best of our knowledge, only once before, and that's in 1965, when American troops had begun to enter in serious numbers"; Davidson, Oral History I, pp. 36–37, LBJ Library.

[15]*PERINTREP*, July 1967, pp. 7, 16, 26. CIA analysts also noted that VC units throughout the country were receiving sapper training; see CIA, Intelligence Information Cable, "Summary of Viet Cong Activities in South Vietnam During July 1967," 30 August 1967, pp. 10–13, 124a, NSF Country File, Vietnam Box 252, 258, 259, LBJ Library. MACV analysts originally reported the improvements in the B-3 front command structure in March 67; see *PERINTREP*, March 1967, p. B-1.

China signed an agreement on China's economic and technical assistance to Vietnam. The U.S. consulate in Hong Kong reported that the agreement included provisions for substantial military assistance and that the North Vietnamese had obtained grants rather than repayable loans, the form of aid previously provided by the Chinese. MACV analysts did not attach any special significance to this new agreement and mentioned it only in passing in their September intelligence summary. In light of the vast influx of recently manufactured Chinese weapons into South Vietnam in late 1967 and early 1968, however, it appears that they missed the most important signal to emerge during August. The change in the terms of the aid might have reflected a willingness on the part of the Chinese to honor a massive North Vietnamese aid request that was beyond the means of the Hanoi regime to repay.[16]

Intelligence analysts also detected what in hindsight appears to be evidence of enemy preparations within South Vietnam for the offensive. Numerous reports had reached analysts about the use of female VC agents, sometimes wearing police uniforms or disguised as members of women's ARVN units, to obtain information about ARVN dispositions, the rural development program, and targets for assassination around Can Tho and the nearby Binh Thuy airbase. Analysts reported that the VC were using female agents to penetrate allied installations in the Saigon area and to elicit information from allied personnel through casual conversation, and they also noted that VC agents had smuggled grenades into the capital by carrying them in a cookie container and concluded that it would be impossible to prevent this type of activity without searching every vehicle and person entering Saigon. They did not, however, attach any particular significance to these reports, which only varied slightly from normal types and levels of enemy activity.[17]

In September the signals generated by preparations for the offensive crossed the threshold of background noise created by typical enemy activity. Two developments were immediately recognized as significant. The first was the publication on 14–16 September of General Giap's "The Big Victory, the Great Task." In his 4 October report to the president, Ambassador Bunker provided a succinct and accurate description of Giap's tactical suggestions:

> Giap calls for intensified guerrilla operations and sophisticated concentrated strikes, and makes a great point of the superiority of Viet Cong tactics over the tactics of United States' forces—particularly artillery

[16]*Command History 1967*, 1:22, 113 n. 11; and *PERINTREP*, September 1967, p. 1.
[17]*PERINTREP*, August 1967, pp. 11–12.

(rocket) units, engineers, and special crack units—to carry out raiding operations and sabotage against carefully selected strategic targets such as logistic and air bases, command posts, and lines of communication. he reports that the tactics (surprise, etc.) of the crack units within the Main Forces are being passed on to guerrilla and Regional Forces as well.[18]

Although Bunker and other senior officials were aware of the tactics advocated by Giap, they tended to interpret the article as a reaffirmation of the communist strategy of protracted war. Bunker noted, for example, that Giap's statement "only by protecting targets and preserving our forces can we create conditions to annihilate the enemy" was evidence of a communist decision to cut losses without suspending offensive activity. Even though the statement was a call to generate forces for the offensive, senior U.S. officials in Saigon interpreted it in light of their belief that communist military capability was on the wane. Similarly, they tended to dismiss as too pat Giap's claim that allied forces would be diverted toward the border and that operations between various communist units would be coordinated. Bunker viewed the strategic prescriptions quite skeptically:

> Giap has listed some difficult requirements. Time will tell whether the Viet Cong can effectively develop coordinated strikes and guerrilla warfare, waged by Main Force and Local Forces with better weapons against professionally selected strategic targets, and whether they can combine this with an intensified political struggle effort to promote and exploit divisions and war weariness among the South Vietnamese People. Giap makes much of the claim that United States' forces have bogged down, failed to win the initiative, and are being pushed into a dispersed, defensive ("passive") posture. All of us here believe he can and will be proven wrong.[19]

Because the beliefs embraced by many U.S. commanders and analysts diverged from Giap's description of the situation, they dismissed as unrealistic Giap's claims and recommendations.[20]

A second development recognized by analysts as significant was the 23 September signing of a new military aid agreement between North Vietnam and the Soviets. In their monthly intelligence summary for September, MACV analysts noted that the agreement "should offer a significant increase in NVN economic development

[18]*Westmoreland v. CBS*, exhibit 846A, p. 7. On 7 October, the entire MACV Saturday "strategy session" was devoted to a discussion of the Giap article; see "General Westmoreland's History Notes, Volume VIII, 21 August–26 December 1967," in ibid., exhibit 912, p. 48.

[19]Ibid., exhibit 846A, p. 7.

[20]Lung, *General Offensives*, pp. 19–20; and Palmer, *Summons*, p. 169.

and defense capability."[21] The fact that MACV analysts recognized the importance of this event is noteworthy as an exception to their tendency to ignore political developments. The U.S. military focused on the event because of their interest in its tactical consequences. In this instance, however, the entire intelligence community seemed to concentrate on the tactical implications rather than the strategic possibilities opened by the treaty. In the absence of information about the actual terms of the agreement, the intelligence community could only speculate about the types of Soviet-supplied weapons that might soon emerge on the battlefield. In November, for example, the National Intelligence Estimate (NIE 14.3–67) stated: "It is possible that Hanoi has sought more sophisticated types of equipment than those now arriving on the scene. These might include cruise missiles and tactical rockets which could be used . . . in the DMZ area and against U.S. warships. . . . we believe that during the coming months the Soviets will continue to supply equipment designed to strengthen air and coastal defenses in North Vietnam and to increase the firepower of both the regular North Vietnamese forces and the Communist forces fighting in the South."[22] This assessment was only half correct. It was wrong about the technological sophistication and defensive nature of the weapons the Soviets eventually supplied, but there were in fact several new relatively unsophisticated but effective Soviet weapons introduced during the Tet offensive. Still, intelligence analysts and commanders did not interpret this trade agreement as evidence of enemy preparations to launch a major offensive. This failure to integrate political and military signals was a problem that would plague MACV officers until the start of the Tet attacks.

Analysts and commanders noticed several other unusual developments in September, but they did not interpret this information as evidence of enemy preparations for a major offensive. In the months that followed, but still before the Tet offensive, they would cite these events as evidence that the communists had adopted a change in strategy. The NLF, for example, announced a new political program. Additionally, the VC initiated a propaganda campaign leading to the Buttercup affair, which succeeded in spreading the rumor that the United States favored the inclusion of the NLF in a coalition govern-

---

[21]Quote from *PERINTREP*, September 1967, p. 1. For the date the agreement was signed, see *Command History 1967*, 1:19.

[22]"SNIE 14.3–67 Capabilities of the Vietnamese Communists for Fighting in South Vietnam, 13 November 1967," in *Westmoreland v. CBS*, exhibit 273, p. 20. For a list of some of the new weapons introduced by the communists during the Tet offensive, see "2/28/68 Note by the Secretaries to the JCS, on the Situation in Vietnam," in ibid., exhibit 693, p. 9.

ment. This propaganda campaign was seen as significant because it created trouble within the alliance. According to Joseph Hovey, analysts also began to receive captured documents and prisoner interrogation reports that referred to a general offensive–general uprising. Hovey claimed that these were the first such references he had seen since his arrival in South Vietnam in 1965, but it would take him two months to formulate his analysis of their implications. Finally, the upward trend in the number of defectors ended: 1,448 of the enemy defected in September compared to 2,131 in August. Given that analysts usually cited the ever-growing number of defectors as a sign of progress in the war, the break in this trend should have alerted them to a change in the communist camp; efforts to generate enthusiasm for the offensive were having an impact on the rank and file. This development was not treated as a cause for alarm by analysts, who tended to interpret the drop as a normal fluctuation produced by relatively low levels of allied activity throughout South Vietnam. As strange at it might appear, increases and decreases in the number of defectors were now interpreted as a positive development from the allied perspective.[23]

Analysts noted an increase in enemy supply and sapper activities in October. The number of truck sightings along the Ho Chi Minh Trail surged from a monthly average of 480 to 1,116. The VC also seemed to be placing a greater emphasis on sapper units in I CTZ, and there were indications that regular infantry formations were being transformed into sapper units. Analysts stated that they had identified three VC battalions that had received specialized training and had already carried out sapper attacks (a key mission during the Tet offensive). ARVN analysts also obtained a document that discussed VC efforts in III CTZ to train troops in sapper tactics and in the operation of ARVN armored vehicles. MACV analysts also detected increased enemy interest in urban operations, ARVN units, and allied installations, important elements in the Tet campaign. They reported that the VC were experiencing difficulty in obtaining the documents needed to gain entry into Saigon. Captured documents revealed that VC cadres in Saigon had requested falsified documents and other "means" and places to hide them. The analysts believed that the word "means" was a veiled reference to weapons and explosives. Captured documents also revealed an increase in enemy interest in ARVN units. The VC had stepped up efforts to place sleepers (agents

---

[23]*Command History 1967*, 1:50; 2:679; Westmoreland, *Soldier*, pp. 311–312; Lung, *General Offensives*, p. 26; and "Joseph Hovey Interview Transcript [with George Crile]" 27 January 1981, in *Westmoreland v. CBS*, exhibit 3, p. 3.

who remained inactive until ordered to carry out their mission) within ARVN. MACV analysts took this threat seriously, noting that the VC had recently succeeded in penetrating ARVN units. A seven-man VC team had been discovered in the ARVN 58th Regional Force Battalion. Another VC team had been identified within a CIDG attached to the U.S. 5th Special Forces headquartered at Da Nang. The mission of the VC inside the CIDG unit was to gather information about the size, defenses, and operations of the 5th Special Forces Group and to obtain ammunition, uniforms, weapons, and rice for the VC.[24]

 In addition to the evidence obtained about the specific targets of the Tet offensive, allied intelligence analysts obtained more general information about enemy objectives. ARVN intelligence obtained a document, dated 1 September, that was intended for middle-level cadres. The document outlined a three-pronged offensive that was supposed to defeat ARVN, destroy U.S. "political and military institutions," and instigate a mass insurrection. The offensive was designated TCK–TCN, or *Tong Cong Kich–Tong Khoi Nghia* (general offensive–general uprising). A similar document, issued on 18 September by the VC, was obtained by CDEC analysts. This document noted that the period between late 1967 and early 1968 was regarded by the communists as a historical phase, a time when the United States would be driven from South Vietnam and a coalition government would seize power from the Thieu regime. These documents, however, apparently failed to elicit a direct response from U.S. analysts. ARVN intelligence also obtained a copy of Resolution 13 of the North Vietnamese Lao Dong party issued in February and March 1967. Even though a former ARVN intelligence analyst stated after the war that the document called for a major offensive to achieve a quick victory, U.S. analysts may not have received a copy of it in October; instead of discussing the military plans contained in the document, they reported a VC defector's interpretation of the document as claiming that American domestic support for the war was weakening and that President Johnson would lose the 1968 election to a "dove" candidate. In effect, MACV analysts suggested that Resolution 13 indicated that the communists would continue in their long-war strategy at least until the 1968 election, the opposite of the policy prescriptions contained in the document.[25]

Throughout November allied intelligence continued to obtain indi-

[24]Pearson, *War in the Northern Provinces*, p. 30; *PERINTREP*, October 1967, pp. 7–9; and Lung, *General Offensives*, p. 33.

[25]Lung, *General Offensives*, p. 33; COMUSMACV to RUHHQA/CINCPAC, 14 October 1967, p. 2, doc. 46, NSF Country File Vietnam, Box 153, Folder: Vietnam Captured Documents Cables, LBJ Library; and *PERINTREP*, October 1967, pp. 8–10.

cations of an increase in unusual forms of enemy activity and documentary evidence about the enemy's Tet plans and objectives. Documents included a propaganda program for the VC winter-spring campaign intended in part to urge the population to engage in the political struggle against government control; an NLF call for a maximum effort during the winter-spring campaign; directives to cadres in Saigon describing the phases (first phase, Oct.–Dec. 1967; second phase, Jan.–Mar. 1968; third phase, Apr.–June 1968) and targets (cities, rear areas, key agencies, warehouses, communication centers, and strategic hamlets) of the coming campaign; and orders for NVA and VC units to carry out coordinated attacks during the winter-spring campaign. The pace of communist logistical and command preparations also quickened during the month. Truck sightings along the Ho Chi Minh Trail again increased dramatically. Compared to 1,116 during October, 3,823 trucks were spotted in November. Logistical preparations within South Vietnam also increased. On 24 November, MACV officers became aware of an order issued by the VC on 17 November to all hamlets in Gia Dinh province. The VC had demanded that each family in the province furnish at least one individual to serve as a porter. Beginning on 25 November, the impressed villagers were to transport ammunition from VC supply areas to locations in the immediate vicinity of Saigon in preparation for the winter-spring offensive. ARVN intelligence operatives also began to pick up indications of communist command reorganizations in the areas around Hue and Saigon, efforts that increased the number of communist units that could operate in the vicinity of these cities.[26]

MACV analysts also obtained evidence of what probably were communist efforts to generate forces for the Tet attacks. Even though analysts had long known that Hanoi often drafted individuals younger than the established draft age of 18, POW and defector reports received during November indicated an acceleration of this trend. Children as young as 14 were being drafted in some provinces of North Vietnam during the late summer of 1967. MACV analysts, however, interpreted this decrease in the draft age and a decline in the amount of training given to infiltrators as evidence of a growing manpower

[26]CDEC Bulletins 7917, 7952, 8015, 8060, 8177, NSF Country File, Vietnam, Folder: Vietnam 1967 Winter-Spring Campaign; COMUSMACV to RUHHHQA/CINCPAC 15 November 1967, doc. 21, NSF Country File Box 153, Folder: Vietnam Captured Documents Cables, LBJ Library; Pearson, *War in the Northern Provinces*, p. 30; Item 21, 0745 24 November 1967, Daily Journal Files, MACV J-2 Command Center; *Long Binh/Saigon Tet Campaign, 199th Infantry Brigade, 12 January–19 February 1968* (Washington D.C., 1968), annex F, p. 1, document obtained at Department of the Army, Office of the Assistant Chief of Staff for Information Management, Alexandria, Virginia; and Lung, *General Offensives*, pp. 34–35.

shortage produced by the air war over North Vietnam and the heavy attrition of NVA forces on the southern battlefield—an interpretation that obviously complemented the beliefs that communist military fortunes were on the decline and that the attrition strategy was succeeding. Moreover, MACV analysts reported that the VC were transferring senior cadre members to relatively low positions in local units. This initiative, probably intended to strengthen VC command arrangements and morale, was interpreted by Westmoreland as evidence of a VC shortage of low-level cadre members.[27]

In a context of increased enemy activity in the western highlands, U.S. forces obtained information that outlined communist plans issued by the B-3 front headquarters. On 2 November, a defector provided allied intelligence with the B-3 front plan of attack in western Kontum province. A document captured on the sixth near Dak To described the winter-spring campaign objectives of the B-3 front. General Abrams, in a cable to Westmoreland dated 15 November, summarized the B-3 front objectives described in the document captured on the sixth: "(1) the annihilation of a major U.S. element in order to force the 'enemy' to deploy as many additional troops in the Western Highlands as possible, and to destroy a large part of the 'Puppet' Army; (2) to encourage units to improve on the technique of concentrated and large-scale attacks; (3) to 'liberate' an important area in order to strengthen the base area of the B-3 Front; and (4) to make a concerted offensive effort in coordination with other units in various battle areas throughout South Vietnam."[28] The document not only ordered the diversionary attacks that had already begun around Dak To but also provided a none-too-veiled reference to the purpose behind the diversion—a coordinated country-wide offensive. Yet Abrams described the diversionary phase of the plan as the main initiative of the B-3 front winter-spring campaign: "The proposed B-3 Front . . . Winter-Spring campaign and recent enemy offensive activities in Western Kontum Province, as well as references made to difficulties in supply, relocation and travel enroute, indicate that the planned prolonged offensive is to be in the Western Highlands." In effect, Abrams's summary highlighted the sections of the document already confirmed by the enemy's behavior on the battlefield and

[27]*PERINTREP*, November 1967, p. 1; and "11/30/67 Department of State Airgram from Embassy Saigon, Subject Assessment of Current Enemy Situation," in *Westmoreland v. CBS*, exhibit 658, p. 3; see also exhibit 831, pp. 18–19; and CIA, "Summary of Viet Cong Activities," pp. 5–6, LBJ Library.

[28]*Westmoreland v. CBS*, exhibit 656; see also exhibit 831, p. 11; Westmoreland, *Soldier*, p. 239; and *PERINTREP*, November 1967, pp. 2–3. Lung dates the capture of the document as 3 November, see Lung, *General Offensives*, p. 34.

downplayed portions that indicated that the November diversion in the western highlands was only the prelude to a future offensive of greater scope. The belief that communist military fortunes were declining—or the belief that most of South Vietnam was safe behind the shield—led Abrams to emphasize the logistical difficulties limiting the scope of the future B-3 front offensive.

Another document—a soldier's notebook captured on 25 November in Quang Tin Province, I CTZ—described the objectives behind the coordinated offensive mentioned in the document captured on 6 November near Dak To: "the central headquarters has ordered the entire army and people of South Vietnam to implement general offensive and general uprising in order to achieve a decisive victory. . . . use very strong military attacks in coordination with uprising of the local population to take over towns and cities. Troops should flood the lowlands. They should move toward liberating the capital city, Saigon, take power and try to rally enemy brigades . . . to our side."[29] The contents of the notebook clearly conflicted with American beliefs about communist military capability, the realization of the shield objective, and the status of the South Vietnamese population. As a result, most analysts dismissed it as a reflection of enemy propaganda.[30]

In addition to the information obtained about the B-3 front's objectives for the winter-spring campaign, MACV analysts received reports of an increase in enemy reconnaissance activity within Saigon and nearby U.S. installations. Analysts obtained a VC form used for a four-part survey for each block, ward, and precinct in Saigon. The first part of the form covered the location of streets, major buildings, police stations, and checkpoints; the second was for listing families and their social class; the third was for recording the names of South Vietnamese officials and other opponents of the VC; and the last section of the survey would identify families whose members were active in South Vietnamese political organizations and the attitudes of these individuals toward the VC. The captured document also emphasized the importance of the survey and the urgent need for its completion. The survey turned out to be an enemy reconnaissance effort for the Tet attacks, but ARVN analysts gave it a less disturbing interpretation. "GVN authorities," according to the monthly MACV intelligence summary, "believe this survey could be the prelude to the planned infiltration of VC cadre and weapons into the area." Apparently, both

---

[29]Braestrup, *Big Story*, 1:71. This document was released by MACV to the press on 5 January 1968.
[30]Ibid.; Lung, *General Offensives*, p. 34; and Palmer, *Summons*, pp. 178–179.

ARVN and U.S. analysts chose not to speculate about how, when, or where these assets would be used.[31]

Similarly, MACV J-2 received a report on 24 November that the VC 165A Regiment headquarters had ordered its 2d Battalion to rendezvous with the Go Mon sapper unit to reconnoiter the U.S. airbase at Ton Son Nhut. The combined force was to select targets to be shelled during the opening of the winter-spring offensive and to identify positions in the surrounding villages to impede allied efforts to destroy VC gun and rocket emplacements. This information apparently was not discussed in any finished intelligence reports.[32]

In effect, by September communist preparations for the offensive had become perceptible. The Americans, who tended to date this apparent change in communist strategy with the publication of Giap's "The Big Victory, the Great Task," failed to realize that the communists had obtained a ten-week head start in their preparations. Moreover, even though by the end of November there were accurate indications of the enemy's objectives, the border battles tended to reduce the apparent threat posed by the nascent communist movement toward southern cities. On balance, when U.S. analysts commented on developments within the communist camp, these changes, no matter how threatening they appear in hindsight, were interpreted as further evidence of allied progress in the war.

ALLIED REACTIONS

As the Hanoi meeting was coming to a close, another strategy session was opening in Saigon. Secretary of Defense McNamara arrived in South Vietnam on 7 July to discuss Westmoreland's most recent request for reinforcements with the MACV staff and Ambassador Bunker. Although the details of the request for additional manpower are not important (the customary compromise over reinforcements between the Department of Defense and MACV eventually emerged), the MACV intelligence briefings given at the meeting reflect the analytical themes that would persist until the Tet attacks. MACV analysts described developments that could be interpreted as signs of an increase in enemy strength as evidence of a decline of the communist military.[33]

[31]*PERINTREP*, November 1967, pp. 8–9.
[32]Item 26, 0945 24 November 1967, Daily Journal Files, MACV J-2 Command Center.
[33]*Pentagon Papers*, p. 539; and *Pentagon Papers, Gravel*, 4:523–527.

MACV analysts pointed to indications of an increase in North Vietnamese infiltration, a growing proportion of NVA troops on the battlefield, and the assumption of command responsibilities by the North Vietnamese along the DMZ and the border areas of II and III CTZ as evidence of heavy losses among communist forces, especially VC units, and of VC recruitment problems in South Vietnam. In response to growing allied pressure, the communists had adopted a "peripheral strategy" by stationing their main-force units along or just across the borders of South Vietnam. The analysts at MACV claimed that, even though the enemy enjoyed a position of strength along the border, the implementation of a peripheral strategy indicated that they were on the strategic defensive. In a good example of the influence of the belief that the communists had abandoned hope of gaining a strategic military victory, U.S. analysts described events that could have been interpreted as an improvement in the enemy's combat capability (the introduction of better equipped NVA soldiers into VC units and centralized command and control arrangements) as evidence of weakness. The movement of NVA and VC main-force units into the border regions, according to the analysts, also demonstrated that the shield objective had been realized. It would now be difficult for the communists to make their main-force presence felt in the heavily populated areas. The possibility of units on the periphery engaging in diversionary operations was mentioned, but evidence that VC forces located near populated areas were weakening made this a hollow threat. In contrast, MACV analysts provided a lengthy description of the possible avenues of attack from the border toward populated areas. They expected that any major communist military initiative would take place along the border of South Vietnam, and this is reflected in the description of MACV operational priorities provided to McNamara during the Saigon visit: "(1) contain enemy at borders; (2) locate and destroy VC/NVA; (3) neutralize enemy base areas; (4) maximum support to RD; (5) open and secure LOC [Lines of Communication]; (6) interdict enemy LOC; (7) secure key installations; and, (8) emphasize Psy Ops."[34]

A major disagreement emerged within the U.S. intelligence community in August over estimates of enemy strength, but the opposing lines in the dispute had already been drawn by July 1967. The proximate cause of the debate was the development of a new order-of-battle estimate for NIE 14.3–67. On one side of the debate stood

---

[34]*Pentagon Papers, Gravel*, 4:518–520. Westmoreland restated the MACV analysts' conclusions in his monthly report on developments in South Vietnam for July 1967; see *Westmoreland v. CBS*, exhibit 827, p. 11.

MACV and Defense Intelligence Agency (DIA) analysts who argued that VC self-defense and secret self-defense forces should not be included in the enemy's order of battle because hard data on the strength of these forces were lacking and because these forces were composed of old people and children and so lacked offensive capability. Members of MACV tended to view these individuals as civilian supporters of the VC and argued that it would be misleading to include them in the enemy's order of battle without including civilian supporters of the South Vietnamese government in the allied order of battle. Senior officers at MACV were concerned that a large increase in order-of-battle estimates would generate public and media criticism, especially in light of MACV reports of progress in the war; they would never be able to convince the press that the increase in the estimate of enemy strength was the result of improved analysis. Instead, the press and public might construe the increase as an inappropriate effort to support recent MACV requests for reinforcements. This concern was not at all far fetched. When improvements in the method of counting enemy-initiated incidents were applied retroactively in early 1967 and produced an increase, as opposed to the previously reported decrease, in enemy-initiated incidents over the past year, the new report prompted a sharp warning to MACV from the chairman of the Joint Chiefs of Staff:

> I note . . . that some feeling exists within your headquarters that there is a relationship between statistical bookkeeping . . . and decisions concerning future strength levels. I feel certain this does not reflect your [Westmoreland's] own views, but for the record, you can assure those who hold such dangerous views that any requirements for additional forces which are well and clearly justified will receive a fair hearing at this and higher levels regardless of the way statistics on enemy activity are running, and that any attempts to "weight the dice" can only result in trouble for us all.[35]

In contrast, CIA analysts argued—based on analyses of captured documents—that the failure to include the approximately 120,000 members of the VC self-defense and secret self-defense forces in estimates of enemy strength would undermine the war effort. They noted that these forces formed a manpower pool that MACV analysts failed to consider as they worked on their "crossover" calculations.

[35]Quotation from "Cable 3/11/67 from Wheeler to Westmoreland," in *Westmoreland v. CBS*, exhibit 233, p. 4. See also "Cable 6/10/67 from Sharp to Westmoreland," "Cable 6/2/67 from Adams to Sandine," "Cable . . . 7/10/67 from Carver to Helms," and "Cable 8/20/67 from Abrams to Wheeler, Sharp, Westmoreland," ibid., exhibits 242, 239, 245, 252.

[159]

MACV, according to CIA analysts, probably subtracted many dead self-defense force members from estimates of the number of individuals in main-force and guerrilla units, thereby skewing the calculations that measured progress toward the attrition objective. The CIA claimed that the inclusion of self-defense and secret self-defense forces in the order of battle would depict a more accurate picture of the strength and nature of communist forces.[36]

Efforts to arrange a compromise between MACV and the CIA broke down on 18 August when the Office of National Estimates included the estimate of 120,000 for the strength of the self-defense and secret self-defense forces in a draft of the National Intelligence Estimate. A flurry of protest arose from Robert Komer, General Davidson, General Abrams, and General Westmoreland. In response to this protest, the Joint Chiefs asked Richard Helms, director of Central Intelligence, to send a team to Saigon to settle the dispute. The CIA team, George Carver, William Hyland, Dean Moor, and Samuel Adams, arrived in Saigon on 8 September. The effort to reach a compromise was about to collapse when Helms, who was anxious to avoid a split National Intelligence Estimate (whereby separate MACV/DIA and CIA figures would be presented), encouraged Carver to reach a compromise. Carver abandoned the CIA objective of including a precise numerical estimate of the strength of the self-defense and secret self-defense forces. Instead, the text accompanying the order-of-battle estimate would note that the estimate did not include VC part-time guerrillas, a force that could conceivably add about 150,000 combatants to the communist cause. Westmoreland agreed to the compromise on 14 September.[37]

The compromise between MACV and the CIA was tenuous at best. Since CIA representatives only succeeded in obtaining MACV's agreement to provide them with a copy of the June 1967 "Crossover memo" (which asserted that the crossover point had been reached) written by the MACV order-of-battle analyst Daniel Graham, they apparently felt shortchanged. Moreover, CIA analysts took a dim view of a proposed MACV October press briefing, which they believed violated the tenets of the September compromise by implying greater certainty over order-of-battle estimates than was justified, further

[36]"Cable 6/2/67 from Adams to Sandine," and "Cable 9/12/67 from Carver to Helms," in ibid., exhibits 239, 258AA.
[37]Ibid., exhibits 250, 251A, 252B, 253A, 255, 220BB, 256B, 258E, 258AA, 259B, 260B; see also "Monograph by Allen [unpublished] 'Indochina Wars—1950–1975'," in ibid., exhibit 313, p. 315; and Daniel O. Graham, Oral History II, pp. 1–2, 4, 13–15, LBJ Library. The same points were made by George Allen in interview with the author, 6 December 1989.

downplaying the role of self-defense and secret self-defense forces, and stating that the intelligence community had overestimated the size of enemy forces arrayed against the allies, whereas NIE 14.3–67 stated that analysts had historically underestimated their strength. CIA representatives suggested that their agency distance itself from what they considered to be the unsupportable statements offered by MACV.[38]

Years after the Tet offensive, charges made by Samuel Adams on the pages of *Harper's*, in front of the Pike committee, before CBS television cameras, and finally during the *Westmoreland vs. CBS* litigation that a conspiracy existed to suppress an increase in order-of-battle estimates tended to blow the dispute between MACV and the CIA out of proportion. There was no conspiracy to limit estimates. Helms even provided President Johnson with a memo that supplied a brief history of the disagreement, the reasons behind the competing estimates, and a warning about the possibility that the order of battle significantly underestimated enemy strength. Helms also repeated his background briefing about NIE 14.3–67 to the cabinet.[39]

Several interesting observations can be offered about the positions adopted by each side in the debate. On the one hand, the CIA claim that the VC self-defense and secret self-defense forces formed a large and significant part of the enemy's war effort—an estimate proved incorrect during the Tet offensive—contradicted the belief, popular in military circles, that the shield strategy was successful. It also demonstrates that these CIA analysts were more willing than the military analysts to explore the political aspects of the war. On the other hand, the MACV position illustrates the belief, held by many members of the military, that NVA units operating along the borders of

[38]*Westmoreland v. CBS*, exhibits 258E, p. 3; 710; 263; 265A; 266. Westmoreland discussed the new order-of-battle estimates with the press on 11 November, and the formal MACV press briefing on the estimate was held on 24 November; see Jones, *War without Windows*, pp. 116–117.

[39]Adams, "Vietnam Cover-up" pp. 41–73; House Select Committee on Intelligence, *U.S. Intelligence Agencies and Activities*, pp. 683–692; "The Uncounted Enemy: A Vietnam Deception," transcript of 23 January 1982 broadcast on CBS Television Network, p. 1, and "11/15/67 Memo From Rostow to LBJ" (including Memo from Helms), in *Westmoreland v. CBS*, exhibits 1; 963, p. 3; Minutes of Cabinet Meeting, 20 November 1967, Cabinet Papers Box 12, Folder: Cabinet Meeting 11/20/67, LBJ Library; Adler, *Reckless Disregard*; Brewin and Shaw, *Vietnam on Trial*; and Cubbage, "Westmoreland vs. CBS: Was Intelligence Corrupted by Policy Demands," in *Leaders and Intelligence*, ed. Michael Handel (London, 1989), especially pp. 138–164. Helms has categorically denied that he was ever asked by the president or members of his administration to develop intelligence estimates to justify ongoing policy: "I would have been so offended if anybody had done that that I would have told them what they could do with it;" Richard Helms, Oral History I, interviewed by Paige Mulhollan, 4 April 1969, p. 31, LBJ Library.

South Vietnam constituted the primary threat to the allied war effort; part-time VC guerrillas did not merit inclusion as combat units in the order of battle.

After receiving the draft MACV press briefing, CIA analysts did more than just distance themselves from the intelligence judgments offered by the members of the intelligence community working in Saigon. They actively sought to deflate what they considered to be overly optimistic and unjustified analyses. Stung by the way MACV analysts took advantage of the September compromise, they became increasingly critical of MACV and what they took to be MACV-influenced intelligence analyses. Because information about the activity of VC guerrillas was viewed in the context of the order-of-battle dispute, a thorough study of VC activity before the Tet offensive would have threatened to turn again into a bureaucratic hot potato, threatening the tenuous compromise over estimates of enemy strength. As a result, MACV and CIA analysts failed to ponder the discrepancy between known communist estimates of their strength, contained in the captured documents employed in CIA analyses, and the estimates produced by the best efforts of the allied intelligence community. The possibility that this discrepancy could reveal a weakness in the enemy's camp—that the communists might have overestimated their support in South Vietnam—was never explored. Ultimately, the order-of-battle controversy would have a detrimental impact on the CIA's interpretation of signals of the impending offensive.

Although the signals obtained during September were not considered to be particularly alarming, enemy pressure along the DMZ forced a modification of U.S. plans. On 7 September, Westmoreland reacted to the increase in enemy attacks against the forces constructing the barrier. He ordered III MAF to develop an alternate plan for the construction of the strong point obstacle system. The main change in the new plan (III MAF OPLAN 12–67) was to stop construction of the obstacle system between strong points until the strong points and base areas were themselves completed and the tactical situation had quieted. Westmoreland justified this change on the grounds that it would result in fewer casualties among construction troops. In addition, he increased the number of allied units involved in protecting construction sites and also informed Sharp that, if the enemy attempted to circumvent the barrier by infiltrating troops farther to the west, he was prepared to move additional U.S. battalions to Lang Ruou, Khe Sanh, and Lang Vei.[40]

Westmoreland's decision to modify barrier plans is the first evi-

---

[40]*Command History 1967*, 3:1097–1098.

dence that communist efforts to divert U.S. forces toward the border were having an impact. In explaining his decision, Westmoreland provided evidence of his increasing receptivity to the communist diversion. His willingness to reinforce the westernmost outposts along the barrier, Khe Sanh and Lang Vei, demonstrates that he had already interpreted possible enemy activity near these bases as an effort to circumvent the antiinfiltration barrier. Westmoreland had interpreted communist pressure as a reaction to barrier construction. In effect, he saw an increase in enemy offensive activity as a defensive response—an interpretation that fit well with the belief that the communists had lost the military initiative.

Westmoreland also reacted to this pressure along the DMZ by requesting the acceleration of troop deployments and by modifying his plans, issued in mid-August, for the northeast monsoon campaign. On 28 September, he asked Sharp if the deployment of the 101st Airborne Division and the 11th Separate Infantry Brigade could be completed by the end of December. He also requested permission to retain the 9th Marine Amphibious Force beyond the planned rotation of the unit to the states because "the situation in I CTZ indicates a continuing requirement for this force through the spring of 1968."[41] Westmoreland informed Sharp about how he would use these additional forces in his modified plan for operations between October and January:

> The prospective early arrival of the 101st Div will not allow for initiation of planned operations in III CTZ while diverting the 1st Cav to I CTZ as required by the intensified enemy situation there. To insure adequate combat ready forces for III CTZ operations, I now plan to delay the movement of additional 9th Div elements to the Delta. . . . These moves are carefully planned to preclude any regression in the vital coastal areas of II CTZ . . . to do what is necessary to relieve and reverse the situation near the DMZ. . . . By this reoriented effort, I desire to pre-empt the enemy strategy of attempting to tie down forces and denude the pacification shield.[42]

---

[41]Quote from *Pentagon Papers, Gravel,* 4:531. According to one of the authors of the *Pentagon Papers,* enemy pressure along the DMZ might not have been the only reason for the acceleration of programed deployments to South Vietnam. The Joint Chiefs were asked what could be done for Westmoreland either before Christmas or 12 March, the day of the New Hampshire primary election. Westmoreland was also concerned about the imposition of a ceiling on the number of U.S. troops in South Vietnam: "A consideration in all accelerated deployments is the possibility of an extended holiday moratorium resulting in an agreement of status quo on force deployments"; ibid., 4:528, 531.

[42]COMUSMACV to CINCPAC, 281500Z, Sep. 1967, in *Command History 1967,* 1:340. Westmoreland's analysis of the purpose behind enemy pressure along the DMZ mir-

This modification of the plans further demonstrates that the enemy's diversion was working. Even though Westmoreland had begun to deploy army units to I CTZ by mid-1967, enemy activity along the DMZ had accelerated this trend and had begun to affect U.S. deployments in the southernmost reaches of the country (the delta). By October 1967, Westmoreland had moved three additional army battalions to I CTZ to reinforce the American Division, which was already deployed there. Westmoreland's underlying explanation for the reorientation of forces toward I CTZ is fascinating: he intended to preempt the enemy strategy of tying down U.S. forces in the border regions by increasing the number of U.S. units engaged in offensive operations in these areas. Westmoreland apparently recognized the enemy effort to divert U.S. forces toward the DMZ—in late October the DIA would again warn that this was at least one purpose behind the NVA attacks along the DMZ—but he intended to counter this effort by moving more units into I CTZ. It seems that Westmoreland's beliefs about the attainment of the shield objectives and the decline in communist military capability prevented him from realizing that his response to pressure along the DMZ would achieve enemy objectives.[43] His revised strategy played directly into the enemy's hands.

Although senior officers sensed during October that the enemy had made a major decision about the conduct of the war, it is difficult to determine what they thought this decision entailed and to what degree their interpretation of events was drawn from information about the enemy. Analysts often claimed that the communists were about to reevaluate their strategy. In August 1966, CIA analysts stated that, if adverse trends continued, the North Vietnamese would be forced "to take stock and consider a change in their basic strategy." Again in January 1967 they had indications that the North Vietnamese were "reviewing their strategy and pondering their prospects." These statements were not, however, solely engendered by available information.[44] The prediction that the communists were making a major decision concerning their strategy was a logical deduction from American

rored the analysis provided by the CIA in May 1967; see "5/23/67, Central Intelligence Agency, 'The Vietnamese Situation: An Analysis and Estimate,'" in *Westmoreland v. CBS*, exhibit 237, p. 2.

[43]Pearson, *War in the Northern Provinces*, pp. 98–99; *Command History 1968*, 1:434; and DIA Intelligence Summary, "Recent Enemy Operations in South Vietnam's Northern First Corps," 23 October 1967, p. 3, doc. 30, DSDUF Vietnam Box 4, Folder: NSF Country File Vietnam 2A (1) I Corps & DMZ Box 66, LBJ Library.

[44]"CIA Report, 8/26/66, 'The Communist Will To Persist,'" and "Memo, 1/9/67, from Office of National Estimates to Director," in *Westmoreland v. CBS*, exhibit 217, p. 21; 225, p. 2; and Kinnard, *War Managers*, p. 70.

beliefs about the allied and communist war efforts. Given assumed allied military strength and declining communist military capabilities, the North Vietnamese would eventually be forced to reevaluate their effort to unite Vietnam through force of arms. In August 1967, for example, Westmoreland stated during a press backgrounder that the time had come for Hanoi to make a "momentous decision" about the conduct of the war; years later, he admitted that this claim was not based on any specific information: "I based my conclusions on logic. They enemy was hurting and he was winning no victories."[45] Similarly, during a press briefing on 4 September, General Davidson, the MACV J-2, gave a detailed description of allied strengths and communist weaknesses and concluded his presentation with the remark: "We believe the enemy is at a point of great decision. The outcome of the [South Vietnamese presidential] elections should shortly reveal to us what he plans to do next."[46] Obviously, Davidson was describing enemy behavior as a reaction to allied initiatives.

One senior official did state during October that the enemy had made a strategic decision. In a 4 October report to the president, Ambassador Bunker stated that the publication of Giap's "The Big Victory, the Great Task" in September was evidence of "a serious and fundamental change in the strategy of the insurgency which merits careful and concentrated analysis."[47] But as Bunker's description of Giap's article demonstrated (see p. 150), he did not interpret Giap's analysis and prescription as an indication of a major offensive. Instead, the Americans, according to the MACV history, interpreted this "decision" as evidence of an enemy effort to avert a slow defeat.[48] What in hindsight appears to be the blueprint for the Tet offensive was interpreted as evidence of a communist decision to reduce the tempo of their activity.

Westmoreland's interpretation of the battles of Song Be and Loc Ninh not only shows that his beliefs influenced his judgments by masking the more disturbing aspects of these engagements but also demonstrates that he was not particularly concerned about the prospect of an increase in communist activity. The attacks at Song Be and Loc Ninh constituted a concerted enemy offensive, evidence of the type of enemy capability that the Americans believed was on the wane. Westmoreland, however, did not focus on this aspect of the battles; instead, he emphasized the surprisingly good performance

[45]Westmoreland, *Soldier*, p. 312.
[46]"10/24/67, Memo from McCafferty to Rostow," in *Westmoreland v. CBS*, exhibit 358, p. 11.
[47]"10/4/67 Bunker Cable to LBJ, No. 23," in ibid., exhibit 846A, p. 6.
[48]*Command History 1967*, 1:75.

turned in by ARVN during the engagements. He passed this interpretation of the battles on to Ambassador Bunker, who included it in one of his weekly reports to President Johnson. It is especially interesting that Westmoreland was aware that the assault at Loc Ninh represented a significant departure from normal enemy behavior. In his monthly report for October, Westmoreland stated that the battle of Loc Ninh was "the first known attempt in the Third Corps to employ multi-regimental forces from two divisions against a single objective." Still, he played down the enemy effort to coordinate main-force units in the attack. The enemy's willingness to employ their main-force units, he explained, could "only hasten the destruction of the main force units and facilitate the expansion of our pacification effort." Westmoreland thus described offensive action by the enemy as an initiative that would ultimately rebound to their detriment, a reflection of his beliefs about the success of the shield and attrition strategies.[49]

Westmoreland's directives for the conduct of future operations also demonstrated his confidence. On 8 October, for example, he responded to the decline in enemy activity around Con Thien by postponing the further reinforcement of I CTZ, instead committing some of the forces previously earmarked for the DMZ to offensive operations in III CTZ. On 29 October, he issued the planning directive that was to guide military operations between 1 November to 30 April. The directive began by summarizing evidence of allied progress in the war: the passing of the crossover point; the successful conduct of South Vietnamese elections in the face of VC pressure; and the failure of the enemy to launch major offensives along the DMZ and the western highlands after the allies conducted several spoiling attacks. Then followed a summary of how in the next six months U.S. forces would exploit their military initiative:

The overall strategy will contain three basic facets: (1) offensives to keep the enemy off-balance; (2) persistent neutralization of enemy base areas with methodical capture/destruction of his supplies and facilities; and (3) improved and expanded territorial security and other pacification programs. . . . Pressure will be applied on all segments of the enemy's external and internal support system to reduce the combat effectiveness of his organized forces and to keep him on the move and away from populated areas. Multi-brigade offensives will be launched against major base areas not previously invaded.[50]

[49]*Westmoreland v. CBS*, exhibits 830B, pp. 5, 8, 10; 846F, pp. 7–8.
[50]COMUSMACV Planning Directive No. 9–67, 29 October 1967, in *Command History*

In both directives, Westmoreland interpreted an event that would have previously been treated as evidence of enemy strength, an increase in offensive activity, as a sign of allied progress. He emphasized allied success in defeating communist offensives rather than the occurrence of the offensive activity itself. His calls for the conduct of U.S. operations against enemy base areas along the border are startling, given his previous concerns about enemy efforts to divert U.S. units away from the populated areas of the country. Westmoreland apparently did not realize that the presence of U.S. forces in these areas would play into the hands of the enemy, whether they were placed there by U.S. initiative or lured there by enemy diversion.

Although the Johnson administration had long been attempting to counter a decline in public support for the war, the climax of the administration's public relations campaign occurred during November. Westmoreland returned to the United States and between 15 and 27 November delivered a series of private briefings and public statements about the war. His assessment was consistently optimistic. Ultimately, however, the administration's presentation of Westmoreland to the American public rebounded to the detriment of the war effort. The general's optimistic reporting in November only added to the shock and disillusionment experienced by the public and by some senior officials after the offensive.[51]

There is no evidence that Westmoreland was unduly pressured by the administration to emphasize successful developments. In fact, it appears that the White House was most interested in discussing future offensive operations in Laos and Cambodia. In his notes prepared for the private briefings delivered to the president, the Joint

---

1968, 1:20–23. For a discussion of the 8 October directive, see *Command History 1967*, 1:341–342.

[51]Karnow, *Vietnam*, pp. 512–513; Palmer, *25-Year War*, p. 75; Oberdorfer, *Tet*, pp. 98–102, 106; Graham, Oral History II, pp. 22–23; and *Westmoreland v. CBS*, exhibit 313, pp. 299–304. The first meeting of the "Wise Men" (a group of distinguished businessmen, former officials, and retired officers), on 2 November 1967, concurred in the need for an increased effort to bolster public support for the war see; Meeting with Foreign Policy Advisors, 2 November 1967, Meeting Notes File, Box 2, Folder: 2 November 67 Meeting with Foreign Policy Advisors, LBJ Library; Schandler, *Unmaking of a President*, pp. 64–65; and Kalb and Abel, *Roots of Involvement*, pp. 199–200. For documentary evidence of a concerted public relations effort undertaken by the Johnson administration, see "8/18/67 notes of meeting with Rusk, McNamara, Wheeler, Rostow in Cabinet Room, from Jim Jones to the President," "Cable, 10/7/67 from American Embassy [Saigon] to Secretary of State," and "Cable, 10/28/67, from Bunker to Rostow," in *Westmoreland v. CBS*, exhibits 249, p. 4; 264; 267. Although the official portion of Westmoreland's trip to the states lasted from 15 to 22 November, he did not return to South Vietnam until 29 November. For a detailed description of Westmoreland's itinerary, see *Westmoreland v. CBS*, exhibits 912, pp. 78–85; 58, pp. 39–41.

Chiefs of Staff, the secretary of defense, and the House and Senate Armed Services committees, Westmoreland highlighted the usual areas of progress: VC manpower and food shortages, the destruction of enemy base areas, and the success of the shield strategy. He privately predicted that, if the United States kept up the pressure, the desirable trends would continue and "in approximately two years or less the Vietnamese Armed Forces should be ready to take over an increasing share of the war thereby permitting us to start phasing down the level of our effort."[52] Westmoreland repeated this claim in a speech to the National Press Club on 21 November.[53]

Although Westmoreland's description of progress would not have surprised his subordinates, the claim that in the foreseeable future the United States could begin to withdraw its forces was a significant departure from the usual assessments of the situation. On 8 November, for example, Vice-President Humphrey, in the aftermath of a trip to Vietnam, told a White House gathering that much progress was evident, but that no estimate could be made about when troop withdrawals could begin. Even as late as 11 November Westmoreland had stated that the decision had not been made to scale down U.S. involvement in the war and refused to speculate about when conditions would permit a reduction in combat strength. In a cable to General Abrams dated 26 November, Westmoreland explained why he decided to adopt this position on his own initiative:

> I believe the concept and objective plan for our forces, as well as those of the Vietnamese, is feasible and as such it should serve as an incentive. The concept is compatible with the evolution of the war since our initial commitment and portrays to the American people "some light at the end of the tunnel." The concept justifies the augmentation of troops I've asked for based on the principle of reinforcing success. . . . The concept straddles the Presidential election of November 1968, implying that the election is not a bench mark from a military point of view. . . . it put emphasis on the essential role of the Vietnamese in carrying a major burden of their war.[54]

Westmoreland implied that his prediction that the United States could soon reduce its involvement in the war followed from the military's

---

[52]"11/67, Westmoreland Notes for Talk with the President," in *Westmoreland v. CBS*, exhibit 283, pp. 1–4.

[53]Memo from Rostow to President, 16 November 1967, 9:30 A.M., doc. 107, and Memo from Rostow to President, 16 November 1967, 11:45 A.M., doc. 43, DSDUF Vietnam Box 3, Folder: NSF Aides File Walt Rostow Memos to the President, vol. 51, LBJ Library; and "11/21/67 Transcript, Westmoreland Speech to National Press Club," in *Westmoreland v. CBS*, exhibit 360.

[54]*Westmoreland v. CBS*, exhibit 285A.

confident assessment of the current situation, but in ordering Abrams to launch a MACV study on implementation of the eventual withdrawal he demonstrated that the announcement constituted a major change in strategy.[55]

Some students of the war have suggested that Westmoreland was unaware of recent developments in South Vietnam when he announced the possibility of troop withdrawals. Westmoreland was kept reasonably well informed, however, about events during his trip. Moreover, by the middle of November he and his subordinates at MACV were advancing different but not contradictory explanations of the developing situation. The assessments advanced by Westmoreland and other military officers tended to focus on explaining enemy motivations for launching individual attacks and did not place the increase in enemy activity in a broad context. These explanations also described the increase in enemy offensive activity and efforts to generate forces as having a positive impact on the allied war effort.[56]

Throughout November, several different explanations for the increase in enemy offensive and logistical activity were advanced. Commanders often explained individual enemy attacks as a reaction to allied initiatives. In responding to questions from reporters following his 21 November remarks to the National Press Club, Westmoreland stated that the communist attack on Dak To was an effort to discredit the South Vietnamese government on the eve of President Thieu's inauguration. Westmoreland also implied that the attacks against Dak To, Song Be, and Loc Ninh were responses to the success of the shield strategy. Similarly, in their monthly intelligence summary for November, MACV analysts claimed that the attacks on Loc Ninh were intended to disrupt preparations for the upcoming U.S. dry-season campaign.[57]

[55]Tom Johnson's Notes of Meetings Box 1, Folder: National Security Council Meeting 8 November 1967, pp. 1, 5, LBJ Library; and "11/11/67 COMUSMACV Backgrounder," in *Westmoreland v. CBS*, exhibit 915, pp. 21–22. Speaking about his November 1967 trip to Washington in 1969, Westmoreland noted that he consciously avoided making any statements that could have involved him in partisan politics and that he would have ignored partisan political questions posed even by the president; see William C. Westmoreland, Oral History I, interviewed by Dorothy Pierce McSweeny, 8 February 1969, pp. 10–11, LBJ Library.

[56]"Walt Rostow 7/29/81 Interview Transcript [with Mike Wallace]" and "Criles' Notes on Charles Morris," in *Westmoreland v. CBS*, exhibits 14, p. 73; 37A. In his memoirs, Westmoreland mentions the receipt of a 15 November cable from Abrams informing him of current war developments; see Westmoreland, *Soldier*, p. 313.

[57]*Westmoreland v. CBS*, exhibit 360, pp. 3, 10; and *PERINTREP*, November 1967, p. 4. Oberdorfer also notes that U.S. commanders believed that the communists attacked Loc Ninh to embarrass Thieu and Ky on the eve of their inauguration. In contrast, months after the Tet attacks, a high-level communist defector told a U.S. general that the Loc Ninh battle had been ordered to test mass-formation tactics in preparation for the Tet attacks; see Oberdorfer, *Tet*, p. 107.

Even though the border battles were interpreted as a response to allied initiatives, this explanation could not account for certain aspects of the engagements. On 25 November, the MACV J-2 assessment of the current enemy situation noted that the enemy had recently engaged in some uncharacteristic activity: "The normal slow and methodical approach to an attack was violated at Son Be, Loc Ninh and Dak To. Even more uncharacteristic was the obstinacy of the Loc Ninh and Dak To attacks in the face of heavy casualties and a growing Allied superiority. The Loc Ninh attack was the first instance in III CTZ of enemy employment of regiments from separate divisions against a single objective. . . . activity in IV corps was unique for that area in the size and coordination of forces involved."[58] MACV analysts also warned that the border battles probably constituted the beginning of the enemy's winter-spring campaign; the attacks fulfilled beliefs about weakened communist capabilities and the success of the shield strategy. Influenced by the belief that the enemy would use truce periods for resupply purposes, they predicted that high levels of enemy activity would continue in the area along the Cambodian border "until the holiday standdowns, but probably not at the high level of recent weeks."[59] Westmoreland even stated that the communists were expending large amounts of material in the border battles because they could use the upcoming truce periods to engage in a massive resupply effort. Analysts also predicted that pressure along the DMZ would increase in early 1968 but warned of the possibility that the NVA would conduct an offensive in this area just before the Christmas truce. MACV analysts were concerned that the communists would intensify their offensive when U.S. units, not their ARVN counterparts, would be most vulnerable to attack.[60]

Even though MACV analysts recognized that the enemy had recently engaged in unusual forms of activity, they still faced the problem of evaluating communist intentions. In their 25 November assessment, they warned that they still had not reached any firm conclusions about the motivations behind the recent increase in enemy offensive activity: "The unusual urgent nature of recent enemy activity and the spate of new reports and documents indicating possible changes in enemy political and military strategies could portend a radical alteration of the situation in the near future. This new information, which is not yet definitive, is under intensive study by the intelligence community."[61] These analysts apparently encountered

[58]*Westmoreland v. CBS*, exhibit 658, p. III-1.
[59]Ibid., exhibit 658, p. I-1.
[60]Ibid., exhibits 658, p. III-4; 831, p. 18.
[61]Ibid., exhibit 658, cover sheet.

some difficulty in understanding the enemy's reasons for launching the border battles. In a letter written on 18 November, James Meacham, an analyst at MACV, claimed that the enemy attack on Dak To was "something of a mystery to everyone." He went on, however, to offer his own analysis of the reasons behind the enemy decision to engage in the border battles:

> The enemy is incredibly stupid and his officers are deceiving themselves and each other at every opportunity. They are desperate for a victory and don't realize how bad off they are. They can't fight on equal terms, but can't go back to the guerrilla phase without losing a great deal. So they go on feeding their men into our meat grinder. . . . The end is near. First the DMZ massacre [Con Thien], then the senseless sacrifice at Loc Ninh, and now this [Dak To]. I look for some more of this, perhaps . . . at an increasing tempo. But they are playing our trump cards for us and the harder they flail at us the sooner it will be over.[62]

Although Meacham did not know it at the time, other officers and analysts were reaching similar conclusions about communist intentions.

Confronted by the need to reconcile an increase in enemy offensive and logistical activity with a belief that communist military strength was sagging, U.S. analysts came to rely on selected aspects of the Dien Bien Phu analogy to integrate their explanations of recent enemy behavior. In a background press briefing given on 29 September, for example, Westmoreland stated that the communists staged the attacks on Con Thien to create the appearance of victory and to "make headlines." Westmoreland argued, however, that Con Thien acted as a magnet, leading to the destruction of NVA units by overwhelming U.S. firepower. On 5 October, Westmoreland again offered this analysis to a reporter—only this time he described the battle of Con Thien as a "Dien Bien Phu in reverse." To prevent any misunderstanding about his use of the analogy, Westmoreland stated that undesirable aspects of the analogy did not apply. He noted that, in contrast to the battle between the French and the Vietminh, Con Thien was a U.S. victory.[63]

The Dien Bien Phu analogy was again used to explain the attacks on Con Thien, Loc Ninh, and Dak To in the 18 December speech given by General Wheeler to the Detroit Economic Club: the communists "hoped that these border engagements would reduce allied

---

[62]"Meacham Letter No. 114 [Dated 18 November 1967]," in ibid., exhibit 214B, pp. 2–4. Bruce Jones, an analyst at CICV at the time, seconds Meacham's description of attitudes within U.S. intelligence agencies; see *War without Windows*, pp. 128–129; see also Betts, "Strategic Surprise for War Termination," p. 161; and Oberdorfer, *Tet*, p. 107.

[63]Palmer, *Summons*, p. 169; and *Westmoreland v. CBS*, exhibit 912, pp. 38, 45.

pressure on the Viet Cong base areas and infrastructure and halt the Saigon Government's efforts to build a cohesive free society. In the process, they sought to increase the attrition on U.S. forces and, if possible, seriously undermine support of the war on the home front by annihilating a battalion or two of our forces in a miniature re-enactment of Dien Bien Phu."[64] These comments are interesting because they integrate the themes used to explain the increase in communist activity. Wheeler placed special emphasis on describing the attacks as a reaction to allied pressure against VC units operating in the more populated areas of Vietnam, the region behind the shield. The 25 November MACV J-2 assessment of the current enemy situation was thus interpreted in light of the belief that communist military fortunes were on the decline and that U.S. forces were achieving their attrition and shield objectives.[65] The border attacks were also explained as an effort to gain a psychological victory, a direct reflection of the belief that the communists realized that they could no longer win a strategic military victory. Many believed that the only logical purpose behind the border battles was to influence public perceptions of the war, the same objective attributed to the communist siege of Dien Bien Phu. Of particular importance is the fact that no type of "initiative" or strictly "military" purpose was attributed to the border battles. In fact, many officers did not view the border battles as an undesirable development. They welcomed the opportunity to use their superior firepower against massed communist troop formations, a view reflected by Westmoreland's interpretation of the fighting around Con Thien. In addition, Westmoreland's description of Dak To as the "beginning of a great defeat for the enemy" is representative of the way many officers viewed the border battles.[66] When these two themes were combined, as they were in Westmoreland's monthly assessment for November, they produced the following analysis: "Have every reason to believe the enemy will continue to expend sizable assets during the Winter months in an attempt to achieve a psychological victory. Such measures will permit us to make maximum use of our superior mobility and firepower in inflicting additional severe losses on the VC/NVA forces."[67] At the end of November, then, many U.S. analysts and commanders continued to embrace an optimistic interpretation of the developing situation.

Even though those at MACV tended to rely on the Dien Bien Phu analogy, Joseph Hovey and other members of the CIA station in

[64]"12/18/67 Address by General Earle C. Wheeler," *Westmoreland v. CBS*, exhibit 697, p. 5.
[65]Ibid., exhibit 658, p. II-8.
[66]Westmoreland quoted in Oberdorfer, *Tet*, p. 108.
[67]*Westmoreland v. CBS*, exhibit 831, p. 23.

Saigon developed a strikingly different interpretation of communist intentions and capabilities. A draft of their analysis was completed on 23 November, and its contents were apparently reviewed by senior officers, including General Westmoreland, by the end of the month. In contrast to the members of MACV, Hovey and his colleagues developed an accurate estimate of the overall strategy and objectives of the 1967 winter-spring offensive. They even predicted that the second phase (Tet attacks) of the campaign would materialize during January 1968.[68]

Several factors separated Hovey's accurate analysis from those of his MACV counterparts. Unlike MACV analysts and commanders, Hovey interpreted military developments on the battlefield in a broad context. He turned to the explanation of recent enemy behavior contained in captured documents, which were translated and initially interpreted by MACV analysts, to guide his analysis and to explain increased levels of enemy offensive and logistical activity:

> Numerous recently captured documents have brought into focus Viet cong (VC) and North Vietnamese (NVN) plans and ambitions for their 1967–68 winter-spring campaign. This campaign is to consist of three phases: a first phase from October to December 1967; a second phase from January to March 1968; and, a third phase from April to June 1968. . . . thus far VC/NVN activity indicates that they are indeed attempting to implement these plans at their intended levels of intensity. . . . the . . . campaign is described by the VC/NVN as the decisive phase of the war, crucial to its ultimate outcome.[69]

In effect, Hovey found that during the border battles the communists had actually implemented the plans for coordinated and sustained attacks contained in captured enemy documents.

After establishing that the first phase of the offensive (the border

[68]Hovey, working with other CIA analysts in Saigon, prepared the first draft of his analysis on 23 November and provided a copy of the memorandum to MACV J-2 analysts on 27 November; see "Adams' William Westmoreland Chrono," in ibid., exhibit 64, p. 23. Additional details provided during an interview with Walt Rostow by author, 7 January 1988. In his memoirs, Westmoreland states that in late November he received "a compilation . . . by the Saigon office of the CIA of various bits of evidence [which] reinforced the case for a more aggressive enemy strategy"; see Westmoreland, *Soldier*, p. 314. Oberdorfer also has referred to Hovey's analysis as a "collection of scraps"; see Oberdorfer, *Tet*, p. 120. The copy of the Hovey memorandum transmitted to the White House (dated 8 December) was, however, far from a collection of scraps. Hovey had divided his analysis into three parts: "Overview of Viet Cong Strategy," "The Viet Cong/North Vietnamese Winter-Spring Campaign," and "The Viet Cong/North Vietnamese Position on Coalition Government"; see "12/15/67 Carver Memo to Rostow, with attached 12/8/67 Memorandum," in *Westmoreland v. CBS*, exhibit 420. For excerpts and commentary on the Hovey memorandum, see Rostow, *Diffusion of Power*, pp. 462–463.

[69]*Westmoreland v. CBS*, exhibit 420, p. II-1.

battles) had taken place, Hovey integrated another factor into his overall analysis, recent political objectives articulated by the NLF. As a result, he was able to describe the overall strategy and objectives behind the campaign:

> The VC/NVN hope to force the redeployment of major Allied military units to the border areas where the VC/NVN enjoy sanctuary and will be able to inflict heavy casualties on them. . . . this will tie the Allied forces down in static defensive positions and . . . will relieve the pressure on the VC/NVN activities in the populated areas. Elsewhere the VC/NVN intend to accomplish the systematic destruction of GVN's administrative apparatus in the rural areas, and to "liberate" most of these areas. A final goal of the VC/NVN is to launch the long-promised "general uprising." To accomplish this, the VC/NVN have set themselves the task of occupying and holding some urban centers in South Vietnam and of isolating many others. . . . if they are successful in the above activities, the conditions will have been created for the overthrow of the present GVN and its replacement by a regime which will consent to form a coalition government. . . . the second major expectation . . . is that if they are successful, this will break the "aggressive will" of the Americans and force them to agree to withdraw from South Vietnam in a short period of time.[70]

Hovey was able to develop an accurate estimate of enemy intentions because, unlike MACV analysts and commanders, he expanded the scope of his analysis to cover both communist military and political objectives. In so doing, he identified one element of surprise, the general uprising, that was embodied in the winter-spring offensive. Mass demonstrations by tens if not hundreds of thousands of partially armed South Vietnamese civilians and defections of whole ARVN units could have altered the military balance between the allies and the communists. Under these circumstances, the communists' Tet objectives appeared realistic.

Hovey's analysis contradicted several beliefs embraced by commanders and analysts: that the shield strategy was working; that the South Vietnamese population would not revolt in support of the communists; and that the communists realized that they could not inflict a strategic military defeat on the allies. He was apparently aware that his analysis contradicted conventional wisdom. In an effort to explain how the communists could have "committed themselves to unattainable ends within a very specific and short period of time," he described at length the communists' optimistic view of the situation. He also warned that it was dangerous to dismiss his description of the

[70]Ibid., pp. II 4–5.

communists' maximum goals because even a partial realization of these objectives could still further the communist cause. Hovey even listed alternate interpretations of the communist campaign that demonstrated that communist gains would result even if they failed to achieve their maximum objectives:

A. A serious effort to inflict unacceptable military and political losses on the Allies regardless of VC casualties during a U.S. election year, in the hopes that the U.S. will be forced to yield to resulting domestic and international political pressure and withdraw from South Vietnam. This would probably involve the commitment of at least some elements of the NVA's reserves to South Vietnam.

B. Negotiations after a major military and political effort to place themselves in an advantageous a position as possible.

C. Reversion to a relatively low-intensity stage of warfare after having inflicted maximum casualties on the Allies and pre-empting any major allied offensive campaign.[71]

Hovey implied that, even though the communists may have miscalculated the relative fortunes of both sides in the conflict, they could still inflict serious damage on the allied war effort.

On 2 December, analysts at CIA headquarters produced a critique of the Hovey memorandum. Even though they admitted not seeing many of the documents used by Hovey (it often took three weeks for the documents screened by the CDEC to reach CIA headquarters), the analysts reacted with disfavor. Perhaps they were still upset by what they believed to be MACV violations of the compromise reached over NIE 14.3–67; their objections focused on some of the analytical themes used by Hovey, themes that were also championed by members of MACV. To the analysts working at CIA headquarters, it must have seemed that their colleagues in Saigon were serving as a mouthpiece for MACV, repeating many of the ideas advanced by the military that fueled the simmering dispute over the National Intelligence Estimate. If CIA analysts placed their stamp of approval on the Hovey memorandum, it could be used by members of MACV to demonstrate that the CIA now agreed with the military's view of the situation in South Vietnam.[72]

[71]Ibid., pp. II 5–6.
[72]For the reaction at CIA headquarters to the Hovey memorandum, see "12/2/67 CIA Memo," in ibid., exhibit 616. After the war, George Allen stated that he and his colleagues at CIA headquarters believed that the Saigon station's analysis of "the argu-

The analysts at CIA headquarters claimed to possess information (not available at the CIA station in Saigon) which undermined some of the conclusions Hovey drew from captured documents (not available at CIA headquarters), but they also took exception to two lines of analysis adopted by Hovey. They objected to the thesis that "the Communists may be about to make 'crucial' new decisions about the course of the war."[73] This prediction, which had been previously made by the CIA and was a favorite of MACV officers and analysts, represented a logical deduction from the belief that communist military fortunes were on the decline. In other words, the analysts at CIA headquarters objected to Hovey's use of one of the facets of the Battle of the Bulge analogy. They stated that the upcoming campaign was not "necessarily a last-ditch desperation gamble [nor did it prove] that the Communists [were] on the verge of collapse." They also objected to Hovey's acceptance of MACV's assertion that the crossover point had been reached, a bone of contention throughout the negotiations over NIE 14.3–67: "The field papers are predicated on the assumption that the present rate of attrition is not acceptable to the Communists, and that they are incapable of checking or reversing the basic trends in the war. We question the validity of these assumptions."[74] This critique, which was included with the memorandum as presented to W. W. Rostow on 15 December, reduced the persuasiveness of Hovey's analysis. Even though analysts at CIA headquarters thought the memorandum provided a "useful and provocative analysis," they basically concluded that Hovey was wrong. Rostow stated that, in light of the CIA critique, he found the Hovey memo to be unconvincing. But at the time, he chose to emphasize to the president one point that both memorandum and critique advanced: "Having gotten the Viet Cong to accept these months as 'decisive' and moving towards peace and victory 'this situation could have serious effects on Viet Cong morale and lead to a substantial increase in defections' if the campaign [the upcoming offensive] fails."[75] Needless to say, this was

---

ments in support of this thesis were not persuasive. Either the VC had been misled by their agents in the cities, or they were merely psyching their troops up to make a major effort in the more traditional offensive we believed was coming"; see ibid., exhibit 313, pp. 320–321.

[73]Quotation from ibid., exhibit 420, p. 3 (Carver's cover letter). Because of similarities in the analysis, Carver's statement was apparently drawn from the critique developed by his subordinates at CIA headquarters; see ibid., exhibit 616, p. 3. To his credit, Allen admitted drafting the 2 December 1967 CIA memo; interview with George Allen by author, 6 December 1989.

[74]Ibid., exhibit 420, p. 2.

[75]Memorandum for the president from Rostow, 16 December 1967, doc. 28, DSDUF Vietnam Box 3, Folder NSF Aides, File: Memos to the President, Walt Rostow, vol. 54, LBJ Library.

an extremely optimistic assessment of the warning contained in the Hovey memorandum.[76]

The history of U.S. responses to information about enemy intentions and capabilities between July and November 1967 shows the influence of entrenched beliefs. Several conclusions can be drawn from this analysis.

Intelligence assessments changed little during the period under consideration. Even though military analysts and commanders had obtained several indications that the communists were preparing a major offensive, they continued to be optimistic. As the evidence accumulated many commanders and analysts became convinced that encouraging trends in the war were accelerating. By the end of November, virtually every signal was being interpreted as a sign of continued progress toward the realization of allied goals, regardless of what it actually conveyed about the enemy. Increases of information only tended to bolster U.S. analysts in their confident estimates. It is not a coincidence that the most optimistic assessments were offered in November, well after most analysts and commanders had realized that the communist units were stirring in their border sanctuaries.

The examples in this chapter demonstrate that a good deal of time usually elapses before the signals generated by an opponent's initiative can break through a threshold of background noise. Even though analysts obtained many signals during July and August that appear in hindsight as preparations for the Tet attacks, at the time these activities seemed normal. Several similar signals had to accumulate before analysts recognized that the new information reflected a change in enemy behavior. It was not until September 1967 that analysts recognized the enemy's "unusual" forms of activity. Even then, analysts and commanders sometimes failed to realize that the preparations needed to undertake these unusual activities often began months before the activity itself was detected. As the next chapter shows, this tendency contributed to an underestimation of the amount of time the communists devoted to generating forces for the Tet attacks.

Intelligence analysts and commanders tended to interpret individual signals or developments sequentially. They often failed to integrate cumulative information, even though they were directly involved in the production of several monthly estimates that would have facilitated the combination of different types of signals into an overall analysis. This tendency made it easier for them to interpret

---

[76]*Westmoreland v. CBS*, exhibit 420, p. 1. For Rostow's post-Tet evaluation of the Hovey memorandum, see Rostow, *Diffusion of Power*, p. 463; and *Westmoreland v. CBS*, exhibit 14, p. 70.

individual developments in terms of simple beliefs; inconsistencies that might have emerged between the assessment of individual events were hidden. A decline in the number of enemy defectors, for example, was explained as a result of a reduction in offensive operations, but the fact that the slowdown was brought about by the surge in enemy activity during the border battles was disregarded. In contrast, Hovey and his CIA colleagues gathered and integrated information about current and planned communist political and military activities from a variety of sources—and in so doing shortened the time lag involved between the generation, detection, and interpretation of signals and developed an accurate description of the 1967 winter-spring campaign.

Developments in the ground war, especially engagements involving U.S. forces, were most salient to Americans. This fixation might be explained by the belief that U.S. units engaged in offensive operations posed the greatest threat to the enemy and constituted the logical target of enemy attacks. The border battles simply confirmed this belief. Moreover, as indications of future communist offensive activity mounted during November, General Westmoreland became concerned about renewed attacks against U.S. units engaged in the shield operation. He worried about the possibility that the main communist offensive would come during the Christmas truce, a period when U.S., not South Vietnamese, troops would be most vulnerable. In contrast, when information indicated that the border battles were a diversion, military analysts and commanders tended to dismiss it as propaganda. When a surprise attack is aimed at an ally, it apparently complicates the already difficult problem of anticipating an offensive. At the same time, the attacks against U.S. units and high-priority initiatives (barrier construction) threatened the targets most important to the U.S. command. When this occurred, commanders usually concluded that the main motivation was to inflict damage on the forces or projects under their direct supervision. They rarely entertained the possibility that the effect of enemy initiatives on U.S. units or projects might have been unintended or part of a larger scheme. Because attacks against U.S. units engaged in border operations and barrier construction affected U.S. forces and strategy, analysts and commanders simply concluded that these actions were intended to hurt their units and plans. They failed to realize that the attempt to prevent the realization of the assumed communist goal of disrupting American border operations actually helped fulfill the enemy's objective, the diversion of U.S. forces away from the populated areas of South Vietnam. As early as 28 September, Westmoreland had stopped the planned movement of elements of the U.S. 9th Infantry Division into the

[178]

densely populated IV CTZ and curtailed planned offensive operations in III CTZ in order to transfer elements of the 1st Cavalry Division to reinforce units operating along the DMZ.

Americans also tended to interpret evidence of enemy offensive and logistical activity as a response to allied initiatives. This interpretation was apparently driven by the belief that the communists had not only lost the military initiative but also recognized that they no longer possessed the military capability to inflict a strategic military defeat on the allies. Increases in enemy activity were interpreted as tactical moves in a defensive strategy, an interpretation that complemented beliefs about declining communist military fortunes. U.S. officers described communist offensives as attempts to gain psychological victories, thereby playing down the possibility that the enemy could still achieve even limited military objectives. The claim that communist attacks were responses to allied initiatives often failed to account for the time lag involved in the enemy's detection and interpretation of signals generated by allied activity; the communists were sometimes credited with an ability to concentrate forces and coordinate attacks on extremely short notice, or with virtually no notice at all. Analysts failed to realize that the allies *always* had just launched or were about to launch an important initiative, and their estimates tended to mistake correlations between allied and enemy actions for causality. The belief that the communists had lost the military initiative prevented them from recognizing this error.

The emergence of the Hovey memorandum demonstrates that U.S. intelligence agencies possessed enough information by the end of November to describe accurately the 1967 winter-spring campaign. Hovey was able to develop his accurate analysis by integrating information provided by a variety of sources, a technique that was rarely employed by members of the military. Moreover, Hovey did not dismiss evidence that indicated that the communists were planning a major offensive, but instead he attempted to discover whether or not the plans outlined in captured documents could be verified in terms of past enemy activity. Yet the question remained: would Hovey's accurate analysis sway U.S. attention away from the communist diversion at Khe Sanh?

[5]

Missing the Signals:
December 1967–30 January 1968

Throughout December 1967 and January 1968, the allies confronted a difficult problem. On the one hand, an ever-increasing amount of information indicated that the communists were preparing to attack urban areas, government installations, and U.S. bases throughout South Vietnam. Captured documents, POWs, defectors, allied agents, and enemy activity provided increasingly detailed insights into the targets, the tactics, and even the timing of the Tet attacks. On the other hand, communist diversionary efforts intended to fix the majority of U.S. units in their normal operating areas increased in intensity. When indications that NVA units were massing near Khe Sanh were confirmed by ground attacks against the firebase on 20 January, reinforcements and the attention of U.S. commanders were directed toward the border. The Dien Bien Phu analogy was readily invoked to explain the motivations behind the siege of the firebase. Senior commanders were convinced, however, that superior American firepower would prevent the communists from reenacting the campaign that had brought them victory against the French.

Although the U.S. command eventually decided that the main communist blow would fall at Khe Sanh, its estimates of enemy intentions and reaction to the dual threat posed by the communists continuously evolved during the period under consideration. This chapter traces this evolution. The first three sections, which chronicle events between 1 December 1967 and 21 January 1968, cover the signals obtained by analysts, the way they were interpreted, and military developments. In the fourth section, covering the period from 22 January through 30 January, all factors under consideration are combined to form a day-by-day analysis of the U.S. reaction to signals of impending attack.

[180]

DECEMBER

Signals

During December, it was evident that an increasing flow of replacements, supplies, and improved weapons were reaching the battlefield; 6,315 trucks were sighted along the Ho Chi Minh Trail during December, up from 3,823 sightings in November. CIA analysts reported on 8 December that the North Vietnamese were transporting, storing, and purchasing supplies in Cambodia. Even though they lacked definitive information, analysts at CIA headquarters claimed to possess indications that the North Vietnamese were using the Cambodian port of Sihanoukville to infiltrate supplies into South Vietnam. By the end of the month, evidence began to mount that more weapons were reaching combat units. AK-47s and RPG-7s, manufactured in China during the last quarter of 1967, were captured in IV CTZ. On 21 December, marine units near the U.S. airbase at Da Nang also captured, for the first time, a complete 122-mm rocket launcher, and POWs and defectors reported that NVA units in South Vietnam were receiving a steady supply of these rockets. MACV J-2 analysts also noted that the communists had used flamethrowers, again for the first time, during a 5 December attack on the Dac Son rural development hamlet in Phuoc Long province.[1]

CIA analysts turned in a mixed assessment of these developments. They correctly concluded that heightened logistical activities and a willingness to expend vast quantities of ammunition during the battle of Dak To demonstrated that the communists could meet the materiel requirements generated by an increase in combat intensity. They suggested that communist main-force units could now engage in sustained combat not only along the DMZ but also in other "remote" areas. In other ways, their analysis was dangerously wrong. They stated that the recent surge in infiltration was prompted by a North Vietnamese effort to replace losses suffered in the attempt to "shake the faith of the rural population" during the border battles and noted that "communist expectations of . . . fomenting a 'general uprising' have almost certainly diminished as a result of continued political stability in Saigon, the establishment of representative government institutions, and the limited nature of communist assets in urban areas."[2]

[1] Pearson, *War in the Northern Provinces*, p. 30; "Interview with General Walt, 4 September 1981" and "12/8/67 CIA Intelligence Memorandum, 'A Review of the Situation in Vietnam'," in *Westmoreland v. CBS*, exhibits 507; 528, pp. V-1–V-3; *Command History 1967*, PERINTREP, December 1967, pp. 5–6.
[2] *Westmoreland v. CBS*, exhibit 528, pp. 2, I-3, II-3.

In contrast to the CIA, which at least noted the increased communist capability to engage in sustained combat, MACV shied away from offering a negative analysis of two developments. First, they reported that captured documents and prisoner interrogations indicated that a command reorganization was under way in III CTZ. The reorganization expanded the area of responsibility of the Military Region 4 headquarters that operated in the vicinity of Saigon. Even though this reorganization increased the number of units attached to the headquarters, thereby increasing the capability of this command to conduct large-scale attacks against Saigon, analysts failed to draw any conclusions from this development. They chose not to confront its disconcerting implications by not speculating about the motivations behind the initiative: "At the present time, no explanation is available as to the reason for this reorganization." In this instance, when the news was bad, no "explanation" (speculation) was "available." Second, MACV analysts reported that General Giap had not been mentioned in official North Vietnamese announcements since October and had been conspicuously absent from several public events in Hanoi. In this instance, analysts offered a positive explanation (speculation) about Giap's whereabouts: they suggested that Giap's protracted war strategy might have been rejected by the North Vietnamese leadership and that he had fallen from favor after losing a policy debate. Even though the analysts' veiled reference to a possible change in communist strategy was correct for the wrong reasons (Giap was one of the architects of the Tet campaign), they interpreted a lack of information about the foremost North Vietnamese strategist in an extremely favorable fashion. Giap's absence from public life could have been explained by his preoccupation with the changes in communist behavior noted by the analysts, preparations that would culminate in the Tet offensive. MACV analysts, however, couched a disturbing reference to a possible shift toward an offensive strategy in a report of the apparent demise of a formidable communist strategist, thereby obscuring the more ominous implications raised by Giap's absence from public life. MACV analysts were apparently more likely to speculate about events in the communist camp that could be interpreted as favorable developments, a clear indication that they attended to information that confirmed their beliefs about the decline of the communist military.[3]

---

[3]*PERINTREP*, December 1967, pp. 1–7. The official government postmortem, however, states that analysts did deduce from the command and control reorganization that the communists were preparing to attack Saigon; see House Select Committee on Intelligence, *U.S. Intelligence Agencies and Activities*, p. 1999.

MACV analysts also played down an intensification of VC propaganda and terrorist activities in Saigon and Cholon, even though they possessed strong indications that the communists were mounting a major operation. Captured documents revealed that the infiltration of cadres into Saigon was supposed to be completed by late January 1968, that the population should be informed, without revealing the exact date of the initiative, that the time had come to stage the general uprising, and that conditions were now ripe to create an "honorable defeat" for the United States. The analysts merely linked the increase in these urban activities to the seventh anniversary of the NLF and the prelude to the holiday truce. They did not, however, elaborate on the relationship between propaganda, terrorist incidents, and holiday truces. Moreover, in their monthly intelligence summary, they described the contents of a captured VC secret document that outlined the use of fifth columnists to foster acts of desertion, defection, and sabotage within ARVN units. The target list described by the document takes on special significance in hindsight: "Main targets of this proselyting program would be personnel assigned to key positions or critical areas such as unit commanders, sentries, and guards at airfields, VIP quarters, cantonments, public offices, harbors, weapons depots and radio broadcasting stations." MACV analysts had unknowingly described many of the primary objectives of the Tet attacks, but they failed to attach any significance to them and chose not to speculate about the relationship between the communist proselyting program and the recent increase in enemy propaganda activity and terrorist attacks in the Saigon area.[4]

The response of MACV analysts to the surge in VC urban activity and efforts to subvert ARVN units is surprising given an additional piece of evidence they possessed about the gravity of the communist threat, the reaction of their South Vietnamese counterparts to the developing situation. In a letter written on 19 December, MACV analyst James Meacham described the reaction of the U.S. command and ARVN officers to the VC campaign: "The word is out that the VC are going to make an all out terrorist effort·against Saigon Americans from now on through Tet. Our ARVN counterparts at CICV are really concerned—the first time in living memory that they have been. This is a bad sign because they know the VC infinitely better than we."[5]

[4]Quote from *PERINTREP*, December 1967, p. 9. CDEC Bulletins 8468, 8319, Folder: Vietnam CDEC Bulletins, vol. 2, and CDEC Bulletin 9026, Folder: Vietnam Captured Documents Cables, LBJ Library.

[5]"Meacham Letter No. 147, Dated 19 December 1967," in *Westmoreland v. CBS*, exhibit 214UU. Bruce Jones, an analyst at CICV, noted that at about this time a VC document was captured that listed not only the Americans and South Vietnamese working at

[183]

U.S. analysts seemed to interpret the reaction of ARVN officers to the VC terror campaign as a rare manifestation of concern about their own personal safety. Even though they were beginning to sense that the communists were planning a major attack, they did not view South Vietnamese concerns that they were being singled out for attack and other information that suggested that urban centers and government installations would be struck as highly specific indications of the exact targets and timing of the offensive. Instead, this information was interpreted as an indication that the communists were simply up to something.

Military Developments

Although the communists launched six large-scale attacks during December, enemy offensive activity remained low throughout much of the country. In I CTZ, enemy units remained in the vicinity of Con Thien and other strong points along the barrier, but offensive activity was limited to artillery attacks. Sporadic contacts with enemy units and information from captured documents, however, led MACV analysts to conclude that enemy activity in I CTZ would increase significantly during January. Intelligence sources in I Corps indicated that the 2d NVA Division was shifting its areas of operation in preparation for an offensive. Other sources reported that the 325C NVA Division had moved back to positions near Hill 881 North (northwest of Khe Sanh), while the 304th NVA Division, which participated in the siege of Dien Bien Phu, had traveled from Laos to positions southwest of Khe Sanh. Small-unit engagements and sightings of enemy reconnaissance parties around Khe Sanh were also interpreted as a possible prelude to offensive action. Analysts even detected the presence of a "front headquarters," which the NVA usually used to direct the operations of two or more divisions, in the vicinity of Khe Sanh. Enemy military activity also remained low in II CTZ during December, but the movement of communist units in the vicinity of Pleiku and Kontum was interpreted as a sign that attacks in the western highlands were again likely in the near future. Throughout the northwestern portions of III CTZ, most enemy units were engaged in resupply efforts, which analysts correctly labeled as preparations for future offensive operations. Communist offensive activity increased in the remainder of III CTZ and in IV CTZ. Analysts attributed this heightened activity to the opening of the 1967 winter-spring campaign in

---

CICV and CDEC but the interior layout of their offices as well. This document might have been the source of ARVN's discomfort; see Jones, *War without Windows*, p. 139.

these areas. MACV analysts, however, gave no indication that they considered this development to be a prelude to an even more intense period of offensive action. Thus, their analysis downplayed the possible intensity of the impending offensive by suggesting that the current level of offensive activity in much of III and IV CTZ constituted the full scope of the dry-season campaign in these areas. In other words, offensive activity in these areas was already considered high in terms of communist military capabilities, and it fulfilled American expectations about the intensity communist attacks would achieve during the 1967 winter-spring campaign.[6]

Reactions

By mid-December, two important developments emerged in the U.S. reaction to signals of impending attack: senior commanders, including General Westmoreland, concluded that the enemy was preparing to launch a major offensive, and the themes used to interpret events were combined into a line of analysis that would persist largely unchanged until the final hours before the Tet attacks.

Even though the year-end summaries turned in by Westmoreland and Admiral Sharp emphasized the progress attained over the preceding twelve months, both men realized that they would soon be facing a major communist challenge. Given the belief that communist military fortunes were on the decline, this was no small development. As late as 11 December, for example, General Depuy had informed General Wheeler that the establishment of the front headquarters near Khe Sanh, "may be in preparation for ultimate negotiations. . . . This would provide a manageable framework for negotiation and ultimate NVA withdrawal." As an afterthought, Depuy added: "It [the command reorganization] also provides a straightforward chain of command for more efficient operations should negotiations not eventuate."[7] Although it is impossible to determine exactly when West-

---

[6]*PERINTREP*, December 1967, pp. 1–5; and Telfer et al., *U.S. Marines in Vietnam*, p. 259. Pearson, Palmer, Shore and the authors of the 1968 command history claim that enemy troop movements were seen as a major indicator of impending attack during December 1967; see Pearson, *War in the Northern Provinces*, p. 30; Palmer, *Summons*, p. 178; Shore, *Battle for Khe Sanh*, p. 29; and *Command History* 1968, 1:390. For a rough location of enemy main-force units on 31 December 1967, see *Command History* 1967, 1:61–65.

[7]Depuy's report quoted (without comment) in memorandum from Robert N. Ginsburgh to Rostow, 11 December 1967, doc. 20, NSF Country File, Vietnam Box 68–69, Folder: Vietnam 2C(2) General Military Activity, LBJ Library. Although Admiral Sharp generally listed areas of allied progress in his end-of-year summary for 1967, he did state that "recent large scale deployments from North Vietnam indicate that the enemy

moreland realized that the enemy was preparing to launch a major attack, by 16 December he had definitely reached some conclusions about where and even when the main communist blow would land. Westmoreland's history notes, which briefly trace out his daily activities, reveal that on that day he traveled to I CTZ to confer with marine commanders and to inspect barrier fortifications along the DMZ: "On Saturday I flew out to I Corps to discuss with General Cushman the construction of facilities to accommodate the 1st Cavalry Division if it becomes necessary to reinforce 3d MAF during the coming months. My analysis is that the enemy's next major effort will be in I Corps and I believe he will be prepared to initiate this by next January. . . . Latest intelligence suggests that we should greatly accelerate these efforts."[8] Westmoreland expected NVA units to attack U.S. forces engaged in shield operations, the troops stationed in relatively well-prepared defensive positions along the barrier. In contrast, he demonstrated that he did not expect an attack against urban centers when he turned over the defense of Saigon to the ARVN 5th Ranger Group on 20 December. In a ceremony commemorating the shift of responsibility, Westmoreland warned the rangers that as a matter of South Vietnamese prestige they had to succeed and that it would be regrettable if U.S. troops were forced to return to protect the capital.[9]

Between 19 and 20 December, Westmoreland sent two cables to Wheeler and Sharp that outlined his analysis of the situation. The first cable, a response to a question—"Why do we fight the enemy near the borders?"—apparently raised by Wheeler, constitutes the ultimate articulation of the shield strategy. It also demonstrates that Westmoreland viewed the border battles and pressure along the DMZ not as a diversion but as a response to the effective deployment of U.S. forces:

> The . . . NVA . . . has chosen to concentrate . . . along the borders . . . so that he can launch major attacks against SVN to gain a psychological and

---

may be seeking a spectacular win in South Vietnam in the near future"; see Sharp, *Strategy for Defeat* pp. 302–303; and *Pentagon Papers, Times* pp. 613–615. Westmoreland also provided an optimistic assessment of allied progress in his year-end report; see *Pentagon Papers, Gravel,* 4:538–539.

[8]"General Westmoreland's History Notes Volume VIII, 21 August–26 December 1967," in *Westmoreland v. CBS,* exhibit 912, p. 99. In his memoirs, Westmoreland states that at the time he believed that the enemy would attempt to overrun the two northern provinces during the Christmas season in order to strike a psychological blow at American public opinion. He also claims that he believed that the enemy would launch attacks throughout South Vietnam in a diversionary effort; see Westmoreland, *Soldier,* p. 313. There is no evidence that Westmoreland took this latter threat seriously at that time.

[9]*Westmoreland v. CBS,* exhibit 912, pp. 101–102; and Stanton, *Rise and Fall* p. 143.

political victory, while at the same time retaining the best hope of disengaging when defeated. He has demonstrated this strategy by his recent incursions near Con Thien, Dak To, and in the Loc Ninh/Song Be areas. In each of these battles, the targets of the enemy attacks, and the big chance for an exploitable psychological victory, were the closest major GVN/US positions to the border and the populated areas surrounding them. . . . When the enemy moves across the borders we must strike him as soon as he is within reach, and before he can gain a victory or tyrannize the local population.

In effect, pressure along the borders provided the allies with an opportunity: "when we engage the enemy near the borders, we often preempt his plans and force him to fight before he is fully organized and before he can do his damage."[10]

On 20 December, Westmoreland elaborated on the previous day's analysis by explaining why the enemy had been driven to stand up to U.S. firepower near the borders. Westmoreland reported that, in late September,

the enemy decided that prolongation of his past policies . . . would lead to defeat, and that he would have to make a major effort to reverse this downward trend. The enemy was forced to this grave decision by the deterioration of his position over the last six months, and a realization that the trends were running heavily against him. His forces were taking heavier losses than he could replace. His coastal divisions were badly hurt. He failed to disrupt the GVN elections. His infiltration could be hampered in the near future by the Muscle Shoals project. Most important, he continued to lose control of the population. . . . His decision therefore was to undertake an intensified country-wide effort, perhaps a maximum effort, over a relatively short period.

Even though Westmoreland provided an accurate prediction of a country-wide offensive, he backed away from this prediction later in the cable: "enemy has already made a maximum effort to achieve *a victory of some sort* in a short period of time."[11]

[10]"Text of Cable From General Westmoreland (MAC 11956)," 19 December 1967, pp. 1, 3, The President's Appointment File Box 89, Folder: 1 Feb. 1968, LBJ Library.

[11]"12/20/67 Cable from Westmoreland to Sharp," in *Westmoreland v. CBS*, exhibit 384, pp. 1, 8 (emphasis added). For a discussion of the Westmoreland cable, see Westmoreland, *Soldier*, p. 314; Oberdorfer, *Tet*, pp. 120–121; and Betts, "Strategic Surprise for War Termination," p. 162. Herbert Schandler points out, however, that Sharp reacted skeptically to the 20 December cable; see *Unmaking of a President*, p. 70. This cable has often been identified as the major warning given to the Johnson administration prior to the Tet offensive and the basis of Johnson's predictions of kamikaze attacks and a surge in enemy activity to the Australian cabinet; see Westmoreland, *Soldier*, p. 239; Betts,

Westmoreland's 20 December cable reflects his prior beliefs. Echoes of the Battle of the Bulge emerge with his justification of the belief that enemy fortunes were on the decline with indications that they were preparing a major attack. His analysis also downplayed the threat posed by a "country-wide offensive" in noting that enemy units in the coastal (populated) areas of the country had been weakened. Westmoreland did not propose initiatives to meet this threat. Instead he highlighted the threat posed by the NVA along the border and proposed a response to this challenge: "To pursue the enemy by fire in the tri border area now, and to execute limited raid operations of Battalion/Brigade size into base areas . . . would put us in a better position as regards the enemy's continued use of the sanctuaries. . . . I strongly recommend this."[12]

In linking the coming offensive to enemy concern over the completion of the Muscle Shoals portion of the barrier, Westmoreland apparently assumed that the communists recognized that the air-supported antipersonnel and antivehicular portion of the barrier that stretched through Laos was being tested. But Muscle Shoals was the section of the barrier that still remained secret, so Westmoreland seems to have based part of his analysis on information that should have been known only by senior U.S. officers and analysts.[13]

Westmoreland also argued that the communists made their strategic decision after the 14–16 September publication of Giap's "The Big Victory, the Great Task" because of the contrast between the article ("proclaiming a protracted war of attrition and conservation of forces") and captured documents issued at a later date that urged enemy units "to make a maximum effort on all fronts (political and military) in order to achieve victory in a short period of time."[14] It seems that Westmoreland not only misinterpreted the portions of Giap's article that described the coming attacks but also failed to recognize the time lag between the generation, detection, and interpretation of signals. He should have realized that, if intelligence analysts were beginning to obtain evidence in September that the enemy had made a major strategic decision, then that decision must have been made long before signals were detected. Westmoreland's ill-considered analysis of the timing of the communists' strategic decision placed a limit on estimates of the time the enemy had devoted to

"Strategic Surprise for War Termination"; Oberdorfer, *Tet*; "William Westmoreland Interview Transcript [with Mike Wallace] 17 May 1981," in *Westmoreland v. CBS*, exhibit 349, pp. 88–89.
[12]*Westmoreland v. CBS*, exhibit 384, p. 8.
[13]For a description of the Muscle Shoals test, see *Command History 1967*, 3:1109–1110.
[14]*Westmoreland v. CBS*, exhibit 384, p. 2.

generating forces for the predicted offensive, thereby limiting estimates of the potential scope and intensity of the upcoming attacks.

Westmoreland also informed Sharp that the communists might attempt to initiate negotiations in conjunction with their upcoming campaign. His concerns about a possible negotiating initiative might have been influenced by the Dien Bien Phu analogy. Westmoreland was worried that the administration might enter into negotiations against the advice of the military. Anticipating this eventuality, he described how current campaign plans—which were directed against the NVA threat along the borders and not against the threat posed by weakened communist units operating in populated areas—would place allied forces in a favorable position if a cease-fire was declared in the near future:

> York operations and concurrent establishment of CIDG camps in Western I CTZ during the period Feb on into early summer will give us presence in a heretofore enemy sanctuary. Our presence, of course, already exists in the populated areas of I CTZ and along the DMZ. In II CTZ our forces have broadly established presence throughout, except in uninhabitable mountainous areas. Yellowstone (War Zone D) will complete the deployment of friendly strength throughout III CTZ. In IV CTZ we now have deployed our forces throughout most of the Corps area. In summary it would be prudent for us to push ahead with all of our current plans so as to establish RVNAF/FWMAF presence on the broadest possible front throughout SVN.[15]

As events were to show, Westmoreland's prediction was accurate and his concerns were well founded; a communist negotiating ploy on the eve of the Tet offensive was partly to blame for the worst decision—to not cancel totally the Tet truce—made by Westmoreland and the Johnson administration in this period. In contrast, Westmoreland's intention to continue to disperse U.S. forces along the borders and to attack communist sanctuaries in response to a possible combined communist offensive and negotiating initiative demonstrates that the enemy's diversionary attacks were succeeding.

Although Westmoreland noted the developing communist threat, he did not modify his offensive plans and even called for permission to conduct operations inside Cambodia and Laos. Operation York, for example, which had been modified in early December and was scheduled to begin in mid-February 1968, consisted of a series of assaults to

[15]Ibid., exhibit 384, p. 4. For a discussion of the continued emphasis on offensive operations along the border of South Vietnam throughout December 1967 and early January 1968, see Thompson, *No Exit from Vietnam*, p. 70.

be launched by the U.S. 1st Cavalry Division into western Do Xa province (York I), the A Shau valley (York II), western Quang Tri province (York III), and eastern Do Xa (York IV). Westmoreland was playing into the hands of the communists by increasing the tempo of offensive operations in the border regions. He even requested that restrictions on the hot pursuit of communist forces into Laos and Cambodia be lifted, an action that would have further removed U.S. forces from the populated areas of South Vietnam. Even though he expected a major offensive, Westmoreland's prescriptions for meeting it did not require the modification of U.S. plans or the taking up of defensive positions. His beliefs about the relative decline of communist military capability were still at work.[16]

Two conclusions stand out about the U.S. interpretation and re-action to signals of impending attack during December. First, despite indications of advanced enemy preparation for a major attack through-out South Vietnam, Westmoreland and many other senior command-ers and analysts seemed most concerned about the possibility of a powerful attack against U.S. positions along the DMZ. The commu-nist diversion toward the border areas was gaining momentum; Khe Sanh would soon begin to loom large in the minds of Americans. Second, the intelligence analysis that emerged in December remained remarkably consistent until the very eve of the Tet attacks. The allies would not realize that southern cities were about to be attacked until it was too late.

30 December–10 January

Signals

The first signal during this period emerged on 30 December, when North Vietnamese foreign minister Nguyen Duy Trinh stated at a public reception that a halt in the bombing of North Vietnam *would* lead to negotiations between Hanoi and the United States. The state-ment, which was repeated by other North Vietnamese officials, was a significant departure in Hanoi's position on negotiations. Previously the North Vietnamese maintained that a halt in the air campaign *could* result in negotiations. Trinh's proposal was, however, a ploy. The change in the North Vietnamese position, which was also announced

---

[16]For a description of the history of Operation York and its status on 20 December, see *Command History* 1968, 1:23–24. In his memoirs, Westmoreland states that the York series was intended to place U.S. forces in a position to invade Laos and support a U.S. landing north of the DMZ; see Westmoreland, *Soldier*, p. 314.

by Radio Hanoi on 1 January, was probably intended to improve the communist military position on the eve of the offensive, add to the surprise of the Tet attacks, and involve the United States in negotiations as the winter-spring campaign unfolded.[17]

MACV analysts continued to obtain information about increasing enemy logistical activity. On 3 January, J-2 duty officers received indications that the VC had positioned weapons around Saigon. The source reported that the VC had buried grenades, rifles, and other more powerful weapons in a cemetery near a crossroads on the outskirts of Saigon. The source also stated that the VC had recently been avoiding the area. Similarly, on 4 January, ARVN discovered a major weapons cache in Dinh Tuong province (IV CTZ). Rifles, rocket launchers, and thousands of rounds of small-arms ammunition were captured. The cache also contained fifty-five 120-mm mortar rounds, confirming for the first time the existence of this weapon in IV CTZ. A POW who claimed to be the executive officer of a VC transportation company operating in the vicinity of the discovery subsequently led ARVN units to forty-one other caches in the area.[18]

The major weapons caches in IV CTZ were, however, not interpreted as evidence of an enemy buildup for an offensive. Even after the Tet attacks, MACV analysts did not speculate about the significance of the weapons caches and only stated that they "indicated [that] the enemy is capable of moving and infiltrating newly manufactured equipment over a long distance in a short period of time."[19] Westmoreland drew the same conclusion. In a cable sent to Wheeler and Sharp on 7 January, he described the contents of the caches captured on 4 January and other weapons that had been accumulating since September. The presence of newly manufactured weapons in IV CTZ was significant, according to Westmoreland, because it pointed to the presence of a new infiltration route into the country: "Although the introduction of newer and larger caliber weapons in IV CTZ has increased the enemy's logistical problem, he has displayed an improved logistical capability, the large volume of supplies and the land distance involved, probably prohibits the use of porters and suggests that the supplies are being moved by ship into Cambodia [Sihanoukville] for subsequent infiltration into South Vietnam." Because of their belief that the enemy had lost the military initiative, Westmoreland

[17]Thies, *When Governments Collide*, p. 198; and Kalb and Abel, *Roots of Involvement*, p. 225.

[18]Item 22 0940 3 January, Item 31 1244 4 January, Item 41 1554 4 January, and Item 46 1715 4 January, Daily Journal Files, MACV J-2 Command Center; and *PERINTREP,* January 1968, p. 3.

[19]*PERINTREP,* January 1968, p. 4.

[191]

and MACV analysts failed to realize that the flow of new weapons into IV CTZ was part of a major offensive. Evidence of offensive activity so far behind the shield of U.S. forces, unlike the NVA concentration along the DMZ, would have contradicted the idea that communist military fortunes were on the wane. Predictably, Westmoreland, on 8 January requested permission to interdict the flow of supplies by attacking enemy base areas inside Cambodia. Although this initiative was never carried out before the Tet offensive, Westmoreland's request again demonstrates that he was not concerned at this time about moving his forces even farther away from the populated areas of South Vietnam.[20]

On 4 January, MACV J-2 obtained further evidence of the enemy's final preparations for the Tet offensive—a report that a VC sapper team had infiltrated the MACV headquarters complex at Tan Son Nhut by securing jobs at the airbase. The sappers reportedly intended to attack MACV between 5 January and "Tet" as one element of a "six part attack on allied installations."[21] Reports of planned attacks against MACV and other allied installations near Tan Son Nhut did not, however, generate much concern among analysts and commanders. Similarly, MACV analysts apparently interpreted a document entitled "Urgent Combat Order Number One," which was captured on 5 January in Pleiku province, as an indication of a threat only against U.S. units in this border province. The operations outlined in the plan culminated in a final assault on Pleiku and called for communist cadres to prepare, before the Tet holidays, to stage mass demonstrations. The document was taken seriously by the commander of the 4th Infantry, Maj. Gen. Charles P. Stone, perhaps because the 4th Infantry Division was directly threatened by the attack. Stone considered the document to be an accurate reflection of enemy intentions, but not evidence of a developing threat against all southern cities. This document, combined with additional information obtained by the 4th Infantry Division, did enable Stone to blunt the attacks on Pleiku when they finally materialized on 30 January.[22]

Other indications of what was to come began on 8 January, when a demonstration against U.S. bombing and aid to South Vietnam was staged in Da Nang (I CTZ). The 84 protesters were led by a VC cadre member who was immediately arrested by the South Vietnamese police. On 10 January, another protest broke out in Lai Nghi hamlet in

---

[20]"6/9/81 Westmoreland letter to Wallace and Crile with Enclosures," "1/8/68 Cable from Westmoreland to Wheeler and Sharp," p. 1, in *Westmoreland v. CBS*, exhibit 390.

[21]Item 24 1053 4 January, Daily Journal Files, MACV J-2 Command Center.

[22]Oberdorfer, *Tet*, p. 126; Westmoreland, *Soldier*, p. 317; Lung, *General Offensives*, p. 35; and *PERINTREP*, January 1968, p. 2.

Quang Nam province (I CTZ). Two hundred villagers called for the United States to stop bombing, firing artillery, and using chemical defoliants near their village. The outbreak of these small demonstrations was probably the first manifestation of open VC efforts to generate popular support for the Tet attacks. Moreover, on 9 January, a document was captured which provided a description of the recent VC command reorganization. The reorganization was effective 1 December. MACV analysts apparently reacted to this information in much the same way that they reacted to previous indications about changes in the communist command: they made no attempt to estimate possible enemy intentions from this initiative. In fact, in their monthly summary for January they simply stated that the reorganization would provide VC local and main-force units "with a greater area of operations and access to Saigon." Even in the aftermath of the Tet attacks, analysts still failed to make the connection between the 31 January attacks on Saigon and the 1 December 1967 VC command reorganization.[23]

Military Developments

Between 31 December and 2 January the New Year's cease-fire was marred by dozens of communist truce violations. The most serious incident occurred at 0514 on 2 January, when elements of the VC 9th Division attacked positions held by the 3d Brigade of the U.S. 25th Infantry Division operating northwest of Saigon. More than 400 VC were killed in an attack that was described by analysts as an effort to prevent the 25th Infantry from continuing Operation Yellowstone, which was designed to eliminate the VC presence in War Zone C.[24] During the night of 2 January, an event confirmed that the 325C and 304th NVA Divisions were near Khe Sanh and that communist interest in the firebase was growing. Six individuals dressed in U.S. Marine uniforms were challenged as they walked near the perimeter of the firebase. When they failed to respond, the marines opened fire and killed five of the six intruders. Documents found on the bodies revealed that the five dead men were NVA officers, one a regimental commander. The marines quickly surmised that the NVA officers were conducting a reconnaissance of the firebase's defenses. U.S. an-

---

[23]*PERINTREP*, January 1968, pp. 6–9; and CDEC Bulletin 9017, doc. 16, NSF Country File, Vietnam, Folder: Vietnam Captured Documents Cables, LBJ Library. The MACV history for 1968 notes the connection between the command reorganization and the Tet offensive; see *Command History* 1968, 1:67, 69.

[24]*PERINTREP*, January 1968, p. 3; Item 34 0553 and Item 58 1303 2 January, Daily Journal Files, MACV J-2 Command Center; and Stanton, *Rise and Fall*, pp. 153, 209.

alysts and commanders, including General Cushman, the commander of III MAF, interpreted this incident as evidence of the enemy's intention to attack Khe Sanh. The incident, which confirmed that the 304th NVA Division, veteran of the siege of Dien Bien Phu, was in the vicinity of Khe Sanh, created a sense of urgency among commanders about improving defenses at the firebase.[25]

Although the NVA reconnaissance of the Khe Sanh perimeter was significant, there were also other important military incidents between 2 and 10 January. In hindsight, it is apparent that these initiatives were either undertaken to practice tactics for the Tet attacks or were last-minute preparations for the offensive. On 3 January, the NVA 368B Artillery Regiment launched 122-mm rockets at the U.S. airbase at Da Nang. The barrage, which was accompanied by ground attacks intended to divert U.S. forces away from the rocket-firing positions, damaged several aircraft. On 10 January, the communists used satchel charges and rockets to attack the U.S. airfield near Kontum (II CTZ). On 5 January, the communists attacked a South Vietnamese police headquarters and prison at An Khe in Binh Dinh province (II CTZ). After penetrating the compound, sappers used satchel charges to blow holes in the wall of the jail, but they failed to free the VC suspects held there. Three significant attacks occurred on 8 January. The VC launched rockets against a U.S. Marine command post near the airbase at Da Nang, damaging the facility and inflicting numerous casualties. The VC, including elements from two sapper units, staged another attack against an ARVN headquarters and provincial defector center in III CTZ. They succeeded in killing or capturing several defectors who were being processed at the facility. MACV analysts noted that the VC apparently also attempted to coordinate a series of attacks in five provinces in IV CTZ.[26]

Allied Reactions

Between 30 December and 10 January, U.S. political and military leaders made decisions that both helped and hindered the allied response to the coming offensive. Members of the Johnson administration were responsible for one of the worst decisions made by Americans during this period when they responded favorably to the

---

[25]Shore, *Battle for Khe Sanh*, pp. 28–29; Westmoreland, *Soldier*, pp. 314–315; and Oberdorfer, *Tet*, p. 109.

[26]*PERINTREP*, January 1968, pp. 1–3; and Item 10 0451, Item 13 0541, Item 16 0701, Item 27 1121, and Item 36 1731 3 January, Item 26 0642 5 January, Item 7 0041, Item 15 0242, Item 34 1003, Item 40 1133, Item 49 1423 8 January, and Item 11 0422, Item 15 0452, Item 19 0612, Item 34 1322 10 January, Daily Journal Files, MACV J-2 Command Center.

negotiating overture of foreign minister Trinh. Since the change in the North Vietnamese position on the prerequisites for negotiations was undertaken in support of the offensive, the U.S. response helped the communists achieve at least two of the three objectives behind the initiative. The Johnson administration fell victim to a communist ruse.[27] It is likely that the primary North Vietnamese objective behind the negotiating initiative was to recreate the conditions that existed during the siege of Dien Bien Phu. The communists hoped to enter into negotiations at a time when their opponents' military fortunes had reached a nadir. Hanoi was attempting to provide the United States with a graceful way to extricate itself from the war in the wake of the expected general uprising, the disintegration of ARVN, and the collapse of the Saigon regime. Because the offensive failed militarily, however, the Trinh initiative never achieved this objective.[28]

The communists probably also hoped that the initiative would gain them some respite from the bombing campaign during the final preparations for the Tet offensive. U.S. officials recognized this as a possible motivation behind Trinh's offer. On 5 January, Rostow told the president that he was concerned about the sharp contrast between the Trinh initiative and "increasingly solid evidence of major North Vietnamese Army buildup against I Corps area." William P. Bundy, assistant secretary of state for Far Eastern affairs, publicly downplayed the importance of the Trinh statement and warned that Hanoi might just be attempting to gain a temporary halt in the bombing to strengthen its military position. Concerns that the initiative was a ploy were not strong enough, however, to prevent the administration from creating conditions conducive to the exploration of Hanoi's new position. Even though Westmoreland voiced his objections on 2 and 7 January, the administration curtailed the air campaign within a five-nautical-mile area around Hanoi and Haiphong. On 16 January, the administration reaffirmed this "prohibition," which remained in effect between 22 January and at least until 28 January, the day Gheorghe Mocovescu, a Romanian go-between, left Hanoi with the North Vietnamese response to the U.S. counteroffer to the Trinh proposal. By securing this partial reduction in the air campaign, the communists partially realized one of the secondary objectives behind the offer to

---

[27]In the aftermath of the Tet offensive, incoming secretary of defense Clark Clifford realized that the Trinh initiative was a ruse: "We have been suckers and we are going to quit being suckers. There is no point in this kind of negotiations. The next time, they come to us, and they had better mean it! San Antonio [President Johnson's standing offer to negotiate with the communists] is the final formula—the furthest we can go"; see Oberdorfer, *Tet*, p. 203; and Thies, *When Governments Collide*, p. 201.

[28]Karnow, *Vietnam*, p. 583.

negotiate. Even though they would have desired that a larger area be excluded from bombing, this temporary respite could still help them prepare to surge supplies south during a holiday truce.[29]

Another possible objective behind the Trinh initiative was to raise hopes that a diplomatic breakthrough was near, thereby causing the United States to forego, in a general sense, a military response to mounting indications of impending attack—to exercise restraint on the eve of the Tet offensive. Here the communists were extremely successful. In late January, senior members of the Johnson administration pressured Westmoreland not only to honor but to not reduce the duration of the Tet cease-fire. Ultimately, the Trinh initiative can be linked to the U.S. decision to aquiesce in a 50 percent reduction in ARVN strength (for holiday leaves) during the Tet celebrations. The failure to cancel the cease-fire was by far the worst action taken by the Americans on the eve of the offensive.

While the Johnson administration responded favorably to the Trinh initiative, Westmoreland increased the military response to the NVA diversion at Khe Sanh. After receiving indications that NVA units were moving toward the outpost, Westmoreland on 5 January initiated the first stage of a two-part operation, code-named Niagara, which would maximize air and artillery support to Khe Sanh in the event of a siege. The operation, built on lessons learned from Operation Neutralize, ultimately proved to be an extraordinary tactical success. In a strategic sense, however, it consumed enormous amounts of resources and preoccupied commanders and analysts, thereby interfering with the U.S. response to the Tet attacks on urban areas.[30]

Operation Niagara I was undertaken to improve the flow of tactical intelligence to marine commanders at Khe Sanh. The operation, which was controlled from a special command center at Da Nang, relied on relatively conventional collection methods: aerial reconnais-

[29]Kalb and Abel, *Roots of Involvement*, p. 225; Thies, *When Governments Collide*, pp. 198–200; *Pentagon Papers, Gravel*, 4:15, 233; Sharp, *Strategy for Defeat*, pp. 205–208; Lung, *General Offensives*, p. 27; Cable From Walt Rostow to President, 5 Jan 68, doc 90, DSDUF Vietnam, Box 3, Folder: NSF Aides File Memos to the President, Walt Rostow vol. 56, LBJ Library; and Westmoreland, *Soldier*, p. 312. Westmoreland's 7 January protest accurately reflected the primary and secondary objectives behind the Trinh initiative: "I believe that his [the enemy's] offensive capabilities and posture relate directly to the recent overtures by . . . Trinh. . . . First, he may use this offensive capability to try to gain an exploitable victory before talks so that he might negotiate from a position of strength. On the other hand, he may enter negotiations without such a victory in order to gain a respite from the bombing in the North and to augment the already significant capabilities of his units in the South. Thus, by political means he could buy time and opportunity to create a formidable threat when hostilities are resumed"; Westmoreland to Sharp and Wheeler, 7 Jan 1968, p. 5, doc. 87, NSF Country File, Vietnam, Box 68–69, Folder: Vietnam 2C(3) General Military Activity, LBJ Library.

[30]Pearson, *War in the Northern Provinces*, p. 31; Westmoreland, *Soldier*, p. 315; and *Command History* 1968, 1:423.

sance, signals intelligence, and vigorous patrolling by marines stationed at Khe Sanh. Niagara I also raised the priority given to providing intelligence support to the defenders of the firebase well before the attacks on Khe Sanh actually materialized. Analysts at CIA headquarters, for example, gave the marines at Khe Sanh pictures of the Vietminh trench system around Dien Bien Phu. These pictures became especially useful when the NVA began to construct a similar trench system around the firebase.[31]

In addition, Niagara I brought a technological innovation that surprised both the marines and the NVA. During January, a test of the seismic and acoustic sensors used in the Muscle Shoals (air-supported) portion of the barrier was under way in the vicinity of Khe Sanh, and these sensors were deployed to cover NVA concentration points and assault routes near the firebase. Experts on the project believed that the system could be adapted to serve a tactical role. Marine commanders at Khe Sanh were apparently unaware of the existence of Muscle Shoals; individuals involved in the program provided extensive briefings on how the system could direct artillery and air strikes on NVA concentrations. The system also came as a surprise to NVA commanders. An acoustic sensor transmitted the reaction of NVA soldiers who discovered the device, but their conversations revealed that they neither knew or cared about what they had found. The system borrowed from Muscle Shoals proved to be highly effective in targeting enemy units before they reached the Khe Sanh perimeter.[32]

Like the Johnson administration's reaction to the Trinh statement, Westmoreland's initiation of Operation Niagara helped to fulfill the major objective of the siege of Khe Sanh. Even though he knew about the increase in enemy preparations for offensive activity throughout South Vietnam, he concentrated his attention and resources on improving the ability of the marines at Khe Sanh to withstand a concerted communist assault. He had apparently decided that the main thrust would come at Khe Sanh, an estimate that reflected his beliefs about the effectiveness of the shield strategy, the communist priority given to attacks on U.S. units, and the applicability of lessons from Dien Bien Phu to this situation. By mobilizing intelligence and military resources for the defense of Khe Sanh, Westmoreland increased the probability of winning a tactical victory if an assault on the firebase materialized. But the decision to set in motion Operation Ni-

---

[31]Nalty, *Air Power*, pp. 15, 90; and Oberdorfer, *Tet*, p. 110. The NVA used the same siege tactics at Dien Bien Phu and Khe Sanh, including artillery placement and tunneling; see Shore, *Battle for Khe Sanh*, pp. 87, 111, 120.

[32]Nalty, *Air Power*, pp. 90–95; *Command History 1968*, 2:921–923. Maclear, *Ten Thousand Day War*, p. 188; and *Command History 1967*, 3:1110.

agara diverted intelligence resources away from other areas of South Vietnam. The communist attempt to fix allied attention on Khe Sanh was succeeding, thereby increasing the possibility of surprise in the Tet attacks on southern cities.[33]

Additional insight into Westmoreland's failure to realize that Khe Sanh was a communist diversion is provided by an 8 January cable to Sharp and Wheeler. Westmoreland minimized the threat posed by the increase in communist logistical activity in Laos, attributing the surge in truck traffic along the Ho Chi Minh Trail to the demands generated by the heightened firepower of NVA units and the need to provide munitions for "present stepped up operations and probably to stockpile sufficiently to cover the period of the next wet season."[34] The belief that the communists had lost the initiative is reflected by Westmoreland's lack of concern that they would use this stockpile in a major offensive throughout all of South Vietnam. At the same time, Westmoreland's belief that the allies still enjoyed the military initiative is reflected in his proposal to cut off the flow of supplies through Laos by sending one ARVN and two U.S. divisions to cut critical road junctures along the Ho Chi Minh Trail. Supported from airfields in I CTZ, including the one located at Khe Sanh, Westmoreland claimed that the operation, which would begin about October 1968, would be the best way to stop the flow of supplies through Laos. The lack of urgency surrounding this proposal shows that Westmoreland still believed that the allies largely governed the pace of offensive operations. Khe Sanh was important to Westmoreland because it served as a base for the next phase of the shield strategy. By defending Khe Sanh, he was laying the groundwork for the next allied offensive. The fact that the defense of Khe Sanh fit into his future objectives made it difficult for Westmoreland to realize that the diversion of resources toward the firebase fulfilled communist objectives too.

In another cable sent to Wheeler and Sharp, Westmoreland described the actions he had already taken in response to the communist efforts that most threatened the allies. In his analysis, Westmoreland implied that NVA units along the borders of I CTZ posed the greatest threat. To respond, he emphasized military operations in I CTZ to eliminate this NVA threat in the future. Barrier construction

---

[33]On 7 January, Westmoreland gave three possible reasons for the NVA buildup in Laos just to the west of Khe Sanh: as an attempt to circumvent the barrier, as a manifestation of the September shift in communist strategy (a reference to Giap's article), or as insurance against a U.S. offensive into Laos; see Cable from Westmoreland to Sharp and Wheeler, 7 January 1968, pp. 3–4, NSF Country File, Vietnam, Box 68–69, Folder: Vietnam 2C(3) General Military Activity, LBJ Library.

[34]"Adams' Notes on William Westmoreland," 1/8/68 Cable from Westmoreland to Wheeler and Sharp, in *Westmoreland v. CBS*, exhibit 191.

was still important, and he intended to launch attacks throughout I CTZ to keep the enemy off balance, reducing their "apparent position of strength" in the area. Westmoreland also described the need for U.S. military operations inside Cambodia and Laos and noted that Operation Niagara could serve as a first step in an allied attack on NVA units operating along the Laotian border in the vicinity of Khe Sanh. Westmoreland also had views on the political threat posed by communist initiatives. The Trinh statement combined with recent NLF calls for a coalition government, according to Westmoreland, lent credibility to recent VC propaganda that claimed that the war would soon end and that a coalition government would be formed. Westmoreland even provided evidence that the VC rumor campaign was effective: ARVN morale was on the decline because soldiers were worried about their fate under a coalition government. VC taxes in the vicinity of Saigon were up, while the number of defectors had recently declined, a sign that the enemy was hedging its bets about the future. In response to this development, he created a special task force to organize an intensive allied propaganda campaign to counter enemy propaganda.[35]

Westmoreland's 8 January analysis demonstrates that the communist effort to divert U.S. attention and resources away from urban areas was succeeding and that the North Vietnamese negotiating ruse was beginning to affect the military response to signals of impending attack. Westmoreland was preoccupied with military operations not only near Khe Sanh and the DMZ but also in Cambodia and Laos. Beliefs that U.S. forces posed the most serious threat to communist units, that the shield strategy was working, and that the allies still possessed the military initiative lay behind Westmoreland's focus on the borders. In contrast, he saw indications of impending attack behind the shield as less threatening and best handled by an intensified propaganda campaign. Moreover, the Trinh initiative apparently affected Westmoreland's interpretation of disturbing information. Lessening defection and increasing VC taxation were not seen as signs of impending attack; instead they showed that the VC had adopted a wait-and-see attitude, an attitude tied to the shift in the North Vietnamese position on negotiations. The Trinh initiative was thus having its intended effect by interfering with the American interpretation of signals of impending attack.

Although the responses of the Johnson administration and West-

---

[35]Ibid., exhibit 390; and *Command History* 1968, 2:785. On 17 January, Ambassador Bunker also noted that the Trinh initiative sparked rumors in Saigon concerning a U.S.–NLF deal leading to a communist takeover of the country; see Bunker's 35th Weekly Message to the President, 17 January 1968, p. 1, NSF Country File, Vietnam, Box 104, 105, 106, Folder: Vietnam 8(B)2[A] 11/67–4/68, LBJ Library.

moreland to the Trinh initiative and the NVA buildup near Khe Sanh demonstrate that the communist effort to divert attention and resources away from the cities of the south was succeeding, General Weyand, the U.S. commander in III CTZ, correctly identified where the main communist thrust would fall in his area of responsibility. In a briefing for Westmoreland and his staff on 10 January, Weyand stated that VC and NVA units were leaving their border sanctuaries and moving toward the populated areas of III CTZ. Weyand predicted that the enemy would attack the cities in III CTZ, including Saigon, and recommended that planned offensive operations along the border be canceled and that allied units be positioned to guard Saigon. On 13 January, General Davidson, the head of MACV intelligence, seconded Weyand's analysis.[36]

How did Weyand develop this accurate, if limited, estimate? Years after the offensive, Davidson noted that Weyand had always opposed Westmoreland's "big-unit war" strategy. Weyand believed that his forces should operate among the people of South Vietnam, not along the border with Cambodia. His advocacy of reinforcing the defenses of Saigon, according to Davidson, "coincided with Fred's natural bent . . . of wanting to concentrate on the populated areas."[37] Still Weyand's 10 January briefing was largely responsible for strengthening the defenses around the cities of III CTZ, including Saigon, and for canceling operations that would have moved U.S. units farther from urban areas. Between 10 and 15 January, Westmoreland set in motion plans to allow Weyand to shift fifteen U.S. battalions to positions near Saigon, a redeployment that greatly inhibited the communist attempt to overrun the city during the Tet attacks. Westmoreland also canceled the first phase of Operation York, allowing the U.S. 1st Cavalry Division to stop preparations for offensive action and take up defensive positions in the vicinity of Hue. Westmoreland also canceled a parachute drop by elements of the 101st Airborne Division and instead used the unit to strengthen existing defensive positions. All told, Weyand's briefing primarily improved the allied defenses in III CTZ and prevented further movement of U.S. units away from southern cities. Davidson admitted, however, that he failed to realize that what Weyand foresaw for Saigon would take place throughout all of South Vietnam. Davidson emphasized that Weyand did not predict that the concentration against urban areas that was occurring in III

[36]Westmoreland, *Soldier*, p. 318; Palmer, *Summons*, p. 184; Gelb, *Irony of Vietnam*, p. 155; Shaplen, *Time out of Hand*, p. 403; Sheehan, *Bright Shining Lie*, pp. 701–702; Daniel O. Graham, Oral History II, pp. 7–9, LBJ Library; and Krepinevich, *Army*, p. 239.

[37]Phillip Davidson, Oral History I, p. 48, LBJ Library; and Sheehan, *Bright Shining Lie*, p. 703.

CTZ would take place throughout the country: "What Fred really foresaw . . . was limited to his own area."[38]

Signals

MACV analysts continued to receive reports about an increase in enemy propaganda and documents that contained VC plans to attack specific targets during the Tet offensive. Late in the evening of 10 January, the South Vietnamese police informed MACV J-2 duty officers that they had received information indicating that VC disguised in ARVN uniforms planned to infiltrate Saigon in three-man teams. The mission of the teams, which were armed with rifles and submachine guns, was to distribute propaganda leaflets and plant explosives in U.S. and South Vietnamese installations. If detected, the VC teams were supposed to use their disguises to escape. Intelligence analysts also obtained several reports of NLF meetings which emphasized the need to convince the population that a major VC victory in the winter-spring campaign would end the war. Further evidence of this intensified propaganda effort was obtained on 15 January when propaganda leaflets were discovered in Saigon. The leaflets called for the population to revolt and seize power in the cities and demand direct negotiations between the NLF and the United States.[39]

Information about another main target, prisons and defector facilities, also became available. On 11 January, an enemy agent caught posing as a defector told intelligence officers that he was part of a large operation that had reconnoitered dozens of defector centers across the country. These agents were to identity not only ARVN personnel working at the centers but also defectors and the location of their assignments after they left the center. Similarly, on 12 January, U.S. advisers assigned to a South Vietnamese prison on Phu Quoc island (IV CTZ) informed MACV J-2 duty officers that they had received reports that VC units were preparing to assault the facility.[40]

---

[38]Quotation from Phillip Davidson, Oral History I, p. 48, LBJ Library. See also Westmoreland, *Soldier*, p. 318; Betts, "Strategic Surprise for War Termination," p. 163; Sharp and Westmoreland, *Report*, p. 157; Palmer, *Summons*, p. 184; William C. Westmoreland, Oral History II, p. 9, LBJ Library; Krepinevich, *Army*, p. 193; *Command History 1968*, 1:238–239; House Select Committee on Intelligence, *U.S. Intelligence Agencies and Activities*, p. 1997; and *Westmoreland v. CBS*, exhibits 349, pp. 13, 65; 399; 400.

[39]Item 50 2100 10 January, Daily Journal Files, MACV J-2 Command Center; and *PERINTREP*, January 1968, p. 9.

[40]Item 58 1900 12 January, Daily Journal Files, MACV J-2 Command Center; and *PERINTREP*, January 1968, p. 7.

On 13 January, MACV J-2 duty officers learned that the VC intended to use rockets and mortars to attack Tre Noc and Binh Tuy airfields in Phong Dinh province (IV CTZ). On 16 January, a VC cadre member working for ARVN intelligence reported that several VC units intended to mortar Ton Son Nhut airbase (III CTZ). On 20 January, fifteen individuals were detained at Da Nang (I CTZ) after ARVN troops captured a VC suspect who confessed to being a member of a 100-man sapper force that had infiltrated the airbase. A search of the facility uncovered over 25 pounds of explosives, other demolition supplies, and weapons. Though analysts apparently did not recognize it, this information about enemy plans to attack airbases provided indications about the scope and timing of the winter-spring campaign. The scope of the Tet attacks was suggested by the fact that the enemy was not concentrating on airbases in a particular area; instead, they planned to attack airbases throughout the country apparently to reduce the ability of aircraft to support ground forces throughout South Vietnam. Moreover, each of the reports stated that the enemy intended to attack the airbases "from now until Tet." "Tet" had been established as the deadline for communist units to complete their mission of damaging U.S. air facilities and aircraft.[41]

On 17 January, analysts at the National Security Agency (NSA) issued the first in a series of intelligence bulletins concerning the analysis of recently collected signals intelligence (SIGINT). According to the NSA analysis, it was likely that NVA units under the control of the B-3 front headquarters were preparing to attack cities in Kontum, Pleiku, and Darlac provinces (western II CTZ), and that units under the control of the MR5 headquarters were preparing attacks against the coastal provinces Quang Nam, Quang Tin, Quang Ngai, and Binh Dinh (southern I CTZ and eastern II CTZ). There were also indications that Hue would be attacked. Documents captured by ARVN units on 20 January which outlined the plan of attack on the cities Ban Me Thout and Qui Nhon (II CTZ) corroborated the 17 January NSA report. SIGINT also picked up signs of an increased enemy presence in the vicinity of Saigon. The U.S. 199th Light Infantry Brigade conducted intensified patrols of the area surrounding the capital between 14 and 25 January, but they failed to make contact with the enemy. These patrols did, however, detect evidence—newly constructed base camps and recently used trails—of an increased enemy presence near

---

[41]Item 9 0945 13 January, Item 24 1225 16 January, Daily Journal Files, MACV J-2 Command Center; and *PERINTREP*, January 1968, p. 8. The MACV history states, however, that the prediction was made that the communists intended launch the sapper attacks at Da Nang during Tet; see *Command History* 1968, 1:143–144.

Saigon.[42] The SIGINT information received by MACV ultimately undermined the effort to anticipate the urban offensive. Because NVA units, especially the units near Khe Sanh, generated more radio signals than the VC units moving toward the cities, pattern analysis indicated that the main enemy blow would fall along the borders. Intelligence analysts relied heavily—too heavily—on this single source of information: without SIGINT to back up captured documents outlining attacks against southern cities, the call for a general uprising was dismissed as propaganda.[43]

Military Developments

Between mid-January and the outbreak of the Tet attacks there was a relative lull in both enemy and allied offensive activity throughout much of South Vietnam. Two major engagements, one initiated by the allies, the other by the NVA, stand out as the only exceptions. The first engagement broke out on 15 January when the 4th Infantry Division, alerted that units attached to the B-3 front headquarters were preparing to attack cities in II CTZ, contacted elements of the 1st NVA Division as they crossed the Cambodian border into South Vietnam. The U.S. division, assisted by the ARVN 42d Regiment and B-52 strikes, prevented all but one NVA battalion from participating in the Tet attacks. General Stone, the commander of the 4th Infantry Division, seems to have been the only allied commander to reduce significantly the impact of the Tet attacks in his area of responsibility.[44]

Events in II CTZ were, however, already being overshadowed by the situation at Khe Sanh. On 16 January, a marine battalion reinforced the garrison. A series of firefights broke out between 17 and 20 January as the marines patrolled between the hilltop outposts that surrounded the firebase. The marines enjoyed a lucky break on 20 January, when a disgruntled NVA lieutenant surrendered and informed them that the NVA would attack two of their main hilltop outposts that evening. The defector also described how this opening attack against Hills 861 and 881 South fit into the NVA plan to overrun Khe Sanh. Col. David E. Lownds, the marine commander, took this information seriously, and consequently the marines were well prepared

[42]"Treatment of Indications in Finished Intelligence: NSA," in *Westmoreland v. CBS*, exhibit 518; Oberdorfer, *Tet*, p. 137; Brewin and Shaw, *Vietnam on Trial*, pp. 204–206; Lung, *General Offensives*, p. 35; and *Long Binh/Saigon Tet Campaign*, p. 6.

[43]Davidson, Oral History I, pp. 17–18, 37; Jones, *War without Windows*, pp. 62–63, 141, 144; Palmer, *25-Year War*, p. 167; and Helm, "The Tet 1968 Offensive," pp. 128–130.

[44]Westmoreland, *Soldier*, pp. 317–318; and Sharp and Westmoreland, *Report*, p. 160.

to meet the assaults that materialized at about midnight 21 January against Hill 861. They even succeeded in breaking up the attacks against Hill 881 South before they materialized.[45]

Although the marines handily defeated the ground attacks against Khe Sanh during the early morning of 21 January, an intense NVA artillery barrage destroyed the main ammunition depot in its opening salvo that same morning. On the same day, the NVA 304th Division attacked the small village of Khe Sanh a few kilometers south of the firebase. Even though the ARVN regional force companies and their U.S. advisers stationed at the village prevented the NVA from overrunning their positions, they abandoned the village and moved to the firebase. By 21 January, it was apparent that the siege of Khe Sanh had begun.[46]

It is difficult to overestimate the impact of the 21 January attack, not only on the way administration officials, senior officers, and intelligence analysts interpreted information even after the Tet attacks, but also on the priority they gave to the defense of Khe Sanh. Although Westmoreland had taken some extraordinary steps to enhance the defenses of the firebase before the attacks, including preliminary efforts to place marine aircraft under air force control, the assault gave Khe Sanh priority over every other allied military operation. In a 21 January cable to Sharp and Wheeler, for example, Westmoreland outlined the actions he had just taken to strengthen the firebase. On 20 January, he sent General Davidson, MACV J-2, to Khe Sanh to coordinate intelligence activities. On 21 January, General Abrams, deputy commander of MACV, arrived at III MAF headquarters to assess the situation. Westmoreland also reassigned aircraft involved in Dump Truck operations (the air-supported antipersonnel barrier over Laos) to supplement the air support for the firebase and canceled all work on the barrier to create reserves for Khe Sanh. Additionally, army reinforcements, including elements of the 101st Airborne Division, were moving toward Hue to help create a marine reserve force for Khe Sanh.[47]

The priority given to the defense of Khe Sanh manifested itself in

[45]Shore, *Battle for Khe Sanh*, pp. 30–42, 48; Nalty, *Air Power*, pp. 23, 25; Palmer, *Summons*, p. 171; Westmoreland, *Soldier*, p. 317; Pearson, *War in the Northern Provinces*, pp. 32–34; *Command History* 1968, 1:378–379; and Item 14 0536, Item 15 0537, Item 35 1331, Item 39 1431, Item 45 1526 January 21, Item 2 011 January 22, Daily Journal Files, MACV J-2 Command Center; and Maclear, *Ten Thousand Day War*, p. 192.

[46]Item 19 0741, Item 41 1443, 21 January, Daily Journal Files, MACV J-2 Command Center; *Command History* 1968, 1:378–379; and Shore, *Battle for Khe Sanh*, p. 44. The ammunition depot at Khe Sanh was destroyed in the opening salvo because it was above ground. According to Graham, "the damn marines never have figured out what that shovel is for that they put on the back of their packs"; Daniel O. Graham, Oral History I, p. 20, LBJ Library.

[47]*Westmoreland v. CBS*, exhibit 402; Shore, *Battle for Khe Sanh*, p. 93; and Maclear, *Ten Thousand Day War*, p. 205.

other small ways. Senior members of the Johnson administration, including the president, exhibited a keen interest in developments at the firebase. A sand model of Khe Sanh and the surrounding countryside was erected in the White House situation room, and at critical periods during the siege the president received reports at 50-minute intervals. Johnson also demanded repeated assurances from the Joint Chiefs that Westmoreland would be able to hold the firebase. In the wake of the destruction of the main ammunition depot, Johnson received reports on the supply situation at the firebase until the stockpile became large enough to last through likely emergencies. Even though Westmoreland often worked 20 hours a day, he allowed a cot to be placed in his office as the siege materialized, a sign that he did not intend to leave his post for the duration of the battle.[48]

The siege received top priority because of the real threat posed by the NVA and because it confirmed many beliefs about North Vietnamese and U.S. strategy. It confirmed American beliefs about the success of the shield strategy; analysts and commanders often referred to it as an effort to penetrate the shield created by U.S. forces, an effort that would allow the enemy to regain an important infiltration corridor into Quang Tri province. The attack on Khe Sanh was also identified as a North Vietnamese attempt to prevent U.S. forces from using the firebase during the next phase of shield operations, the extension of the defensive perimeter into Laos and Cambodia.[49]

U.S. commanders were also mesmerized by the similarities between the Vietminh siege of Dien Bien Phu and the NVA attacks on Khe Sanh. They readily recalled Dien Bien Phu to explain the communist siege of the firebase. On 22 January, for example, Westmoreland cabled Washington: "I believe that the enemy sees a similarity between our base at Khe Sanh and Dien Bien Phu and hopes, by following a pattern of activity similar to that used against the French, to gain similar military and political ends." The reliance on the Dien Bien Phu analogy even raised the issue of tactical nuclear weapons in defense of the base in the minds of both President Johnson and Westmoreland. The willingness to apply the Dien Bien Phu analogy to the situation at Khe Sanh, however, was not driven solely by physical

[48]Nalty, *Air Power*, pp. 16–18; Oberdorfer, *Tet*, p. 110; Shore, *Battle for Khe Sanh*, p. 102; Palmer, *Summons*, p. 170; Maclear, *Ten Thousand Day War*, p. 194; Notes of the President's Meeting with the National Security Council 24 January 1968, pt. 2, p. 9, Folder: 24 January 1968 1pm *Pueblo* II, and Notes of the President's Meeting with the Democratic Leadership, 30 January 1968, p. 8–9, Folder: 30 January 1968 *Pueblo* 10 Congressional Leadership Breakfast; both in Tom Johnson's Notes of Meetings, Box 2, LBJ Library; and Palmer, *25-Year War*, p. 40.

[49]Shore, *Battle for Khe Sanh*, pp. 45, 47; Broyles, "The Road to Hill 10," p. 102; Lung, *General Offensives*, p. 9; "Letter from Westmoreland to E.H. Simmons, 27 May 1978," in *Westmoreland v. CBS*, exhibit 215B, p. 4; and Westmoreland, *Soldier*, p. 336.

and geographic similarities. The NVA siege also confirmed the belief that the communists no longer possessed the military capability to inflict a strategic defeat on the allies. Senior officers and analysts interpreted the siege as an effort to inflict a "public-relations" defeat, thereby eliminating public support for the war. U.S. commanders were, however, eager to prove that U.S. firepower and logistical expertise could succeed where the French had failed.[50]

The tactical lessons offered at Dien Bien Phu facilitated the defense of Khe Sanh. Unlike the French, the marines were never in danger of running out of supplies or losing the artillery–air duel with the communists. In a strategic sense, however, the acceptance of the Dien Bien Phu analogy produced disastrous results. Senior U.S. commanders, including Westmoreland, estimated that the main communist attack would materialize at Khe Sanh and that increased communist activity throughout South Vietnam was a diversion intended to draw attention and resources away from the firebase. In a cable sent to Sharp and Wheeler on 23 January, Westmoreland warned: "It is prudent to expect that enemy activities may be initiated simultaneously elsewhere in RVN in an attempt to divert and disperse our strength to levels incapable of country wide success. As the Quang Tri [province] battle develops there will be those quick to advocate abandonment of 'indefensible and unimportant positions' [Khe Sanh]. I unreservedly maintain that Khe Sanh is of significance: strategic, tactical, and most importantly, psychological."[51] In effect, the North Vietnamese diversion at Khe Sanh, enhanced by memories of Dien Bien Phu, focused American attention on events at the firebase. They expected that the main communist blow, when it finally materialized, would fall at Khe Sanh.[52]

Allied Reactions

Although evidence about impending enemy attacks against urban areas continued to accumulate, by mid-January attention was again riveted on I CTZ and Khe Sanh. On 13 January, Westmoreland described the actions he had taken to counter the enemy's capability to attack Khe Sanh "before Tet," leading Rostow to remark to the president that "Westy has Khe Sanh on his mind as much as we do." On

---

[50]Quotation from 22 January 1968 MAC 00967 (Westmoreland's assessment of situation), p. 2, NSF Country File, Vietnam, Box 68–69, Folder: Vietnam 2C(3) General Military Activity, LBJ Library. See also Westmoreland, *Soldier*, pp. 316, 338; Lewy, *America in Vietnam* p. 128; Kinnard, *War Managers*, p. 78; Maclear, *Ten Thousand Day War*, pp. 195–196; Nalty, *Air Power*, pp. 21, 31; and *Westmoreland v. CBS*, exhibit 313, p. 326.

[51]*Westmoreland v. CBS*, exhibit 390.

[52]Westmoreland, *Soldier*, p. 316; Herring, *America's Longest War*, p. 186; Palmer, *Summons*, p. 180; and *Westmoreland v. CBS*, exhibits 313, p. 321; 327, p. 103; and 64, p. 25.

15 January, Westmoreland told Sharp and Wheeler about the deployment of additional forces to I CTZ and his efforts to concentrate B-52 strikes to support Khe Sanh. He intended to preempt enemy attacks in I CTZ and recognized that the redeployment of forces from II CTZ toward the DMZ constituted a calculated risk. He also stated that the allies maintained sufficient forces in III CTZ "to continue operations generally as planned." In effect, Westmoreland had decided that the main enemy thrust would land in I CTZ. In his 15 January cable, however, Westmoreland also made a prediction about when the main enemy attacks would occur. "The odds are 60–40," said Westmoreland, "that the enemy will launch his planned campaign prior to Tet."[53] General Davidson offered a slightly different estimate. He predicted that there was a 60–40 chance that the main blow would fall after the Tet holidays. Needless to say, neither of the men predicted that the main attacks would come during the Tet celebration.[54] Faced with information indicating that a major enemy attack was about to develop, both Westmoreland and Davidson relied on beliefs based on past enemy behavior during truce periods and the importance of the Tet holidays to the Vietnamese people. In this manner, they were able to eliminate the Tet holidays as a time for the attack. They were not alone in this estimate; there are no indications that anyone in the allied command predicted that the main blow would materialize during Tet.

The Westmoreland and Davidson estimates do, however, raise an extremely important question. Did Westmoreland attempt to cancel the Tet truce, a cease-fire that resulted in a significant reduction in ARVN readiness and force levels, because he thought the enemy would attack before the Tet holidays? Long before January, senior officers had repeatedly expressed their misgivings about participation in holiday cease-fires because they allowed the communists to intensify resupply efforts unimpeded by U.S. airpower. In fact, they began building their case early against the series of truces that would start in December 1967. During a 9 October mission council meeting, Westmoreland went on record against allied participation in cease-fires during the upcoming Christmas, New Year's, and Tet holidays. He recognized, however, that political considerations might necessitate participation in a truce. In this situation, he recommended that the allies observe only a 24-hour Christmas truce, refuse to honor a New

---

[53]Memo From Walt Rostow to the President, 13 January 1968, p. 4, DSDUF Vietnam, Box 4, Folder:NSF Country File Vietnam 2A(1) I Corps and DMZ Box 66, LBJ Library; and *Westmoreland v. CBS*, exhibit 400.

[54]Westmoreland, *Soldier*, p. 318; Oberdorfer, *Tet*, p. 121; Maclear, *Ten Thousand Day War*, p. 204; Palmer, *Summons*, p. 183; and *Westmoreland v. CBS*, exhibits 313, p. 322; 349, p. 6.

Year's truce, and limit the Tet truce to 48 hours. Westmoreland also recommended that the allies begin advanced planning so that they would not have to move men and supplies during truces. This suggestion was an attempt either to pressure the communists into not using future truces to surge supplies to combat units or to begin building the case for the cancellation of a truce if such activity occurred. Westmoreland would eventually have second thoughts about this latter recommendation. On 11 December he informed Ambassador Bunker that he wanted to make sure that the announcement of the Christmas cease-fire did not contain a reference to any freeze on the movement of allied troops and supplies during the truce. Westmoreland was worried about setting a precedent that could work to the disadvantage of the allies.[55] On 8 December, Westmoreland argued specifically against participation in the Tet truce. In a meeting with General Vien, the chairman of the JGS, he suggested that they both recommend against allied participation in a Tet cease-fire. Vien was sympathetic to Westmoreland's arguments; he agreed that past truces had been hoaxes, and he did not expect any change in enemy behavior during a cease-fire. He argued, however, that the absence of the traditional Tet respite for his troops would create a morale problem. In any event, Vien and Westmoreland split the difference and agreed to recommend that the Tet truce be reduced from 48 to 24 hours.[56]

True to their agreement, Westmoreland and Vien, without informing Ambassador Bunker, approached President Thieu on 16 January with their recommendation. Once again, a decision on the truce's duration was reached by splitting the difference. Thieu agreed to limiting the Tet truce to 36 hours. The Westmoreland-Vien initiative, however, raised a furor within the Johnson administration, which had just extended the "prohibition" on bombing around Hanoi and Haiphong in an effort to send an encouraging signal to North Vietnam in the wake of the Trinh initiative. It was argued that reducing the length of the truce would send the wrong signal to Hanoi. In a memo sent to the president on 18 January, Rostow summarized the arguments raised by Rusk and McNamara against shortening the cease-fire:

Hanoi could regard it as our changing rules of the game in the middle of a tense period of communications;

We could be criticized further for toughening up our behavior in a deli-

---

[55]*Westmoreland v. CBS*, exhibit 912, p. 49.
[56]Ibid., exhibit 390; and Braestrup, *Big Story*, 1:75 n. 30.

cate, potentially pre-negotiation situation. (There is apparently some criticism of your State of the Union message along these lines.)

Therefore, Secretaries Rusk and McNamara would like to go back to Bunker and Westy and reverse the decision, reinstalling the 48-hour Tet truce. Both do this reluctantly out of respect for Westy, and having whipsawed Thieu once already on this matter.

Once again, the Trinh initiative was having its intended impact, albeit in unforeseen ways, by impeding the U.S. response to signals of impending attack.[57]

On the behalf of Westmoreland, the Joint Chiefs of Staff quickly responded to the concerns of the secretaries of state and defense. On 19 January, they supplied Rostow with a short DIA analysis of how a 12-hour difference in the Tet truce would affect the war: "It can be estimated that the logistic difference to the North Vietnamese between a 36 hour and 48 hour cease-fire period could be as much as 10,000 tons of material. This difference being represented by the ability or lack of ability to employ WBLC [waterborne logistic craft] to any great extent."[58]

In a memo to the president dated 19 January, Rostow summarized and commented on the argument for shortening the truce:

—Present rules of engagement permit strikes against "abnormally great resupply activities" during a standown. These rules are meant to protect against the kind of resupply our people in Saigon fear. The argument in the attached paper is really for no truce rather than a 12-hour reduction.

—There is a strong case for excluding the Khe Sanh area from the truce. It is relatively unpopulated. Given the evidence that the North Vietnamese are assembling forces for a massive attack I believe it would be unwise for us to give them even 36 hours of free movement of forces and supplies in the Khe Sanh area.

—With the Khe Sanh exception and the freedom of action Westy already has to deal with abnormal supply movements, I don't think the 12 hours matter much one way or the other.[59]

In effect, the Joint Chiefs relied on their traditional argument—that the enemy used truces to resupply—to respond to the administration's concern that minimizing the truce would send the wrong signal to Hanoi.

[57]Quote from *Westmoreland v. CBS*, exhibit 980; see also exhibit 390; and Braestrup, *Big Story*, 1:75 n. 30.
[58]"1/19/68 Memo from Rostow to LBJ," enclosure "DIA Estimate," in *Westmoreland v. CBS*, exhibit 982.
[59]Ibid. exhibit 982.

Although Rostow did not find the arguments offered in support of a limitation of the Tet truce to be particularly convincing, Westmoreland directly entered the debate by sending a lengthy cable to Wheeler and Sharp on 20 January in which he outlined past enemy behavior during truces, Vien and Thieu's support for a limitation of the cease-fire, and an argument that tied the military situation to the truce issue: "The enemy is presently developing a threatening posture in several areas in order to seek victories essential to achieving prestige and bargaining power. He may exercise his initiatives prior to, during or after Tet. It is altogether possible that he has planned to complete his offensive preparations during the free world cease-fire. He has used past truce periods for this purpose and can be expected to do so again."[60]

Despite the passing reference to the possibility that the communists would attack during the Tet holidays, the core of Westermoreland's argument was the expected communist use of the cease-fire to resupply in preparation for their offensive. Thus he did not directly address the Johnson administration's concerns. The debate had reached an impasse by 20 January.

The 21 January attack on Khe Sanh forced a resolution of this stalemate. The Johnson administration apparently responded favorably to Westmoreland's 20 January call for a 36-hour truce and a 24 January suggestion from Bunker and Westmoreland to cancel the cease-fire in the vicinity of Khe Sanh. On 25 January, in a cable sent to Wheeler and Sharp, Westmoreland stated that Thieu had agreed to cancel the Tet cease-fire in I CTZ. On 28 January, Westmoreland informed his component commanders and the commanding general of III MAF that the Tet cease-fire (1800 29 January to 0600 31 January) would be canceled in I CTZ and that the announcement of the cancellation would not be made before 1200 29 January. Until then, they were to inform no more than three key staff members of this change in plans. Allied participation in the Tet cease-fire in all but I CTZ began on schedule at 1800 29 January. In contrast, the communists had claimed that they intended to honor a Tet cease-fire from 27 January to 3 February.[61]

[60]Ibid., exhibit 390; and Westmoreland, *Soldier*, p. 318.
[61]*Westmoreland v. CBS*, exhibits 401; 390; 64, p. 26; Pearson, *War in the Northern Provinces*, p. 37; Text of Cable from Bunker (Saigon 16851), 24 January 1968, President's Appointment File, Box 88, Folder: Appointment File, 24 January 1968, LBJ Library; William Colby, *Lost Victory* (Chicago, 1989), p. 228; and Sharp and Westmoreland, *Report*, p. 158. Graham notes that ARVN commanders responded differently to the order to limit leaves to 50 percent. Some officers canceled all leaves, while others allowed more than 50 percent of their forces to return home for the holiday; see Graham, Oral History II, pp. 9–10.

What is surprising about the debate over allied participation in the Tet truce is that Westmoreland failed to stress the possibility that the enemy was about to launch a major attack either before, after, or during the Tet holiday and instead relied on the usual arguments against participation in cease-fires. The fact that Westmoreland worked so diligently to limit the duration of the truce and still failed to marshal this additional argument in favor of his position demonstrates how strongly he believed that the communists would engage in intensified logistical operations rather than launch a major attack.

The North Vietnamese negotiating ruse ultimately succeeded in reducing the readiness of ARVN units, responsible for the security of most urban areas, during the Tet holidays. Westmoreland's long effort to eliminate allied participation in the truce, or at least to reduce its duration, was hampered by the administration's effort to accommodate the Trinh initiative. Without executive support for cancellation, Westmoreland was forced to compromise with the South Vietnamese. Because of the perceived political costs of canceling the truce, Westmoreland could not prevent the reduction in ARVN readiness that followed.

22–30 JANUARY

22–25 January

Although three separate terrorist incidents occurred in Saigon and its environs on 22 January, indicating an increased VC presence in the area, senior commanders still concentrated on the developing situation in I CTZ, especially at Khe Sanh. The firebase was subjected to sporadic artillery and mortar fire throughout the day, and another U.S. Marine battalion arrived to reinforce the garrison. Refugees from Khe Sanh village also began to arrive at the base. Air support intensified on 22 January: 96,000 tons of ordnance were dropped near the marine positions. Ultimately, air support inflicted an estimated 49–65 percent casualty rate among the NVA units encircling the base. Operation Niagara II prevented NVA units from concentrating the forces needed to overwhelm the Khe Sanh perimeter in a major ground assault.[62]

Westmoreland issued public and private warnings concerning Khe

---

[62]Item 12 0416, Item 20 1046, Item 37 1615, Item 48 1926 22 January, Daily Journal Files, MACV J-2 Command Center; Shore, *Battle for Khe Sanh*, p. 48; Pearson, *War in the Northern Provinces*, pp. 34–35; *Command History 1968*, 1:423–426; Nalty, *Air Power*, pp. 82–88; and Maclear, *Ten Thousand Day War*, p. 197.

Sanh on 22 January. In an interview for NBC television, he discussed the movement of NVA units from Laos toward Khe Sanh: "I think his [the enemy's] plans concern a major effort to win a spectacular battle-field success on the eve of the Tet festival next Monday."[63] The same day, Westmoreland provided Sharp and Wheeler with a more de-tailed assessment: "I believe that the enemy will attempt a country-wide show of strength just prior to Tet, with Khe Sanh being the main event. In II Corps, he will probably attack Pleiku and Kontum cities, and I expect attacks on the Special Forces camps at Da Seang, Duc Co, and Dak To. In III and IV Corps, province towns are likely targets for renewed attacks by fire. Terrorism will probably increase in and around Saigon."[64] By the close of 22 January, Westmoreland still expected the main enemy blow to land at Khe Sanh while diversion-ary attacks were launched elsewhere in I CTZ. A surge in terrorist incidents in and around the capital (but not a direct ground attack) and "attacks by fire" (mortars, small arms, but no ground attack) would also be staged to divert U.S. forces away from Khe Sanh. Given this interpretation of communist intentions, it is easy to under-stand why Westmoreland did not react strongly to indications that southern cities would be attacked. He wanted to be better prepared for the main attack at Khe Sanh.

In contrast to 22 January, the twenty-third was an uneventful day in South Vietnam. Throughout the country the battlefield was rela-tively quiet. Although one policeman was shot attempting to prevent a group of youths from raising the NLF flag on a Saigon street corner, terrorist activity in Saigon had definitely declined from the previous day. Westmoreland and Sharp spent most of the day at the airbase at Da Nang discussing Khe Sanh.[65] Events in South Vietnam on this day were overshadowed by the North Korean seizure of the USS *Pueblo*. The degree to which events on the Korean peninsula alarmed and distracted senior members of the Johnson administration cannot be overemphasized. Speculation abounded about possible Soviet in-volvement in the seizure of the ship. Officials also worried that the incident presaged the renewal of hostilities along the 38th parallel.

[63]Westmoreland quoted in Braestrup, *Big Story*, 1:76–77. Westmoreland implies that this interview was given to counter the efforts of senators Fulbright and Kennedy to halt all bombing of North Vietnam in response to the Trinh statement; see Westmore-land, *Soldier*, p. 318.

[64]Quotation from "Memo from Rostow to LBJ, 22 January 1968 4:45 PM [LBJ copy of MAC 01049 January 22, 1968]," in *Westmoreland v. CBS*, exhibit 1510. Both Schandler and Westmoreland leave out the reference to Khe Sanh in quoting the first sentence in this passage; see Schandler, *Unmaking*, p. 71; and Westmoreland, *Soldier*, p. 320.

[65]Item 22, 1006 23 January, Daily Journal Files, MACV J-2 Command Center; and Sharp, *Strategy for Defeat*, p. 208.

Initially, the administration reacted by transferring some aircraft from South Vietnam to Korea, sending additional B-52s to reinforce the U.S. bomber fleet in the Far East, and calling up 15,000 air force and navy reservists. On balance, these actions eventually worked to the benefit of U.S. forces in South Vietnam; aircraft sent to reinforce the South Koreans, including the additional B-52s, were soon used to support ground forces during the Tet offensive. The seizure of the *Pueblo* did, however, provide Westmoreland with a few difficult moments. On 1 February, for example, General Wheeler, concerned about the seizure and a North Korean terrorist attack on the South Korean presidential residence, ordered Westmoreland to begin contingency planning for the withdrawal of the South Korean contingent fighting in the country (two and one-third divisions) "in the shortest time without regard to a cessation of hostilities in Vietnam."[66] In response, Westmoreland objected to the withdrawal of the Korean forces unless they were replaced on a one-for-one basis by other troops.[67]

Americans in Washington and South Vietnam saw the North Korean actions as attempts to divert U.S. attention away from Vietnam, and the link between events in Korea and Vietnam was solidified in the minds of U.S. commanders after the Tet attacks. On 1 February, for example, Rostow asked Westmoreland and Bunker if they believed that there was a relationship between activities in South Vietnam and those in Korea. Westmoreland, responding for both himself and Bunker replied: "It would seem to us that there is a relationship." President Johnson, McNamara, and Rostow concurred in this observation.[68]

[66]Quotation from "[William Westmoreland] Memo Origins of Post-Tet Plans for Additional American Forces in RVN [9 November 1970]," in *Westmoreland v. CBS*, exhibit 508, p. 13.

[67]Nalty, *Air Power*, pp. 60, 83; Betts, "Strategic Surprise for War Termination," p. 160; Kinnard, *War Managers*, p. 121; Notes of the President's Meeting with the National Security Council, 24 January 1968, Tom Johnson's Notes of Meetings, Box 2, Folder: 24 January 1968 1 PM *Pueblo* II, and Meeting at the State Department on the *Pueblo*, 24 January 1968, Meeting Notes File, Box 2, Folder: 24 January 1968 Meeting at State, LBJ Library; and "Adams' Richard Helms Chronology," *Westmoreland v. CBS*, exhibit 53, p. 17. The USS *Pueblo*, designated an auxiliary general environmental research (AGER) ship, was a converted World War II light cargo ship with a top speed of 13 knots. At the time of its capture, the mission of the 170-foot-long SIGINT vessel was to "(1) determine the nature and extent of naval activity of North Korean ports; (2) sample electronic environment off the east coast of North Korea; and (3) intercept the communications of and conduct surveillance of Soviet naval units"; see Jeffrey Richelson, *The U.S. Intelligence Community* (Cambridge, Mass., 1985), p. 128; and *American Espionage and the Soviet Target* (New York, 1987), pp. 158–159.

[68]*Westmoreland v. CBS*, exhibit 508, p. 13; Walt Rostow interview with Author, 7 January 1988; Memorandum from President to Secretary of State, Secretary of Defense, and

On 24 January the allies received a variety of signals generated by both the communist preparations to attack the southern cities and the diversion at Khe Sanh. There were several indications of an increasing VC presence in urban areas. NSA analysts reaffirmed an earlier report that units assigned to the B-3 and MR5 headquarters would attack urban areas in II CTZ and southern I CTZ. Even though they could not determine exactly when these attacks were to occur, NSA analysts warned that they were imminent. MACV J-2 duty officers also obtained several indications of intensified VC activity in Saigon. A South Vietnamese policeman and a U.S. serviceman were shot on the streets of Saigon. At 2242, MACV J-2 duty officers received a report from ARVN's CMD headquarters concerning VC plans for Saigon that night: "VC plan to attempt to launch political campaign in the city tonight by concentrating armed propagandists, dropping leaflets, displaying flags, setting up slogans, beating drums, and radio broadcasting. They are preparing to move into city an amount of weapons such as sub-machine guns and grenades to support mission they have. Further, they have instructions to annihilate Military Police."[69] This activity did not take place that night, but the report does provide an accurate characterization of one type of operation undertaken by the VC during the Tet attacks. The fact that this unusual rumor was circulating in Saigon should have alerted analysts to the possibility that the VC were planning some sort of action in the immediate vicinity of the capital.[70]

At the same time, analysts received ominous signals about the situation at Khe Sanh. MACV J-2 learned at 1151 that a Laotian army outpost near the South Vietnamese border had been overrun by elements of the NVA 325C Division and that refugees from the outpost were heading toward the special forces camp at Lang Vei west of Khe Sanh. By 2041 that evening, there were approximately 6,000 refugees, including the remnants of the Laotian 33d Royal Elephant Battalion, in the immediate vicinity of Lang Vei. The Laotian soldiers reported that the NVA had used tanks in the assault on their base, and this report was confirmed when a U.S. reconnaissance aircraft spotted five

---

Director, Bureau of the Budget, 31 January 1968, p. 1, NSF Country File, Vietnam Box 68–69, Folder: 2C(3) Vietnam General Military Activity, and [White House] Meeting of Congressional Leaders, 31 January 1968, p. 2, Meeting Notes File Box, 2, Folder: 31 January 1968 Meeting with Congressional Leaders, LBJ Library. On 2 February, President Johnson admitted that he had no proof, but he still linked the seizure of the *Pueblo* to the Tet offensive; see Nalty, *Air Power*, p. 105.

[69]Item 56 2242 24 January, Daily Journal Files, MACV J-2 Command Center.
[70]*Westmoreland v. CBS*, exhibit 518; and Item 37 1736, Item 52 2216 24 January, Daily Journal Files, MACV J-2 Command Center.

tanks moving along Route 9 toward the South Vietnamese border. The destruction of the Laotian base and the sighting of NVA tanks moving toward Khe Sanh obviously indicated that the NVA was tightening the ring around the firebase.[71]

U.S. preparations to meet an attack in I CTZ, especially at Khe Sanh, were at their height on 25 January. Westmoreland authorized the creation of MACV forward to establish a headquarters for the army units that had been transferred to I Corps. By this time, he had also requested permission from Sharp to begin planning for an amphibious landing north of the DMZ to relieve pressure on Khe Sanh. He informed his immediate subordinates that the Tet truce would be canceled in I CTZ and his superiors in Washington that the situation at Khe Sanh had become critical and was now a turning point in the war.[72]

Information obtained on 25 January reinforced the decision to further prepare for a major enemy attack in I CTZ. The NSA, for example, issued a SIGINT report entitled "Coordinated Vietnamese Communist Offensive Evidenced" which clearly warned of a major attack. The report, citing an "almost unprecedented volume of urgent messages . . . passing among major [enemy] commands," predicted imminent coordinated attacks throughout all of South Vietnam, especially in the northern half of the country.[73] Moreover, by this time Westmoreland apparently had been told by members of his staff that NVA units were moving toward the city of Hue, even though this information was not passed on to the U.S. forces working in the small MACV compound located in that city.[74]

26–30 January

Although there was a relative lull on the battlefield on 26 and 27 January, two types of enemy activity still demonstrated that the VC were present in the capital, around other cities, and near allied instal-

---

[71]Item 21 1151, Item 46 2041 24 January, Daily Journal Files, MACV J-2 Command Center; *PERINTREP*, January 1968, p. 5; Pearson, *War in the Northern Provinces*, pp. 34–35; and Nalty, *Air Power*, p. 26.

[72]Sharp and Westmoreland, *Report*, p. 172; Pearson *War in the Northern Provinces*, p. 66; *Command History 1968*, 1:217, 219. CINCPAC approved the MACV request to begin work on Operation Pacific Grove (CTF 76 Oplan 128-68), the amphibious landing north of the DMZ on 26 January; see *Command History 1968*, 2:781–782; and *Westmoreland v. CBS* exhibit 64, p. 26.

[73]NSA report quoted in *Westmoreland v. CBS*, exhibit 64, p. 26.

[74]House Select Committee on Intelligence, *U.S. Intelligence Agencies and Activities*, p. 1999. In addition to the 25 January report, the NSA issued ten other warnings before the offensive that indicated that VC and NVA units were preoccupied with preparations for imminent attack; see *Westmoreland v. CBS*, exhibit 518; and Westmoreland, *Soldier*, p. 319.

lations in III CTZ. VC terrorists struck once in Saigon during the night of the twenty-sixth, killing a South Vietnamese civilian in his home. On the twenty-seventh, VC assassinated two South Vietnamese civilians, one the chief of Binh Thuan hamlet located 6 kilometers west of Saigon. Communist units also attacked two allied airbases in II CTZ. At 0100 on the night of the twenty-sixth, communists launched a mortar barrage against the U.S. airfield at the An Khe base camp in Binh Dinh province. During the barrage, enemy sapper units cut the perimeter wire surrounding the airfield and used satchel charges to destroy aircraft and vehicles and to damage several buildings. Similarly, at 0002 on the morning of the twenty-seventh, the communists attacked the U.S. complex at Pleiku, damaging the 71st Evacuation Hospital and communication facilities.[75]

On the morning of the twenty-seventh, General Davidson briefed Westmoreland, predicting major country-wide attacks and specifically naming the towns of Kontum and Pleiku. Even though Westmoreland claimed years after the war that this briefing increased his concerns about the security of Saigon, the initiatives he undertook at this time still demonstrated his preoccupation with Khe Sanh. For example, he ordered Col. Reamer Argo, the MACV military historian, to conduct a "thorough military analysis of the Dien Bien Phu battle and a comparison thereof to the analogous Khe Sanh situation in order to ensure that all possible counteractions were taken by US/FWMAF forces."[76] Two studies were eventually produced: "Lessons of Dien Bien Phu (1954) Analogous to Khe Sanh (1968)," which was completed by 13 February, and "Final Report, Dien Bien Phu Analogous to Khe Sanh," which was completed by 10 March. Westmoreland apparently received more than he bargained for in authorizing the study. In a preliminary briefing, Argo stressed a factor that emerged at Dien Bien Phu and in most sieges throughout history: the defender usually succumbed after losing all initiative. Westmoreland responded to Argo's briefing, which shocked the MACV staff, by thanking him for presenting a worst-case analysis and stating, "We are not, repeat not going to be defeated at Khe Sanh. I will tolerate no talking or even thinking to the contrary."[77] The outcome of the siege

[75]Item 17 0532, Item 26 0912, Item 55 2256 26 January, Item 9 0213, Item 21 0545, Item 65 2246 27 January, Daily Journal Files, MACV J-2 Command Center.

[76]*Command History 1968*, 2:785.

[77]Westmoreland, *Soldier*, p. 338. Given Westmoreland's response to Argo's initial findings, it is not surprising that years after the war General Davidson was able to remark: "I don't think anybody ever worried at MACV nor at . . . [III MAF] . . . that Khe Sanh was in any great danger. I never heard one word in all the weeks saying 'We're liable to lose it'"; Davidson, Oral History II, pp. 12–24, LBJ Library.

of Dien Bein Phu was one element of the analogy that Westmoreland had no interest in applying to Khe Sanh.[78]

Although General Davidson was at least wavering in his preoccupation with Khe Sanh by the morning of the twenty-seventh, on 28 January an incident convinced many ARVN commanders and possibly some senior U.S. officers that major attacks on urban areas were about to occur. Responding to information about VC plans to hold several meetings in the coastal city of Qui Nhon (II CTZ), ARVN military police conducted several cordon and search operations and apprehended eleven VC cadre members. Included in captured propaganda materials were two tapes. The tapes, which were to be played over captured radio stations, announced that "the forces struggling for peace and sovereignty" had occupied the cities of Saigon, Hue, and Da Nang, and that southerners should rise up and overthrow the government. Under interrogation, the VC prisoners disclosed that the communists intended to attack urban areas during the Tet holidays. After listening to the tapes, L. Col. Pham Minh Tho, the local province chief, alerted ARVN troops in Qui Nhon and then played the tape on the telephone for officers at the JGS in Saigon. Information about the content of the tapes, however, probably did not reach MACV J-2 until the afternoon of 29 January.[79]

Meanwhile, during the early morning of the twenty-ninth, MACV J-2 received an ominous report from the officers responsible for analyzing sensor signals near Khe Sanh. At 0115, the following message was received from the Dutch Mill facility at Nakhon Phanom, Thailand: "Lot of activity in Khe Sanh. Many troop movements of large and small units from Laotian border as far S[outh] as 10 miles below Khe Sanh. All movements toward Khe Sanh. Seems to be Big Push."[80] By 0530, two NVA troop concentrations had also been positively identified, one within 10 kilometers west-northwest of the firebase.[81]

[78]"3/10/68 MACV Memo, 'Promulgation of Strategic/Tactical Study," in *Westmoreland v. CBS*, exhibit 677; Westmoreland, *Soldier*, p. 320; and *Command History 1968*, 2:785–786. Senior commanders and analysts had Dien Bien Phu in mind when they made the decision to defend Khe Sanh, even though these studies were initiated well after the decision was made to defend the firebase; see Nalty, *Air Power*, p. 19. For a copy of a comparison of Dien Bien Phu and Khe Sanh given to Rostow by a "knowledgeable American officer" on 21 February 1968, see Rostow, *Diffusion of Power*, pp. 694–696 n. 18.

[79]Lung, *General Offensives*, pp. 35, 43; Westmoreland, *Soldier*, p. 320; Palmer, *Summons*, p. 179; and Oberdorfer, *Tet*, pp. 127–128. In their monthly intelligence summary for February, MACV analysts qualified their description of the Qui Nhon tapes with the word "reportedly," which suggests that they had not yet received a translation of the tapes; see *PERINTREP*, February 1968, p. 13.

[80]Item 4 0115 29 January, Daily Journal Files, MACV J-2 Command Center.

[81]*Command History 1968*, 2:911; and Item 15 0900 29 January, Daily Journal Files, MACV J-2 Command Center.

Other last-minute warnings began to accumulate during the twenty-ninth, but it is difficult to determine how many of these were passed on to senior commanders and MACV J-2 analysts. The U.S. 199th Light Infantry Brigade, which had taken up positions around Saigon on 25 January, captured two VC who revealed that local force companies were supposed to guide VC and NVA main-force units in an attack on the capital. Several company-size enemy units were spotted moving near Saigon. Residents of a suburb of Bien Hoa (III CTZ) informed ARVN units that communist forces were in the vicinity, confirming earlier reports that one artillery and two infantry regiments were moving into an area north of the city. Moreover, at about this time a South Vietnamese agent working for the national police turned over information about the communist plan of attack on the U.S. complex at Da Nang. This information facilitated the marine's defense of the installation.[82]

Westmoreland, apparently in response to signs of enemy activity near urban areas, informed his superiors that "there are indications that the enemy may not cease military operations during Tet." He did not waver, however, from his preoccupation with the situation in I CTZ. He noted that the enemy was apparently attempting to "dig his way into Khe Sanh [to avoid] our tremendous firepower (as he did at Dien Bien Phu)." He also claimed that the enemy might attempt to isolate the two northernmost provinces of the country at any time. Westmoreland concluded: "I have no doubt that the enemy plans to launch widespread activity to deter reinforcement of northern I Corps." Indications of the impending urban attacks were interpreted by Westmoreland as evidence that the main blow of the offensive would materialize along the DMZ.[83]

In any event, at 1800 29 January the allied cease-fire went into effect in all of South Vietnam except I CTZ. President Thieu, unmoved by an intelligence briefing concerning indications of impending attack against urban areas, left Saigon soon after the declaration of the cease-fire to spend the Tet holidays at the coastal city of My Tho (IV CTZ). Less than two hours later, however, Lieutenant General Weyand sent the following message to his subordinate unit commanders in III CTZ: "There are a number of positive intel [intelligence] indications that EN [enemy] will deliberately violate truce by attacking FRD [friendly] installations on Corps wide basis during

---

[82]*Long Binh/Saigon Tet Campaign* p. 3; Lung, *General Offensives*, p. 37; House Select Committee on Intelligence, *U.S. Intelligence Agencies and Activities* p. 698; Betts, "Strategic Surprise for War Termination," p. 163; and Oberdorfer, *Tet*, p. 125.

[83]Cable from Westmoreland to Sharp, 29 January 1968, NSF Country File, Vietnam, Box 68–69, Folder: Vietnam 2C(3) General Military Activity, LBJ Library.

night 29 Jan or early 30 January, initiation time 0130H. Addressees take action to insure maximum alert posture thru TET. Be particularly alert for EN deception involving FRD vehicles and FRD uniforms."[84] Weyand's alert order, issued at 2037, came forty-five minutes after MACV J-2 analysts recorded the first communist truce violation, which took place in II CTZ.[85]

At this point, the allies benefited from a major communist mistake. The Tet attacks were probably scheduled to begin at about 0300 on the morning of 30 January, but difficulties encountered by some units in reaching their staging areas forced the postponement of the attacks by 24 hours. For some reason, however, the MR5 headquarters failed to pass news of this postponement to the units under its control. Consequently, units attached to the MR5 headquarters launched a series of attacks in I and II CTZ during the early morning hours of 30 January. Major attacks started to erupt at about 0135, and by 0500 the province capitals of Pleiku, Khanh Hoa, Darlac, and Quang Tri were all under heavy attack. Sappers also attacked U.S. installations at Da Nang, Nha Trang, and Cam Rahn Bay.[86] Such events could not go unnoticed by senior commanders and analysts. At dawn on the morning of the thirtieth, General Davidson informed Westmoreland that similar attacks would materialize throughout South Vietnam during the following night (30–31 January). At 0945 that morning, the South Vietnamese government canceled the Tet truce throughout the country. U.S. units were simultaneously informed about the South Vietnamese cancellation of the cease-fire and ordered to resume full operations.[87]

[84]Item 37 2037 29 January, Daily Journal Files, MACV J-2 Command Center.

[85]Lung, *General Offensives*, pp. 37, 43; Stanton, *Rise and Fall*, p. 220; Item 35 1952 29 January, Daily Journal Files, MACV J-2 Command Center; and Shaplen, *Time out of Hand*, p. 402.

[86]Shaplen, *Time out of Hand*, p. 405; *PERINTREP*, January 1968, pp. 15–18; Oberdorfer, *Tet*, p. 124; Westmoreland, *Soldier*, p. 322; Stanton, *Rise and Fall*, pp. 231–232, 240–241; *Westmoreland v. CBS*, exhibit 64, p. 26; Items 2 through 58 30 January, Daily Journal Files, MACV J-2 Command Center; Memorandum for the President, 30 January 1968, NSF Country File, Vietnam, Box 68–69, Folder: Vietnam 2C(3) General Military Activity, LBJ Library; and Graham, Oral History II, p. 32.

[87]Westmoreland, *Soldier*, p. 323; Oberdorfer, *Tet*, pp. 131–133; Shaplen, *Time out of Hand*, p. 402; House Select Committee on Intelligence, *U.S. Intelligence Agencies and Activities*, p. 1997; Lung, *General Offensives*, p. 44; and Item 46 0945, Item 50 1030 30 January, Daily Journal Files, MACV J-2 Command Center. Given the scope, intensity, and the apparent outcome of the premature attacks, Westmoreland did not seem particularly alarmed by the prospect of renewed urban attacks the following evening. After describing the premature attacks, he predicted a renewal of the urban attacks, but he concluded: "The enemy displayed what appears to be desperation tactics, using NVA troops to terrorize populated areas. He attempted to achieve surprise by attacking during the truce period. The reaction of Vietnamese, US and Free World Forces to the

At this time, the situation became confused as U.S. commanders and their ARVN counterparts scrambled to generate forces to meet the coming attacks. Even though U.S. forces had supposedly been put on alert 36 hours before Tet, at 1125, Maj. Gen. Walter Kerwin, Westmoreland's chief of staff, sent a "flash priority message" to all U.S. unit commanders: "Effective immediately all forces will resume intensified operations and troops will be placed on maximum alert with particular attention to the defense of headquarters complexes, logistical installations, airfields, population centers, and billets. All units will be particularly alert to deception measures by the enemy and be poised to aggressively pursue and destroy any enemy force which attacks."[88] Moreover, Westmoreland either saw or telephoned every senior U.S. commander in the country "to discuss the likelihood of immediate widespread attacks" and then informed Sharp and Wheeler that "all my subordinate commanders report the situation well in hand."[89] Westmoreland's method of communicating his concerns was not, however, unique and would not have been viewed as particularly alarming by senior commanders. On 31 August 1967, for example, Westmoreland had telephoned every senior U.S. commander in the country to alert them to the possibility that the communists would attempt to disrupt the South Vietnamese elections. On 28 October he had telephoned senior officers to tell them to be on alert during Vice-President Humphrey's trip to Vietnam. In fact, he had telephoned every senior commander in the country on his departure and return from his November 1967 trip to Washington, D.C.[90]

ARVN also tried to generate forces for the anticipated attacks, especially in the vicinity of Saigon. Units located in the CMD were placed on alert at 1200 30 January. ARVN units were confined to their barracks, one airborne battalion was designated as a reserve force for the capital, a company was deployed at the Chi Hoa prison and the Saigon national radio station, and security was tightened at all major

situation has been generally good. Since the enemy has exposed himself, he has suffered many casualties. As of now, they add up to almost 700. When the dust settles, there will probably be more"; see Cable from Westmoreland to Sharp and Wheeler, 30 January 1968, 1255Z, pp. 2–3, NSF Country File, Vietnam, Folder: Vietnam 2C(3) General Military Activity, LBJ Library.

[88]Oberdorfer, *Tet*, p. 133.

[89]Westmoreland, *Soldier*, p. 323; Cable from Westmoreland to Sharp and Wheeler, 30 January 1968, 1255Z, p. 3, NSF Country File, Vietnam, Folder: Vietnam 2C(3) General Military Activity, LBJ Library.

[90]*Westmoreland v. CBS*, exhibits 64, p. 26; 912, pp. 11, 69, 76, 85; Statement of Lt. Gen. Daniel O. Graham and letter from Westmoreland to Congressman Milford, in House Select Committee on Intelligence, *U.S. Intelligence Agencies and Activities*, pp. 1663, 1666, 2009.

access routes to Saigon. Starting at 0945 30 January, Saigon radio announced the cancellation of the Tet truce throughout the country and broadcast an urgent plea for all ARVN troops on leave to return to their units. U.S. units in the CMD also went on "red alert" at about 1630.[91] These late efforts were not an outstanding success. In terms of increasing ARVN readiness, they were far too late. Even though ARVN units were on alert during the Tet truce, 50 percent of all ARVN soldiers were allowed to go on leave during the Tet holiday. The ARVN command structure was probably incapable of recalling these troops on short notice, and ARVN soldiers generally ignored the orders they received to return to their units. In IV CTZ, for example, provincial officials simply filed the orders canceling the cease-fire and continued celebrating the holiday. The "point of no return" had been reached for ARVN; actions taken to increase ARVN readiness would now only produce diminishing results.[92]

U.S. officers reacted only slightly better than their ARVN counterparts to orders placing them on maximum alert. The command structure was incapable of passing the warning to all units on such short notice; the communications network simply could not provide enough detailed information to commanders of small units in the field to convince them of the gravity of the situation in time for them to take appropriate defensive measures. Since the summer of 1967, U.S. forces had been on maximum alert nearly 50 percent of the time, so the cancellation of the Tet truce was not especially alarming. Even in the immediate vicinity of Saigon, the U.S. reaction to the warning was mixed. Security forces were placed on alert at Ton Son Nhut, a step that saved the airbase from being overrun. In contrast, three instead of two guards were stationed at the U.S. embassy that evening, and no extra precautions were taken at many other U.S. facilities, including the MACV compound in the capital. A good indication of the concern generated by the alerts sent by MACV is the fact that approximately 200 colonels, all assigned to MACV J-2, spent the evening of 30 January attending a pool party at bachelor officer quarters (boq) 1 in the heart of Saigon. According to James Meacham, an analyst at CICV who attended the party, "maybe Westy knew about Tet, but not the people down below. I had no conception Tet was

[91]Shaplen, *Time out of Hand*, p. 402; Lung, *General Offensives*, pp. 43–44; "Richard McArthur Interview [with George Crile, 25 February 1981]," in *Westmoreland v. CBS*, exhibit 2; and Westmoreland, *Soldier*, p. 323.

[92]Westmoreland, *Soldier*, p. 319; Stanton, *Rise and Fall*, p. 220; testimony of Samuel A. Adams and William E. Colby, in House Select Committee on Intelligence, *U.S. Intelligence Agencies and Activities*, pp. 1706, 1716; see also p. 1996; and Meyerson, *Vinh Long* pp. 128–129.

coming, absolutely zero. I'm categorically sure of that. Of the 200-odd colonels, not one I talked to knew Tet was coming. Without exception." Meacham spent the next day manning a machine gun on the roof of the bachelor officer quarters.[93]

Although Americans received an ever-increasing amount of detailed information about the targets, tactics, and even timing of the Tet attacks, they generally downplayed the threat posed against urban areas, government installations, ARVN units, and U.S. facilities during December 1967 and January 1968. Until the very eve of the 31 January attacks, their actions and analyses demonstrated their preoccupation with Khe Sanh. The diversion at Khe Sanh succeeded in focusing attention and resources on the firebase, thereby reducing the ability of the allies to meet the Tet attacks when they finally materialized. An obvious question is, why?

The communists' multiple threats throughout the country indeed posed a difficult problem. U.S. units could not be in two places at the same time; they would have to rely on ARVN to defend the cities, a prospect that did not fill them with confidence. But instead of confronting the problem squarely, commanders belittled the threat against urban areas. External factors intervened to reduce the momentum of Westmoreland's efforts to shorten the cease-fire, but he did not rely on the one argument that might have convinced the Johnson administration that the truce would hurt the allies—that ARVN and southern cities might be attacked during the holiday. None of the allies confronted the grim situation facing them; consequently, ARVN, which bore the brunt of the offensive, was at half strength when the attacks materialized.

One explanation for the U.S. preoccupation with Khe Sanh lies in the difference between the signals generated by the firebase diversion and those generated by the impending attacks against urban areas. The communists actually attacked the firebase before the Tet offensive, and it was certainly easier to place credence in estimates of enemy intentions based on actual military developments. An NVA ground assault against the firebase provided extremely salient evidence that the communists placed a high priority on the siege of Khe Sanh; in contrast, possible attacks against urban areas were still a military "non-event." Moreover, signals of an impending attack against southern cities lacked a certain military quality; indications that gov-

---

[93]Quote from "Adams' James Meacham Chronology," in *Westmoreland v. CBS*, exhibit 58, p. 44; see also House Select Committee on Intelligence, *U.S. Intelligence Agencies and Activities*, p. 1997; and Oberdorfer, *Tet*, pp. 7–8, 10, 134.

ernment officials in the vicinity of Saigon had been executed, that the VC intended to beat drums in the streets of the capital, or that ARVN soldiers were disturbed by VC rumors concerning the formation of a coalition government were just not considered to be as threatening as the battle already joined at Khe Sanh.

Americans beliefs also greatly influenced their interpretation of events prior to the Tet attacks. The concentration of NVA units around the firebase, interpreted as an effort to penetrate the perimeter formed by U.S. forces along the DMZ, testified to the effectiveness of the shield strategy. The siege also supported the belief that U.S. units posed the greatest threat to the communists and would constitute the likely targets of a major offensive. Most officers believed that they could readily exploit the willingness of the communists to stand up to superior U.S. firepower. The defense of Khe Sanh facilitated the further realization of the attrition strategy. When combined, however, these beliefs led most to downplay the threat posed against the targets of the 31 January attack. Indeed, by the time of the Tet attacks, more than 50 percent of U.S. combat battalions had been moved to I CTZ, and as late as 30 January elements of the 101st Airborne Division were still in transit toward I CTZ. The success of the shield and attrition strategies, it seemed, reduced the capability of VC units operating behind U.S. units; if attacks against cities materialized, they would pale in comparison to the situation at Khe Sanh.[94]

The belief that the communists had lost the military initiative increased the willingness of U.S. commanders to draw on analogy between Dien Bien Phu and Khe Sanh. In embracing the analogy, they stressed the public-relations aspects of the French defeat. In their view, the French were not dealt a defeat of strategic proportions at Dien Bien Phu, and Khe Sanh was an attempt to inflict a psychological not a strategic military defeat on the allies—an interpretation that complemented the belief that the communists realized that they lacked the military capability needed to win in Vietnam. Given the justifiable confidence most Americans had in the ability of their firepower to stop any NVA assault, they readily accepted the opportunity to inflict a Dien Bien Phu in reverse on the communists. The firepower and logistical weaknesses that doomed the French garrison were never a significant factor in the defense of Khe Sanh. Ultimately, U.S. commanders would continue to hope for an opportunity to defend Khe Sanh against a major assault until NVA units began to withdraw from the vicinity of the firebase during the middle of March 1968.

[94]Jones, *War without Windows,* p. 161; and Helm, "The Tet 1968 Offensive," p. 207.

[223]

[6]

Reacting to the
Tet Offensive

Although Americans expected the communists to attack during the night of 30–31 January, it is apparent that they failed to anticipate the intensity, scope, and nature of the offensive. Awakened by the sound of gunfire in Saigon during the night, officers were shocked to learn the VC had entered the capital. It soon became apparent, especially to the press corps, that the allies had failed to stop the main thrusts of the urban offensive directed at Saigon and the old imperial capital at Hue. Weeks of bitter house-to-house fighting would occur before the communists were cleared from these cities, one the center and the other the symbol of government power in South Vietnam. By the end of 31 January, the allies had lost the military initiative to the communists.

The communists, however, also encountered a few unpleasant surprises during the attacks. Even though most ARVN units were at half strength, they did not desert to the communists. Instead, they fought valiantly and ultimately drove the VC out of dozens of cities and towns. The communists soon discovered that they were not welcomed as liberators. Civilians ignored the call to stage a general uprising and generally failed to cooperate with the communists. Some civilians even jumped at the first opportunity to inform authorities of the whereabouts of VC units or to volunteer information about VC plans. The Tet offensive definitely failed to unfold as anticipated.

TET ATTACKS

[225]

THE TET ATTACKS

Assault on the Cities

Although field units continued to obtain indications of impending attack during the night of 30–31 January, there was no longer enough time to analyze and disseminate this information. At 2246 30 January, MACV analysts were informed that a VC soldier, captured near Saigon at 2115, revealed that the VC intended to attack Ton Son Nhut airbase and various targets in the capital that night. Similarly, at 0210 31 January, analysts learned that during interrogation an ARVN deserter revealed that the VC intended to disguise themselves as members of the 5th ARVN Ranger Battalion (the use of ARVN uniforms by the VC was common during the offensive), board vehicles that routinely entered Ton Son Nhut airbase, and attack the base that evening. During the night, analysts received detailed information about the objectives of the previous night's attacks in I and II CTZ. These reports all indicated that ARVN installations, government facilities, radio stations, and U.S. airbases were priority targets in the premature attacks. In the time remaining, forces could not be generated to meet the attacks that were about to develop against similar targets throughout the country. These last-minute warnings arrived too late.[1]

In contrast, some late indications obtained by field units were used successfully by local commanders. Elements of the 199th Light Infantry Brigade, stationed near the U.S. complex at Long Binh and to the southwest of Saigon, received several warnings from a long-range reconnaissance patrol and from impressed civilians who managed to escape the VC. In the final moments before the attacks, a breakdown of noise-discipline (the practice of moving quietly into position) among VC units also provided warning. Alerted, the brigade prevented some VC units from reaching their attack positions and quickly suppressed the VC's preliminary rocket and mortar barrage. It kept several VC units from either entering or leaving Saigon, but it could not stop the VC units already in the capital from launching their attacks as planned.[2]

---

[1]House Select Committee on Intelligence, *U.S. Intelligence Agencies and Activities*, p.2000; Item 87 1701, Item 113 2246 30 January, Item 3 0012, Item 7 0210 31 January, Daily Journal Files, MACV J-2 Command Center; Lung, *General Offensives*, p. 37; Richard C. Kriegel, "Tet Offensive, Victory or Defeat?" *Marine Corps Gazette*, December 1968, p. 25. Robert Shaplen states that the VC soldier was captured at 2215, not at 2115; see *Time out of Hand*, p. 403.

[2]*Long Binh/Saigon Tet Campaign*, p. 1, and annex F; *Command History 1968*, 2: 895. The 199th Infantry obtained information from civilians, but in general few South Viet-

Allied forces operating near Hue failed to respond effectively to last minute warnings. An ARVN reconnaissance patrol operating about 4 kilometers southwest of the Hue reported that at least two NVA battalions were heading toward the city about one hour and forty minutes before the attacks against the old imperial capital developed. Even though the local ARVN commander alerted his forces, U.S. officers stationed at the MACV compound in the city were not informed about this development. Moreover, divisions in the command structure impeded the defense of the city; calls for assistance sent by officers at the MACV compound had to be relayed by ARVN's I Corps, III MAF, and 1st Marine Division headquarters before they reached the 1st Marine Division forward headquarters. Messages became so garbled in transmission that the senior U.S. commander in the vicinity of Hue lacked a clear idea of the extent of the NVA presence in the city throughout 31 January.[3]

Beginning at about 0300 on the morning of the thirty-first, the communists launched coordinated attacks in I, III, and IV CTZ. By the end of the day, 27 of South Vietnam's 44 provincial capitals, 5 of its 6 autonomous cities, 58 of its 245 district towns, and more than 50 hamlets had been attacked. Although most of these assaults failed to penetrate the defenses of these urban centers, between 30 and 31 January the communists either infiltrated or fought their way into Quang Tri, Hue, and Da Nang in I CTZ; Nha Trang, Qui Nhon, Kontum, and Ban Me Thuot in II CTZ; Saigon in III CTZ; and My Tho, Can Tho, and Ben Tre in IV CTZ. In most cases, the communists were driven from these urban areas within two or three days. Very heavy fighting continued for some time, however, in Kontum, Ban Me Thout, Can Tho, and Ben Tre. In Saigon and Hue, the battle was protracted. In a matter of days, the communists also delivered a stiff setback to the pacification program in the countryside.[4]

---

namese provided information before the offensive; see "House Select Committee on Intelligence, *U.S. Intelligence Agencies and Activities*, p. 2000. Civilians probably did not come forward because of VC threats. In a hamlet in Vinh Long province on 27 January, for example, leaflets informed the inhabitants that the VC would be using the village for a while "and that anyone who went to the authorities would be decapitated"; see Meyerson, *Vinh Long*, p. 128.

[3]Nolan, *Battle for Hue*, pp. 6, 9–10; and Westmoreland, *Soldier*, p. 329.

[4]*Command History 1968*, 1:129; Shaplen, *Time out of Hand*, p. 415; Sharp and Westmoreland, *Report*, p. 159; Karnow, *Vietnam*, pp. 523–525; and National Military Command Center, Memorandum for the Record, Subject: Enemy attacks South Vietnam, 30 January 1968 1658 EST, doc. 56; Central Intelligence Agency, Intelligence Memorandum, 30 January 1968, 1630 EST, The Situation in South Vietnam, doc. 5; Central Intelligence Agency, Intelligence Memorandum, Spot Report on the Situation in Hue 31 January 1968, 1530 EST, doc. 2a; and Cable from Sharp to Wheeler, 31 January 1968, doc. 34 in NSF Country File Vietnam, Box 68–69, Folder: Vietnam 2C(3) General Military Activity,

The Tet attacks shared several characteristics. The communists usually concentrated on destroying ARVN installations, government facilities, command centers, airbases, lines of communication, and prisons. AK-47s, RPG-7s, and 120-mm mortars were used widely. Tear gas was also used, a development that surprised the allies. Two weapons were used for the first time during Tet: 122-mm rockets and PT-76 tanks. The communists also tried to convince ARVN units to either surrender or defect. In IV CTZ, for example, the VC held the commander of the 7th ARVN Division and his family hostage in an unsuccessful attempt to convince his entire division to defect. Cadres usually began to exhort the population to revolt as soon as they gained a foothold in an urban area. If the communists retained control for more than a few days, however, exhortation changed to coercion. In Hue, 3000 bodies were discovered and 2000 people were missing after the communists settled old scores and eliminated "enemies of the people."[5]

Probably the worst and definitely the most spectacular fighting took place within and around Saigon and Hue. Fighting began near Saigon at 0430 when the VC attempted to destroy the ammunition depot at Long Binh and to capture a POW compound maintained at the facility. Elements of the U.S. 199th Infantry Brigade removed most of the demolition charges and surrounded the VC units by 0600. VC sappers destroyed only about 5 percent of the ammunition stored at the base. At about the same time, the VC attacked Bien Hoa airbase, destroying several aircraft, penetrating the base perimeter, and bringing the III Corps headquarters under fire. Even though air operations were curtailed between 0300 and 1300 on 31 January, allied reinforcements drove the VC from the base by the late afternoon of the thirty-first. Similarly, the perimeter of Ton Son Nhut airbase was penetrated at about 0321, but the VC were driven from the base by 1219.[6]

LBJ Library. Evaluations of the impact of the offensive on the pacification program vary. The setback was apparently temporary, but its severity was overestimated in the immediate aftermath of the offensive; see Phillip Davidson, Oral History I, pp. 69–70; Daniel O. Graham, Oral History II, pp. 27–29; Don Oberdorfer, Oral History II, p. 20; and Cable from Bunker to President, 15 February 1968, Thirty-ninth Weekly Message, p. 5, Folder: Vietnam 8B(2) [B], NSF Country File, Vietnam, Boxes 104, 105, 106, LBJ Library.

[5]Shaplen, *Time out of Hand*, p. 415; Westmoreland, *Soldier*, p. 327; PERINTREP, February 1968, pp. 3, 7–8; Nolan, *Battle for Hue*, p. 184; Lewy, *America in Vietnam*, pp. 274–275; Herring, *America's Longest War*, p. 187; and House Select Committee on Intelligence, *U.S. Intelligence Agencies and Activities*, p. 1996.

[6]*Command History* 1968, 2:895–898; Stanton, *Rise and Fall*, pp. 227–231; *Long Binh/Saigon Tet Campaign*, pp. 7–12; PERINTREP, February 1968, pp. 4–5; Shaplen, *Time out of Hand*, pp. 410–411; and Lung, *General Offensives*, p. 69. Bruce Palmer, however, claims that fighter aircraft could not use Bien Hoa airbase until 48 hours after the Tet attacks; see *25-Year War*, p. 77.

Inside Saigon and its suburb Cholon the VC opened fire at about 0210 on the morning of the thirty-first, just as the final volley of Tet fireworks was ending. At 0247 elements of the VC C-10 Sapper Battalion, a unit whose members lived in Saigon, breached the wall of the U.S. embassy and attacked the main building with rocket-propelled grenades and automatic weapons. Defense of the embassy was initially fragile—embassy security guards and military police almost ran out of ammunition at 0636—but reinforcements helped to secure the compound by 0900. By 0426, approximately 4000 VC emerging from hiding in the capital had brought installations throughout Saigon under small-arms and mortar fire. The situation inside Saigon worsened throughout the day. At 1445, for example, MACV J-2 analysts logged a report that illustrated the chaos reigning in the city:

New Embassy Hotel in SAIGON near ROK [Republic of Korea] Embassy, has an estimated VC company using it as a strong point. Have machine guns on roof. Approximately 20 US and local police and ROK MPs pinned down by enemy. Doubt they can hold out after dark. RACE TRACK AREA: Capital Military District forces driving VC in direction of PX warehouse. Warehouse lightly held by civilians and unarmed American personnel. 1 platoon (US) on way to warehouse for reinforcement. BOQ [bachelor officer quarters] #3: US relief force still fighting a company size enemy force, enemy holding out in houses near BOQ. Wounded (US) removed from street. Dead in street. Town situation not getting better. Sporadic shooting all over city. [some abbreviation in original removed][7]

By the end of the day, the 6th and 7th national police precinct headquarters, the South Vietnamese JGS compound, and the studios of the national broadcasting station were also attacked.[8]

Although allied units reacted quickly to the Saigon attacks, their response was hampered by a lack of preparedness to fight inside the capital. The U.S. 716th Military Police Battalion, which operated in Saigon, lacked a contingency plan to deal with widespread fighting in the city. As a result, the military police implemented their "disaster plan" intended to deal with isolated bombings or rioting in the city. The U.S. military police suffered heavy casualties when they were

[7]Item 87 1445 31 January, Daily Journal Files, MACV J-2 Command Center.
[8]*Command History 1968*, 2:898–899; Item 71 0306, Item 72 0315, Item 75 0426, Item 76 0436, Item 82 0655 31 January, Daily Journal Files, MACV J-2 Command Center; "Adams' Tet Chronology," in *Westmoreland v. CBS*, exhibit 628; Stanton, *Rise and Fall*, pp. 219–227; Westmoreland, *Soldier*, pp. 323–328; Sharp and Westmoreland, *Report*, p. 159; Palmer, *Summons*, pp. 190–191; Shaplen, *Time out of Hand*, pp. 405–409; Lung, *General Offensives*, pp. 45, 53–63; and *PERINTREP*, January 1968, p. 17.

dispatched throughout the capital in open trucks. The U.S. forces also lacked a headquarters for the conduct of military operations within the CMD and were forced to improvise at the height of the battle; a separate headquarters, "Hurricane Forward," was created by 1100 31 January and placed under the command of the deputy commander of II FFV, Maj. Gen. Keith L. Ware. Additionally, operations at the MACV headquarters were impeded because the fighting prevented most of its off-duty personnel from returning to their posts. The effort to prepare a hasty defense of the MACV headquarters also interfered with its efficient functioning, and a surge in communications traffic as the Tet attacks developed further complicated matters. U.S. Army Vietnam headquarters at Long Binh, which was designated as the MACV alternate command post, picked up the slack in operations.[9]

Several developments worked in favor of the allies, reducing the communists' ability to gain and hold their objectives in the capital. A shortage of transport aircraft left the 1st and 8th ARVN Airborne Battalions stranded in Saigon when the Tet attacks erupted. The battalions, originally slated for deployment to I CTZ, were quickly thrown into the battle. Allied units also succeeded in blocking most routes into the city, preventing the communists from reinforcing units already in the capital. In contrast, the allies moved five additional battalions to Saigon during the first 24 hours after the Tet attacks. Moreover, rigid plans, a lack of withdrawal routes, and the disintegration of the VC command structure hurt the communists relatively early in the battle. Some commanders of VC reserve units even decided not to attack because of the failure to gain initial objectives. Still, a few isolated pockets of VC remained in Saigon on 5 February, and sporadic fighting continued until a COSVN forward command post was destroyed on 11 February. By 16 February, Richard McArthur, an analyst in the order-of-battle section at MACV J-2, was able to inform his parents that the "town [Saigon] seems to be getting back to normal."[10]

On 16 February, however, the situation was far from normal in

[9]Stanton, *Rise and Fall*, pp. 222–223; *Command History 1968*, 1:219, 2:726, 899; Eckhardt, *Command and Control*, pp. 80–81; Palmer, *25-Year War*, pp. 74, 76; Sharp and Westmoreland, *Report*, p. 170; "James Meacham Interview [3/2/81]," "Russell Cooley Interview [4/9/81]," "Adams' James Meacham Chronology," and "Handwritten Letter from McArthur to His Parents, 6 February 1968," in *Westmoreland v. CBS*, exhibits 8, p. 19; 11, pp. 42,44; 58, p. 44, 247H.
[10]Quote from "Handwritten Letter from McArthur to His Parents, 16 February 1968," *Westmoreland v. CBS*, exhibit 2471; Stanton, *Rise and Fall*, p.219; Lung, *General Offensives*, pp. 42–43, 70–71; Shaplen, *Time out of Hand*, pp. 411–412; Westmoreland, *Soldier*, p. 328, 332; Maclear, *Ten Thousand Day War*, p. 204; *Long Binh/Saigon Tet Campaign*, Annex F, pp. 6–8; and Sharp and Westmoreland, *Report*, p. 159.

Hue, where the communists virtually overran the city before the allies realized that they were under attack. The 4th and 6th NVA Regiments, the 12th VC and Hue City VC Sapper Battalions, and approximately 500 of the 2500 prisoners released from the Hue jail controlled the city except for the 1st ARVN Division headquarters and the MACV compound. By 0800 31 January, the NLF flag was flying over Hue. In contrast to the battle for Saigon, about five days passed before U.S. forces prevented the NVA from reinforcing units already inside the city. Thus ARVN and U.S. Marine units confronted the grim job of dislodging the NVA from their fortified positions inside the city, a task made all the more difficult by an initial prohibition on the use of heavy weapons and air support issued to limit damage to Hue. Even though the most vicious street fighting had ended by 25 February, allied units continued to destroy isolated NVA positions until 2 March. By that time, the ancient imperial capital, which had previously been untouched by the war, had been largely destroyed. At least 5000 communists died in the battle, and over 500 allied servicemen were killed regaining control of the city.[11]

The Battle for Khe Sanh

Although fighting raged throughout most of South Vietnam on 31 January, the situation was relatively calm at Khe Sanh. In fact, it was not until the early morning of 5 February that the sensor field around Khe Sanh detected the movement of NVA units toward marine positions on top of Hill 881S. Artillery strikes broke up the enemy's assault before it reached the hill, but the communists succeeded in launching a ground attack against a different outpost. At 0305 the NVA assaulted marine positions on Hill 861A and captured the forward trench line. The marines quickly counterattacked, and in less than a half hour the position was again in U.S. hands. A second NVA assault on Hill 861A began at approximately 0610 but was quickly broken up by artillery and airstrikes.[12]

The situation at Khe Sanh heated up again at 0042 7 February when

[11]Lt. Col. Phan Van Khoa, the mayor of Hue and province chief of Thua Thien province, was warned about the attacks two days in advance but failed to pass on this information until he emerged from hiding on about 6 February; see Shaplen, *Time out of Hand*, p. 414. The attack on Hue started at approximately 0340 31 January. For a description of the battle, see Nolan, *Battle for Hue*, passim; Stanton, *Rise and Fall*, pp. 232–240; Lung, *General Offensives*, pp. 75–85; Pearson, *War in the Northern Provinces*, pp. 39–48; Westmoreland, *Soldier*, pp. 329–330; Palmer, *Summons*, pp. 192–195; *Command History 1968*, 1:378, 2:886–887.

[12]Oberdorfer, *Tet*, p. 111; Stanton, *Rise and Fall*, p. 250; Shore, *Battle for Khe Sanh*, pp. 64–66; Pearson, *War in the Northern Provinces*, p. 73; and Nalty, *Air Power*, p. 31.

an officer at the U.S. special forces camp at Lang Vei, about 9 kilometers to the southwest of Khe Sanh, radioed that the camp was being attacked by tanks. Within thirteen minutes, nine PT-76 tanks had penetrated the camp's perimeter. Justified fears of an NVA ambush along the road to Lang Vei combined with the danger posed by NVA tanks, which were now positioned in the areas suitable for helicopter landing zones, forced the marines to forego a rescue attempt. By 0243, the remaining defenders of Lang Vei had buttoned themselves up in their bunkers and called in artillery strikes on their own positions. At first light, the survivors managed to break through the NVA ring around the camp and moved about 500 meters east to the site of an older camp. A few hours later they were rescued by helicopter, but more than 3000 Laotion refugees who had also been present at the camp were forced to make their way to Khe Sanh on foot. They reached the firebase at about 0800 on 8 February but were denied entrance to the base until each could be searched.[13]

The NVA also renewed its assault on Khe Sanh on the eighth. At 0420, a regiment from the 325C Division penetrated the marine positions on top of Hill 64. By 0900, a relief force had reached the hill, and within fifteen minutes it drove the NVA off the crest. The NVA again were subjected to a withering fire as they retreated. During the next two weeks, NVA activity around Khe Sanh was limited to sniping incidents and small-scale probes against the perimeter of the firebase. Intelligence analysts noted that the movement of NVA forces toward Khe Sanh had slowed drastically and that the communists were apparently consolidating their positions for a major assault. Although the communists launched a company-sized probing attack against the firebase on 21 February and subjected it to a major artillery barrage on the twenty-third, the sheer weight of U.S. artillery and air power stopped a major NVA assault on Khe Sanh on 29 February. At 2130, 2330, and 0315 (1 March), elements of the NVA 304th Division attempted to penetrate the Khe Sanh perimeter, but they were cut down before they reached the outer defenses of the firebase.[14]

The 29 February attack was the last major NVA assault against the firebase. With the clearing weather, U.S. airpower began to inflict increasing casualties on the NVA units surrounding the marine positions. Even though shelling and probes of the firebase perimeter continued throughout March, marine intelligence began to obtain evi-

[13]Sharp and Westmoreland, *Report*, p. 164; Nalty, *Air Power*, pp. 32–33; Maclear, *Ten Thousand Day War*, p. 195; *Command History 1968*, 1:156, 379; Stanton, *Rise and Fall*, pp. 250–254; *PERINTREP*, February 1968, p. 7; and Shore, *Battle for Khe Sanh*, pp. 66–69.
[14]Stanton, *Rise and Fall*, pp. 254–255; Shore, *Battle for Khe Sanh*, pp. 69–71, 121–125; *Command History 1968*, 1:156; and Nalty, *Air Power*, p. 38.

dence that several NVA units were beginning to move away from the firebase by the middle of the month. At the same time, marine and ARVN units began conducting patrols at increasing distances from the perimeter of the firebase. These patrols would eventually form the basis of Khe Sanh's contribution to operation Pegasus, the "relief" expedition intended to open the land lines of communication to the firebase. Pegasus began on 1 April 1968. Planning for Pegasus had started on 25 January, but the operation was delayed by two factors: the tremendous amount of supples and manpower needed to retake Hue, and the transformation of MACV Forward, which became operational on 9 February, into a corps headquarters designated Provisional Corps, Vietnam on 10 March. This latter development apparently caused turmoil within the command, because U.S. units under the command of Provisional Corps, Vietnam, slated for Pegasus were scheduled to operate in I CTZ, which was under the jurisdiction of III MAF. By 14 April, however, the operation opened a land route to the firebase. Ultimately, overwhelming U.S. air and artillery power, a superior tactical intelligence collection capability based on the sensors designed for the Muscle Shoals portion of the barrier, and a massive aerial resupply effort saved Khe Sanh from the fate that befell the garrison at Dien Bien Phu.[15]

THE ALLIED REACTION TO THE TET OFFENSIVE

Although General Davidson predicted during the morning of 30 January that the communists were about to launch attacks throughout South Vietnam, officers and analysts were nevertheless surprised by the scope and intensity of the Tet offensive. Davidson himself, for example, returned home during the night of 30–31 January, an action

[15]Shore, *Battle for Khe Sanh*, pp. 126–147; Stanton, *Rise and Fall*, 255–258; Sharp and Westmoreland, *Report*, p. 186; Palmer, *25-Year War*, p. 80; Nalty, *Air Power*, pp. 96–100; Eckhardt, *Command and Control*, pp. 74–75; Tolson, *Airmobility*, pp. 169–180; Pearson, *War in the Northern Provinces*, pp. 81–89; and *Command History 1968*, 1:378–380. Used to target artillery and airstrikes, the Muscle Shoals sensors and SIGINT had a devastating impact on the NVA near Khe Sanh. On 30 January, SIGINT located the NVA headquarters near Khe Sanh, leading to its destruction in a massive B-52 strike. NVA radio operators refused to broadcast because any transmission resulted in a massive artillery barrage. In fact, it is impossible to estimate how many times the NVA actually attempted to storm the firebase because many units simply vanished after massive airstrikes were launched in response to activations of the Muscle Shoals sensors; Montagnard tribesmen asked for shelter at Khe Sanh because they could no longer stand the stench of dead NVA soldiers. See Daniel Graham, Oral History I, pp. 20–21; Phillip Davidson, Oral History II, p. 5; Cable from Westmoreland to Sharp, 30 January 1968, doc. 34, Folder: NSF Aides File Memos to the President, Walt Rostow, vol. 58, DSDUF Vietnam, Box 3, LBJ Library; and Jones, *War without Windows*, p. 168.

that demonstrates that senior officers still underestimated the intensity of what was about to unfold. The surprise experienced by U.S. forces in South Vietnam, however, paled in comparison to the shock that the attacks produced in Washington, D.C. Senior members of the administration were far less informed about the situation than senior officers in Vietnam. The Johnson administration, unlike Westmoreland, who benefited from Davidson's 30 January briefing, never received a last-minute warning about the impending attack.[16] Even after the premature attacks on the night of 29–30 January, senior members of the administration still did not realize that the main blow would fall during the next night. At 1145 on 30 January (Washington time), for example, Rostow provided Johnson with a memo describing the attacks that had taken place in I and II CTZ during the previous night. The memo failed to draw the all-important conclusion that similar attacks were about to erupt throughout the rest of South Vietnam (the attacks actually began about three hours after this memo was drafted). Similarly, a memo prepared for Johnson at 0630 31 January (Washington time) provided only a sketchy picture of the situation in South Vietnam during the previous night. The 0630 memo even failed to mention the enemy's attack on Hue. Prior to and during the opening days of the Tet attacks, a time lag of about 18 hours apparently existed between developments in Vietnam and the receipt of information and analysis in Washington.[17]

Johnson and his senior advisers also lacked an appreciation of the tense atmosphere that pervaded the upper levels of the U.S. command just before the Tet attacks. According to the official government investigation of the performance of the intelligence community before Tet, "finished intelligence disseminated in Washington did not contain the atmosphere of crisis present in Saigon. . . . The information available was transmitted and duly analyzed, but atmosphere is not readily passed over a teletype circuit. Although senior officials in Washington received warnings in the period 25–30 January, they did not receive the full sense of immediacy and intensity which was present in Saigon." Unlike senior commanders in South Vietnam, who were able to brace themselves for the main attacks, officials in Washington were unprepared for the emotional shock produced by the offensive, especially since they were still hoping for an encouraging exchange with the North Vietnamese over the Trinh initiative. As late as

---

[16]Phillip B. Davidson, *Vietnam at War* (Novato, Calif., 1988), pp. 474–475; and Betts, "Strategic Surprise for War Termination," p. 162.

[17]"1/30/68 [11:45 AM] Rostow Memorandum for the President" and "1/31/68 [6:30 AM] Rostow Memorandum for the President," in *Westmoreland v. CBS*, exhibits 481, 480.

31 January, Johnson still wanted to see "what the Romanian brings us tomorrow" (the North Vietnamese answer to the U.S. reply to the Trinh initiative) before selecting a response to the offensive.[18]

Meanwhile, in Saigon, Westmoreland was awakened at home at 0300 31 January by a call from MACV headquarters that informed him about the offensive, including the assault on the U.S. embassy. Westmoreland remained at his quarters until about 0830, when he was driven to the embassy compound, which had just been secured. After reporting by phone to Ambassador Bunker and to Philip Habib at the State Department, Westmoreland conducted an impromptu press conference in an unsuccessful attempt to reassure reporters that the offensive would end in a communist defeat. Even though Westmoreland's prediction would eventually prove correct, he admitted in his memoirs that he still did not know about the full extent of the offensive until he arrived at MACV headquarters at Ton Son Nhut airbase after his trip to the embassy.[19]

Westmoreland spent the remainder of 31 January at MACV headquarters monitoring incoming information about the developing battle, but there was little he could do to influence the situation. The MACV J-2 log demonstrates that confusion reigned for at least the first 24 hours after the attacks. Information about the communist attacks was often delayed. J-2 duty officers on 1 February were still logging reports of incidents that occurred in Saigon on 31 January. Moreover, initial reports were often sketchy. A press release issued by MACV on 31 January, which probably reflects the information possessed by Westmoreland at the time, provides a relatively optimistic assessment of only some of the day's major attacks. It also is clear that on 31 January the allies had lost the initiative and were forced to react to the communist attacks. Senior U.S. commanders were initially unable to control the overall allied response to the offensive. As a result, officers at MACV headquarters probably devoted most of their efforts to gathering the reinforcements needed to drive the VC from Saigon. On 31 January, the battle was in the hands of individual unit commanders.[20]

[18]Quotations from House Select Committee on Intelligence, *U.S. Intelligence Agencies and Activities*, pp. 1997–1998; and Memorandum to Secretary of State, Secretary of Defense, Director, Bureau of the Budget, from the President, 31 January 1968, Folder: Vietnam 2C (3) General Military Activity, NSF Country File Vietnam, Boxes 68, 69, LBJ Library.

[19]Westmoreland, *Soldier*, pp. 323–325, 328; Oberdorfer, *Tet*, p. 34; and Braestrup, *Big Story*, 1:95–96.

[20]See delayed entries Item 91 310735, Item 92 310736, Item 93 311036, Item 94 311045, Item 95 311115, Item 96 311236, Item 97 311246, all logged at approximately 2037 1 February, Daily Journal Files, MACV J-2 Command Center; Davidson, Oral History I,

By the end of 1 February, the military situation had started to stabilize. At 0625 Westmoreland took the first step toward regaining the military initiative by advising his FFV and MAF commanders to pursue the communists as they attempted to withdraw from urban areas. A pattern began to emerge in the way that MACV J-2 duty officers reacted to information about the enemy. They became highly sensitive to information about enemy intentions toward urban areas following the Tet attacks. POW interrogations revealed that the U.S. complex at Bien Hoa was to be attacked during the night of 1 February, for example, and U.S. forces responded rapidly. In this case, information that would have been considered unremarkable before the offensive was now interpreted to be extremely significant. Once the idea that the communists could attack urban areas became salient, it was easy to identify indications of additional urban attacks. Even though the incidence of false alarms about imminent local attacks increased—no small matter given that during February it was rumored that the attacks would be renewed on 10, 15, 21, 27 February, 15 March, 1 April, or 1 May—heightened vigilance usually paid dividends, especially if the intelligence could be quickly exploited. For example, allied units were warned that the VC were using Buddhists and other civilians as human shields in their attacks. This information helped to save many civilians. ARVN units also captured a large weapons cache as information about its whereabouts was quickly exploited. At the tactical level, allied intelligence began to function more effectively in the aftermath of the attacks.[21]

At the senior level, however, officers and officials continued to interpret the situation in terms of beliefs held before the Tet offensive. As early as 0918 on 31 January, Westmoreland informed Wheeler that the attacks against urban areas were "diversionary efforts while the enemy prepares for his major attack in northern I CTZ."[22] Westmore-

---

pp. 59–60, LBJ Library; and "News Release, Office of Information, U.S. Military Assistance Command, Vietnam, APO San Francisco 96222, January 31, 1968," in Braestrup, *Big Story*, 2:45–52.

[21]COMUSMACV to III MAF et al., 010625Z Feb. 1968, in *Command History 1968*, 1:25; Item 47 1204, Item 75 1737, Item 111 2133 1 February, Daily Journal Files, MACV J-2 Command Center; and Victoria Pohle, *The Viet Cong in Saigon: Tactics and Objectives during the Tet offensive* (Santa Monica, Calif., 1969), p. 41. The performance of U.S. intelligence agencies was still not flawless. The POW interrogations indicating that the 274th and 275th VC Regiments intended to attack the Bien Hoa complex during the night of 1 February were false alarms. An Operation Niagara report that indicated the presence of tracked vehicles and "prime movers" 25 kilometers northwest of Lang Vei was received by MACV J-2 on 1 February, but the U.S. Special Forces unit at Lang Vei was still surprised by the 7 February NVA tank assault; see Item 2 0100, Item 13 0330, and Item 66 1627 1 February, Daily Journal Files, MACV J-2 Command Center.

[22]MAC 01448, 310918Z January 1968, General Westmoreland to General Wheeler, partially quoted in Schandler, *Unmaking of a President*, p. 85.

land's interpretation of the Tet attacks given in a 1 February press conference was remarkably consistent with his earlier evaluation of enemy intentions and capabilities. He claimed that the decision to launch the Tet attacks was made in September 1967, and that the overall North Vietnamese campaign plan was divided into three phases: a psychological campaign lasting from October 1967 through January 1968; the Tet attacks, which served as a diversion; and finally major attacks in Thua Thien and Quang Tri (I CTZ). Westmoreland thus still believed that the enemy's main attacks would fall on Khe Sanh, other barrier outposts, and the western border of I CTZ. Similarly, General Wheeler, while talking to reporters on 1 February, noted that the Tet attacks were largely a failure because they did not force Westmoreland to divert forces from "the critical Khe Sanh–DMZ area."[23]

On 2 February, events followed a similar pattern. MACV analysts received information concerning VC withdrawal routes from Saigon, a description of the uniform worn by most VC soldiers (a blue scarf), and a copy of the VC plan of attack for Saigon. The allies also broke up an attack on a communication facility 5 kilometers southwest of Saigon by quickly exploiting intelligence to guide airstrikes against VC staging areas. Meanwhile, in Washington, General Wheeler, following his daily telephone call to Westmoreland, denied that the United States had suffered a failure of intelligence before the offensive. He also noted that the communist decision to violate the Tet holidays, a "sacrilegious" act in the eyes of the Vietnamese, was evidence of "the utter desperation tactics that they employed in mounting these attacks." Secretary of Defense McNamara emphasized that the allies had prevented the communists from securing their military objectives, and that it was now imperative that the communists be prevented from securing their only remaining goal, "a psychological or propaganda victory." President Johnson, while emphasizing the connection between the North Korean seizure of the *Pueblo* and the Tet attacks, also noted in a press conference that it was important to deny the communists a psychological victory and that the allies still faced "a major enemy offensive in the area of Khe Sanh and generally around the Demilitarized Zone."[24]

---

[23]"Secretary of Defense Robert S. McNamara and Chairman of the Joint Chiefs Gen. Earle G. Wheeler, Interview following Appearance before the Senate Armed Services Committee, February 1, 1968," in Braestrup, *Big Story*, 2:68; "Press Briefing, General William C. Westmoreland, Saigon, February 1, 1968," in ibid., 2:62–66; and Oberdorfer, *Tet*, p. 165. Westmoreland took the time to deliver a press briefing at this critical juncture because he was ordered to by the president on 31 January; see Schandler, *Unmaking of a President*, p.83.

[24]"McNamara and Wheeler following Appearance," in Braestrup, *Big Story*, 2:73–74,

Between 3 and 4 February, MACV analysts obtained documents concerning the targets of the Tet attacks in Saigon, information about the location of VC units, and reports from civilians about VC intentions. Before the offensive, analysts tended to dismiss this latter type of information as rumor circulated by the VC to undermine South Vietnamese morale. Now, however, information volunteered by civilians was taken seriously. On 3 February, MACV analysts responded to a report turned in by the West German air attache who was told by South Vietnamese friends to stay away from certain areas of Saigon because of impending VC activity. On 4 February, analysts received reports from civilians that a NVA unit might be operating near Saigon. Members of the unit wore a distinctive uniform on which the words *Sinh Bac Tu Nam–Sinh Daes Tuws Nam* (Born in the North–Die in the South) were embroidered. Of course, much of the information volunteered by civilians turned out to be erroneous. Even though reports of the NVA unit persisted until 8 February, for example, allied units were unable to locate it. Aircraft dispatched on 3 February also failed to locate a VC battalion supposedly operating near Ton Son Nhut airbase. Still, by 4 February, MACV analysts, undeterred by the increase in false alarms, turned to a wider variety of sources as they looked for information about the enemy.[25]

Senior officers and officials offered candid assessments of the attacks and enemy intentions. On 3 February, Brig. Gen. John Chaisson, director of MACV's combat operations center, admitted that the U.S. military was surprised by the coordination, intensity, and large commitment of communist resources during Tet. Chaisson also warned that the biggest concentration of communist forces to date was currently near Khe Sanh and along the DMZ. Senior officers expected the communists to synchronize attacks in this area with attacks in other areas of South Vietnam, but Chaisson claimed that no firm conclusions had been reached on when these attacks would materialize. Even though early reports indicated that communist losses had been extremely heavy, Chaisson noted that the enemy could launch more urban attacks by "recycling" units.[26]

Chaisson's concerns about the possibility of an NVA attack against Khe Sanh or across the DMZ were repeated in a warning delivered by

---

28; "News Conference, President Lyndon Johnson, The White House, February 2, 1968," in ibid., 2:76, 77–85; and Kalb and Abel, *Roots of Involvement*, pp. 205–206.

[25]Item 53 1840, Item 50 1830, Item 61 2030 3 February, Item 39 1801 4 February, Item 66 2330 8 February, Daily Journal Files, MACV J-2 Command Center; and Pohle, *Viet Cong in Saigon*, p. 19.

[26]"Press Briefing, Brig. Gen. John Chaisson, USMC, Saigon, February 3, 1968," in Braestrup, *Big Story*, 2:89–94.

Westmoreland to his senior subordinates on 4 February: "The enemy's current country-wide major offensive has been blunted and stopped. The forces he initially committed have been turned back with enormous losses. . . . the enemy has withheld many of his main force and NVA units. . . . Consequently, he [the communists] continues to maintain a strong capability to re-initiate attacks country-wide at the time and place of his choosing, and most probably in conjunction with what I believe will be his ultimate efforts; a major offensive in the Khe Sanh/Cam Lo/Con Thien area."[27] The same day, Westmoreland repeated this assessment in a message to Wheeler: "We must accord him [the enemy] the capability of a second cycle of attacks either against the populated areas or most likely, in the DMZ and other areas of NVA concentration." In fact, Wheeler, Westmoreland, and Bunker repeatedly warned—and senior administration officials fretted—about Khe Sanh until the end of February.[28]

Ambassador Bunker, in his weekly cable to President Johnson transmitted 4 February, repeated Westmoreland's warning that remaining communist forces could be committed to a second wave of attacks, especially along the DMZ. In addition, Bunker admitted that "there was some failure of intelligence on our side." As evidence of this failure, he correctly noted that "a sizeable number" of ARVN soldiers and government officials were on leave when the offensive erupted. Bunker also offered an assessment of the communist motivations behind the offensive, which he developed after consultations with President Thieu: "It seems to me that the primary purpose of this particular operation was probably psychological rather than military, that it was designed to put Hanoi in a strong position for negotiations by demonstrating the strength of the Viet Cong while shaking the faith of the people in South Vietnam in the ability of their own government and the U.S. to protect them. This would be consistent with the determination on their part to press toward peace talks."[29]

[27]COMUSMACV to III MAF et al., 040655Z Feb. 1968, in *Command History* 1968, 1:26.
[28]Quotation from "Memo Origins of Post-Tet Plans, 9 November 1970 [by William Westmoreland, with endorsements from Earle Wheeler and U.S. Grant Sharp]," in *Westmoreland v. CBS*, exhibit 508, pp. 4–5. See also Notes of the President's Meeting with the National Security Council, 7 February 1968, pp. 3–5, Folder: February 7, 1968 National Security Council Meetings, Tom Johnson's Notes of Meetings, Box 2; Cable from Bunker to President, 15 February 1968, Thirty-ninth Weekly Message, pp. 7–8, Folder: Vietnam 8B(2) [B], National Security File, Country File, Vietnam, Box 104, 105, 106; Cable from Bunker to President, 22 February 1968, Fortieth Weekly Message, pp. 2,5, Folder: Vietnam 8B(2) [B], National Security File, Country File, Vietnam, Box 104, 105, 106; Rostow Cable to Wheeler and Westmoreland, 23 February 1968, Folder: NSF Country File, Vietnam 2C(7) General Military Activity, DSDUF Vietnam, Box 4; and Earle G. Wheeler, Oral History II, p. 4, LBJ Library.
[29]*Westmoreland v. CBS*, exhibit 846G, pp. 2, 5.

Evidence supporting Bunker's analysis of the relationship between fighting and negotiating in Hanoi's strategy was provided the same day. North Vietnamese diplomats offered to begin negotiations with the United States. The offer was repeated on Radio Hanoi four days later.[30]

Although between 5 and 18 February analysts continued to obtain information about the communists' Tet objectives and battle plans, events in Washington began to overshadow battlefield developments, with one exception. MACV analysts received indications that the communists were planning a new series of urban attacks. On 7 February, interrogation reports revealed that the VC intended to renew "all offensives," but POWs provided different dates for the attacks: 11 and 16 February. On 10 February, ARVN captured a document outlining VC plans for the movement of supplies and reinforcements into the capital. On the same day, MACV analysts received a report that the VC intended to attack that evening. The fact that civilians believed the report was apparently considered significant. The VC also let it be known that they had made a mistake in the first attacks. They now intended to wear red arm bands and to distribute red arm bands to all civilians to increase confusion and civilian casualties. Civilians took this threat seriously, a development analysts also noted. Even though reports of an attack during the night of 10 February turned out to be false, analysts informed units to prepare for a renewed enemy assault. As a result, allied forces were relatively well prepared to meet the new round of attacks that eventually materialized in Saigon during the night of 17–18 February.[31]

FINAL ISSUES

The failure of intelligence before the Tet offensive ultimately led to a general reassessment of the administration's policies for the prosecution of the war, but officers, officials, and analysts also addressed four more specific issues: problematic divisions in the allied command; shortcomings in the analysis of enemy intentions; the communists' objectives behind Tet and their own assessment of their success; and estimates of enemy strength.

---

[30]Thies, *When Governments Collide*, p. 203.
[31]Item 33 1627 7 February, Item 36 1317, Item 55 1935 10 February, Daily Journal Files, MACV J-2 Command Center; PERINTREP, February 1968, p. 5; Sharp and Westmoreland, *Report*, p. 161; Lung, *General Offensives*, pp. 74–75; Palmer, *Summons*, p. 200; and Stanton, *Rise and Fall*, p. 227.

Many of the weaknesses in the allied war effort highlighted by the communist attacks were corrected, with one notable exception: virtually nothing was done to rectify the problems created by the divisions in the allied command. Following the offensive, U.S. officials recognized that the destruction of ARVN had been given a high priority by the communists. In a memo written to President Johnson on 7 February, for example, Rostow described how ARVN had been singled out for special attention: "One technique was to try to render [ARVN] units leaderless. In several cases, enemy forces were given the specific mission of killing or kidnapping various high-ranking commanders and paralyzing command posts (the Joint General Staff compound itself was one specific object of the attack) in the belief that the units concerned would then defect to the Viet Cong/North Vietnamese Army side."[32] Westmoreland, in messages to Wheeler on 9 and 12 February, also noted that the destruction of the South Vietnamese "political and military control apparatus" was a primary communist objective during the 31 January attacks.[33]

There was also evidence that communication delays were produced by the separate command structure maintained for U.S. advisers assigned to ARVN units. A 6 February entry in the MACV J-2 command log demonstrates that communication delays created by command divisions often led to lost opportunities: "At unk [unknown] time, a sector advisor requested a railway zone advisor to relay the following: 1 VC Co with heavy wpns [weapons] in Ba Dain market area, in the vic [vicinity] XS758982."[34] In this instance, the need to relay messages from one adviser to another produced delays that allowed the VC to escape before they could be engaged.

Even though these kinds of problems were readily apparent after Tet, Westmoreland still rejected McNamara's February 1968 proposal to reduce the divisions within the command by increasing the commander of MACV's authority over allied units. Virtually nothing was done to prevent the communists from again exploiting the differences in allied command arrangements, areas of operation, and missions which left ARVN vulnerable to renewed attempts to single it out for destruction. A more surprising example of the failure to rectify such deficiencies concerns Hurricane Forward, the emergency command center created in Saigon during Tet. Hurricane Forward was kept in operation for only fifteen days. When a new wave of urban attacks, known as mini-Tet, began in May 1968, it was reestablished, again

---

[32]*Westmoreland v. CBS*, exhibit 696, p. 1.
[33]Ibid., exhibit 508, p. 2.
[34]Item 57 2215 6 February, Daily Journal Files, MACV J-2 Command Center.

under emergency conditions. It was not until after mini-Tet that the allies took measures to establish permanent command facilities for the coordination of allied operations in the CMD.[35]

In contrast to the failure to respond to the command problem, there was a dramatic improvement in the performance of U.S. intelligence organizations after Tet. In part, this improvement was brought about by the flood of information produced when the VC exposed themselves during the attacks. For example, a VC intelligence operation consisting of a tunnel complex under an ARVN intelligence center in Kontum province was uncovered during the offensive. New enemy units were identified and thousands of documents and prisoner interrogation reports were received by analysts. More important, the way information was analyzed changed significantly after Tet.[36]

MACV analysts took advantage of communist efforts to correct the problem of premature attacks in the Tet campaign. Communist commanders disseminated the mini-Tet battle plan much earlier than they had issued the Tet attack orders, and thus allied analysts obtained the plan earlier too. The first indications of the coming attacks were, however, from a source the MACV analysts would have ignored before the Tet offensive: VC propaganda. Analysts noted an increase in VC propaganda in rural areas during March 1968 in which the VC told the people that they intended to launch a second attack against cities. In early March 1968, a VC propaganda team that had been ordered to generate support among the population for the next round of attacks was captured in Pleiku. The team did not know the date for the attacks, but it was supposed to complete its mission by May. Analysts also learned that VC propaganda teams in Khanh Hoa province (II CTZ) were to complete their mission by 1 May.[37]

During the first week of April, Col. Tran Van Dac, the deputy political commissar of the MR4 headquarters, defected and told ARVN intelligence about the renewed offensive. According to Dac, the communists intended to renew the offensive on 22 April, but difficulties would probably delay the offensive about two weeks (to about 1 May). Dac stated that Saigon was the primary objective and that the main assault would be against Ton Son Nhut airbase. He also warned of two supporting attacks against the southern and western portions of the capital. On April 26, a notebook taken from a captured VC surgeon revealed that the attacks were to begin at 0210 28 April. In-

[35]*Command History 1968*, 1:219–222.
[36]Item 18 0542 3 February, Daily Journal Files, MACV J-2 Command Center; and *PERINTREP*, February 1968, pp. 8–14.
[37]*Command History 1968*, 1:29; Sharp and Westmoreland, *Report*, pp. 166–167; and *PERINTREP* March 1968, pp. 10, 13.

formation about the impending attacks was dispatched promptly to Washington, so the administration was not surprised by mini-Tet.[38]

In response to this information, commanders took a variety of actions by the beginning of May to blunt the new round of attacks. U.S. and Australian units took up defensive positions around Saigon to disrupt communist preparations. ARVN units operating within the CMD also took up defensive positions and stepped up their efforts to prevent infiltration into Saigon. With these preparations already completed, the allies were able to take advantage of two last-minute warnings. On 3 May, an ARVN intelligence agent who had penetrated the VC infrastructure informed III CTZ headquarters that the communists would attack during the night of 4 May. The next day, a VC sapper captured after a successful car bomb attack in Saigon revealed that news reports of his attack transmitted by government radio stations were intended to serve as the signal for the start of the main attack.[39]

When the attacks began during the night of 4–5 May, the allies engaged many of the communist units while they were still several kilometers outside the capital. VC units that had already infiltrated the capital were destroyed expeditiously. In one incident, the allies even surprised the VC after they had moved into Saigon. ARVN intelligence agents reported that a VC battalion was assembling at the French cemetery near Ton Son Nhut airbase. An ARVN airborne battalion dispatched to the vicinity engaged only a small enemy unit. The ARVN commander decided to set an ambush, and the next day a battalion of the VC 9th Division was decimated by his unit. As it turned out, the VC were delayed in reaching their assembly point because of difficulty in contacting local guides. In this incident, the prompt exploitation of intelligence allowed the allies to beat the VC at their own game; the allies never fully lost the initiative during mini-Tet.[40]

Heavy communist losses during Tet limited the intensity of mini-Tet, but the excellent use of information about enemy intentions eliminated the element of surprise from the renewed attacks. Analysts

---

[38]Memorandum for the Secretary of Defense from Earle Wheeler, 23 April 1968, and Memo from Rostow to President, 27 April 1968, Folder: NSF Aides File Memos to the President, vol. 73, DSDUF Vietnam, Box 3; CIA Intelligence Memorandum, "Indications of Forthcoming Communist Offensive Activity in South Vietnam, 27 April 1968," Folder: NSF Country File, Vietnam 2C(9) Box 71, General Military Activity, DSDUF Vietnam Box 5, LBJ Library; Lung, *General Offensives*, p. 93; and Shaplen, *Time out of Hand*, pp. 417–418.

[39]Lung, *General Offensives*, p. 94; and Stanton, *Rise and Fall*, pp. 273–274.

[40]*Command History 1968*, 1:28, 132; Westmoreland, *Soldier*, p. 360; Sharp and Westmoreland, *Report*, p. 167; and Lung, *General Offensives*, pp. 95, 97.

profitted from their failures during Tet in two ways. For one, they were by now well aware that VC units had both the capability and inclination to launch attacks on southern cities. Because their beliefs about enemy intentions and capabilities changed, they were far more successful in interpreting indications of a renewed urban offensive. Analysts also now seriously considered information obtained from a wider variety of sources. The contents and conduct of VC propaganda was used to uncover enemy intentions. Critical indications of the timing of mini-Tet contained in the orders provided to VC propaganda teams were not ignored this time. In sum, information about renewed urban attacks was extremely salient to analysts following the Tet offensive. This sensitivity formed the basis of the successful allied response to mini-Tet.[41]

Whatever Happened to the General Uprising?

As the initial shock of the Tet attacks began to wear off, Americans addressed two questions: What were the objectives behind the Tet offensive? Did the communists believe that they had been successfully achieved?

Analysts and officers in South Vietnam were most interested in identifying the enemy's Tet objectives in order to predict future communist plans. Westmoreland launched Operation Leapfrog, a comprehensive survey of senior ARVN officers' assessments of the enemy's objectives. The survey team, apparently headed by General Abrams, began its work on 3 February and visited every ARVN division except for the 1st Division, which was heavily engaged at Hue. The consensus of opinion among senior ARVN officers was that the offensive was politically motivated, intended to strengthen the communists' position at future peace talks. A minority held that the VC intended to discredit the allies by demonstrating their inability to protect civilians. ARVN officers agreed that the communists had used all available resources to launch an all-out offensive in every area except III CTZ, where some VC units had been withheld from the 31 January attacks. Since the VC carried only between three and eight days' sup-

---

[41]U.S. Embassy Saigon to Secstate, 20 May 1968, Folder: NSF Country File, Vietnam 2C(10) General Military Activity Box 71, DSDUF Vietnam, Box 5, LBJ Library; Stanton, *Rise and Fall*, p. 275; and testimony of Lt. Gen. Daniel O. Graham, in House Select Committee on Intelligence, *U.S. Intelligence Agencies and Activities*, p. 1684. George Allen has noted that only in comparison to Tet can mini-Tet be considered weak in intensity; see "Monograph by Allen 'Indochina Wars—1950–1975'," *Westmoreland v. CBS*, exhibit 313, p. 331.

plies with them in the attacks, ARVN officers reasoned that they intended to succeed within that time frame.[42]

Senior members of the Johnson administration were most interested in determining whether the communists believed that they achieved their objectives. They apparently believed that recent battlefield events might lead to a softening of the North Vietnamese negotiating position. During the immediate post-Tet period, Rostow kept the president well informed about the developing estimate of the enemy's Tet objectives and potential communist assessments of the attacks. On 6 February, for example, he provided the president with answers to three questions: "1. Did the VC/NVA troops expect the Vietnamese populace to rise up and support them in their attacks? 2. Did the VC/NVA have any known plans for retreat or withdrawal? 3. What is the VC/NVA evaluation as to success or failure of the campaign?"[43] To answer these questions, Rostow turned to information gleaned from POW interrogation reports and captured documents that had accumulated since 31 January. Rostow answered the first question in the affirmative. The enemy had expected a general uprising during Tet, but the revolt never materialized. In support of this conclusion, which he repeated to the president on 7 February, Rostow cited information obtained from three POWs captured in Bien Hoa. The POWs claimed "that they had believed that the population would assist in an uprising against the GVN and U.S. forces and in their opinion the anticipated support from the population had not been forthcoming." In discussing these reports, however, Rostow failed to comment on a point made by most POWs; they did not believe that the local population in *their* area would revolt in support of the attack, but they carried out their orders in the hope that their own assault would help to instigate the general uprising in other areas. These POW statements indicate that, even though local commanders in South Vietnam knew that civilians in their area of operations did not overwhelmingly support their cause, senior communist commanders still launched the Tet offensive in the hope of instigating a general uprising. The communist military leadership apparently ei-

[42]Pearson, *War in the Northern Provinces*, pp. 49, 97; and "Background Press Briefing, Gen. Creighton W. Abrams, USA, Saigon, February 8, 1968," in Braestrup, *Big Story*, 2:123–139.

[43]Quotation from *Westmoreland v. CBS*, exhibit 427, p. 1. See also CIA Directorate of Intelligence, 1 February 1968, Intelligence Memorandum, Spot Report on Situation in Vietnam; Rostow to President, "Copy of Intelligence Report TDCS 314-01890-68 (advance)" 2 February 1968; Memorandum from Rostow to President, 2 February 1968, Folder: National Security File Memos to the President from Walt Rostow, vol. 59, DSDUF Vietnam, Box 2, LBJ Library.

ther ignored or never requested or received the accurate estimates of the likelihood of a general uprising that could have been provided by their field commanders. Rostow replied in the negative to the second question. There was no evidence that the communists provided withdrawal plans to their assault units, which were often told to gain and hold their objectives at all costs. POWs captured on 30 January in the assault on Pleiku, for example, had orders to "take Pleiku city or not return." Rostow also noted that it was still to early to tell whether the communists believed that the Tet attacks had succeeded, but there were strong indications that their offensive did not unfold as anticipated. Although on 6 February it was still too early to tell, by 7 February Rostow informed the president that the offensive was most definitely a failure from the communist perspective. Even though he warned the president on 14 February that the NVA was still preparing a major offensive to capture the two northern provinces of South Vietnam, Rostow concluded that the absence of a general uprising during the Tet attacks must have come as a blow to the communists. On 7 February, he pointed to a variety of indications that the communists expected a general uprising and the disintegration of ARVN during Tet. Captured documents, VC efforts to induce ARVN defections, the establishment of revolutionary organizations to take over government functions, the absence of withdrawal plans, and the tenacity with which the enemy defended captured areas all indicated that the communists had expected a popular revolt in support of the offensive. Morever, by 20 February detailed interrogation reports from high-ranking POWs confirmed not only that the communists were counting on a general uprising at Tet but that they had realized that the Tet attacks had been a failure. Captured enemy postmortems of the Tet failure, reports of motivational meetings held for cadres, and evidence that NVA soldiers were actually moving back up the Ho Chi Minh Trail accumulated in the months after Tet, confirming Rostow's February conclusion that the communists' believed that the offensive was a failure.[44]

[44]See *Westmoreland v. CBS*, exhibits 398; 427, pp. 1–4; 429; 696; Cable from Bunker to President, 15 February 1968, Thirty-ninth Weekly Message, p. 1, Folder: Vietnam 8B(2) [B], National Security File, Country File, Vietnam, Box 104, 105, 106; Memorandum for the President From Rostow, 16 February 1968, Folder, NSF NSC History March 31st Speech, vol 3, tabs. A–Z and AA–QQ, NSF NSC History Box 47; Davidson, Oral History II, pp. 15–19; Graham, Oral History I, p. 15; and CDEC Bulletins 11,279, 12,472, 12,560, Folder: Vietnam, CDEC Bulletins vol 3, 8,733, NSF Country File, Vietnam, Box 154, LBJ Library. A captured notebook, which records an exchange during a VC motivational meeting held toward the end of April 1968, is worth quoting, because it illustrates the fundamental problem the communists faced when they failed to deliver on their promise of victory to the rank and file: "During this political indoctrination, some members

Rostow's conclusion that the communists had failed to achieve their objective of instigating a general uprising was correct. Throughout the entire offensive, only several thousand Montagnards staged a few demonstrations in Pleiku and Darlac provinces. There was apparently only one known incident of treachery within an ARVN unit during the offensive. A regional force position in Hau Nghia province (III CTZ) was overrun with heavy loss of life. A relief unit reported that the firing wires for the unit's claymore mines had been cut, and survivors reported that the soldiers manning the unit's light machine guns did not fire when their position was attacked. In contrast to the few incidents of collaboration, most civilians failed to cooperate with the VC, and within days many ARVN soldiers on Tet leave made their way back to their units.[45]

How Many VC Were There?

The Tet attacks revived the long-simmering dispute between MACV and CIA analysts over the VC/NVA order of battle. In the minds of administration officials and MACV analysts, who were eager to identify the positive elements in a deteriorating situation, the large losses suffered by the enemy raised the possibility that communist units had virtually destroyed themselves during the Tet assault. In a memo to the president dated 11 February, however, Rostow explained why this line of analysis was not valid. In January 1968, MACV analysts had changed the way they calculated total VC strength, dropping estimates of self-defense forces, secret self-defense forces, and political cadres (the types of VC units that Samuel Adams claimed pushed total NVA/VC strength in South Vietnam to 600,000) from their estimate of the enemy's order of battle. These changes, described by Rostow as "bookkeeping [in] character," reduced the MACV estimate of total NVA/VC strength from 286,438 in December 1967 to 235,941 in January 1968. Rostow did not quarrel with the January 1968 MACV estimate, but he did state that the enemy's Tet losses could not be subtracted from the January estimate. The January order of battle did not include the NVA soldiers (approximately 27,000) op-

---

of the unit expressed their confusion in the VC terminology for general counterattacks and general uprising. Vinh of Unit 122 believed that this was supposed to be a final operation intended to seize power in a matter of a few days. Other members . . . thought that there should be no phases in the general counterattack and general uprising"; see CDEC Bulletin 12,433, 17 May 1968, Folder: Vietnam Troop Morale, NSF Country File, Vietnam, Box 154, LBJ Library.

[45]Kriegel, "Tet Offensive, Victory or Defeat," p. 27; Item 44 1633 6 February, Daily Journal Files, MACV J-2 Command Center; and "Background Briefing, Gen. Abrams," in Braestrup, Big Story, 2:127.

erating near Khe Sanh or the forces generated by the VC on the eve of Tet: "Because of numerous indications of significant increases in the strength of enemy combat units throughout the country just prior to and since the beginning of the Tet offensive, we believe it would be premature to attempt any recomputation of enemy combat strength on the basis of the casualties reported since 29 January."[46]

CIA analysts also took a dim view of MACV's efforts to recalculate the enemy strength estimates by subtracting the enemy's Tet losses from the January 1968 order of battle.[47] But unlike Rostow, they did not accept the order of battle. In February 1968, they provided their best estimate of enemy strength on the eve of the Tet offensive: "A preliminary review of available evidence suggests that the Communist organized manpower base as of 30 January 1968 probably numbered between 515,000 to 580,000. This base would include estimates for main and local forces, guerrillas, administrative services, self defense militia (secret and overt) and political cadre."[48] In fact, CIA analysts believed that information offered by prisoners captured during the offensive could settle the debate over the existence and strength of the self-defense and secret self-defense forces. In a cable to the CIA station in Saigon dated 18 February, for example, George Carver described the types of enemy units CIA analysts believed were responsible for the attacks: "Recent events indicate that we should reopen the question of excluding from numerical military order of battle holding all communist components other than Main and Local Force, Admin Service and Guerrillas, strictly defined. We strongly suspect that much of recent urban excitement was caused by personnel drawn from Secret Self-defense components, perhaps the Assault Youth, and other elements currently written out of the record by J-2 MACV on the ground that they 'have no military significance'."[49] Carver also suggested that CIA analysts in Saigon place top priority on using information provided by recently captured POWs to determine the kinds of units that participated in the offensive. Carver warned field analysts, however, that "we should let said prisoners tell us how the enemy organizes his force structure and not impose our organization breakdown on this new body of evidence."

[46]"2/11/68 Memo from Rostow to LBJ Re: Infiltration," in *Westmoreland v. CBS*, exhibit 632, pp. 1,2.
[47]"1/19/68 Cable from Saigon Station to Director" and "Cable 2/20/68 from Carver to Saigon," in ibid., exhibits 297A, 463.
[48]"Memo for the Record, 2/27/68, Re: Preliminary Views of the Office of Economic Research on the Communist Organized Manpower base in South Vietnam, 1/30/68," in ibid, exhibit 298, p. 1.
[49]Ibid., exhibit 296A.

The Tet offensive would not, however, produce compelling evidence supporting Adam's claims about the existence of the self-defense and secret self-defense forces or his estimate of 600,000 for total enemy strength in South Vietnam. Most of the evidence contradicted Adams's analysis. Apparently none of the POWs captured during the offensive claimed to be members of the VC self-defense force, secret self-defense force, or assault youth, the units (the "insurgency base") Adams claimed MACV failed to count in their estimates. In a 22 April cable to Sharp, for example, Westmoreland explained: "we questioned a representative cross section of prisoners we picked up during the Tet offensive. Not one has admitted to being a member of any of the organizations which CIA would quantify as 'the insurgency base'." Westmoreland also made a crucial observation about the failure of the units identified by Adams to materialize during Tet: "If there were these thousands of people armed and in sympathy with the enemy, that is, in the 'insurgent base', then I think that they would have joined the enemy during the recent Tet offensive. On the contrary, the population rejected the VC; they did not flock to their cause."[50] The fact that the VC units identified by Adams failed to help instigate the general uprising, the crucial point in the communist war effort, indicates that they probably existed only on paper.

Estimates of the number of NVA and VC soldiers who participated in the Tet attacks also contradicted Adams's analysis. Estimates varied, but none of them posited that more than 85,000 fought during Tet. An intelligence memorandum produced by the CIA's Directorate of Intelligence on 21 February 1968, for example, stated that the communists committed approximately 58,000 soldiers in attacking urban centers and military installations between 30 January and 13 February. Rostow, Wheeler, the Australian ambassador to South Vietnam, and the MACV command history estimated that the enemy committed about 60,000 soldiers during the offensive. Because the communists mounted a major, if not a "go-for-broke," effort during Tet, they probably committed most of their available manpower. Thus, if Adams was correct, more communist soldiers should have participated in the offensive.[51]

---

[50]Ibid., exhibit 403, p. 2.

[51]"2/68 CIA Memo on Communist Units Participating in Tet Offensive," in ibid., exhibit 713, p. 1; Ranelagh, *The Agency*, p. 470; Rostow Cable to Wheeler and Westmoreland, 23 February 1968, p. 2, doc. 52, and Cable from Australian Ambassador to Saigon, 7 February 1968, p.2, 73A, Folder: NSF Country File Vietnam 2C(7) General Military Activity, DSDUF Vietnam, Box 4; Graham, Oral History I, p. 11; and Davidson, Oral History II, p. 12, in LBJ Library; and *Command History 1968*, 2:906. Renata Adler has already posed the obvious question: "What were the remaining five hundred

Even though Adams's estimate of 600,000 for the total communist strength in South Vietnam was probably double the number of combatants (in the broadest sense of the word) available to the enemy, his error raises an intriguing possibility. Senior communist commanders were misinformed about the sympathies of the southern population; they might also have been unsure about the actual strength of the VC. In one report, dated 16 November 1967, for example, a cadre stated that 22,800 civilians would take part in the political struggle in just one district of Quang Nam province, and that 4,950 of these individuals could be considered hard-core supporters. In contrast, Colonel Dac, a NVA defector, stated after Tet that the North Vietnamese did not know much more about the strength of VC irregulars than did the allies; the irregular units he was supposed to lead in battle were nowhere to be found. Senior communist commanders might have relied on the same documents (VC reports of recruiting efforts and unit strength) that Adams used in his analysis when they decided to instigate the general uprising. If Adams had used a different analytical "hook" in his estimate of enemy strength (that it was an accurate reflection of an erroneous enemy estimate of their order of battle), it might have lent credibility to reports of communist intentions to attack urban areas and create a general uprising. MACV analysts, who argued that Adams had been taken in by communist propaganda, might have been persuaded that the communist leadership actually believed the numerical estimates of VC strength contained in the documents that Adams used in his analysis. In an atmosphere charged with bureaucratic animosity, however, this type of intellectual give and take was impossible. Without the aid of hindsight, it would have been extraordinary.[52]

Even though a few last-minute warnings helped some units resist the communist assault, the allies failed to anticipate the onslaught against southern cities. The fact that the communists enjoyed their greatest, albeit temporary, success in Saigon and Hue demonstrates the intelligence failure to recognize the true nature of the offensive.

---

and fifteen thousand [communist troops] doing during Tet?" *Reckless Disregard*, p.202. Wheeler stated that 67,000 soldiers and 17,000 impressed civilians participated in Tet; see Cabinet Meeting of February 28, 1968, p. 2, Folder: Cabinet Meeting 2/28/68, Cabinet Papers Box 12, LBJ Library.

[52]CDEC Bulletin 8613, 24 December 1967, Folder: Vietnam CDEC Bulletins, vol. 2, NSF Country File Vietnam, Box 153; Davidson, Oral History II, p. 11; Graham, Oral History II, p. 17, LBJ Library; and T. L. Cubbage II, "Westmoreland vs. CBS: Was Intelligence Corrupted by Policy Demands?" (Paper presented at the Intelligence and Military Operations Conference, U.S. Army War College, May 1987, n. 96).

U.S. analysts and officers had signals that accurately reflected what was about to unfold, but they did not anticipate fully the targets, intensity, coordination, and timing of the Tet attacks.

The Tet offensive was an unprecedented form of military activity during the U.S. involvement in the ground war, but it failed to discredit the beliefs embraced by many officers and administration officials about communist intentions and capabilities. After Tet, predictions of further enemy behavior continued to reflect ideas that should have been discredited by the offensive. Many officers and officials, for example, still believed that the major engagement of the offensive would take place at Khe Sanh. They failed to realize that the threat to Khe Sanh was primarily a diversion for the urban attacks. Without a general uprising, a concerted assault on Khe Sanh no longer constituted the straw that would break the back of the allies. Given the failure of the urban attacks, the communists apparently decided that seizing Khe Sanh was either no longer necessary or impossible.

In contrast, analysts at MACV attempted to rectify the weaknesses in their estimates. Fully alerted to the obvious enemy interest in urban areas, they became sensitive to indications of a renewal of the offensive against southern cities. Sources and information that would have been dismissed as inconsequential prior to the offensive were scrutinized after the attacks for indications of communist intentions. High false alarm rates were tolerated in an ultimately successful effort to predict when and where the communists would next attack.

Finally, the absence of the general uprising and information about the number of soldiers and types of units participating in the Tet attacks undermined the CIA estimates of the VC/NVA order of battle. Even though MACV analysts may have underestimated total enemy strength in South Vietnam by as much as 20 percent, they were closer to the mark than CIA analysts. VC/NVA strength in South Vietnam was probably slightly less than 300,000 at the time of the Tet offensive, about half the number of combatants the CIA claimed were fighting in the south.

Conclusion: Explaining
the Failure of Intelligence

Although evaluations of the Tet attacks have changed repeatedly over the past twenty years, the passage of time has also served to illuminate the problems faced by the allies on the eve of the 1967 winter-spring offensive. Hindsight does little to diminish the complexity of the communist plan for the offensive, replete with its accurate reading of allied weaknesses, multiple threats, deceptive measures, and miscalculation. Even though it took years for the communists to respond to intervention by U.S. combat units in the war, they attempted to integrate all instruments at their disposal in a well-planned and concerted effort to inflict a defeat of strategic proportions on the allies. The offensive failed to achieve its primary objective, the quick termination of the war on the communists' terms; yet, in a manner unanticipated by the communists, it initiated a chain of events that led to the demise of the Saigon regime and the failure of U.S. policies in South Vietnam.

History has also demonstrated that U.S. intelligence organizations failed to develop an accurate and timely estimate of enemy intentions and capabilities before the offensive. The North Vietnamese diverted U.S. attention from the impending urban offensive by launching attacks along the DMZ, especially against Khe Sanh. The U.S. command incorrectly predicted that the main communist blow would land at Khe Sanh, with diversionary attacks against southern cities. These predictions reversed the importance the enemy placed on the two offensives, thereby facilitating the communist effort to surprise the allies. Ultimately, an explanation for the failure of intelligence suffered by the allies can be tied to the beliefs embraced by many Americans concerning the status of the allied and communist war efforts. The threat of a major offensive against U.S. positions along the DMZ coincided far better with these beliefs than did the possibility of significant attacks against urban areas, so enemy activity along the DMZ was viewed as more threatening than indications of impending attacks on southern cities.

DECEPTION AND MISCALCULATION IN THE COMMUNISTS' PLANS FOR TET

An evaluation of communist plans must begin with two observations. First, the offensive was an all-out affair that used every asset possessed by the communists and even some that literally existed only in the minds of senior officials. Second, the enemy relied heavily on the element of surprise in their attack. Deception loomed large in communist plans for the offensive.

In their preparations for the offensive, the communists demonstrated a familiarity with the factors that make up successful deceptive strategies. Before September 1967, they apparently relied on secrecy to hide their preparations. The decisions made during the July 1967 strategy session were not disseminated immediately to low-level cadres and officers. At this stage, many individuals involved in rudimentary preparations did not need to know the ultimate purpose of their activities. Secrecy was all that was required to hide these relatively normal activities from the sophisticated collection capabilities of the allies. Even in hindsight, only a few signals available to allied analysts before September 1967 can be linked to the Tet offensive, and even these do not reflect a significant change in communist activity. Secrecy, in conjunction with other deceptive tactics, was applied right until the outbreak of the Tet attacks. This emphasis on secrecy, however, ultimately conflicted with the coordination of dozens of urban attacks. Restrictions on information within the communist hierarchy, combined with the need to transmit rapidly attack orders once they were released for dissemination, apparently overwhelmed enemy communications, thereby contributing to premature attacks in I and II CTZ.

The communists seemed to realize that, given the offensive's scope, secrecy alone could not hide preparations from allied intelligence. A concerted effort was undertaken in September 1967 to divert attention away from the impending urban threat. Border battles, which constituted the primary element of this deceptive strategy, shifted both U.S. attention and combat capability away from the cities. It is probably no coincidence that the border battles erupted at about the same time that U.S. analysts began to sense a shift in communist strategy.

[253]

New or unusual developments such as the publication of Gen. Giap's "The Big Victory, the Great Task" were linked by analysts and commanders to increasing communist activity along the borders.

As the Tet offensive approached, communist diversionary attacks along the borders of South Vietnam, especially on the U.S. firebase at Khe Sanh, increased in intensity. While high-quality indications of an imminent attack on southern cities became apparent, so did increasing noise generated by the diversionary attacks. Because this deception took the form of actual combat, the noise it generated made the signals about impending urban attacks appear pale in comparison. The difference between the intensity of the noise generated by the ongoing diversion and the signals created by preparations for urban attacks produced a dilemma that contributed to the surprise suffered by the allies. Most U.S. commanders considered the attack on southern cities a diversion and expected the primary blow to fall along the DMZ, probably at Khe Sanh.

The communists paid a price for this successful diversion. To be convincing, the diversion along the DMZ and border areas had to be intense. The effort to stage major attacks throughout South Vietnam, however, ultimately strained communist capabilities beyond their limit. Because of a remarkable communist miscalculation, the offensive violated the principle of concentration of forces. By simultaneously attacking everywhere, the NVA and VC lacked the numerical superiority they needed to succeed; as a result, they were defeated piecemeal. If the offensive had unfolded as planned, the principle of concentration of forces would not have been violated. But as the attacks developed, a large portion of the force the communists included in their plans failed to materialize on the battlefield; South Vietnamese civilians did not stage a general uprising in support of the offensive. A general uprising might have allowed the communists to secure their primary objective, a quick and successful conclusion of the war. Faced with the disintegration of ARVN and isolated by a hostile and partially armed population, the United States might have been left with no alternative but to abandon South Vietnam. In such a situation, NVA commanders might have attempted to hasten U.S. forces on their way by accepting the tremendous costs of storming Khe Sanh. But without the added strain on allied resources created by a general uprising, such an NVA effort would have been suicidal.

Communist miscalulation about the likelihood of a general uprising added an extremely difficult element to the problem faced by U.S. intelligence analysts. Because they possessed superior information about the sympathies of the southern population, they interpreted communist calls for a general uprising as incredible. In fact, analysts and officers even claimed that propaganda calling for a general uprising was an encouraging development, since the communists would be discredited when the revolt failed to materialize. U.S. analysts accurately estimated that, without the manpower provided by a general uprising, the communists would lack the resources needed to pose overwhelming multiple threats throughout the country. The communist plan made no sense from the allied perspective; it violated the principle of concentration of forces. Communist miscalculation about the likelihood of a general uprising thus created an interesting irony. On the one hand, it greatly contributed to the successful diversion of U.S. forces toward the border and maximized the element of surprise in the attacks against urban areas. On the other hand, it ultimately doomed these urban attacks to failure.

The communists also used cover operations in the strategy of deception, especially as preparations reached an advanced stage. Perhaps they recognized that secrecy and diversionary attacks could not prevent the allies from detecting the burst of signals generated by the final preparations for the offensive. They apparently realized that cover operations were needed to create confusion and hesitancy among the allies as they attempted to respond to indications of impending attack. The Tet holiday itself constituted the primary cover. The possibility exists that the North Vietnamese realized that they had established a pattern of activity during previous truce periods, leading to a sense of security among the allies about the likelihood of a major attack during the Tet truce. It was no coincidence that the communists, not the allies, proposed an extended truce for the 1968 Tet holidays. Even though attacking during a truce constitutes a classic cover operation, the communists also may have anticipated that the allies would expect them to conduct final preparations for the offensive during the truce. The communists probably expected to catch the allies off guard by attacking during the truce, abandoning their standard practice of using truces to resupply. The Trinh initiative was also a successful cover operation, even though its basic purpose was to lay the groundwork for a negotiated end to the war following a successful offensive. Because the offensive failed to destroy ARVN or spark a general uprising, the Trinh initiative also failed in its main objective. But it still achieved its secondary objective, by provoking a highly cooperative, albeit unanticipated, allied response. In reaction to the initiative, the United States restricted its bombing of North Vietnam. The Trinh initiative can also be linked to the 50 percent reduction in ARVN strength during the Tet truce. In comparison to other allied acts of omission or commission, the absence of these ARVN forces contributed most to the military setbacks suffered by the allies during Tet.

In sum, the communist plans for the Tet offensive constituted a military tour de force in identifying and exploiting allied weaknesses. They exploited divisions in the allied command structure, differences in the missions of various allied forces, and the distance that usually separated U.S. units from their ARVN counterparts. Thus, the communists responded to U.S. intervention in the ground war by tying down and isolating powerful U.S. units in order to attack directly the government infrastructure and relatively weak ARVN units. The communists succeeded in circumventing the shield provided by U.S. units, leaving them to play a peripheral role during the Tet offensive. Communist miscalculation about civilian sympathies helped to gain the element of surprise during Tet, but it also doomed the offensive to failure. Ironically, the communists, like the Americans, were far better at identifying the vulnerabilities of their enemy than the weaknesses in their own alliance.

THE LOCATION OF THE FAILURE OF U.S. INTELLIGENCE

Because the effort to anticipate and respond to information about an impending attack is a multifaceted enterprise, identifying the exact location of the failure of U.S. intelligence is the first step in explaining why the communists surprised Americans during the Tet offensive. A number of possible explanations for the failure of intelligence can be dismissed by identifying the tasks that were adequately fulfilled prior to the offensive. The explanation of the failure of U.S. intelligence must begin with an anaysis of four factors: (1) the collection of information, (2) the analysis of signals, (3) the response to warnings, and (4) the dissemination of warning of impending attack.

Collection of Information

The failure of U.S. intelligence was not caused by shortcomings in the collection of information about enemy intentions and capabilities. The intelligence organizations responsible for this task obviously missed some information they might have collected, but their performance exceeded realistic expectations. With the aid of hindsight, dozens of pieces of information collected by allied intelligence organizations provide a concise description of communist motivations and objectives behind the offensive, as well as when, where, and how the attacks would materialize. Even without hindsight, however, four pieces of information collected by the allies provided accurate warning of how, where, and when the offensive would unfold.

First, U.S. intelligence organizations within South Vietnam obtained a document during November 1967 that not only indicated that a major offensive was imminent but also stated how and where the attacks would take place. The key passage of the document, which was even released to the press on 5 January 1968, is worth repeating because of its accurate description of the nature and general location of the impending attacks: "The central headquarters has ordered the entire army and people of South Vietnam to implement general offensive and general uprising in order to achieve a decisive victory. . . . Use very strong military attacks in coordination with uprisings of the local population to take over towns and cities. Troops should flood the lowlands. They should move toward liberating the capital city, Saigon, take power and try to rally enemy brigades . . . to our side."[1] The document provided little indication of when the general offensive–general uprising would take place, but it does demonstrate that U.S. intelligence organizations had hard evidence of where and how the impending offensive would unfold about two months before Tet.

Second, information about where and when the offensive would erupt was provided by the NSA in a series of reports issued to MACV between 17 and 25 January 1968. The NSA's sophisticated SIGINT collection facilities detected an almost unprecedented volume of urgent messages passing among major communist commands before the offensive. The finished intelligence reports that resulted from this collection, admittedly a form of analysis from the NSA's perspective, confronted MACV analysts and officers with indications that attacks throughout South Vietnam were imminent. At least six days before the offensive, the NSA provided a specific and accurate warning of when the offensive would materialize and an accurate prediction about the location of the attacks.

The "Qui Nhon" tapes, combined with the information obtained from the individuals who were caught with them in their possession, also support the conclusion that shortcomings in the collection of information did not cause the failure of intelligence. The tapes and interrogation reports, which were obtained by ARVN officers and intelligence analysts on 28 January, provided compelling evidence that the enemy intended at a minimum to attack and occupy the cities of Saigon, Hue, and Da Nang and hoped that civilians would support the offensive by launching a general uprising. Furthermore, the information obtained at Qui Nhon specified that the attacks would materialize during the Tet holidays. It is doubtful that the information obtained at Qui Nhon was disseminated throughout the allied command before the offensive, but the existence of the tapes and in-

---

[1]Passage from a soldier's notebook cited in Braestrup, *Big Story*, 1:71.

terrogation reports shows that the allies possessed information about the location and timing of the offensive three days before the attacks erupted.

Finally, the premature attacks that occurred throughout I and II CTZ during the early morning of 30 January provided the allies with a preview of the offensive that would take place throughout the remaining portions of South Vietnam the following morning. Information about these attacks, collected by allied combat units engaged with the enemy, provided a compelling indication of future enemy behavior. Premature attacks constitute one of the clearest signals that can be collected by intelligence organizations before a major attack. Because of a major breakdown in the communist command structure, the allies possessed virtually unambiguous indications of where, when, and how the communists would attack 24 hours before the main blow of the Tet offensive materialized.

In sum, the captured Tet attack order, NSA intercepts, Qui Nhon tapes and prisoner interrogation reports, and premature attacks all independently provided accurate and specific information concerning how, where, and when the Tet attacks would develop. Information from these sources required little analysis; the signals that each provided could stand alone and still offer accurate insights into the coming offensive. The premature attacks provided an extremely unambiguous signal of communist intentions. Intelligence organizations did not, then, fail to collect accurate information about where, when, and how the communists would attack. The source of the failure of intelligence suffered by the allies lies outside the realm of intelligence collection.

Analysis

In contrast to the successful collection effort, the U.S. analysis of information was far more problematic. In the strictest sense, the allies did not suffer a complete failure of intelligence analysis before Tet. Senior officers ultimately accepted analyses that identified the general parameters of the Tet attacks before they materialized, but they did so too late to reduce the military and psychological impact of the attacks.

The existence of four highly accurate analyses of enemy intentions supports the conclusion that the allies did not suffer a failure of analysis. The first of these finished intelligence reports, produced by CIA analyst Joseph Hovey, accurately described the offensive nearly two months before Tet. Moreover, Hovey's analysis was circulated widely. The memorandum was provided to intelligence analysts at MACV headquarters, CIA analysts in Washington, D.C., senior U.S.

officers in South Vietnam, including General Westmoreland, and senior administration officials, including Walt Rostow and President
Johnson. But Hovey's analysis contradicted the prevailing analytical
consensus of the time and was not accepted as a realistic estimate of
future enemy behavior by either the intelligence community or senior
officers and officials. Nevertheless, the Hovey memorandum demonstrates that someone in the U.S. command provided an accurate estimate of enemy behavior well in advance of the offensive.

The briefings delivered to Westmoreland by General Weyand on 10
January and by General Davidson on 13 January also provided accurate and timely predictions of specific communist attacks. Weyand's
analysis, which was subsequently supported by Davidson's estimate,
warned that communist forces were moving toward Saigon and that
urban attacks in III CTZ were imminent. In response to these warnings, Westmoreland canceled several offensive operations and ordered U.S. units to move into position to defend Saigon. The threat
against the cities of III CTZ, however, was soon overshadowed by the
eruption of major fighting at Khe Sanh, the main communist effort to
divert allied attention from the impending attacks against urban
areas. Westmoreland's decision to strengthen the defenses of Saigon
ultimately prevented the communists from occupying the city, but
preparations to strengthen the city lost momentum as the NVA threat
against Khe Sanh increased.

The final accurate, if not timely, analysis supplied to senior U.S.
commanders was the briefing delivered by General Davidson on the
morning of 30 January. Davidson told Westmoreland that the attacks
against urban areas in I and II CTZ which had occurred earlier that
morning would be replicated throughout the rest of South Vietnam
within 24 hours. Even though this assessment was accepted fully by
Westmoreland and disseminated to senior U.S. commanders throughout South Vietnam, not enough time remained to put it to good use.
Senior commanders and a few MACV analysts received and, more
important, accepted a relatively specific and accurate description of
the Tet attacks hours before they materialized, but this acceptance
came too late to reduce significantly the impact of the offensive.

In one sense, therefore, senior officers at MACV headquarters were
not surprised by the 1967 winter-spring offensive; they knew about it
before it happened. In another sense, however, a failure of intelligence analysis did take place. The acceptance of accurate estimates
of the outlines of the offensive just hours before the attacks did little
to improve the allies' ability to meet the coming onslaught. U.S. intelligence agencies ultimately failed to overcome the disadvantage inherent in the process of producing and responding to intelligence.

[259]

Forced to play "catch up" in their race to anticipate communist plans from relatively old information, they succeeded in anticipating the Tet offensive before it materialized, but not by a margin wide enough to allow this information to be used successfully. The communists had gained the advantage of surprise.

The critical moment when this inherent disadvantage determines whether efforts to anticipate an impending attack will be successful varies from situation to situation. For the allies, this "point of no return" was passed at 1800 29 January, when ARVN strength was reduced 50 percent for holiday leaves. The joint U.S.–South Vietnamese decision to allow ARVN soldiers to depart on Tet leave marks the allies' last opportunity to avoid reducing their ability to respond to the impending attacks. Even though U.S. units had excellent mobility, it was virtually impossible in the time remaining to move U.S. forces deployed to counter the diversionary attacks along the borders into positions from which they could interfere significantly with the coming urban offensive. U.S. analysts almost overcame the disadvantage inherent in intelligence production: only about 12 hours elapsed between the commencement of ARVN holiday leaves and Davidson's 30 January briefing. After 1800 29 January, however, the benefits provided by accurate estimates of enemy intentions rapidly diminished. If the time lag between discovery and action is taken into account, then there was a failure of intelligence analysis before Tet.

Response

Senior U.S. commanders' responses to the warnings they received raise several questions. After all, even the best informed of them—generals Westmoreland and Davidson—returned to their quarters during the night of 30–31 January, a sign that they still underestimated the gravity of the urban attacks. Indeed, both men must have regretted this decision the next morning when they were delayed in returning to their posts by street fighting in Saigon. Kerwin's 1125 30 January alert to U.S. units failed to mention the size of the impending urban attacks, leaving it up to local commanders to determine the magnitude of the threat posed against areas under their jurisdiction. The way Westmoreland informed his immediate subordinates about the impending attacks was not unique and would not have been interpreted as particularly alarming by senior commanders. Westmoreland was in the habit of telephoning all senior commanders over relatively mundane matters, such as receiving updates on developments after returning from his trips outside South Vietnam. Given the fact that U.S. units were on alert nearly 50 percent of the time, officers at

[260]

MACV would have had to develop some type of extraordinary response to communicate the gravity of the situation to their subordinates. Even though senior officers at MACV accepted indications of impending attack on the eve of the offensive, their response to this information, in the form of the warning they issued, was ineffective.

Outside the small circle of senior officers and analysts at MACV headquarters, who benefited from the latest finished intelligence reports, a pronounced awareness of the impending offensive did not exist. The method chosen by senior officers to respond to the impending attack failed to communicate the gravity of the situation; the alerts issued by MACV headquarters on the morning of 30 January could have easily been interpreted as a confirmation of the recently rejected estimate of enemy intentions: that the communists were about to launch relatively minor diversionary attacks to support their assault on Khe Sanh. In effect, the response selected by senior officers to the impending offensive contributed to the communist success. The various alert messages were not particularly alarming. Moreover, because analysts failed to overcome the disadvantage inherent in intelligence production, there was no longer enough time to communicate even this minimal warning to most small-unit commanders. Shortcomings in the analysis of information were responsible for overtaxing the command structure. Senior officers selected a mundane response to predictions of impending attack, but the failure of intelligence—the failure to overcome the disadvantage inherent in intelligence production—had already been produced by shortcomings in the analysis of information.

Dissemination of Warning

Shortcomings in the dissemination of information directly contributed to the failure of intelligence suffered by the allies during Tet. The stage was set for such failure by senior commanders' tardy acceptance of accurate estimates of enemy behavior. For example, the attempt at 0945 30 January to recall the ARVN soldiers who had already left on leave was hopeless. By the time Maj. Gen. Kerwin sent his "flash priority message" at 1125 30 January, senior U.S. commanders had already begun to lose control. They would not begin regaining the initiative and asserting a degree of central control over the U.S. response to the battle for two days.

Marginal improvements in the ability of U.S. units to meet the coming attacks might have been achieved, but the small-unit commanders who could have profited from warning were not adequately informed about the coming attacks. Even though the advanced communication

[261]

network could transmit Kerwin's message to senior officers in the time remaining before the offensive unfolded, it was unable to provide the thousands of specific messages to individual officers needed to create credible warning. A generic warning of impending attack made little sense in a local context in which troops and officers were expecting the respite brought by the Tet holidays.

Further evidence that a failure to disseminate warning occurred within the command is provided by the fact that some allied commanders prepared their units to meet the attacks whereas others only became aware of the attacks as their positions were being overrun. Differences in unit readiness were apparently largely determined by the collection and analysis of information by local commanders. Lt. Col. Pham Minh Tho, whose forces obtained the Qui Nhon tapes and related prisoner interrogation reports, for example, placed his units on alert on 29 January. Even without the benefit of Kerwin's 30 January warning, Major General Stone, the commander of the 4th Infantry Division, responded to information collected by members of his command and blunted the premature attacks against Pleiku. In contrast, commanders in Hue, who lacked first-hand information, were never warned of an impending attack. They learned of the attack only after the NVA had surrounded their command post. The unevenness of the response turned in by small-unit commanders indicates that they failed to receive a precise or convincing warning about the coming attacks from senior U.S. commanders.

EXPLAINING THE FAILURE OF ANALYSIS

A failure of analysis was responsible for the surprise suffered by the United States during the Tet offensive. To explain this failure, it is necessary to identify how Americans responded to the six empirical issues involved in intelligence analysis. In other words, were the Americans surprised because they failed to: (1) identify the adversary; (2) estimate the probability of attack; (3) determine the type of action involved; (4) identify the location of the attack; (5) predict the timing of the attack; and (6) determine the motivation behind the initiative?

The Opponent

Logic and common wisdom both dictate that the enemy should become readily apparent during war. Combat itself produces an intimate awareness of the opponent or coalition of opponents faced on the battlefield. One of the ways failure of analysis can occur, then, should be insignificant. The need to identify the opponent should not constitute a serious challenge during a war.

Before Tet, Americans tended to follow this common wisdom. It was assumed that the coalition of NVA and VC, which had been fighting the allies for years, was the adversary. But the Tet offensive became an exception to the common wisdom. The communists tried to add new elements to their coalition by enlisting civilians and ARVN defectors. They not only hoped to use the widespread turmoil produced by a general uprising as a force multiplier but also intended to introduce a new type of combatant, an urban guerrilla, during the offensive. Furthermore, they believed that ARVN units might actually join the general uprising, turning their weapons on U.S. units or moving against South Vietnamese forces loyal to the government.

As the offensive actually unfolded, the U.S. intelligence identification of the opponent proved to be correct. The general offensive failed to materialize, and civilians and ARVN did not join the coalition facing the allies. But this accurate, timely identification of the opponent actually impeded estimates of when, where, and how the communists would attack. In an example of the highly complicated nature of intelligence production, an accurate estimate in one dimension of intelligence analysis undermined the overall estimate of future communist behavior.

U.S. analysts and officers possessed indications that the communists intended to launch a general uprising during the Tet holidays, and that another nation (North Korea) might support the impending attack with its own military operations. They were also aware that the introduction of new forces onto the battlefield was one component of the general uprising called for by the communists. But the allies had better information about civilian and ARVN sympathies than their opponents, and consequently they tended to interpret the call for a general uprising as mere propaganda that would rebound to the communists' detriment when the revolt failed to materialize. The extreme divergence between communist expectations and the reality of the situation, reflected by the information possessed by the allies, should have raised suspicions about the possibility of communist miscalculation. Intelligence agencies were puzzled by the call to stage a general uprising, but their interest in the subject waned after they determined that it was unlikely that the revolt would materialize.

The allies even possessed indications of the sources of the communist mistake behind the call for a general uprising. Samuel Adams's estimates, based on captured documents, of the type and size of enemy forces supported the notion that the communists had the resources to launch a general uprising. Adams estimated that there were about 600,000 combatants available to the communists, slightly more than twice the number that MACV analysts claimed were present on the southern battlefields. Even though Adams's analysis ultimately proved to be incorrect, it is possible that Adams and senior communist commanders relied on the same kinds of information to develop their troop counts. MACV never entertained the possibility that Adams's analysis offered insights into the enemy's estimate of their situation, and Adams was accused of falling victim to communist propaganda. MACV analysts and officers reacted harshly to Adams's analysis because it contradicted their beliefs about the achievement of the U.S. shield and attrition objectives as well as widely shared assumptions about who should be called a "combatant." Because these beliefs led to the dismissal of Adams's analysis in its entirety, a possible explanation for the apparently irrational call for a general uprising was overlooked. MACV analysts lost sight of the fact that leaders are not all disingenuous cynics and that they sometimes believe their own propaganda.

Americans were more receptive to indications that the North Koreans were preparing some sort of military or political initiative to support the liberation of South Vietnam. Even though this sensitivity was most pronounced among senior administration officials, U.S. officers were also alert to a North Korean exploitation of a communist offensive in South Vietnam for their own purposes. They were cognizant of abnormal North Korean activity because the memory of Chinese intervention in the Korean War made them sensitive to developments indicating that other communist nations might aid the North Vietnamese. Thus, following the seizure of the USS *Pueblo*, they reopened the problem of identifying likely adversaries—but they still ignored the possibility that new opponents might emerge directly on the southern battlefield. The Korean analogy helped to channel attention away from some of the implications of the communist call for a general uprising by increasing preoccupation with events off the Korean coast.

Although they correctly identified the coalition they would face during Tet, the willingness of U.S. intelligence analysts to entertain the possibility that new opponents might emerge on the battlefield illustrates the impact of beliefs on even the relatively simple task of identifying the adversary. They knew that new opponents might enter the battle either through a general uprising or as the result of a North Korean initiative. Because the Korean analogy influenced their interpretation of North Korean activity, many worried about the possibility of North Korean intervention in the war. In contrast, because of their superior understanding of South Vietnamese sympathies and their beliefs about the success of U.S. strategy, MACV analysts and officers rejected Adams's analysis and dismissed calls for a general uprising as propaganda. If their beliefs had been different, or their information about South Vietnamese sympathies had been less persuasive, they might have closely scrutinized signs that the communists intended to use a general uprising to strengthen their coalition, thereby forcing officers to take the possibility of a country-wide offensive more seriously.

Ironically, the accurate identification of the opponent had a detrimental impact on the overall effort to anticipate the offensive. Since analysts and officers determined that it was unlikely that the general uprising would materialize, they calculated that the communists lacked the manpower to pose significant threats throughout South Vietnam. Without the additional forces supplied by the general uprising, it made no military sense for the communists to attack southern cities. Thus the accurate identification of the membership of the opposing coalition influenced U.S. estimates of when, where, and how the communists would attack.

Probability of Attack

During war, analysts can safely assume that the enemy will attack. U.S. analysts and officers put this rule of thumb to good use; they quickly determined that they would face a major offensive. Before the offensive, they remained highly sensitive to signs of impending attack and were quick to label unusual enemy activity as preparations for offensive action. This accurate estimate of communist intentions was not, however, a foregone conclusion. Americans had to overcome a strong tendency to treat their opponent as a nearly defeated adversary. For one thing, beliefs about the attainment of the shield and attrition objectives in U.S. strategy influenced assessments of the ability of the communists to launch a major offensive. During the fall of 1967, for example, the allies often claimed that a military victory was beyond the grasp of the communists. Instead, the communists could now only pursue propaganda, political, or psychological victories. For another, senior officers and officials had begun to state repeatedly during the fall of 1967 that years of effort were finally paying dividends. There was light at the end of the tunnel. They were hopeful that their policies would soon be successful, that the loss of human life, especially American life, would soon come to an end. This perspective, which can be summarized by the phrase "the boys will be home by Christmas," can make it extremely difficult for those who hold it to recognize information about impending attack.

[265]

Unlike other commanders in similar situations, U.S. officers were aware of the pitfalls of treating an unbeaten opponent as a defeated adversary. The Battle of the Bulge loomed large in their minds. It illustrated the dangers of underestimating an apparently defeated enemy and warned that desperation could produce an irrational response from a struggling adversary. By analogy, U.S. officers were able to justify their beliefs about the decline in communist military fortunes with evidence that the enemy was preparing to attack. The analogy dictated that desperate opponents can launch all-out attacks to retrieve a losing situation, but that these attacks marked the beginning of the end for the opponent.

Location of the Attack

U.S. intelligence failed to make an accurate and timely estimate of where the enemy attack would take place. Moreover, unlike the identity of the enemy and the probability of offensive action, this issue is not superficial during wartime. In fact, communist efforts at deception, centered on the conduct of military operations, increased the complexity of determining where the main attack would occur. Analysts were presented with signs that the communists would attack urban areas and other signs that they would attack U.S. units operating near the borders, forcing them to differentiate between competing threats.

Two factors influenced the incorrect determination that the main attack would fall along the northwestern border of the country, especially at Khe Sanh. First, MACV officers and analysts were highly sensitive to battlefield events. This sensitivity aided communist efforts to fix U.S. forces far away from southern cities with diversionary attacks. Officers and analysts interpreted the threat posed by communist units that had already engaged U.S. forces to be far greater than a threat against urban areas that had not yet erupted in actual combat. Moreover, information obtained about impending attacks against cities also tended to be less threatening, in a military sense, than the NVA operations underway along the border. Evidence that the VC planned to move into Saigon to distribute propaganda leaflets, display flags, beat drums, and attack military police installations paled in comparison to the more than 20,000 NVA soldiers that had already laid siege to Khe Sanh.

The Americans failed to pay attention to a key element of deceptive strategies: diversionary attacks tend to succeed when they create the impression that they are of greater scope and intensity than the impending main offensive. Diversionary attacks that come before the main blow are by definition of greater scope and intensity than attacks that have not yet materialized. The U.S. command failed to pay sufficient attention to this truism because they were predisposed to believe that the main enemy blow would fall along the border, especially at Khe Sanh. This predisposition, the second factor influencing predictions of attack location, was the product of several entrenched attitudes. Many believed that the U.S. shield and attrition objectives had been realized, thereby reducing the number of communist combatants behind the American lines. Many failed to realize, thanks to their beliefs about command problems, that ARVN units could be singled out for attack. Because they also believed that U.S. forces posed the greatest threat to the communists, they assumed that U.S. units were the logical target of a major attack. Similarly, U.S. officers were quite sensitive to threats against units under their direct command; in contrast, the protection of South Vietnamese cities was primarily an ARVN responsibility. Because Khe Sanh loomed large in plans to cut the Ho Chi Minh Trail, senior officers interpreted the siege of the firebase as a sensible communist effort to disrupt the planned allied offensive, despite the fact that these offensive plans remained, or at least should have remained, secret. Finally, U.S. officers relied on an analogy with Dien Bien Phu to help identify a communist "win-the-war offensive." The siege of Khe Sanh completely matched expectations based on this analogy. Americans had long expected the enemy to try to replicate its victory over the French garrison, and the similarities between Dien Bien Phu and Khe Sanh appeared overwhelming to officers, analysts, and administration officials.

Communist efforts to fix U.S. forces far from the cities were aided by two of their opponent's predispositions. First, the fact that U.S. units, the most capable allied contingent in the viewpoint of senior commanders, were available to meet an offensive along the DMZ and at Khe Sanh influenced estimates of the location of the coming offensive. Moreover, U.S. units were relatively well prepared to meet an attack along the DMZ because they had already manned defensive positions (the barrier fortifications) and because the relaxed rules of engagement in the area permitted full use of their superior firepower. Estimates of the location of the attacks were thus influenced by a conception of a "preferred enemy strategy." U.S. units, the best available troops, were most prepared to meet an attack along the DMZ. Signs of a major attack against U.S. units along the DMZ were accepted because an offensive in this area posed the least serious threat to the war effort. Second, because U.S. commanders were directly responsible for the safety of U.S. units, they were sensitive to indications that these forces were about to be attacked. They tended to interpret signals of an impending offensive, regardless of their content, as indications of impending attack against high-value targets (U.S. units) in their areas of responsibility.

The explanation of the failure to predict the location of the Tet offensive is straightforward. Because of their predisposition to expect an attack against U.S. units stationed along the borders, most commanders and analysts readily accepted indications that the communists were preparing to launch a major offensive along the DMZ, especially at Khe Sanh. Officers misinterpreted indications of imminent attacks against southern cities as evidence of a communist diversion away from the main offensive along the DMZ; they mistook the main attack for the diversion and the diversion for the main attack.

Timing of the Offensive

U.S. analysts did not determine, until too late, when the offensive would materialize. The explanation for this analytical shortcoming is similar to that for the failure to identify the location of the main attack. The focus on U.S. units can explain the lack of sensitivity to the problem of ARVN vulnerability during the Tet holidays. From the U.S. perspective, an attack during the Tet truce did not place U.S. units at a particular disadvantage; U.S. troops would not celebrate the holiday. Senior officers realized that the communists could attack during truce periods in which U.S. troops did celebrate a holiday, catching them at a disadvantage; Westmoreland was concerned, for example, that an attack would come during the Christmas cease-fire. But it made no sense for the communists to attack U.S. units during Tet, because the celebration did not reduce singificantly the readiness of U.S. ground forces.

U.S. analysts also believed that a violation of the Tet holiday would hurt the communists' cause. The Vietnamese treated Tet as a sacred event and would deeply resent any interference in holiday celebrations. The analysts failed to realize that throughout their history the Vietnamese had violated the sanctity of the holiday to surprise an enemy (the Chinese) who also celebrated Tet. They did not recognize that the North Vietnamese might run the risk inherent in spoiling the Tet celebrations to attack ARVN while it was at a reduced state of readiness. Because they believed that U.S. units were the main target of the impending attacks and that ARVN units were relatively secure behind the U.S. shield, they did not consider that by attacking during Tet the communists could catch ARVN at a disadvantage.

Assumptions about communist activity during truces also contributed to the failure to estimate the timing of the main assault. The enemy always had taken advantage of restrictions, enforced during cease-fires, on the U.S. interdiction campaign by increasing logistical activity. The communists were expected to again use the Tet truce for logistical purposes. It made sense for the enemy to conduct final preparations for a major assault during a reduction in the bombing campaign. The possibility that the communists would recognize and capitalize on their established pattern of truce activity was not considered.

Not only were U.S. commanders wrong in predicting when the attacks would materialize (if not before, then after the Tet cease-fire), they actually eliminated the holiday from consideration. Even without the aid of hindsight, it is remarkable that they could ignore, until it was too late, the vulnerability of ARVN units during the holiday. In the final analysis, only their preoccupation with the status of U.S. units can explain the lack of sensitivity to threats against an important member of the alliance.

Nature of the Attack

Expectations of how the enemy intended to attack were largely determined by conclusions about membership of the enemy coalition and when and where the attack would come. In terms of this dimension of intelligence analysis, U.S. analysts did not face a particularly pressing problem. The communists lacked many of the options available to modern armies. Their offensive would not take the form of an air, naval, amphibious, airborne, or nuclear attack. In all likelihood, it would be an attack by ground forces, the only type of communist unit available in significant numbers. In spite of the evident capacities of their opponent, U.S. analysts turned in a mixed performance in their effort to determine how the communist attack would develop. They produced a remarkably accurate prediction of how the diversionary siege of Khe Sanh would unfold, but it is doubtful that they ever came to any firm conclusions about how the communists would carry out the urban attacks.

For the Khe Sanh attack, the Dien Bien Phu analogy accurately predicted tactical developments. Superficial similarities between communist operations against the French and U.S. outposts aroused suspicions. The fact that General Giap was rumored to be near Khe Sanh and that several of the same units that participated in the siege of Dien Bien Phu were surrounding the marine positions, however, offered little concrete information about how the siege would develop. To their credit, U.S. analysts looked beyond these surface similarities to find similarities of great tactical importance: the NVA use of the same siege techniques as at Dien Bien Phu. Yet, in a strategic sense,

[269]

the prediction of how the siege of the firebase would develop may have damaged the estimate of overall enemy intentions and capabilities; it tended to reinforce analysts and officers in their conviction that the main thrust of the offensive would be directed at the firebase.

The nature of the urban attacks received relatively little attention. In contrast to their emphasis on Operation Niagara I, the intelligence effort for Khe Sanh, analysts barely speculated about the attacks against urban areas. Before the offensive, they seemed to believe that a diversion would materialize in a series of frontal assaults to occupy urban areas. There is little evidence to indicate that analysts realized that the communists also intended to use infiltrators to occupy key positions and stage daring attacks to spark a general uprising; they were surprised by their widespread use. Moreover, the initial confusion produced by the urban attacks certainly did not clarify U.S. estimates. Efforts to determine the objectives the communists hoped to achieve during the offensive (i.e., spark a general uprising), remained a high intelligence priority weeks after the attacks.

Enemy Motivations

The desire to reverse a deteriorating military situation seems to have been the primary communist motivation behind the Tet offensive. By the close of the 1966 winter-spring campaign, both North Vietnamese and VC leaders admitted to themselves that communist units were suffering an erosion of combat capability. Troop morale was on the decline, and the logistics system in the south was being slowly eliminated. If current trends continued, the communists would eventually lack the resources for an offensive large enough to affect the outcome of the war. In a sense, the communists faced a "use it or lose it" situation.

U.S. analysts identified this primary motivation. Influenced by their beliefs about the achievement of the attrition and shield objectives, they were quick to accept evidence that the enemy was in dire straits. By the fall of 1967, many claimed that the communists had lost the military initiative and were encountering increasing difficulties on the battlefield. They tended to invoke the Battle of the Bulge analogy to predict how the communists would react to their deteriorating military situation.

In contrast, analysts and commanders never identified a second factor apparently underlying the decision to launch the offensive. They recognized that U.S. military operations had a severe impact on communist forces, but they failed to realize that by intervening in the conflict they forced the enemy to search for a new way to meet the allied threat. When no strategic innovation materialized immediately after U.S. intervention in the ground war, officers and analysts no longer attempted to anticipate novel communist solutions to the problem posed by U.S. units. Given that they believed U.S. military units to be the best in the world, they should have realized that it would take time for an opponent to develop a response. Instead, they tended to believe that U.S. units could not be neutralized by any strategic innovation. They violated the rule of thumb that dictates that an opponent should never be underestimated in wartime.

A third communist motivation, the desire to exploit divisions within the allied command, was also not anticipated. U.S. commanders believed that shortcomings in the command structure were an internal problem but not an external vulnerability. As a result, they were at a marked disadvantage in seeing this particular motivation behind the Tet offensive; from their perspective, indications were that the communists intended to exploit a nonexistent allied weakness. The Americans, like their opponents, were better at detecting shortcomings in the opposing coalition than in their own alliance.

U.S. analysts recognized the defensive motivations behind the Tet offensive (to reverse a deteriorating military situation), but they failed to identify its offensive motivations (to develop an innovative response to American strengths and to exploit allied weaknesses). If they had realized that the communists were still capable of innovation, they might have been more sensitive to the possibility that a traditional operation, the siege of Khe Sanh, for example, was not the enemy's primary objective but part of a deception. Accurate perceptions of alliance weaknesses might have helped them identify communist innovation and offensive objectives: the isolation and destruction of ARVN units.

THE IMPACT OF SITUATIONAL FACTORS

Although the disadvantage inherent in intelligence production played a major role in the analytical failure experienced by the Americans, additional observations can be made about the effect of this handicap on American estimates. U.S. analysts often failed to realize that information about ongoing communist activity sometimes reflected enemy decisions made months before the activity was detected; they failed to recognize that their current analysis did not reflect the present state of affairs within the communist camp. A good example of this mistake is provided by Westmoreland's interpretation of the publication of General Giap's "The Big Victory, the Great Task" in September 1967. In the months following the publication of the article, Westmoreland claimed that the communists had decided to launch a major offensive in mid-September 1967, when Giap's "unusual" article surfaced. He failed to account for the time lag between the generation and the collection of signals related to changes in the communist war effort. Clearly, weeks, if not months, might have elapsed between an actual communist decision to launch a major offensive and the emergence of a North Vietnamese public statement providing cadres with the outlines of the operation. At a minimum, the production of this article would have been a time-consuming task because of the editorial demands involved: operational details still needed to be withheld from cadres and the enemy. At a maximum, the North Vietnamese could carry out months of preparation following such a decision without informing vast numbers of cadres who lacked a need to know about the policies adopted in Hanoi. Westmoreland's remarkable interpretation of the article reduced the estimate of the amount of time the communists had devoted to preparing their offensive, thereby influencing U.S. assessments of its scope and intensity.

Similarly, a tendency to rely heavily on battlefield developments as indicators of enemy intentions and capabilities tended to exacerbate the disadvantage inherent in intelligence production. More effort was often devoted to explaining why the communists had decided to engage the allies in a particular area than to predicting where they would next attack. "Current" intelligence estimates were often just histories of recent enemy battlefield activity. The "hard" data gleaned from the battlefield proved to be more salient than "soft" data (indications of potential activity) used to predict initiatives. Explanations of what had already happened were thus confused with predictions of future events. By relying on past or ongoing battlefield events as the basis of current intelligence, MACV analysts and officers simply reinforced the inherent disadvantage they faced in predicting enemy behavior.

In a rather strange example of the way beliefs influenced estimates of enemy behavior, officers and analysts often failed to realize that the communists also faced an inherent disadvantage in predicting allied initiatives. Explanations of communist behavior often credited the opponent with an ability to respond immediately, or in an extremely short period, to U.S. initiatives. Attacks against Khe Sanh, for example, were interpreted as an effort to disrupt a U.S. offensive. The offensive, however, barely existed on paper and was not scheduled to take place until the late fall of 1968. Moreover, U.S. officers often interpreted attacks as a response to secret U.S. initiatives. The assault against barrier fortifications in the fall of 1967, for instance, was interpreted as an effort to disrupt the final stages of barrier preparation. But the communists had no way of knowing that barrier construction was moving into its final stages. Information that defined the final phase of barrier construction—specifically, the tests of the air-supported portions of the barrier—was available only to the U.S. command.

This tendency to discount the inherent disadvantage faced by the communists in predicting future allied activity is especially intriguing because it consistently reflected U.S. beliefs about the decline of communist military fortunes. Americans forgot the disadvantage faced by the enemy when they were confronted with evidence of communist offensive activity. Before Tet, they often labeled attacks or preparations for offensive activity as a defensive response to allied initiatives. They did not seem to realize that the communists might not know about allied initiatives that remained in the planning stages, or that the simultaneous occurrence of allied and enemy initiatives was coincidental. By denying the existence of the inherent disadvantage faced by the communists, Americans were able to preserve their belief that the enemy had lost the initiative.

It is difficult to determine the influence of the "intelligence-to-please" syndrome on the development of U.S. intelligence reports. MACV analysts and officers tended to produce estimates that supported existing policy and the preferences of senior administration officials. But officers, MACV analysts, and senior administration officials shared policy preferences and beliefs about progress in the war effort. With the exception of a few CIA activities, distinctions between intelligence analysis and policy formulation had evaporated by the time of the Tet offensive. Because shared beliefs were so pervasive, it is impossible to determine whether MACV analysts and officers produced intelligence to please themselves or senior administration officials. They tended to produce intelligence that confirmed beliefs about the decline of the communist military, thereby pleasing everybody except a few pessimists at the CIA.

On the other hand, there is virtually no evidence that senior administration officials pressured officers and analysts to produce estimates that supported their preferences or existing policy. The only possible exception occurred during Westmoreland's visit to Washington, D.C. in November 1967. For reasons that still remain obscure, Westmoreland, on the spur of the moment, informed the president and the public that the United States could begin to withdraw its forces from South Vietnam in approximately two years. It remains unclear whether the president asked Westmoreland to provide some tangible evidence of progress or Westmoreland sensed that such a statement was needed to counter a decline in public and congressional support for the war effort. In any event, Westmoreland recognized that the announcement would surprise MACV analysts and officers; he quickly sent them a cable explaining his decision to announce publicly that there was "light at the end of the tunnel." In general, then, the breakdown in the division of labor between intelligence analysts and policy makers before Tet may have led to the emergence of the "intelligence-to-please" syndrome prior to the Tet offensive. MACV analysts and officers produced estimates that confirmed their beliefs about the decline in communist military fortunes, thereby supporting the preferences and policies of the Johnson administration. Given this situation, members of the administration did not have to exert overt pressure on analysts and officers to provide estimates supporting existing policies.

It appears, however, that U.S. analysts did fall victim to the "ultra" syndrome, the tendency to rely on sources of information that have a reputation for providing accurate and timely information. In early 1968, SIGINT revealed the movement of NVA units as they massed along the DMZ and the western border of South Vietnam, especially near Khe Sanh. In contrast, the VC units that were surrounding and infiltrating southern cities remained relatively quiet (they did not generate much radio traffic). As U.S. intelligence agencies became increasingly mesmerized by the electronic image generated by the NVA, they tended to downplay captured documents and prisoner interrogation reports that indicated a VC attack against the cities of the south. Lacking SIGINT evidence, they dismissed other information that indicated that the communists intended to attack cities during the Tet holiday.

The "cry-wolf" syndrome also affected the U.S. response to the Tet offensive, but in a somewhat unusual manner. Analysts did not issue and thus policy makers and senior officials did not need to respond to repeated false alarms. Instead, there was a gradual increase in the specificity and gravity of intelligence warnings, culminating in General Davidson's 30 January prediction of the Tet attacks. In a sense, analysts and those responsible for responding to warning solved the dilemma posed by the "cry-wolf" syndrome in an extremely unproductive fashion: they shifted the responsibility for discriminating among warnings to field commanders. In the months preceding Tet, U.S. units were placed on alert nearly 50 percent of the time. This high alert rate reduced field commanders' responsiveness to warning. Even more damaging, senior commanders were apparently unaware that officers in the field might treat accurate warnings as just another false alarm. Field commanders were forced to rely on their own devices: those who collected and analyzed information that indicated a threat against their units responded to the Tet alert; those in an apparently quiet sector dismissed warnings issued by MACV as just another false alarm.

U.S. intelligence analysts and policy makers charged with anticipating and responding to communist initiatives faced a difficult problem on the eve of the Tet offensive. The North Vietnamese and VC had implemented a sophisticated deceptive strategy that included serious multiple threats throughout South Vietnam. Confronted with evidence of increasing enemy activity in the vicinity of urban areas and along the borders of the country, the allies were forced to decide where, when, and how the main blow would fall. They were unsuccessful in this effort.

Although it would be misleading to place the blame on any one event or shortcoming for the disaster experienced by the United States in Vietnam, the Tet offensive does represent a turning point in the war. After Tet, U.S. policy toward Southeast Asia shifted, reducing American involvement in Vietnam. But the offensive was more than just a critical event in the Vietnam War; it also constituted a unusual incident in the history of surprise attack. It was the shock produced by the Tet attacks, not the military consequences of surprise, which led to the reassessment of American policy. When viewed in this way, the Tet offensive represents an extraordinarily successful instance of surprise attack. Surprise itself altered the balance of political will between the combatants.

The story of the intelligence failure also highlights the herculean task faced by officers, analysts, and policy makers as they strove to complete the intelligence cycle. Remarkably, the Americans almost succeeded in anticipating their opponents' moves in time to avoid the military consequences of surprise, despite their underestimation of the weaknesses in their alliance, the resourcefulness of their opponents, and the handicaps they faced in completing the intelligence cycle. But two factors ultimately slowed them in their race to predict the future: the influence of beliefs that could no longer account for events and their inability to anticipate the mistakes made by their opponents. The failure to anticipate an attack in wartime, when Americans could have assumed that their opponents would do everything in their power to hurt the allied war effort, testifies to the difficulty inherent in avoiding failures of intelligence.

Centuries ago, the Chinese philosopher Sun Tzu summarized these conclusions far more succinctly: "Know the enemy and know yourself; in a hundred battles you will never be in peril."[2] The Tet offensive demonstrates how difficult it is to achieve these simple goals.

---

[2]Sun Tzu, *The Art of War*, trans. Samuel B. Griffith (Oxford, 1963), p. 84.

Bibliography

BOOKS

Acheson, Dean. *Present at the Creation*. New York: W. W. Norton, 1969.

Adler, Renata. *Reckless Disregard*. New York: Alfred A. Knopf, 1986.

Allison, Graham T. *Essence of Decision: Explaining the Cuban Missile Crisis*. Boston: Little, Brown, 1971.

Axelrod, Robert. *Structure of Decision: Cognitive Maps of Political Elites*. Princeton: Princeton University Press, 1976.

Baldwin, Hanson. *Battles Lost and Won*. New York: Harper & Row, 1966.

Berman, Larry. *Lyndon Johnson's War: The Road to Stalemate in Vietnam*. New York: W. W. Norton, 1989.

Betts, Richard. *Surprise Attack*. Washington, D.C.: The Brookings Institution, 1982.

Blaufarb, Douglas S. *The Counterinsurgency Era: U.S. Doctrine and Performance*. New York: Free Press, 1977.

Bradley, Omar N. *A Soldier's Story*. New York: Henry Holt, 1951.

Braestrup, Peter. *Big Story*. 2 vols. Boulder, Colo.: Westview Press, 1977.

Braken, Paul. *The Command and Control of Nuclear Forces*. New Haven: Yale University Press, 1983.

Brandon, Henry. *Anatomy of Error*. Boston: Gambit, 1969.

Brewin, Bob, and Sydney Shaw. *Vietnam on Trial: Westmoreland vs. CBS*. New York: Atheneum, 1987.

Brodie, Bernard. *War and Politics*. New York: Macmillan, 1973.

Clodfelter, Mark. *The Limits of Air Power: The American Bombing of North Vietnam*. New York: Free Press, 1989.

Colby, William, *Lost Victory: A Firsthand Account of America's Sixteen-Year Involvement in Vietnam*. Chicago: Contemporary Books, 1989.

Cole, Hugh M. *The Ardennes: Battle of the Bulge*. Washington, D.C.: Office of the Chief of Military History, Department of the Army, 1965.

Coleman, J. D. *Pleiku: The Dawn of Helicopter Warfare in Vietnam*. New York: St. Martin's Press, 1988.

Collins, J. Lawton. *War in Peacetime: The History and Lessons of Korea*. Boston: Houghton Mifflin, 1969.

Cruickshank, Charles. *Deception in World War II*. Oxford: Oxford University Press, 1979.

[277]

Davidson, Phillip B. *Vietnam at War, the History: 1946–1975*. Novato, Calif.: Presidio Press, 1988.

de Silva, Peer. *Sub Rosa*. New York: New York Times Book Co., 1978.

Drew, Dennis M. *Rolling Thunder 1965: Anatomy of a Failure*. Cadre Paper AU-ARI-CP-86-3. Maxwell Air Force Base, Ala.: Air University Press, 1986.

Duiker, William J. *The Communist Road to Power in Vietnam*. Boulder, Colo.: Westview Press, 1981.

——. *Vietnam: Nation in Revolution*. Boulder, Colo.: Westview Press, 1983.

Eckhardt, George S. *Command and Control*. Washington, D.C.: Department of the Army, 1974.

Eisenhower, David. *Eisenhower at War, 1943–1945*. New York: Vintage Books, 1987.

Eisenhower, Dwight D. *Crusade in Europe*. New York: Doubleday, 1948.

Eisenhower, John S. D. *The Bitter Woods*. New York: G. P. Putnam's Sons, 1969.

Enthoven, Alain C., and K. Wayne Smith. *How Much Is Enough?* New York: Harper and Row, 1971.

Ewell, Julian J., and Ira A. Hunt, Jr. *Sharpening the Combat Edge: The Use of Analysis to Reinforce Military Judgment*. Washington, D.C.: Department of the Army, 1974.

Fall, Bernard B. *Hell in a Very Small Place: The Siege of Dien Bien Phu*. New York: Da Capo Press, 1985.

——. *Street without Joy*. New York: Schocken Books, 1972.

FitzGerald, Frances. *Fire in the Lake: The Vietnamese and the Americans in Vietnam*. Boston: Little, Brown, 1972.

Gallucci, Robert L. *Neither Peace nor Honor*. Baltimore: Johns Hopkins University Press, 1975.

Garthoff, Raymond. *Reflections on the Cuban Missile Crisis*. Washington, D.C.: The Brookings Institution, 1989.

Gelb, Leslie, with Richard K. Betts. *The Irony of Vietnam: The System Worked*. Washington, D.C.: The Brookings Institution, 1979.

George, Alexander L. *Presidential Decisionmaking in Foreign Policy: The Effective Use of Information and Advice*. Boulder, Colo.: Westview Press, 1980.

George, Alexander L., and Richard Smoke. *Deterrence in American Foreign Policy: Theory and Practice*. New York: Columbia University Press, 1974.

Giap, Vo Nguyen. *People's War People's Army*. New York: Praeger, 1962.

Halperin, Morton H., with Priscilla Clapp and Arnold Kanter. *Bureaucratic Politics and Foreign Policy*. Washington, D.C.: The Brookings Institution, 1974.

Handbook for Military Support of Pacification. Saigon: MACV, February 1968.

Handel, Michael. *The Diplomacy of Surprise: Hitler, Nixon, Sadat*. Cambridge: Center for International Affairs, Harvard University, 1981.

——. *Military Deception in Peace and War*. Jerusalem Papers of Peace, Problem no. 38. Jerusalem: The Leonard Davis Institute of International Relations, 1985.

——. *Perception, Deception and Surprise: The Case of the Yom Kippur War*. Jerusalem: The Leonard Davis Institute of International Relations, 1976.

Herken, Gregg. *Counsels of War*. New York: Alfred A. Knopf, 1985.

Herring, George, C. *America's Longest War: The United States and Vietnam, 1950–1975*. New York: John Wiley and Sons, 1979.

Hoopes, Townsend. *The Limits of Intervention*. New York: David McKay, 1969.

Hosmer, Stephen T., Konrad Kellen, and Brian M. Jenkins. *The Fall of South Vietnam*. New York: Crane, Russak, 1980.

Janis, Irving L., and Leon Mann. *Decision Making: A Psychological Analysis of Conflict, Choice and Commitment*. New York: Free Press, 1976.

Jervis, Robert. *Perception and Misperception in International Politics*. Princeton: Princeton University Press, 1976.

Jervis, Robert, Richard Ned Lebow, and Janice Gross Stein, eds. *Psychology and Deterrence*. Baltimore: Johns Hopkins University Press, 1985.

Johnson, Lyndon Baines. *The Vantage Point*. New York: Holt, Rinehart and Winston, 1971.

Jones, Bruce E. *War without Windows: A True Account of a Young Army Officer Trapped in an Intelligence Cover-up in Vietnam*. New York: Vanguard Press, 1987.

Kahin, George McT. *Intervention: How America Became Involved in Vietnam*. New York: Alfred A. Knopf, 1986.

Kahn, David. *Hitler's Spies*. New York: Macmillan, 1978.

Kalb, Marvin, and Ellie Abel. *Roots of Involvement: The U.S. in Asia, 1784–1971*. New York: W. W. Norton, 1971.

Kam, Ephraim. *Surprise Attack: The Victim's Perspective*. Cambridge: Harvard University Press, 1988.

Karnow, Stanley. *Vietnam: A History*. New York: Viking Press, 1983.

Kinnard, Douglas. *The War Managers*. Hanover, N.H.: University Press of New England, 1977.

Knorr, Klaus, and Patrick Morgan, eds. *Strategic Military Surprise*. New Brunswick, N.J.: Transaction Books, 1983.

Kolko, Gabriel. *Anatomy of a War: Vietnam, the United States, and the Modern Historical Experience*. New York: Pantheon Books, 1985.

Komer, Robert. W. *Bureaucracy at War*. Boulder, Colo.: Westview Press, 1986.

Krepinevich, Andrew F., Jr. *The Army and Vietnam*. Baltimore: Johns Hopkins University Press, 1986.

Laqueur, Walter. *A World of Secrets*. New York: Basic Books, 1985.

Layton, Edwin T., Roger Pineau, and John Costello. *"And I Was There": Pearl Harbor and Midway—Breaking the Secrets*. New York: William Morrow, 1985.

Lebow, Richard Ned. *Between Peace and War*. Baltimore: Johns Hopkins University Press, 1981.

——. *Nuclear Crisis Management: A Dangerous Illusion*. Ithaca, N.Y.: Cornell University Press, 1987.

Leckie, Robert. *Conflict: The History of the Korean War, 1950–53*. New York: G. P. Putnam's Sons, 1962.

Levite, Ariel. *Intelligence and Strategic Surprises*. New York: Columbia University Press, 1987.

Lewy, Guenter. *America in Vietnam*. New York: Oxford University Press, 1978.

Lomperis, Timothy J. *The War Everyone Lost—and Won*. Baton Rouge: Louisiana State University Press, 1984.

Lung, Hoang Ngoc. *The General Offensives of 1968–69*. Washington, D.C.: U.S. Army Center for Military History, 1981.

——. *Intelligence*. Washington, D.C.: U.S. Army Center for Military History, 1976.

Luttwak, Edward N. *The Pentagon and the Art of War*. New York: Simon and Schuster, 1984.

McChristian, Joseph A. *The Role of Military Intelligence 1965–67*. Washington, D.C.: Department of the Army, 1974.

McGarvey, Patrick J. *Visions of Victory*. Stanford, Calif.: Hoover Institution on War, Revolution and Peace, 1969.

Maclear, Michael. *The Ten Thousand Day War*. Toronto: Methuen, 1981.

Marshall, S. L. A. *Ambush*. New York: Cowles, 1969.

Meyerson, Harvey. *Vinh Long*. Boston: Houghton Mifflin, 1970.

Morison, Samuel Eliot. *History of United States Navel Operations in World War II*, vol. 4: *Coral Sea, Midway and Submarine Actions*. Boston: Little, Brown, 1949.

——. *The Two-Ocean War*. Boston: Little, Brown, 1963.

Nalty, Bernard C. *Air Power and the Fight for Khe Sanh*. Washington, D.C.: Office of Air Force History, United States Air Force, 1973.

Neustadt, Richard E., and Ernest R. May. *Thinking in Time*. New York: Free Press, 1986.

Nolan, Keith W. *Battle for Hue, Tet 1968*. Novato, Calif.: Presidio Press, 1983.

Oberdorfer, Don. *Tet!* Garden City, New York: Doubleday, 1971.

Orr, George E. *Combat Operations C³I: Fundamentals and Interactions*. Maxwell Air Force Base, Ala.: Air University Press, 1983.

Osgood, Robert Endicott. *Limited War: The Challenge to American Strategy*. Chicago: University of Chicago Press, 1957.

Palmer, Bruce. *The 25-Year War*. Lexington, Ky.: University of Kentucky Press, 1984.

Palmer, Dave Richard. *Summons of the Trumpet*. San Rafael, Calif.: Presidio Press, 1978.

Pearson, Willard. *The War in the Northern Provinces*. Washington, D.C.: Department of the Army, 1975.

The Pentagon Papers as Published by The New York Times. New York: Bantam Books, 1971.

The Pentagon Papers, Senator Gravel Edition, vol. 4. Boston: Beacon Press, 1971.

Pike, Douglas. *History of Vietnamese Communism 1925–1976*. Stanford, Calif.: Hoover Institute Press, 1978.

——. *PAVN: People's Army of Vietnam*. Novato, Calif.: Presidio Press, 1986.

——. *Viet Cong*. Cambridge: MIT Press, 1966.

Podhoretz, Norman. *Why We Were in Vietnam*. New York: Simon and Schuster, 1982.

Pohle, Victoria. *The Viet Cong in Saigon: Tactics and Objectives during the Tet Offensive*. Santa Monica, Calif.: Rand Memorandum RM-5799-ISA ARPA, January 1969.

Powers, Thomas. *The Man Who Kept the Secrets: Richard Helms and the CIA*. New York: Alfred A. Knopf, 1979.

Prange, Gordon W. *At Dawn We Slept*. New York: McGraw-Hill, 1981.

——. *Miracle at Midway*. New York: Penguin Books, 1982.

Race, Jeffrey. *War Comes to Long An*. Berkeley: University of California Press, 1972.

Ranelagh, John. *The Agency: The Rise and Decline of the CIA*. New York: Touchstone Books, 1987.

Richelson, Jeffrey. *American Espionage and the Soviet Target*. New York: William Morrow, 1987.

——. *The U.S. Intelligence Community*. Cambridge, Mass.: Ballinger, 1985.

Rogers, Bernard W. *CEDAR FALLS–JUNCTION CITY: A Turning Point*. Washington, D.C.: Department of the Army, 1974.

Rostow, W. W. *The Diffusion of Power*. New York: Macmillan, 1972.

——. *The United States in the World Arena*. New York: Harper & Brothers, 1960.

Schandler, Herbert Y. *The Unmaking of a President*. Princeton: Princeton University Press, 1977.

Shafer, D. Michael. *Deadly Paradigms: The Failure of U.S. Counterinsurgency Policy*. Princeton: Princeton University Press, 1988.

Shaplen, Robert. *Time out of Hand*. New York: Harper & Row, 1969.

Sharp, U. S. Grant. *Strategy for Defeat*. San Rafael, Calif.: Presidio Press, 1978.

Sharp, U. S. Grant, and William C. Westmoreland. *Report on the War in Vietnam*. Washington, D.C.: U.S. Government Printing Office, 1968.

Sheehan, Neil. *A Bright Shining Lie: John Paul Vann and America in Vietnam*. New York: Random House, 1988.

Bibliography

Shore, Moyers S. *The Battle for Khe Sanh*. Washington, D.C.: Historical Branch, G-3 Division Headquarters, U.S. Marine Corps, 1969.

Snyder, Glenn, and Paul Diesing. *Conflict among Nations*. Princeton: Princeton University Press, 1977.

Sobel, Lester A., ed. *South Vietnam: U.S.–Communist Confrontation in Southeast Asia*. Vol. 2. New York: Facts on File, 1969.

Spector, Ronald H. *Advice and Support: The Early Years of the U.S. Army in Vietnam, 1941–1960*. New York: Free Press, 1985.

Stanton, Shelby L. *The Rise and Fall of an American Army*. Novato, Calif.: Presidio Press, 1985.

Stein, Janice Gross, and Raymond Tanter. *Rational Decision-Making*. Columbus: Ohio State University Press, 1980.

Summers, Harry G. *On Strategy*. Novato, Calif.: Presidio Press, 1982.

Sun Tzu. *The Art of War*. Translated by Samuel B. Griffith. Oxford: Oxford University Press, 1963.

Tang, Truong Nhu., David Chanoff, and Doan Van Toai. *A Viet Cong Memoir*. New York: Vintage Books, 1985.

Telfer, Gary L., Lane Rogers, and Keith V. Fleming. *U.S. Marines in Vietnam Fighting the North Vietnamese, 1967*. Washington, D.C.: History and Museums Division Headquarters, U.S. Marine Corps, 1984.

Thies, Wallace J. *When Governments Collide*. Berkeley: University of California Press, 1980.

Thompson, Robert. *No Exit from Vietnam*. New York: David McKay, 1969.

Tolson, John J. *Airmobility 1961–1971*. Washington, D.C.: Department of the Army, 1973.

Tra, Tran Van. *Vietnam: History of the Bulwark B2 Theatre*, vol 5: *Concluding the 30-Years War*. Ho Chi Minh City: Van Nghe Publishing House, 1982. Translated by Foreign Broadcast Information Service. JPRS 82783, 2 February 1983.

Truman, Harry S. *Years of Trial and Hope*. New York: Doubleday, 1956.

Truong, Ngo Quang. *RVNAF and U.S. Operational Cooperation and Coordination*. Washington, D.C.: U.S. Army Center of Military History, 1980.

Tsou, Tang. *America's Failure in China*. Chicago: University of Chicago Press, 1963.

Van Creveld, Martin. *Command in War*. Cambridge, Mass.: Harvard University Press, 1985.

Vien, Cao Van, and Dong Van Khuyen. *Reflections on the Vietnam War*. Washington, D.C.: U.S. Army Center of Military History, 1980

Westmoreland, William C. *A Soldier Reports*. Garden City, N. Y.: Doubleday, 1976.

Whaley, Barton. *Codeword BARBAROSSA*. Cambridge: MIT Press, 1973.

Whiting, Allen S. *China Crosses the Yalu: The Decision to Enter the Korean War*. Stanford, Calif.: Stanford University Press, 1960.

Wohlstetter, Roberta. *Pearl Harbor: Warning and Decision*. Stanford, Calif.: Stanford University Press, 1962.

ARTICLES AND UNPUBLISHED MATERIALS

Adams, Samuel. "Vietnam Cover-up: Playing with Numbers." *Harper's*, May 1975.

Betts, Richard K. "Intelligence for Policymaking." *The Washington Quarterly* 3 (Summer 1980).

——. "Strategic Surprise for War Termination: Inchon, Dienbienphu, and Tet." *Strategic*

Military Surprise. Edited by Klaus Knorr and Patrick Morgan. New Brunswick, N.J.: Transaction Books, 1983.

Brodie, Bernard. "Tet Offensive." *Decisive Battles of the Twentieth Century*. Edited by Noble Frankland and Christopher Dowling. London: Sidgwick and Jackson, 1976.

Broyles, William, Jr. "The Road to Hill 10." *The Atlantic Monthly*, April 1985.

Clifford, Clark. "A Vietnam Reappraisal." *Foreign Affairs* 47 (July 1969).

Cubbage, T. L. "Westmoreland vs. CBS: Was Intelligence Corrupted by Policy Demands." *Leaders and Intelligence*. Edited by Michael Handel, London: Frank Cass, 1989.

Cubbage, T. L. "Westmoreland vs. CBS: Was Intelligence Corrupted by Policy Demands?" Paper Presented at the Intelligence and Military Operations Conference, U.S. Army War College, May 1987.

Dunn, Peter M. "The American Army: The Vietnam War, 1965–1973." *Armed Forces & Modern Counter-Insurgency*. Edited by Ian F. W. Beckett and John Pimlott. London: Croom Helm, 1985.

George, Alexander L., "Warning and Response: Theory and Practice." *International Violence: Terrorism, Surprise, and Control*. Edited by Yair Evon. Jerusalem: Hebrew University, Leonard David Institute, 1979.

Gordon, Bernard K. "The Third Indochina Conflict." *Foreign Affairs* 65 (Fall 1986).

Handel, Michael. "Intelligence and the Problem of Strategic Surprise." *Journal of Strategic Studies* 7 (September 1984).

——. "The Politics of Intelligence." *Intelligence and National Security* 2 (October 1987).

Helm, Glenn E. "The Tet 1968 Offensive: A Failure of Allied Intelligence." M.A. thesis, Arizona State University, December 1989.

Holsti, Ole R. "The Belief System and National Images: A Case Study." *Journal of Conflict Resolution* 6 (1962).

Jervis, Robert. "Political Decision Making: Recent Contributions." *Political Psychology* 2 (Summer 1980).

Jungermann, Helmut. "The Two Camps on Rationality." *Judgement and Decision Making*. Edited by Hal R. Arkes and Kenneth R. Hammond. Cambridge: Cambridge University Press, 1986.

Kriegel, Richard C. "Tet Offensive, Victory or Defeat?" *Marine Corps Gazette,* 52 (December 1968).

Latimer, Thomas. "Hanoi's Leaders and Their South Vietnam Policies, 1954–1968." Ph.D. dissertation, Georgetown University, 1972.

Lebow, Richard, "Windows of Opportunity: Do States Jump through Them?" *International Security* 9 (Summer 1984).

Macdonald, Douglas. "'Adventures in Chaos': Reformism in American Foreign Policy. Ph.D. dissertation, Columbia University, 1987.

Pike, Douglas. "The Tet Offensive: A Setback for Giap, but Just How Big?" *Army* 18 (April 1968).

Snyder, Jack. "Civil-Military Relations and the Cult of the Offensive, 1914 and 1984." *International Security* 9 (Summer 1984).

Staudenmaier, William O. "Vietnam, Mao and Clausewitz," *Parameters* 7:1 (1977).

Weyand, Fred C. "Serving the People: The Basic Case for the United States Army." *CDRS Call* (May-June 1976).

DOCUMENTS

Combined Intelligence Center, Vietnam (CICV), *Strategy since 1954*, Study 67-037. Headquarters, U.S. Military Assistance Command Vietnam, Office of Assistant Chief of Staff J-2, 29 June 1967.

Commander, United States Military Assistance Command, Vietnam. *Command History 1966*. Prepared by the Military History Branch, Office of the Secretary, Joint Staff Headquarters, USMACV, Saigon, Vietnam: 30 June 1967.

Commander, United States Military Assistance Command, Vietnam. *Command History 1967*, 3 vols. Prepared by the Military History Branch, Office of the Secretary, Joint Staff Headquarters, USMACV, Saigon, Vietnam: 16 September 1968.

Commander, United States Military Assistance Command, Vietnam. *Command History 1968*, 2 vols. Prepared by the Military History Branch, Office of the Secretary, Joint Staff Headquarters, USMACV, Saigon, Vietnam: 30 April 1969.

Daily Journal Files of MACV J-2 Command Center, record group 334, accession number 70A0738, box number S 1–2 of 11. National Records Center, Suitland, Maryland.

Documents presented to North Vietnam by W. Averell Harriman, May 1968. Film W1484. Government Documents Collection, Widener Library, Harvard University.

Long Binh/Saigon Tet Campaign, 199th Infantry Brigade, 12 January–19 February 1968. Washington, D.C.: Department of the the the Army, 1968.

Oral History, National Security File, and Vietnam Country File Collections. Lyndon Baines Johnson Library, Austin Texas.

"The P.L.A.F. Control Tan Canh Urban Centre, Overrun the Puppet 'Special Forces' Base Camp, and Pound Nearly All Enemy's Bases in Dac To Region." *Vietnam Courier*, 4 December 1967.

Statement of Mission, Composition and Functions, I Corps Joint Coordinating Council, 31 January, 1967, record group 319, accession number 71A4237, box number 10 of 15, folder number 6. National Records Center, Suitland, Maryland.

Vietnam: A Documentary Collection—Westmoreland v. CBS. New York: Clearwater, 1985.

Viet-Nam Documents and Research Notes (VDRN), Saigon: United States Mission in Vietnam, 1967–68.

U.S. Congress, House Select Committee on Intelligence. *U.S. Intelligence Agencies and Activities: Risks and Control of Foreign Intelligence*. 94th Cong., 1st sess., 1975, pt. 5.

U.S. Congress, Senate. *Stalemate in Vietnam*. Report to the Committee on Foreign Relations United States Senate by Senator Joseph S. Clark on a study mission to South Vietnam. 90th Cong., 2d sess., 1968.

USMACV AC of S J-2. *PERINTREP*. February 1967–June 1968. Vietnam Collection, U.S. Army War College, Carlisle Barracks, Pennsylvania.

Index

Abrams, Creighton, 90–91, 155–156, 160, 168–169, 204, 244
Adams, Samuel, 160–161, 247–250, 263–264
Aleutians, 3
allied command arrangements, 87–95, shortcomings of, 95–98
allied military operations; Attleboro, 42, 113; Cedar Falls, 42, 113; Fairfax, 116; Golden Fleece, 43; Hastings, 43; Junction City, 42, 97, 113, 125; Leapfrog, 244; Masher/White Wing/Thang Phong II, 33; Neutralize, 143–144, 196; Niagara I & II, 196–199, 211, 270; Paul Revere IV, 42; Pegasus, 233; Prairie, 43; Sea Dragon, 107–108; Thayer II, 42; Yellowstone, 193; York, 189–190, 200
Analogies, 9. *See also* Battle of the Bulge analogy; Dien Bien Phu analogy; Korean War analogy
An Giang province, 148
Ardennes. *See* Battle of the Bulge analogy
Argo, Reamer, 216
Army of the Republic of Vietnam (ARVN) units; 1st Airborne Battalion, 230; 8th Airborne Battalion, 230; 1st Division, 97, 244; 5th Division, 145; 7th Division, 228; 9th Infantry Regiment, 144; 5th Ranger Battalion (Group), 116, 186, 226; 37th Ranger Battalion, 116; 42nd Regiment, 203; 58th Regional Force Battalion, 153
Assault Youth, 248

B-3 (highlands) Front Command headquarters, 144–145, 148, 202–203, 213; and attack on Dak To, 75, 155–156
Barbarossa, 3
barrier, the, 120–124, 178, 198, 272. *See also* Dump Truck; Muscle Shoals
Battle of Britain, 3
Battle of the Bulge analogy, 88, 129–132, 176, 188, 266, 270
Betts, Richard, 12, 17–18
Bien Hoa, 122, 218, 245; and III CTZ headquarters, 79; and VC attack on airbase, 228, 236
Bien Hoa province, 245
Binh Dinh province, 31, 33, 45, 75–76, 107, 194, 202, 216
Binh Duong province, 46
Binh Long province, 69
body count, 34, 117, 126
border battles, 81, 147, 170–171, 173–174, 253, 157. *See also* Con Thien; Dak To; Gio Linh; Khe Sanh; Loc Ninh; Song Be
Buddha, 107, 109
Buddhists, 26, 54, 236
Bundy, William, 195
Bunker, Ellsworth, 150, 157, 165–166, 208, 210, 213, 235, 239
"Buttercup affair," 70, 151–152

Cambodia, 42, 67, 72, 75, 105, 113, 121, 141, 144–146, 170, 181, 200; and North Vietnamese concerns about invasion of, 58; and North Vietnamese 1965 offensive, 31–32; and U.S. plans for in-

Library of Congress Cataloging-in-Publication Data

Wirtz, James J., 1958—
   The Tet offensive: intelligence failure in war / James J. Wirtz.
     p.   cm. — (Cornell studies in security affairs)
   Includes bibliographical references and index.
   ISBN 0-8014-2486-0 (alk. paper)
   1. Tet Offensive, 1968.   2. Vietnamese Conflict, 1961–1975—Military intelligence.
3. Vietnamese Conflict, 1961–1975—United States. I. Title. II. Series.
DS559.8.M44W57   1991
959.704′38—dc20   91-55048